Toleration in Enlightenment Europe

Grell and Porter

The Enlightenment is often seen as the great age of religious and intellectual toleration, and this volume offers the first systematic European survey of the theory, practice, and very real limits to toleration in eighteenth-century Europe. A distinguished international team of contributors demonstrates how the publicists of the European Enlightenment in fact developed earlier ideas about toleration, gradually widening the desire for religious toleration into a philosophy of freedom seen as a fundamental attribute of and a pre-condition for a civilized society. Nonetheless, Europe never uniformly or comprehensively embraced toleration during the eighteenth century: although religious toleration remained central to the Enlightenment project, advances in toleration of all kinds were often fragile and short-lived.

This volume is the successor to the acclaimed study of *Tolerance and Intolerance in the European Reformation*, edited by Ole Peter Grell and Bob Scribner and published by Cambridge in 1996.

OLE PETER GRELL is affiliated lecturer in the Faculty of History, University of Cambridge.

ROY PORTER is Professor of the Social History of Medicine at the Wellcome Institute for the History of Medicine, London.

Toleration in
Enlightenment Europe

Edited by Ole Peter Grell and Roy Porter

CAMBRIDGE
UNIVERSITY PRESS

#40912708

PUBLISHED BY THE PRESS SYNDICATE OF THE UNIVERSITY OF CAMBRIDGE
The Pitt Building, Trumpington Street, Cambridge, United Kingdom

CAMBRIDGE UNIVERSITY PRESS
The Edinburgh Building, Cambridge CB2 2RU, UK http://www.cup.cam.ac.uk
40 West 20th Street, New York, NY 10011-4211, USA http://www.cup.org
10 Stamford Road, Oakleigh, Melbourne 3166, Australia

First published 2000

Printed in the United Kingdom at the University Press, Cambridge

Typeset in Times 10/12 pt. [wv]

A catalogue record for this book is available from the British Library

Library of Congress Cataloguing-in-Publication Data

Toleration in Enlightenment Europe/edited by Ole Peter Grell and Roy Porter.
    p.   cm.
ISBN 0 521 65196 4 (hardback)
1. Religious tolerance–Europe–History–18th century. 2. Toleration–Europe–History–18th century. 3. Enlightenment.
I. Grell, Ole Peter. II. Porter, Roy.
BR735.T66 1999
323.44′2′09409033–dc21 99–22488 CIP

ISBN 0 521 65196 4 hardback

Contents

Contributors

Justin Champion, Department of History, Royal Holloway College,
University of London
Nicholas Davidson, St Edmund Hall, Oxford
Martin Fitzpatrick, Department of History, University of Wales,
Aberystwyth
Ole Peter Grell, Department of History and Philosophy of Science,
University of Cambridge
Jonathan I. Israel, Department of History, University College, London
Henry Kamen, CSIC Institución Milá y Fontanals, Barcelona, Spain
Marisa Linton, Faculty of Human Sciences, Kingston University, Surrey
Michael G. Müller, Department of History, Martin-Luther-University,
Halle-Wittenberg, Germany
Roy Porter, Wellcome Institute for the History of Medicine, London
Sylvana Tomaselli, Hughes Hall, Cambridge
Karl Vocelka, Institute for Austrian History, University of Vienna, Austria
Ernestine van der Wall, Department of Church History, University of
Leiden, The Netherlands
Joachim Whaley, Gonville and Caius College, Cambridge
Robert Wokler, Department of Politics, University of Exeter

Preface

These essays have emerged out of a conference held in Corpus Christi College, Cambridge, 17–19 September 1997, which was the culmination of a series of academic symposia which began in 1988 during the William and Mary Tercentenary, and which has resulted in the publication of two previous volumes: O. P. Grell, J. I. Israel and N. Tyacke (eds), *From Persecution to Toleration: The Glorious Revolution and Religion in England* (1991); and O. P. Grell and Bob Scribner (eds), *Tolerance and Intolerance in the European Reformation* (1996).

The issue of toleration still remains as important today as it was during the Enlightenment. The continuous conflict in the former Yugoslavia, with its horrific examples of intolerance between different religious and ethnic groups, which started in Bosnia and has now moved on to Kosovo, reminds us that toleration cannot simply be a passive response, something akin to indifference. We are reminded that, if it is to have any meaning, toleration will occasionally mean active intervention to protect those who are exposed to intolerance and persecution. Edmund Burke's 200-year-old dictum: 'For evil to succeed it only takes good men to do nothing' remains as relevant as ever.

The editors are grateful to all the contributors for their cooperation in transforming conference papers into published essays, aided by constructive referees' reports provided by Cambridge University Press, and the encouragement of Richard Fisher of the Press.

We are beholden to the William and Mary History of Toleration Committee and the British Academy for their generous financial support of the conference which made this volume possible. For administrative aid, the editors wish to thank Frieda Houser.

Ole Peter Grell
Roy Porter
Cambridge/London, November 1998

1. Toleration in Enlightenment Europe

Ole Peter Grell and Roy Porter

Prehistory

The invention of printing, the Protestant Reformation and the reactions of princes and popes brought furious struggles, theological and political, over conscience and coercion, faith and freedom. Throughout the Reformation and Counter-Reformation eras, Europe remained uncompromisingly a 'persecuting society', even if arguments for toleration, both on principle and as a *politique* necessity, were also advanced.[1]

The publicists of the Enlightenment further developed such pleas for toleration, and in the process their basis and character was transformed, with the original religious rationales becoming incorporated within a wider philosophy of freedom conceived as a fundamental human attribute and precondition for civilized society. *Liberté* would head the Rights of Man of 1789, just as religious freedom – guaranteed by the absence of an established church – was one of the shibboleths of the Constitution of the United States, whose third president, Thomas Jefferson, boldly proclaimed the 'illimitable freedom of the human mind'. Toleration was thus to acquire a secular cast as, in liberal ideologies, freedom of thought and speech became definitive of human rights, alongside other cherished freedoms like *habeas corpus*.[2]

In reality, however, the eighteenth century saw toleration nowhere unequivocally and comprehensively embraced in either theory or practice; and where it gained ground, it was partial, fragile, contested and even subject to reversal. No clear and distinct metaphysics underpinned toleration claims, nor was there a single, classic, foundational text, commanding universal assent. It will be the aim of this book, therefore, to address the ambiguities, limits and fluctuations no less than the extension of toleration in the Enlightenment.

One point, moreover, must first be stressed. Religion did not merely retain a powerful presence throughout eighteenth-century Europe, it was central to the Enlightenment project itself. Some historians have claimed that the *philosophes* crusaded for 'atheism' or 'modern paganism'[3] and atheists there were indeed. François-Marie Arouet de Voltaire (1694–1778), the most notorious critic of Christianity, made his ultimate rallying-cry *écrasez*

1

l'infâme – 'crush the infamous' – and he attacked not only Catholicism but also the shallow natural religion and Optimism of the rationalists. His own liberal views were set out in his *Traîté de la tolérance* (1763). Most activists, however, wished to see religion not abolished but reformed, with 'bigotry' and 'superstition' yielding to a God of reason and Nature, compatible with science, morality and civic duties. Immanuel Kant claimed the Enlightenment meant *sapere aude*, having the courage to think for oneself in all things, including matters of religion.[4] The fact that the French Revolution enthroned its Goddess of Reason in Nôtre Dame shows how religion continued to provide the vestments in which enlightened values were ceremonially clad. 'The coherence, as well as the confidence of the Enlightenment', Norman Hampson has maintained, 'rested on religious foundations'.[5]

Nor must it be forgotten that while the cause of toleration was fundamental to freethinkers and Deists, it might weigh no less heavily with sincere Christians. The English polymath Joseph Priestley (1733–1804), for instance, combined materialist philosophy with a distinctive model of Protestant Dissent. His *Lectures on History* (1788) vindicated the superiority of modern times over the ancient in faith, science, government, manners and happiness, discerning therein the hand of God. In his providentialist scenario, the future progress of religion and rationality required total toleration and the separation of Church and State would be its guarantee.[6]

But if many of them were pious and even Christian, *Aufklärer* across Europe were disgusted by worldly and extravagant church establishments, by 'priestcraft', and by preposterous pontifications: 'I knew a real theologian once', wrote Voltaire:

He knew the Brahmins, the Chaldeans ... the Syrians, the Egyptians, as well as he knew the Jews; he was familiar with the various readings of the Bible ... The more he grew truly learned, the more he distrusted everything he knew. As long as he lived, he was forbearing; and at his death, he confessed he had squandered his life uselessly.[7]

Divisions within Christianity, and the bloody wars of truth they sparked, brought disillusionment. The endless squabbling among the children of God was contrasted with the harmony supposedly brought by the 'new philosophy', notably the Newtonian science which was revealing the fundamental laws of Nature. There were, Voltaire quipped, no sects in geometry.

Thinking Tolerance

The early modern centuries advanced many arguments for toleration. Every advocate denounced tyranny, the persecution of the faithful and the suppression of truth. The Inquisition, the *Index Librorum Prohibitorum* (initiated in 1559), judicial torture and the Augustinian maxim '*compellare intrare*' all drew vehement denunciations. The irenic Erasmus, along with fellow Christian humanists, had reminded the faithful that the Gospel message was peace; Christ had preached love, and war-mongering popes like Julius II were like Antichrist. Sceptical towards witch persecution, Michel Montaigne famously deemed that 'it is putting a very high price on one's conjectures to have a man roasted alive because of them'.

> On a huge hill, cragg'd and steep, Truth stands
> And hee that will reach her, about must and about must goe,

declared John Donne, likewise intimating that no candid Christian should presume to possess a monopoly on that commodity.[8]

For all that, Catholics and Protestants alike continued to maintain that the True Church was duty-bound to extirpate evil and error, if necessary with fire and faggots. Thomas More declared the 'carbuncle' of heresy had to be surgically excised lest it infect the rest of the *corpus Christi*. Was it not preposterous to tolerate the disciples of the Devil or of Machiavelli? Witches, unbelievers, atheists and apostates were rebels against the Lord who must be converted, punished or annihilated. Only a few brave and persecuted groups, like the Anabaptists or Socinians, proclaimed toleration as an ideal – toleration, it has been remarked, was long a loser's creed.

Building upon what had come before, Enlightenment champions were to recast the emergent claims to toleration. New individualistic models postulated an original autonomy for natural man anterior to Church and State. If, as John Locke and many others were to insist, man was born free under universal law in a state of Nature, how could the prince come by any legitimate authority to constrain the mind? Faith was not to be forced: 'For what obeys reason is free, and Reason He made right', sang John Milton, developing a tolerationism hingeing on a pious image of reason as a divine light, which complemented the anti-censorship arguments developed in *Areopagitica*.[9]

If freedom and toleration were thus essential to the pursuit of inquiry, both religious and secular, doubts were at the same time being voiced in the early Enlightenment about the authenticity of any transcendental tablets of Truth to which the Godly had privileged access. The seeds of such scepticism might be found in Renaissance Pyrrhonism – Montaigne's *'que scais je?'*; in the temper of Christian fideists; in the Cartesian call to systematic doubt; and in the adiaphoristic teachings of Anglicans and Dutch Remonstrants, who pared down to the core the truths essential for subscription and accepted a penumbra of 'things indifferent' about which forbearing Christians could agree to disagree.

Enlightened minds ventured further. Philosophy, philology and textual scholarship were persuading critics like Pierre Bayle that human erudition was irremediably imperfect, be it in respect of the migrations of the descendants of Noah, the occurrence of miracles or the theology of salvation. The corruption of sources, the depredations of time and the quarrels of authors meant that teachings would never cease to be in dispute. In the late seventeenth-century 'crisis of European consciousness', the 'Ancients versus Moderns' *querella* challenged old certainties. William Temple's *Essay upon the Ancient and Modern Learning* (1690) maintained the superiority of Greek philosophy and science; William Wotton's *Reflections upon Ancient and Modern Learning* (1694) countered that, in the sciences at least, the 'Moderns' had surpassed the 'Ancients'. This battle of the books was especially corrosive because its arguments were manifestly extendable to the sacred writings themselves. What then of Scripture truth? Was it self-evident for all to see? Was it literal or figurative? Did it have to be elucidated by the erudite? And, if so, who were the authorized interpreters?[10]

This scepticism accompanied a new problematization of the well-known fact that the human scene was a world of difference. Travellers and armchair anthropologists alike found themselves confronted by a kaleidoscope of beliefs and customs amongst the peoples of mankind. Might such differences in manners and morals best be understood not – as traditionally – in terms of truth and error but as marks of mere heterogeneity? Indeed, might such human variability be natural or even desirable? The histories of nations showed that one prime site of divergence was religion. The globe presented a cabinet of diverse faiths – Buddhism, Hinduism, Judaism, Islam, Christianity, with all their sects and schisms, to say nothing of polytheistic cults. Confrontations with such radical heterogeneity fostered the deistic conviction that there must be many ways to God, discoverable through Nature, each acceptable to the Supreme Being, and hence deserving of tolerance.[11] In his *L'Esprit des lois*, that magisterial account of human diversity and the laws governing it, Montesquieu implied that the true philosopher would be indifferent to difference.

In short, philosophical doubt swept through the world of letters in the early Enlightenment. Diversity did not, it goes without saying, unequivocally clinch the case for toleration. For Hobbes, after all, no less than the Pope, the enforcement of uniformity was necessary to obviate anarchy. But the philosophy of tolerance could be supported by pragmatism. Voltaire thus suggested the utility of diversity:

Take a view of the *Royal Exchange* in *London*, a place more venerable than many courts of justice, where the representatives of all nations meet for the benefit of mankind. There the Jew, the Mahometan, and the Christian transact together as tho' they all profess'd the same religion, and give the name of Infidel to none but bankrupts. There the Presbyterian confides in the Anabaptist, and the Churchman depends on the Quaker's word. And all are satisfied.[12]

The ties of trade, in other words, rendered religious heterodoxy unthreatening in a nation in which 'every man goes to heaven by which path he likes'. Voltaire's was only one of many voices which made the economic case for toleration: pluralism promoted prosperity. Conversely, had not intolerance proved calamitous and counterproductive? Far from stamping it out, persecution had bred heresy; the Inquisition had created martyrs, its flames had lit freedom's torch. Wars of religion had discredited the faith.

With the Peace of Westphalia ending the Thirty Years War in 1648, and the Restoration bringing down the curtain on twenty years of mayhem in Britain, the mood of Europe's ruling orders swung decisively against those who had boldly shed blood in the name of infallibility, divine right, prophetic revelation or the Bible. As the dictates of popes and presbyters grew challenged by arguments historical, philosophical and moral, it could now even be claimed that religious dogmatism did not only create *civil* disorder but was even symptomatic of *mental* disorder: the *soi-disant* saints were literally out of their minds. Physicians pointed to affinities between sectaries and lunatics – speaking in tongues, seizures, visions and violence. In individuals such aberrations had long been blamed on demonic possession; now it was the turn of entire religious sects to be 'demonized' on medico–philosophical authority, with scientific rationality thus playing a regulatory no less than a liberating role.[13] And all the while satirists were making laughing-stocks of Puritans and other zealots:

> Such as do build their faith upon
> The holy text of pike and gun
> Decide all controversies by
> Infallible artillery . . .
> As if religion were intended
> For nothing else but to be mended.[14]

Critiques of Catholic superstition and Puritan enthusiasm (or self-divinization) thus had many sources and took many forms. The smouldering anti-clericalism fuelling them even occasionally became enshrined in official policy, witness the eventual expulsion of the Jesuits from all Catholic countries – hardly in itself a triumph of toleration!

The philosophical basis of toleration

In a political situation in which freedoms were endangered by the ambitions of the Sun King, Enlightenment philosophies of toleration were elucidated which construed man as a thinking being whose rationality demanded freedom of thought and expression. John Locke's *Essay Concerning Human Understanding* (1690) developed an empiricist model of the mind as a *tabula rasa* on which the raw data of experience were registered.[15] Book IV spelt out the epistemology of religion. Discussing the existence of God, Locke rejected the Cartesian assumption that man is born with an innate idea of the Deity. God is rather a complex idea built up in the mind by taking ideas already acquired – e.g. 'existence and duration, knowledge and power, pleasure and happiness' – and projecting them to infinity. Simple ideas are built up from the senses, and the mind organizes and 'enlarges' them until it arrives at the highest complex idea of all, that of God. Such notions were further developed in *The Reasonableness of Christianity* (1695), where Locke explained that faith for its part is, properly, trust in the powers of reason. Revelation contains verities which do not come from reason but which must be subjected to its bar, since it is a divine gift and therefore our final arbiter.

Locke's thinking on toleration chimed with his epistemology. A substantial but unpublished essay on toleration, dating from 1667, contains the essential principles later to be expressed in the *Letters on Toleration* published during the reign of William III. In his 1667 essay, Locke held that the 'trust, power and authority' of the civil ruler was vested in him solely for the purpose of securing 'the good, preservation and peace of men in that society'. That is, the sphere of the state extended solely to external matters and not to faith, which is internal, a matter of conscience.

To elucidate the limits of those civil powers, Locke divided opinions and actions into three kinds. First, there were speculative views and forms of divine worship which did not concern the polity at all. Second, there were those opinions and actions which were neither good nor bad in themselves, but which impinged upon others and thus were public concerns. Third, there were actions which were good or bad in themselves – namely, virtues and vices.

Beliefs and behaviours of the first kind had 'an absolute and universal right to toleration'. This derived from the fact that they did not affect society, being either wholly private or concerning God alone. Opinions of the second sort – for instance conceptions about divorce – 'have a title also to toleration, but only so far as they do not tend to the disturbance of the State or do not cause greater inconvenience than advantage to the community'. But, Locke added, while the magistrate could prohibit *publishing* such opinions if they might disturb the public good, no man ought to be forced to renounce his opinion, or assent to a contrary opinion, for such coercion would only breed hypocrisy.

As for the third class – actions good or bad in themselves – Locke maintained that civil rulers had 'nothing to do with the good of men's soul or their concernments in another life'. God would reward virtue and punish vice, and the magistrate's job was simply to keep the peace. Applying such principles to the political situation of the 1660s, Locke held that Catholics could *not* be tolerated, because their opinions were 'absolutely destructive of all governments except the Pope's'. Neither should toleration include atheists, since any oaths of loyalty and allegiance which they took would carry no conviction.

Exiled in the Dutch Republic in the 1680s, Locke wrote a *Letter on Toleration* which was published in Latin in 1689. Echoing the 1667 arguments, this denied that Christianity could be promoted or defended by force. Christ was the Prince of Peace; He had used not coercion but persuasion; persecution could not save men's souls. Persecution was anti-Christian, since love of fellow men is the essence of Christianity.

Civil government must be distinguished from the Church. The business of civil government was to secure men's lives, liberty, health and possessions, whereas the salvation of souls was the concern of religion. Hence churches should be voluntary societies and the ecclesiastical authority ought to have no physical sanction other than excommunication.

Locke's tolerationism was contested by High Churchmen, while his latitudinarian attempt to defend Christian belief by reason drew criticism from traditionalists. Bishop Stillingfleet, for example, expressed his fear as to the erosion of belief which was bound to follow from the denial of innate ideas. 'An universal toleration is that Trojan Horse', he proclaimed, 'which brings in our enemies without being seen'.[16] At the same time, Locke's opinions were being driven down more radical roads by embarrassing deistical and freethinking allies, notably John Toland (1670–1722). Reputedly the son of an Irish Catholic priest, Toland had run away to England as a young man, becoming a Protestant of a sort. A brilliant scholar, he was known in Oxford as 'a man of fine parts, great learning, and little religion'. In 1696, he published his *Christianity not Mysterious: Or a Treatise Shewing that there is Nothing in the Gospel Contrary to Reason, Nor above it: And that no Christian Doctrine can be Properly call'd a Mystery*. Religion, he claimed, requires no mysterious explanation, and the Christian gospel stands by the use of reason independent of divine revelation. He expressed his belief in a Supreme Being, verified, as Justin Champion shows in the chapter entitled 'Toleration and Citizenship in Enlightenment England' (see pp. 133–56, this volume), on broadly rationalist principles. The religion of which Toland had little was conventional Christianity; and while he roundly denounced clergy of all denominations, his true *bêtes noires* were the Puritans with their scriptural dogmatism.

Though just a year separated Toland's book from Locke's *The Reasonableness of Christianity*, the intellectual gulf was vast. Locke aimed to make Christianity acceptable to all reasonable men; Toland taught that the mysterious and miraculous elements of Christianity must be trashed. His book caused an uproar, being condemned by the Irish parliament, attacked by divines and burned by the public hangman.

Only the most anglocentric historian would maintain that toleration and rational religion blossomed on English soil alone. The French Calvinist, Pierre Bayle, exiled in the Netherlands, was hugely influential. His first major work was a critique of Catholic intolerance, published in 1682 as *Letter on the Comet*, and republished the next year as *Diverse Thoughts on the Comet*. In *New Letters from the Author of the General Critique* (1685), he expanded on ideas about the rights of conscience mentioned in that earlier work, showing – contrast Locke! – that a society of atheists could live by honour and civility, and even surpass idolatrous and superstitious nations in orderliness.

Bayle then reacted to the revocation of the Edict of Nantes with his outraged *Philosophical Commentary on the Words, 'Compel Them to Come In'*, published in 1686. To compel men to profess religion in which they did not believe was immoral; it was also irrational, because it discouraged the discovery of truth. No one, he maintained, had a right to claim such complete possession of truth as not to need to engage in rational argument with others.[17]

According to Jonathan Israel's 'Spinoza, Locke and the Enlightenment battle for Toleration' (see pp. 102–13, this volume), whilst discussion of toleration has tended to focus on Bayle, Locke and the English freethinkers, it was actually the Dutch Jew, Benedict Spinoza, who launched the most radical, and historically most momentous, justification. For such contemporaries, toleration remained essentially a matter of freedom of religion. Spinoza's slogan, *libertas philosophandi*, by contrast embodied a barely concealed revolutionary implication: the absolute freedom to philosophize, entailing the right to reject *all* revealed religion and to base human values, along with social and political principles, not on faith or priestly authority, but on rational philosophy.

The battle for *religious* toleration was crucial, since the flames of ecclesiastical persecution had been so fierce. But for Enlightenment thinkers more was to be at stake. Censorship in any shape or form denied man's dignity as a rational being. Social progress depended upon reason being free to apply itself wheresoever – to the natural sciences, to legislation, morality and politics. In a Europe still disgracefully backward, advance would be impossible without the ferment of knowledge and modernization of attitudes which the free exercise of reason alone would stimulate. How absurd that regimes were still burning books and clapping authors in irons! Why such dread of knowledge? The *philosophes* endlessly rehearsed Galileo's fate as an object lesson in the arrest of progress by religious bigotry. Where inquiry was free, as in England, science leapt ahead – witness Newton. Prometheus became the hero of those championing dauntless defiance of authority – other myths, from Dr Faust to Dr Frankenstein, were, of course, waiting in the wings as reminders of the nemesis looming for humans behaving like gods.[18]

Toleration and its tensions

The *philosophes* loved portraying themselves as paladins of freedom, combating censorship and intolerance, and as the tutors of enlightened rulers, notably Frederick the Great. Himself an unbeliever, Frederick perceived the value to Prussia of encouraging immigrants of all faiths, Jews included. 'All must be tolerated', he proclaimed in a celebrated letter of 1740, 'here everyone must be allowed to choose his own road to salvation'.[19] In reality the situation was far more complicated than these idealizations suggest.

There was, for one thing, no agreement even within the republic of letters as to precisely what toleration entailed and what its limits should be. Was it a means or an end? Must the intolerant be tolerated? Was curbing bigots itself an act of bigotry? Above all, realists like Locke divined that toleration had to be guaranteed by a civil power, which evidently would not tolerate deadly enemies like Papists. Voltaire notoriously would not allow atheism to be talked of in front of the servants.

As Quentin Skinner has recently intimated, building upon earlier discussions by Isaiah Berlin, the eighteenth century might be viewed as a watershed in philosophies of liberty. An earlier tradition of 'liberty before liberalism' – it has variously been called Machiavellian, neo-Harringtonian, civic humanist or republican, and is now styled by Skinner 'neo-Roman' – envisaged liberty in terms of citizen participation in a free and virtuous commonwealth. Nineteenth-century liberalism by contrast, as typified by John Stuart Mill, espoused what Berlin has dubbed 'negative liberty', that is a state of legal protection from external hindrances ('freedom from'). Enlightenment thinkers rang the changes upon these respectively 'positive' and 'negative' ideas of liberty. In the context of the present discussion, the point is that both of these tenets, and all positions intermediate, tended to assimilate the case for religious toleration within a wider temporal politics of (positive or negative) liberty.[20]

This is not to imply that the status of freedom itself was beyond controversy. That great fly in the ointment, Jean-Jacques Rousseau, insisted that the health of a republic might necessitate 'forcing people to be free' – why tolerate the selfishness and depravity which would cause a polity to corrupt and collapse? In that light it made perfect sense for the Genevan to condemn the setting up of a theatre in his native city, since such licenciousness would sap virtue. Quite apart from Rousseau, powerful primitivist currents hankered after the sincerity and simplicity associated with moral solidarity. Holding cohesion essential to political vitality, some *philosophes* advocated a civil religion to counter sordid, sinister, selfish factionalism. For Rousseau, those refusing to accept the civil religion would be banished. In such circumstances, tolerance might be represented as the atrophy of collective moral will.[21]

The dilemma of how personal and public freedoms could be balanced also loomed large, albeit within a different moral framework, in Immanuel Kant's analysis of the relations between rationality, freedom and the public sphere. It was, Kant insisted, man's duty to break free of his self-imposed chains and dare to think. But his *Was ist Aufklärung?* (1784) also maintained the individual's paramount duty of public obedience to his prince; subjects had a duty to restrain expression of individual judgments in the interests of upholding the ruler's will and thus forestalling chaos.[22] As Kant's dilemma and other examples make clear, in the Enlightenment the bottom line in questions of toleration ultimately lay in decisions of state, even *raison d'état*. Thus the journalist and moralist Daniel Defoe allowed Robinson Crusoe to argue the case for toleration from the perspective of enlightened Absolutism in his best-selling novel of the same name, published in 1719. Here Crusoe stated:

My island was now peopled, and I thought myself rich in subjects; and it was a merry reflection, which I frequently made, how like a king I looked. First of all, the whole country was my own mere property, so that I had an undoubted right to dominion. Second my people were perfectly subjected; I was absolutely Lord and Law-giver; they all owed their Lives to me, and were ready to lay down their Lives, *if there had been occasion for it*, for me. It was remarkable too, we had but three Subjects, and they were of different Religions; my man *Friday* was a Protestant, his father was a *Pagan* and a *Cannibal*, and the *Spaniard* was a Papist; however, I allowed Liberty of Conscience throughout my Dominions.[23]

For the poet and philosopher Samuel Taylor Coleridge, the argument for toleration, however, was a negative one, namely the proven historical failure of persecution. As he put it:

The only true argument, as it seems to be, apart from Christianity, for a discriminating toleration is, that *it is of no use* to attempt to stop heresy or schism by persecution, unless perhaps, it be conducted upon the plan of direct warfare and massacre. You *cannot* preserve men in the faith by such means, though you may stifle for a while any open appearance of dissent. The experiment has now been tried and it has failed; and that is by a great deal the best argument for the magistrate against a repetition of it.[24]

So much for the theories, but how did eighteenth-century rulers handle the practical issue of toleration?

Toleration and the State

The histories of states reveal very different political stances toward toleration, and different degrees of its *de facto* or official practice.[25] At least in terms of the subjects' ability to think and worship as they wished, it was the Dutch

Republic and England which were most advanced. Yet as two essays in this book insist, there were significant limits to the toleration granted even in those nations.

From the early seventeenth century, the United Provinces enjoyed informal toleration. But in 'Toleration and Enlightenment in the Dutch Republic' (see pp. 114–32, this volume), Ernestine van der Wall shows that the Dutch Republic was none the less later to be shaken by a series of toleration controversies, revolving around the basic question: how far should one go? Their vehemence is explained by the specific religio–political role of the Dutch Reformed Church – while not 'established', it nevertheless enjoyed privileged status – and this had far-reaching consequences both religiously and temporally, since non-Reformed citizens were often treated as second-rate citizens. From 1750 onwards, the non-Reformed denominations campaigned for a greater measure of toleration, or even for equal rights. Such goals were resisted as a toleration too far, but were later to be realized in 1796 when, in the new Batavian Republic, Church was officially separated from State, signalling the end of the Reformed Church as a dominant body.

In the 1760s and 1770s the 'limits of toleration' question was voiced in the Netherlands in the context of speculations about the salvation of virtuous pagans. This so-called 'Socratic War', in which attitudes towards non-Christian religions played an important role, brought into sharp focus the conceptual and practical problems of toleration in eighteenth-century Dutch society.

Parallels may be drawn with Erastian England, where the Church of England remained established but the Act of Toleration (1689) granted freedom of worship for Nonconformists and most other religious minorities (excepting Unitarians) at the price of the continuation of certain civil disabilities – a political compromise (a mere *exemption*, not a *right*) for the time being acceptable to Protestant Dissenters but, in later decades, increasingly insupportable to a vocal minority. In 'Toleration and Citizenship in Enlightenment England' (see pp. 133–56, this volume), Justin Champion highlights the intellectual and political conflicts which arose over the toleration of Judaism in the first half of the eighteenth century: as in the United Provinces, how far were tolerationist imperatives to be extended to non-Christians? Ranging up to the political controversy surrounding the proposed Bill for the Naturalization of the Jews in 1753, Champion analyzes the relationships between Enlightenment ideas about faith, citizenship and toleration.

It was the Deists who made capital out of the debate, above all John Toland. His *Reasons for Naturalising the Jews* (1714) has been celebrated by historians as a liberal and even philo–semitic work, representing an unambiguous defence of rights to toleration – it was, after all, Toland who coined the phrase 'the emancipation of the Jews'. By setting this work in the broader context of Toland's other accounts of Judaism, notably his materialist history of the Mosaic polity, Champion brings out the non-confessional premises of Toland's arguments. In the process, comparing Toland's views with clandestine works such as the *Traité des trois imposteurs* (1719), he also highlights points of difference between English polemics and 'High Enlightenment' theorists. Far from being mere abstract theories, English toleration arguments were rooted in a practical political agenda aimed at reconfiguring the relationship between the political and the religious. In eighteenth-century discourse, Champion concludes, a coherent theory of toleration could be constructed only from non-confessional parameters: for all religions to be tolerated, they had to all be considered equally false.

If the Dutch and the English enjoyed a substantial, but far from complete, toleration, certain other regimes set their face squarely against it – at least officially. In his 'Inquisition, Tolerance and Liberty in Eighteenth-Century Spain' (see pp. 250–58, this volume), Henry Kamen wryly notes that the Iberian world has not figured large in discussions of toleration, and Spain has usually been pictured as the archetypically persecuting society, obediently served by the Inquisition. Enforced orthodoxy and cultural unity – as evidenced by the expulsions of the Jews (1492, 1497) and Muslims (1609) – created a monolithic society in the expectation that 'unity makes peace': there was therefore no 'problem' of social tolerance that might call either for fresh thinking or new legislation. In other words, in the wake of the expulsions, toleration was not a living issue. If shedding some of its notoriety, the Inquisition continued during the eighteenth century to play its accustomed role in upholding censorship.

But even the Spanish story, apparently so clear-cut, proves more complex. Kamen shows that debate continued to simmer as to the fate of cultural minorities, including those earlier expelled, and with respect to discrimination against minorities on such matters as blood-purity. He further examines the philosophical and political attitudes held by progressive members of the elite who challenged dogmatism in science and faith, and had minds open to the possibility of religious pluralism. He also raises the issue of receptivity to Enlightenment outlooks amongst those who travelled abroad, notably their absorption of French and English rationalism.

If Spain is often ignored, Nicholas Davidson's 'Toleration in Enlightenment Italy' (see pp. 230–49, this volume) similarly reminds us that, despite the prodigious labours of Franco Venturi and other Italian historians, all too many anglophone scholars remain unfamiliar with the dynamics of the Italian Enlightenment.[26] Sketching in bold strokes developments in different centres, he examines the institutional framework upholding religious intolerance, including the operation of the Index and the Inquisition. He then explores the case for toleration as advanced by Enlightenment propagandists including

Pietro Giannone, Alberto Radicati, Cesare Beccaria and Gaetano Filangieri, before comparing similar views amongst Jansenists and Catholic reformers, including Pope Benedict XIV and Pietro Tamburini. We need to learn more, counsels Davidson, about the relationship between Enlightenment authors and discussions on toleration within the Italian Catholic Church: were changes in the institutional framework of religious intolerance a response, or a prelude, to those intellectual debates?

In Enlightenment France the toleration question was dominated by the revocation of the Edict of Nantes in 1685, that high-point of the politico–religious ambitions of Louis XIV. Marking the end of a century of *politique* bi-confessionalism, the post-1685 expulsions of the Huguenots signalled a new era of religious persecution in the name of *un roi, une foi, une loi*. In 1691 Bishop Bossuet was thus proud to boast that Catholicism was the least tolerant of all faiths. In her 'Citizenship and Religious Toleration in France, 1685–1787 (see pp. 157–74, this volume), Marisa Linton relates the theoretical positions adopted in the French toleration debate to the changing political predicament of religious minorities and official attitudes towards them. One reason why the Bourbon monarchy upheld a confessional state lay in the fear that those whose religious affiliations lay elsewhere would also be disloyal to the Throne. Assessing the position of Protestants who stayed in France after 1685, she notes that, while revocation marked a reversal of an earlier, more tolerant, politics, there remained a certain measure of *de facto* toleration of Protestant minorities in local communities.

Linton also teases out some of the complexities of French Enlightenment attitudes towards toleration – its equivocations and limits. Turning to the theoretical position on toleration adopted by Montesquieu, Voltaire and other *philosophes*, she emphasizes that a key justification was derived from the natural law concept of freedom of conscience.

Casting her eye more widely, Linton then enquires into the relationships between ideologies and politics, in particular considering how the equivocal theoretical position of Jansenists within the French state after the Bull *Unigenitus* skewed the terms of the debate and encouraged pro-tolerationist arguments on the basis of citizenship. Could religious minorities be virtuous citizens and play a supportive role in public life, thereby permitting matters of religious affiliation to be left to private conscience? Such questions were played out in the Paris *parlement* in the *billets de confession* issue in the 1750s and the 1780s debate on the toleration of Protestants. Although the number of actual Jansenists in the *parlement* was small, they were highly influential and played a vital role in developing political consciousness; and disputes over religion were to prove a major source of tension between monarchy and *parlement*. Jansenists increasingly used arguments based on citizenship and patriotism to justify their participation in the State, and the citizenship card was also played by other religious minorities; the campaign to vindicate the memory of Jean Calas, for example, derived moral force from the claim that he, like his fellow-Calvinists, was a good family man and a loyal citizen.[27]

Linton thus draws attention to the growing currency of the idea that citizenship implied the right to religious toleration. Eventually the monarchy itself acquiesced in this change in public opinion, and some civic rights were formally conceded to Protestants in 1787 – and the Revolutionaries were, of course, to take the logic of this position much further.

Every kingdom has its own distinctive toleration tale. In some, the forces of Enlightenment came to prevail, albeit partially and sometimes temporarily. Habsburg Austria offers a case in point. In 'Enlightenment in the Habsburg Monarchy: History of a Belated and Short-lived Phenomenon' (see pp. 196–211, this volume), Karl Vocelka notes that Austrian historiography has traditionally defined the reigns of Maria Theresa, Joseph II and Leopold II as the period (1740–92) of 'enlightened absolutism'. Although they already enjoyed a certain influence at the dawn of the eighteenth century through Prince Eugene de Savoy and the Emperor Joseph I, enlightened ideas remained restricted to the elite. The religious struggles of the seventeenth century had undermined the influence of Protestantism and established Catholicism as the state religion in Austria and Bohemia, and the traditional Protestant stress on education and literacy was replaced by a Counter-Reformation focus on fine arts and music. This, together with a stagnant economy, meant that the cultural climate was not congenial to Enlightenment ideas, which in any case lacked a broad social base.

Maria Theresa remained baroque in her attitudes in most respects. While she prided herself upon conducting 'enlightened' policies against peasant superstition, particularly in her non-Austrian territories,[28] and initiated reforms in administration, law and education, religious toleration as such was anathema to her. Working towards the creation of a uniformly Catholic state, she deported many thousands of her Bohemian Protestant subjects.

Joseph II (who ruled for only ten years, although he also had some influence on the politics of his mother) and Leopold II (who ruled for just two years) did, however, put enlightened ideas into action. Joseph brought in a Patent of Toleration – for Protestants, Greek-Orthodox and Jews – and a number of reforms regarding the Catholic Church, such as a reduction of ceremonies, pilgrimages and brotherhoods, the dissolution of monasteries, etc. Quite unlike his mother, Joseph believed toleration would actually bolster the political strength of the state. 'With freedom of religion', he wrote to her in June 1777, 'one religion will remain, that of guiding all citizens alike to the welfare of the state. Without this approach we shall not save any greater number of souls, and we shall lose a great many more useful and essential people'.[29] Toleration thus was politically expedient. The outbreak of the French Revolution led, however, to a return to reaction under Francis I, who succeeded Leopold II in 1792. Reforms ceased, Revolutionary sympathizers were persecuted, and the brief period of Enlightenment in the Habsburg Monarchy ended abruptly.

While Austria seemed to be moving towards toleration, other nations were veering in the opposite direction, if for complex reasons. In 'Toleration in Eastern Europe: the Dissident Question in Eighteenth-century Poland–Lithuania' (see pp. 212–29, this volume), Michael Müller focuses on religious conflict in the period before the partitions, examining the reasons for the erosion of toleration in Eastern Europe and the emergence of a new 'neo-confessionalism'.

In Poland and elsewhere in the East, the Enlightenment was not necessarily instrumental in consolidating already existing, or producing new models of, multi-confessional coexistence. The ideal of religious unity played an important role in processes of proto-national integration or, as in Catherine the Great's Russia, in the shaping of an identity of late-absolutist statehood. Eighteenth-century politics tended to instrumentalize religious issues in the context of great power relations – in other words, religion became nationalized. The fate of toleration, Müller emphasizes, lay in tensions between secularization and re-confessionalization.

Other political entities embodied toleration of a sort, but independently of avowed enlightenment ideologies – realities counting more than rhetoric. In his 'A Tolerant Society? Religious Toleration and the Holy Roman Empire, 1648–1806' (see pp. 175–95, this volume), Joachim Whaley observes that the Peace of Westphalia had brought to a conclusion over a century of often violent confessional struggle dividing the Holy Roman Empire. Primarily a religious peace, it set the judicial framework for relations between the three main Christian denominations, and hence for religious coexistence generally, in the German lands for the next 150 years.

Whaley addresses the Imperial problem at several levels. In terms of politics, the provisions of the Peace of Westphalia were designed to neutralize religion as an issue liable to unsettle the relations between the members of the Empire. At the same time, however, by specifying in great detail the rights of various Christian confessions in designated territories, the Treaty created a check to change, since its opponents could always appeal to the sanctity of the Empire's fundamental law.

Nevertheless, many factors bred demands for change. Jurists such as Thomasius, looking back to precedents from pagan Rome, promoted the view that rulers and regents had no authority in religious matters, and such jurisprudential arguments were given greater force during the eighteenth century by the influence first of English and later of French writings on toleration. In some localities purely pragmatic considerations – both political and, above all, economic – prompted legislation granting rights to religious minorities including radical sects, Mennonites and Jews, none of whom had been mentioned in the Peace of Westphalia.

Whaley examines the interplay between ideals and necessities in stimulating legislation first in the Protestant territories and later in many of the Catholic principalities. This legislation commonly involved granting licences to specific groups for specific purposes. After the 1770s this piecemeal approach was itself condemned as inadequate by enlightened critics who regarded licences as simply another, if disguised, form of intolerance. Contemporaries such as Goethe and Schiller protested that they were living in an intolerant age. In Goethe's judgement, to tolerate was itself to insult, rather as Tom Paine contended that the very notion of toleration was inherently intolerant, since it implied its granting as an act of grace and favour, whereas in truth freedom of thought and conscience was a basic right.

Such criticisms did little, however, to bring about more general change. That was the product of the reform period after 1800, in which the Holy Roman Empire and its restrictive legislation were destroyed. A reduced number of larger German states emerged, with confessionally more mixed populations: for the first time the principle of legal equality between individuals of different denominations became a functional prerequisite of the new polities.

Despite some examples of *de facto* toleration of a limited number of immigrant Reformed communities in the Lutheran states of Scandinavia from the late sixteenth through the early seventeenth centuries, neither Denmark nor Sweden proved particularly receptive to Enlightenment toleration.[30] French Enlightenment ideas were advanced in Denmark and neighbouring Sweden by the influential philosopher and playwright, Ludvig Holberg (1684–1754), who was particularly influenced by the writings of Montaigne. Like his French mentors Holberg was hostile to the established clergy and learned theology. Despite his adherence to a modern Deism he never became an advocate of religious toleration. According to Holberg, articles of faith which went against common sense had to be rejected. Thus Catholicism with its emphasis on transubstantiation had to be discarded as dangerous superstition, while Calvinism with its emphasis on predestination undermined God's justice and mercy. *Raison d'état*, argued Holberg, could not allow such denominations or atheists to be publicly tolerated. However, the fact that Holberg was convinced that everyone had a duty to examine their faith and accepted religious dogma critically, meant that while he could not support freedom of worship he came down strongly in support of freedom of conscience and speech.[31] Even if, by the mid-eighteenth century, Holberg and French Enlightenment authors such as Voltaire and Montesquieu had a considerable readership in Denmark, as well as in Sweden, where the writings of Locke and Hume seem to have been particularly popular, their views never appear to have reached beyond the urban upper classes and the educated gentry, and they had little if any immediate practical effect. If anything, in the short term Enlightenment ideas, together with the pressures from Pietist circles, led to greater intolerance spurred on by the increasingly beleaguered Lutheran state churches of Scandinavia.[32]

In 1770 when the Court physician Johann Friedrich Struensee became chief minister in Denmark it seemed to many contemporaries that the Enlightenment had finally arrived in the North. They were confirmed in their beliefs when in September 1770 Struensee's government removed all censorship. Even if some restrictions were re-introduced the following year, this freedom of the press gave rise to a host of pamphlets of a highly heterodox nature, many of which were particularly hostile to the established Lutheran clergy who were portrayed as fat and greedy priests. Struensee also proceeded to demolish many of the moral laws, cancelling the fines which had hitherto been imposed on people found involved in extra-marital sex, while instructing the Lutheran Church to offer similar baptismal treatment to illegitimate as well as legitimate children. Such moral relativism, however, caused considerable hostility among the conservative and orthodox establishment who needed little justification to take action against a man whom they did their utmost to portray as a dangerous atheist. Struensee's fall in January 1772 and subsequent execution meant that his Enlightenment project was short-lived and of little consequence.[33]

Towards the end of the eighteenth century there was a growing support for toleration in Denmark and Sweden even among Lutheran theologians, many of whom supported some form of toleration. Locke's *Letters on Toleration* was translated into Swedish in 1793, while Sweden received its toleration act (*Religionsfrihetslag*) in 1781. It had, however, clear limitations, for example only extending the right to stand for parliament to those of the Reformed faith. Schooling still remained the prerogative of the Lutheran Church in Sweden, while Catholic proselytism was explicitly forbidden. Jews were excluded and regulated by the so-called *Judenreglement* issued the following year. Despite such changes and initiatives toleration was never fully and sincerely embraced by the ecclesiastical and political leadership in Scandinavia during the Enlightenment period.[34]

Conclusions

What generalizations do these different national experiences prompt? We must, for one thing, always be careful not to confuse rubrics and realities. As Robert Darnton has shown, though *ancien régime* France officially maintained a system of strict censorship, it was an open secret that censorship was at best uneven, and Malesherbes, one of the *Directeurs de la Librairie* – that is, chief censor – was not a little sympathetic towards the *philosophes*. Clandestine manuscripts circulated widely, and banned books were constantly smuggled into the country from the United Provinces and the Swiss cantons.[35] Nicholas Davidson likewise shows that in various Italian states censorship, though officially rigorous, was in actuality lax, corrupt or erratic. No regime had the power, even if it possessed the will, to enforce absolute unity of worship or prohibitions on print.

In his wide-ranging 'Multiculturalism and Ethnic Cleansing in the Enlightenment' (see pp. 69–85, this volume), Robert Wokler observes how, during the past 200 years, critics of the 'Enlightenment Project' have decried its philosophy for its shallow rationalism, its uniformitarian conceptions of human nature and the alleged sinister application of its political doctrines by totalitarian regimes.[36] Addressing the charge that leading Enlightenment thinkers were as intolerant of religious and social diversity as the orthodoxies they denounced, Wokler appraises the commitment to multiculturalism in the philosophical anthropologies of such protagonists as Voltaire, Hume, Diderot, Kant and Condorcet. Above all he identifies a principle of toleration at the heart of the Enlightenment, which he views as an intellectual movement which did not *prefigure* but rather attempted to *forestall* the grandiose schemes of ethnic cleansing which have been so prevalent throughout the twentieth century.

A somewhat dissimilar assessment is offered by Sylvana Tomaselli. Her 'Intolerance, the Virtue of Princes and Radicals' (see pp. 86–101, this volume) holds that scrutiny of seventeenth- and eighteenth-century writings reveals that toleration was not particularly prized as a virtue. Toleration was not even routinely portrayed by its advocates as a good in itself – mostly it was considered as a means to an end. For Montesquieu, it was a necessary route to prosperity and peace, rather than a neglected virtue.

To understand why this was so, we need, Tomaselli contends, to examine further the texts and contexts in which toleration was discussed. The two most important political theorists around 1700, Bossuet and Fénelon, provide an appropriate starting-point for her elucidation of the moral status of toleration for eighteenth-century minds.

Overall, according to Martin Fitzpatrick's survey, 'Toleration and the Enlightenment Movement' (see pp. 23–68, this volume), there are many ways of exploring the themes of freedom and repression in the Enlightenment. Fitzpatrick discounts the triumphalist whiggism which would trace an inevitable rise of toleration through the Enlightenment and beyond, but he equally challenges the pessimistic view that the Enlightenment, in its attacks on the *ancien régime* confessional state, cleared the way for the imposition of new and more stringent mind and behavioural controls. The truth lies, he suggests, somewhere between both positions.

That is why, Fitzpatrick contends, it is necessary to probe ambivalences in the thinking of the *philosophes*, and in so doing he raises major questions. What sort of prejudices did they attack, and which were they content to leave in place? What was the relationship between their editorializing and their actions? What prejudices did they themselves retain? Finally, by the vigour of their attack on intolerance, did they not create a new sort of intolerance, one favourable to enlightened uniformity? Did Voltaire, for instance, envisage a new 'Church'? Did reason dictate a new dogmatism? Was new *philosophe* but old priest writ large?

Through posing such questions, Fitzpatrick moves on to the relationship between campaigns for religious toleration, understood in the restricted terms of freedom of worship, and the trend to demand toleration as a 'right'. Did such changes in discourse mean a real shift in programme, moving ultimately away from a concern with toleration towards a pluralistic society, and the implied acceptance of moral and religious relativism? Did religious claims finally become swallowed up in the specifications of the modern state?

This book does not suggest that the Enlightenment was some predestined stage in the triumph of toleration: far from it. But, as John Gray has recently stressed, it was the thinkers of the Enlightenment who most clearly voiced those arguments for toleration, in all their strengths and weaknesses, which continue to envelop us in our present multicultural and multireligious societies. Here, as in so many other ways, we are the children of the Enlightenment.[37]

Notes

1 For introduction to the sixteenth- and seventeenth-century debates, see O.P. Grell and B. Scribner (eds), *Tolerance and Intolerance in the European Reformation*, Cambridge, 1996; O.P. Grell, J.I. Israel and N. Tyacke (eds), *From Persecution to Toleration: The Glorious Revolution and Religion in England*, Oxford, 1991; W.K. Jordan, *The Development of religious Toleration in England*, 4 vols., Cambridge, Mass., 1932–40; reprint Gloucester, Mass., 1965; E. Labrousse, 'Religious Toleration', in P.P. Wiener (ed.), *Dictionary of the History of Ideas*, 5 vols., New York, 1974: IV, 112–21; H. Kamen, *The Rise of Toleration*, London, 1967; J.C. Laursen and C.J. Nederman (eds), *Beyond the Persecuting Society*, Philadelphia, 1998. See also R.I. Moore, *The Formation of a Persecuting Society: Power and Deviance in Western Europe AD 950–1250*, Oxford, 1986.

2 From a letter of 1820, quoted in R. Shattuck, *Forbidden Knowledge. From Prometheus to Pornography*, New York, 1996: 35. The transition from religious to political frameworks in the Enlightenment is well discussed in Michel de Certeau, *The Writing of History*, trans. Tom Conley, New York, 1988: 149–91 ('The Formality of Practices').

3 Peter Gay's *The Enlightenment: An Interpretation* is subtitled *The Rise of Modern Paganism*, London, 1966; see also his *The Enlightenment: An Interpretation*, II: *The Science of Freedom*, London, 1969; and the excellent discussion in D. Outram, *The Enlightenment*, Cambridge, 1995: 31ff. For atheism see M. Hunter and D. Wootton (eds), *Atheism from the Reformation to the Enlightenment*, Oxford, 1992.

4 J. Schmidt (ed.), *What is Enlightenment? Eighteenth Century Answers and Twentieth Century Questions*, Berkeley, 1996.

5 N. Hampson, *The Enlightenment: An Evaluation of Its Assumptions, Attitudes and Values*, Harmondsworth, 1968: 106; J. Byrne, *Glory, Jest and Riddle: Religious Thought in the Enlightenment*, London, 1996.

6 J.G. McEvoy and E. McGuire, 'God and Nature: Priestley's Way of Rational Dissent', *Historical Studies in the Physical Sciences*, VI, 1975: 325–404; J.G. McEvoy, 'Enlightenment and Dissent in Science: Joseph Priestley and the Limits of Theoretical Reasoning', *Enlightenment and Dissent*, II, 1983: 47–67.

7 F.M.A. de Voltaire, *Philosophical Dictionary*, 1764, article 'Theologian'.

8 For Montaigne see M.A. Screech (ed.), *The Essays of Michel de Montaigne*, Harmondsworth, 1991: Book III, Essay 11, 'On the Lame': 1166. For Donne, see C.A. Patrides (ed.), *The Complete English Poems of John Donne*, London, 1983: 228.

9 John Milton, *Paradise Lost*, Book IX, lines 351–2, in D. Masson (ed.), *The Poetical Works of John Milton*, 3 vols, London, 1874: I, 351.

10 P. Hazard, *The European Mind 1680–1715*, trans. J.L. May, Harmondsworth, 1964; R.F. Jones, *Ancients and Moderns: A Study of the Background of the Battle of the Books*, St. Louis, 1936; Joseph Levine, *The Battle of the Books: History and Literature in the Augustan Age*, Ithaca, 1991.

11 On Deism see J.A.I. Champion, *The Pillars of Priestcraft Shaken: The Church of England and its Enemies, 1660–1730*, Cambridge, 1992; Peter Gay, *Deism: An Anthology*, Princeton, 1968; M.C. Jacob, *The Radical Enlightenment: Pantheists, Freemasons and Republicans*, London, 1981.

12 F.M.A. de Voltaire, *Letters Concerning the English Nation*, London, 1733: 44.
   Sir William Temple's *Observations upon the United Provinces of the Netherlands* (1673) had earlier developed similar arguments. Temple stated that 'the great and general end of all religion, next to men's happiness hereafter, is their happiness here'. Since 'the way to our future happiness has been perpetually disputed throughout the world, and must be left at last to the impressions made upon every man's belief and conscience', our 'happiness here' is alone of public concern. The rulers of the United Provinces had grasped that. There

> men live together like citizens of the world, associated by the common ties of humanity and by the bonds of peace, under the impartial protection of indifferent laws, with equal encouragement of all art and industry and equal freedom of speculation and enquiry, [wherein] will appear to consist chiefly of the vast growth of their trade and riches, and consequently the strength and greatness of their state.

   Sir William Temple, *Observations upon the United Provinces of the Netherlands*, ed. G.N. Clark, Oxford, 1972: 99–100, 106–7; see Kamen, *Rise of Toleration*: 223.

13 M. Heyd, *'Be Sober and Reasonable'*: the Critique of Enthusiasm in the Seven-

teenth and Early Eighteenth Centuries, Leiden, 1995; J.G.A. Pocock, 'Post-puritan England and the Problem of the Enlightenment', in P. Zagorin (ed.), *Culture and Politics from Puritanism to the Enlightenment*, Berkeley, 1980: 91–111.

14 S. Butler, *Hudibras, Parts I and II and Selected Other Writings*, ed. J. Wilders and H. de Quehen, Oxford, 1973, lines 193–5, 203–4, p. 7.

15 For the following on Locke, see John Dunn, 'The Claim to Freedom of Conscience: Freedom of Speech, Freedom of Thought, Freedom of Worship?', in O.P. Grell, J.I. Israel and N. Tyacke (eds), *From Persecution to Toleration*: 171–94; M. Cranston, *John Locke: A Biography*, London, 1957; Kamen, *Rise of Toleration*: 231f.

16 Kamen, *The Rise of Toleration*: 204; see also J. Yolton, *John Locke and the Way of Ideas*, Oxford, 1956.

17 J.C. Laursen, 'Baylean Liberalism: Tolerance Requires Nontolerance', in J.C. Laursen and C.J. Nederman (eds), *Beyond the Persecuting Society*, Philadelphia, 1998: 197–215. For discussion see Kamen, *Rise of Toleration*: 236ff.

18 R. Shattuck, *Forbidden Knowledge*, passim.

19 Quoted in H.W. Koch, *A History of Prussia*, London, 1978: 41.

20 Q. Skinner, *Liberty Before Liberalism*, Cambridge, 1997; I. Berlin, *Two Concepts of Liberty*, Oxford, 1958; J.G.A. Pocock, *The Machiavellian Moment. Florentine Political Thought and the Atlantic Republican Tradition*, Princeton, 1975; *idem*, 'Machiavelli, Harrington and English Political Ideologies in the Eighteenth Century', in *Politics, Language and Time: Essays in Political Thought and History*, London, 1972: 104–47. The question of the importance of Locke to Enlightenment liberalism has been fiercely disputed: see J.G.A. Pocock, 'The Myth of John Locke and the Obsession with Liberalism', in *John Locke: Papers Read at a Clark Library Seminar, 10 December, 1977*, Los Angeles Clark Library, 1980: 1–24; I. Kramnick, *Republicanism and Bourgeois Radicalism*, Ithaca, 1990. The modern implications of these Enlightenment debates about proto-liberalism are brilliantly developed in J. Gray, *Enlightenment's Wake: Politics and Culture at the Close of the Modern Age*, London, 1995: 19–27 ('Toleration: A Post-Liberal Perspective').

21 For the claim that Enlightenment opinion created despotisms of its own, see J.L. Talmon, *The Rise of Totalitarian Democracy*, Boston, 1952.

22 M. Foucault, 'What is Enlightenment?', in Paul Rabinow (ed.), *The Foucault Reader*, New York, 1984: 32–50; Outram, *The Enlightenment*: 2.

23 D. Defoe, *The Life and Strange surprizing Adventures of Robinson Crusoe*, ed. J.D. Crowley, Oxford, 1972: 241.

24 S.T. Coleridge, *Table Talk*, 'Toleration – Calvin – Servetus – Norwegians' (3 January 1834), London, 1884: 271.

25 For analysis of national divergences, see R. Porter and M. Teich (eds), *The Enlightenment in National Context*, Cambridge, 1981.

26 F. Venturi, *Settecento Riformatore*, Torino, 1987; *idem, Utopia and Reform in the Enlightenment*, Cambridge, 1971; and S. Woolf (ed.), *Italy and the Enlightenment*, London, 1972.

27 D. Bien, *The Calas Affair; Reason, Tolerance and Heresy in Eighteenth-Century Toulouse*, Princeton, 1960. See also G. Adams, *The Huguenots and French Opinion: The Enlightenment Debate on Toleration*, Waterloo, Ontario, 1991.

28 G. Klaniczay, *The Uses of Supernatural Power: The Transformation of Popular*

Religion in Medieval and Early-Modern Europe, trans. S. Singerman, Princeton, 1990.

29 A. von Arneth, *Maria Theresa und Joseph II: Ihre Correspondenz*, 3 vols, Vienna, 1867: II, 141–2.

30 See O.P. Grell, 'Exile and Tolerance', in Grell and Scribner (eds), *Tolerance and Intolerance*: 164–81.

31 F.J. Billeskov Jansen, *Dansk Litteratur Historie*, I, Copenhagen, 1967: 324–34 and 367–76.

32 S. Lindroth, *Svensk Lärdomshistoria. Frihetstiden*, Stockholm, 1978: 497–557 and O. Feldbaek, 'Tro, viden og holdninger 1730–1814', in A.E. Christensen *et al.* (eds), *Danmarks Historie*, IV, Copenhagen, 1982: 228–52. Volumes dealing specifically with the Enlightenment in Denmark/Norway and Sweden/Finland have yet to be written, even if some useful information can be obtained from S. Holm, *Filosofien i Norden før 1900*, Copenhagen, 1967.

33 See S. Cedergreen Bech, *Struensee og hans tid*, Copenhagen, 1972; and L. Koch, *Oplysningstiden i den Danske Kirke 1700–1800*, Copenhagen, 1914.

34 See N. Hope, *German and Scandinavian Protestantism 1700 to 1918*, Oxford, 1995: 300–6.

35 R. Darnton, *The Business of Enlightenment. A Publishing History of the Encyclopédie, 1775–1800*, Cambridge, Mass., 1999; *idem, The Literary Underground of the Old Regime*, Cambridge, Mass., 1982; *idem, The Forbidden Best-Sellers of Pre-Revolutionary France*, London, 1996.

36 For modern critiques of Enlightenment rationality which cast it as intolerant, see M. Horkheimer and T. Adorno, *The Dialectic of Enlightenment*, trans. J. Cumming, London, 1983; J. Baudrillard, *Symbolic Exchange and Death*, trans. I. Hamilton Grant, London, 1993; Z. Bauman, *Mortality, Immortality and Other Life Strategies*, Cambridge, 1992.

37 Gray, *Enlightenment's Wake*. See also S. Mendus (ed.), *Justifying Tolerance: Conceptual and Historical Perspectives*, Cambridge, 1988.

2. Toleration and the Enlightenment Movement

Martin Fitzpatrick

It has become increasingly difficult to write about the Enlightenment. The topic has been the subject of great academic interest over the last half century. Although it was accepted that the general features of the Enlightenment were well known, it was felt that there was still a great deal to learn about the variety of its manifestations.[1] Interest was also stimulated by the attempt to understand the way in which the progressive hopes associated with the Enlightenment, not least the desire to create more tolerant societies, foundered so badly in the first half of the twentieth century. The consequence of much energetic research has been to dissolve old certainties, to find Enlightenment in the most unlikely places, to see national characteristics in the Enlightenment, and to make one wonder whether the Enlightenment was a movement at all.[2] In 1987, J.G.A. Pocock, speaking at the Seventh International Congress on the Enlightenment at Budapest, suggested that one should not use the definite article – The Enlightenment – because 'it creates the [inaccurate] presumption of a single unitary process, displaying a uniform set of characteristics'. His view was cited by L.G. Crocker in his introduction to *The Blackwell Companion to the Enlightenment*. He also followed Norman Hampson in arguing that although the use of the word Enlightenment is justified, it cannot be defined satisfactorily:

All [definitions] fail because the complexities and inconsistencies of historical reality overflow the rationally convenient reduction to a definition, which is by definition, a limit ... To use a definition, as Hegel said, immediately exposes what contradicts it. The penalty is historical distortion.[3]

However, some of the greatest students of the Enlightenment have been prepared to take the risk. One of the most recent, Peter Gay, in his magisterial two-volume study published in 1966 and 1969, argued that although the philosophic movement was 'rich, various and sometimes contradictory', it was essentially united: it was a 'loose, informal, wholly unorganized coalition of cultural critics, religious sceptics, and political reformers ... united in a programme of secularism, humanity, cosmopolitanism and freedom'. It was predominantly French, and so it reached its climax in the mid century when the great *philosophes* were at the height of their powers, and when Voltaire began campaigning for law reform. This was when the *philosophes* began to translate their ideas into action and became the 'party of humanity'.[4]

Although there were limitations in Gay's views, not least in his failure to appreciate the religious dimensions of the Enlightenment, there is something to be said for reviving his notion that the Enlightenment was a movement with some sort of programme based on a set of philosophic assumptions. Recently Robert Darnton has argued along similar lines. He suggests that the Enlightenment movement centred on France and within France on Paris. It was crucially French not because of the originality of the ideas of the *philosophes* but because 'that is where the movement came together and defined itself as a cause'. Although there had been earlier examples of groups of thinkers working for a cause, the *philosophes* represented something new:

Men of letters acting in concert and with considerable autonomy to push through a programme . . . They were marked as a group by persecution, just enough to dramatize their daring and not enough to deter them from undertaking more. They developed a strong sense of 'us' against them; men of wit against the bigots, honnêtes hommes against exclusive privilege, the children of light against the demons of darkness.

They were an elite who sought the ear of kings and queens, the patronage of the rich and powerful and the approval and support of a burgeoning middle-class public. They orchestrated a republic of letters which stretched throughout Europe. This is what Voltaire called 'the church'. Many foreign *philosophes* made the pilgrimage to Paris, where they often felt slightly ill at ease. Nor did they necessarily learn a great deal from the journey. As Darnton remarks, 'Thinkers in Stockholm and Naples did not need to read Voltaire in order to learn about tolerance and natural law.'[5] None the less, they looked to the *philosophes* as leaders of the movement to which they adhered.

Adopting this 'deflationary' view of the Enlightenment for our discussion means that the focus will be on France. But not exclusively, because the movement can be extended at both ends and given a broader western European context, on the understanding that those involved must have a sense of participating in a movement, an awareness of persecution, a sense of grievance against the powers that be and be actively involved in trying to change things, either by precept or example, or both. What Darnton calls the pre-Enlightenment in England and the Low Countries, can be viewed alternatively as the first phase of the Enlightenment, and one which was absolutely crucial in associating the Enlightenment with the cause of toleration. It contained an important exilic component, most crucially French Huguenots, but also English dissident Whigs and Dissenters. They all belonged to the republic of letters which Pierre Bayle was so anxious to foster.[6] Questions relating to toleration were central to it. A.M. Wilson has enumerated fifteen characteristics of the Enlightenment all of which occurred first in England.[7] Five of these are relevant to the question of toleration in the broadest sense. Wilson argues that the English set the example of toleration, tolerance, freedom of the press, freedom from arbitrary arrest and the theory and practice of liberal constitutionalism, and that these examples all had a direct influence on the *philosophes*. Moreover, the English undoubtedly had a sense of being part of a movement which, like that of the *philosophes*, was for a period under threat. Although by the mid eighteenth century the centre of the Enlightenment movement was undoubtedly France, that in Britain, notably in Scotland in the mid century and England later in the century, contributed crucial dimensions to the movement: in Scotland especially through the development of the science of man; in England through the exposition of more radical political ideas, which were very much linked with the American Revolution, and which would in turn find expression in the United Provinces. Indeed, what R.R. Palmer has described as the age of the Democratic Revolution which embraced Europe and America may be regarded as the final phase of the Enlightenment.[8]

Viewing the Enlightenment as a movement enables one to recapture the contemporary sense of enlightened virtue spreading far and wide, while the impetus and focus remained in western Europe and, towards the end of the century, in America.[9] This was a characteristic of both the earlier and later phases of the Enlightenment. Writing in 1706, the third Earl of Shaftesbury declared, 'There is a mighty light which spreads over the world, especially in those two free nations of England and Holland, on whom the affairs of all Europe now turn.'[10]

Voltaire himself contributed to this view of things in his *Letters Concerning the English Nation* (1733) published a year later as the *Lettres philosophiques*, in which the English were portrayed as the most enlightened nation setting an example of constitutionalism, liberty and tolerance to the rest of the civilized world.[11] At the end of the century, Richard Price, in his *Discourse on the Love of Our Country* (1789), combined the Voltairean notion that the English set the example in granting subjects their essential liberties in the Glorious Revolution through the Bill of Rights and the Act of Toleration, with homage to key figures of Enlightenment in France – Fénelon, Marmontel, Montesquieu and Turgot. They had sown seeds which were about to bear fruit in 'a glorious harvest'.[12] That harvest represented the emancipation from political and intellectual tyranny, which had kept mankind in darkness. In his conclusion, he resorted to the metaphor of the spreading light. Praising the philosophers of the Enlightenment, he enthused, 'Behold the light you have struck out, after setting America free, reflected to France and there kindled into a blaze that lays despotism in ashes and warms and illuminates Europe!'[13]

Price was perhaps being unduly parochial, for this feeling of the illumination of Enlightenment found its greatest cultural manifestation in Mozart's *The Magic Flute*, in which the light of the Enlightenment spread throughout the universe, and mankind everywhere would benefit from it rays.[14]

The light of the Enlightenment, unlike the traditional Christian idea of light as an inner light, as a light of faith, was an external light, the light of knowledge and of truth, which would emancipate man, and transform him and his conditions of existence. The Enlightenment as a movement was sustained by the related notions that the development of enlightened ideas would enable man to throw off the yoke of intellectual oppression and that these ideas would not only change ways of thinking but ways of behaving. Central to such notions of transformation was the belief that governments could be persuaded to grant toleration to differing religions and societies could be educated to grow more tolerant. Voltaire enjoyed a unique role in this process on account of his towering status as a *philosophe* and of his trail-blazing campaigns against intolerance. The perceived power of his influence and the general optimistic naivety concerning the power of ideas was demonstrated in an English advertisement for subscription to a complete edition of his works.

he [Voltaire] has done more, singly, to dispose the mind for the elegant and rational use and enjoyment of life: for the peace of mind and good order of society: for the dispelling the clouds of ferocity, superstition and fanaticism, and brightening the atmosphere of the mind, than all other writers collectively.

There followed a footnote:

Was Voltaire read in Spain, there would be no Inquisition, no Auto da fé. Had his work been Universally known and perused in the British Empire, there would be no rebellion: nor would the Metropolis lately have been at the eve of destruction and general conflagration.[15]

Such confidence may seem naïve, but it is important to acknowledge that the actual power of ideas about toleration rested in part upon it. I shall return to Voltaire in due course, but first I wish to examine the Enlightenment agenda as regards toleration.

Any student of ideas of toleration will soon discover that many of them were of ancient origin. For example, some of the central ideas relating to conscience, including the need to give ease to tender consciences, to allow conscience to operate free of the interference of the state, and the suggestion that conscience could not be forced, could all be found in the early Christian church. Such notions would be repeated in early-modern arguments for toleration. Indeed they gained a special urgency as a result of the religious conflict caused by the Reformation and of the growth of the power of the confessional state. During this period there emerged at least six approaches, both intellectual and practical, to the issue of toleration. These were not self-contained, their ideas often overlapped, and they were usually closely related to context and circumstance, but there is a sense in which, over the early-modern period, they became identifiable traditions. Eighteenth-century ideas and practices of toleration drew on these traditions, but rarely singularly, as the chapters in this volume indicate clearly. At the risk of oversimplifying, these traditions may be outlined as follows.

At the core of the religious tradition of toleration was the imperative to obey one's conscience understood in the light of scripture, and the concomitant right to obey one's conscience. This was powerfully reinforced by Luther's conscientious stand at Worms. To turn this into a truly tolerant tradition, this tradition usually had to be mixed with others, for in most instances, religions were reluctant to concede the rights of conscience to others that they claimed for themselves. However, in the hands of some Socinians and Anabaptists it led to self-contained arguments for toleration. They argued that faith could not be compelled, that the state should not interfere in the religious beliefs of its subjects or citizens, and that complete freedom of religious enquiry was necessary for the discovery or recovery of Christian truth and for conscientious sincerity in religion.

The irenic tradition was present in Renaissance humanism. As a consensual and peace-loving tradition it grew in reaction to the fierce conflict brought about by the Reformation. It sought to reduce religion to essentials, to emphasize the core of common truths in Christianity in whatever organizational form it existed, and to direct attention away from theological disputatiousness to Christian moral virtue.[16] In the seventeenth century this came to be associated with Latitudinarianism in Britain and Arminianism in the United Provinces. It was fortified by the natural law tradition which sought to create a new moral order which would 'gain the consent of all Europeans', irrespective of their confessional differences. Although it was less concerned with dissent than with unity, it witnessed the gradual realization that that could not be obtained without toleration of diversity within *and* of dissidence without. In that sense it can be seen as developing out of the late medieval concern to secure *pax et concordia* as well as out of humanist universalism.[17]

The sceptical humanistic tradition, closely related to the irenic tradition, challenged the view that a single rational understanding of Christian religion was possible. It argued that everyone was orthodox to himself, that human arbitration in matters of religious truths could not be relied upon, and that the connection between faith and morality was uncertain. Every Christian, therefore, should be allowed to find his/her own way to God. Some went further and included Deists and atheists in the right to toleration. In radical hands this embraced freethinkers who accepted the need for civil religion, but believed the educated few should be able to pursue truth in whatever direction it led, so long as they formally assented to civil religion and did not seek to undermine it in their publications. Such freethinkers drew on the sceptical *libertin* tradition which accepted that an enlightened elite in private could behave and think in ways which contravened orthodox theology, religion and morality, provided that they were obedient to public authority. It developed in the late sixteenth century in France and was expounded by Michel de Montaigne in his *Essais* (1580 and 1588) and by his disciple, Pierre Charron, in his *De la sagesse* (1601), both profoundly influential works.[18] Later the notion of the privately emancipated intellectual formed a key aspect of the meaning of a *philosophe* as defined by the *Académie Française* in its first dictionary published in the late seventeenth century (1694).[19]

Although the anticlerical and anti-religious potential in the sceptical humanist tradition was considerable, it had a strong religious and especially fideist dimension. There were, however, two other tolerationist traditions whose preoccupations were secular. These were the republican and *politique* traditions. The former stressed the value of religion to civil society as a communal bond and moral cement. It accepted that within the bounds of a few agreed doctrines, usually a belief in one God, in His Overruling Providence and in a future life in which the good will be rewarded and the wicked punished, there should be a toleration of a variety of beliefs and practices. This tradition accepted that a minimalist religious belief was a necessary qualification for citizenship, but that apart, complete toleration should be allowed. This tradition looked back to classical times for inspiration, and would in some eighteenth-century formulations seem quite cynical, the most famous of which being Edward Gibbon's, in volume I of his *Decline and Fall of the Roman Empire* (1776), 'The various modes of worship, which prevailed in the Roman World, were all considered by the people, as equally true; by the philosopher, as equally false; and by the magistrate, as equally useful.'[20]

The *politique* tradition was a response to religious conflict in the sixteenth century. In the face of irreducible divisions, it accepted that compromises had to be made with religious minorities which could not be forcibly converted, and that the attempt to enforce uniformity had seriously disruptive political and/or economic consequences. On pragmatic grounds therefore, it favoured limited toleration for religious minorities, notably the Huguenots in France, while often retaining the aspiration for a conversion by persuasion, so that the ideal of a state united in religion could be attained. The *Politique* party was formed by Michel de L'Hôpital, chancellor to Catherine de Medici. Although the tradition to which it gave birth was attractive in absolutist states which were severely affected by religious conflict, the pragmatic attitude with which it was infused and its secular assessment of the need for toleration would find sympathy in other states and societies.[21] Similarly, aspects of the republican tradition would appeal to those who favoured a comprehensive church on religious as well as secular grounds, and who thought the threat of irreligion more serious than that of sectarian Christianity, however reprehensible that might be. One could amplify this, but the essential point, as the essays in this volume exemplify, is the flexibility of the arguments and traditions in favour of toleration. Different languages and logics would be employed side by side. Even when some in the late eighteenth century wanted to go beyond tolerationist arguments to argue instead in favour of a complete equality of religious and civil rights, they would mix the new Enlightened language of rights and the older languages in which toleration was implicitly or explicitly a dispensation or favour.

Few would argue for the originality of Enlightenment ideas of toleration, yet neither were they completely derivative nor without special significance. Not only were the circumstances in which they were used different in the period of the Enlightenment from those of the Renaissance and Reformation, which is fairly obvious, but also the conjunction of ideas and the thrust of argument were new. The intellectual world changed so much as a result of the scientific revolution that those who argued for freedom of enquiry and pursuit of truth had gained confidence and conversely appeared more threatening to those who wished to maintain eternal verities (as they understood them to be) and the subservience of subjects. Moreover the combination of rationalism and empiricism which characterized so many aspects of advance in natural philosophy could be turned with good effect to questions concerning toleration. The Enlightenment saw the development of the science of society, especially in Scotland, and this lent new emphasis to the practical impact of toleration. The analogy of the free market had been used before the development of Smithsonian economics, but Smith's assertion that individuals allowed to choose their own economic self-interest would make choices of benefit not only to themselves but also to society, gave the idea of free trade in religion a warmer glow even though few advocated a complete free trade in such matters.[22] It is none the less observable that absolutist states which began to relax economic controls in the later eighteenth century also began to relax religious ones.

Not only did the Enlightenment generally impact upon notions of toleration by changing the understanding of the relationship between the state and society, it also helped to change the self-perception of religions. The first uneasy steps were taken towards understanding religion in a comparative and anthropological way. Montesquieu's best-selling *Lettres persanes* (1721) encouraged Europeans to look at themselves with the same distance and sense of curiosity as Persian travellers to the continent, and mused aloud whether it was necessary for states to have one religion.[23] Yet if the Enlightenment changed the intellectual environment in which toleration was discussed and debated, it is as well to remember, as William Doyle has reminded us, that it was not until the later eighteenth century that many came to believe that toleration rather than discrimination was the more likely to promote religious harmony.[24] Indeed the immensely destructive Gordon riots in 1780 underlined the need to proceed with the introduction and/or extension of toleration with the utmost caution. Maria Theresa believed them to be the 'result of liberty' and a salutary reminder of the need for 'religion and discipline'. Her death in the same year may have saved the Habsburg Empire from a revival of religious intolerance.[25]

Despite such fears and prejudices one might suggest that it was the growing power of the state and the reappraisal of *raison d'état*, in itself influenced by the Enlightenment, which enabled statesmen to feel more confident that toleration might be the best policy. Generally one might wish to argue that, in those states which were most authoritarian and in those societies which were least open, toleration was introduced predominantly on grounds of *Realpolitik*. There is much evidence for this interpretation in this volume, and it fortifies Sylvana Tomaselli's criticism of Enlightenment ideas of toleration in this volume. The alternative thesis put forward by Lord Acton that toleration, along with self-government and democratic rights, was slowly extracted from the increasingly powerful modern states by the 'combined efforts of the weak', is attractive but simplistic.[26] Crucial decisions relative to toleration were taken by those who had the power to influence or control state policy, therefore the role of the State in advancing or retarding toleration depended upon the nature of the polity of any given state. Toleration could only be gained in 'opposition' to the State, if the political community was sufficiently broad and developed for it to be safe for minorities to campaign for change and for that campaigning to have an impact upon state policy. Since it was in the more liberal polities that the Enlightenment was strongest, it also follows that the Enlightenment had the greatest opportunities there for campaigning for wider toleration. It would, however, be misleading to set up polarities in which, in relatively liberal states, toleration developed through idealistic campaigning, and, in the more absolute states, it developed through liberal statesmanship. It has already been noted that arguments for toleration often overlapped despite logical inconsistencies. To this one should add that they were made within varying contexts and historical circumstances. Legislation concerning toleration was often bewilderingly complex. The supreme example of that was the Holy Roman Empire as Joachim Whaley's expert dissection of the situation there amply demonstrates. Even within 'liberal' Britain the law was by no means clear. The famous Toleration Act of 1689 did not make any new law as regards toleration, rather it suspended 'pains' and 'penalties' for orthodox Protestant Dissent. Technically such Dissent was a crime until the famous Mansfield verdict in the case of Allen Evans in

1767. It is worth quoting Mansfield's language on that occasion, for it is a wonderful example of how more enlightened ideas of religion, philosophy and needs of state taken together were coming to prevail.

There is nothing certainly more unreasonable, more inconsistent with the rights of human nature, more contrary to the spirit and the precepts of the Christian Religion, more iniquitous and unjust, more impolitic, than Persecution. It is against Natural religion, Revealed Religion, and sound Policy.[27]

Yet that verdict clarified only one point of law. When the Protestant Dissenters began to campaign for the repeal of the Test and Corporation Acts in 1787, they consulted their lawyers to find out the legal situation. This was partly because those acts were for much of the time suspended by annual indemnity acts.[28] But the fact that they had to ask was indicative of another feature of the period, namely that oppressive legislation was only fitfully enforced. Tacit toleration could be found in many countries in Europe, yet it did not lead to complacency. In England, Rational Dissenters defined persecution in such a way as to include all discrimination on the grounds of belief.[29] It is in the light of the growing liberality of ideas on toleration that real physical persecution caused such a shock to enlightened opinion. When, in 1762, the Huguenot, Jean Calas, was broken on the wheel on a wrongful conviction for the murder of his son, Marc Antoine, the *philosophes*, led by Voltaire, launched an unprecedented campaign, under the banner of *écrasez l'infâme*, to persuade governments to acknowledge injustices perpetrated, to reform discriminatory laws against dissenters and to dispel public prejudices. It was their ability to use discreet influence, combined with an appeal to public opinion, which justifies the focus for the remainder of this chapter on ideas and issues relating to tolerance and toleration in the mainstream Enlightenment movement as it has been defined.

The classic study of toleration in the early-modern period by Henry Kamen, *The Rise of Toleration*, closes at the end of the seventeenth century. One might be forgiven for wondering whether toleration had 'risen' by then, when one of the most significant events in the history of religious intolerance, the revocation of the Edict of Nantes, happened in 1685. It was also the time when England suffered the worst period of intolerance of the later Stuart period, when Protestant Hungarians suffered a new burst of persecution, and dissent was being finally eradicated in Italy and Spain. These very points are noted by the author; his case is that 'practice lagged behind theory'. He cites W.K. Jordan's view that theory of toleration was 'substantially complete by 1660' and argues that the 'leading philosophers in Europe tended to agree that a large measure of toleration was not only advisable and just but also right'.[30] It is also true that the conditions under which religions would seek toleration were changing, as states asserted their power over the churches. A large measure of religious peace had been created by the Treaty of Westphalia in 1648. The treaty by extending the doctrine of *cuius regio eius religio* to Calvinism accepted the power of the State to control religious policy, and completed an essentially legalistic imperial settlement. It was not accepted by the Papacy, although it later received some measure of tacit acceptance. Religion was now playing second fiddle to the State. There is thus a paradox in that as the confessional state reached its apogee under the Sun King, it was also tolling its own death knell. The sanctification of the French State and of Louis XIV, who was not only deified but placed virtually on a par with Jesus Christ in obsequious verses composed by the Jesuits for his coronation, did not lead to a new phase of religious intrusion into politics, rather the reverse.[31] The State was using religion as a unifying force. The Ultramontanism of the latter half of his reign may have had a personal religious dimension for Louis, but essentially it was a device, and a supremely ineffective one, for repressing Jansenism.[32] However intolerant established churches were, it was increasingly clear that it would be the State which chose whether or not established intolerance was vital to its character and interests.

The fact that toleration was increasingly a matter of secular politics would affect the arguments for and against toleration. Opponents of toleration emphasized the dissidence of dissent, the disqualifications of dissenters to be good citizens or good subjects. Proponents of toleration now looked beyond the solution of confessional disputes, whether theological, liturgical or organizational. There was less concern now as to whether intolerance was unchristian (although that remained an argument in the armoury of those who sought toleration) or conversely whether the imperative of a particular confessional truth was such as to require the compulsion of consciences. The debate on toleration moved away from the virtue of a particular religion or the virtue of tolerance, even though such matters were of vital concern in eighteenth-century religion. Not only was there an increasingly secular emphasis in discussions of the issue but those discussions were affected by an increasingly empirical outlook. Both proponents and opponents of toleration would spend a good deal of time trying to prove its benefits or hazards to the State and society.

One consequence of this change of emphasis is that whether one stressed the role of the State in providing toleration, or suggested that the State should not interfere in matters of religion, proponents of conservative or radical theories of toleration all believed that their policies were beneficial in secular terms. This change of emphasis can be witnessed early in the Enlightenment. It led to a lively historical debate in relation to the persecuted Huguenots, a debate which included French, English and Dutch participants and which stretched into the eighteenth century. The Huguenots faced insuperable problems in arguing that they were deserving of toleration. In France, the dominant theory of the divine right of kings demanded submission from subjects to the powers that be, which were ordained of God; it was necessary to obey 'not only for wrath, but also for conscience sake'.[33] Yet more than submission was in fact required. It was religious uniformity. That was a requisite which the Huguenots could not fulfil. Although they had been loyal during the Frondes, they had been reluctant to convert to Catholicism and, rather than remain loyal to an increasingly persecuting state had preferred to seek exile in states which were Louis's principal enemies, many with their own histories of rebelliousness. The Huguenots could not win the argument for toleration by justifying their past conduct, for they could hardly prove their loyalty by explaining their disloyalty, nor prove their credentials for toleration by exonerating their own intolerant conduct. History could hardly provide an impartial adjudication on such divisive issues. No wonder the Huguenot Pierre Bayle complained, 'history is prepared a little like meats in a kitchen; each nation, each religion, each sect takes the same raw facts where they can be found, prepares and seasons them according to his taste . . .'[34]

Nonetheless, even as history provided a new battleground for proponents and opponents of toleration, it changed the parameters of debate, shifting discussion away from apologetics to a more objective account of confessional history. Whether it provided arguments for seeking to regulate and enlighten 'enthusiasts' as it did with Hume,[35] or greater understanding of religious differences as it did with Mosheim,[36] history provided vital information for thinking about the way confessional differences might have been handled differently, and how they might be treated in the contemporary world. Issues of toleration might be related to circumstance, and considered empirically. Questions such as the right to conscience could be viewed less as abstract claims than as pleas for consideration, leading to the discussion of those situations in which it might be appropriate to concede rights of conscience, and of the criteria by which one should judge the worthiness and sincerity of claims for toleration. If the appeal to history did not solve the charges of dissidence and disaffection, the detailed debate about them moved the focus of concerns about toleration to secular considerations. What was actually done in the name of religion was more important than the theological claims of the disputants. In the Enlightenment, the debate about religious toleration would be crucially about the moral worthiness of dissenters, and about their credentials not only as good subjects but increasingly as citizens in a modern sense.[37] From the claimants' point of view, a shift was effected from disputes between Churches and sects to petitioning the State for toleration. Established Churches sought to maintain their authority within the State, dissenters sought to weaken the confessional state. But it was the State which was the focus of attention. Religious solutions to the problem of toleration notably through comprehension were not entirely abandoned, but they became less and less convincing. Toleration was coming to be decided by secular political considerations. In Britain, the clergy after the Glorious Revolution aligned themselves on party lines and fought out their struggles through parliament. In France they would align themselves with the court or the *parlements*. Neither of these developments was entirely new, but they do indicate that at the very time the confessional state reached its apogee, it was perhaps the weapon of its own destruction. Much as it tried to spiritualize its role, its power was of this world. In the eighteenth century, anticlericalism was often an accompaniment to arguments for toleration as a means of attacking those who used clerical influence to keep the confessional state on the straight and narrow. The assault on the Jesuits which spread through the Protestant as well as the Catholic world was the supreme manifestation of this. Although assumptions about the confessional state were not thereby destroyed, they co-existed uneasily with secular ideas about the State and about the monarch's role within it. The reiteration of Louis XVI's role as protector of the Catholic religion in the Edict of Toleration, which accorded civil status to the Huguenots in 1787, is evidence of this, just as a few years later he found it impossible to shed notions of the state being his patrimony.[38] In the debate(s) on the French Revolution, older ideas about the sanctity of the State would be reiterated, and they would also be to a degree transformed by romantic organic notions of the State. Fear of the Revolution resurrected older fears of religious dissidence. Nonetheless, it was during the Revolutionary and Napoleonic period that confessional states would lose their power to dictate the terms upon which Dissenting religions were tolerated or not, and the era 'altered for ever the terms on which religious establishments ... must work'.[39] Chateaubriand would finally pronounce the desacralization of the monarchy in the Chamber of Peers on 7 August, 1830 when he declared, 'monarchy is no longer a religion'.[40] However, the *philosophes* were not to know all this. Their arguments were shaped by the continuing power of religion in the State and society, a power which permeated everyday life. At the same time, the future they envisaged was of a predominantly secular state, with religion as subordinate to it, or as separated from it.

It is generally agreed that one of the great legacies of the Enlightenment has been the right to freedom of conscience and freedom of thought. Although the Enlightenment debate on toleration did not centre exclusively on those great issues, it is true that by the end of the eighteenth century there was growing agreement amongst the educated that in an *ideal* enlightened society both should be conceded. For many, the prerequisite for greater toleration was greater enlightenment. Yet that is not the whole story, for some of the leading thinkers in the late Enlightenment, including Immanuel Kant and the Marquis de Condorcet, believed that freedom of enquiry was necessary for the development of Enlightenment. So the issue of toleration was also an issue of enlightenment strategy about which there was considerable disagreement. Enlightenment came to be deployed as a tool of State progress, and even the more authoritarian states began to appeal to a wider public as part of the process of conversion to enlightened policies. In the process, states created a new arena for the criticism of government, and the arguments for wider toleration which they promoted would increasingly become associated with those for freedom of thought, which they opposed. Indeed, it became increasingly difficult to separate the issues. Within the Enlightenment both conservative and radical thinkers linked the issue of religious toleration with freedom of thought, the tangible expression of which was the discussion of the freedom of the press and censorship. Naturally, statesmen whose priority was the use of enlightenment for modernizing the state, and conservative thinkers who feared the social disruption of the propagation of radical ideas, avoided the abstract arguments for toleration and gave increasing currency to pragmatic and utilitarian arguments for toleration and wider freedom of thought.[41] The result was that all the traditions touched on earlier were in some way implicated in the Enlightenment debate on toleration. Within the new context of expectations of the growing enlightenment of society, and growing power of the State, they would acquire new meaning and significance. Most were deployed to find a solution to the problems of toleration within the framework of what has been described as jurisdictional toleration, that is a solution in which the state did not abdicate its right to have an established church and to regulate Dissent. The alternative solution, put forward by some radical Enlightenment thinkers was to separate Church and State.[42] But this was not the only radical solution, and it was possible to satisfy the needs of conscience, of enlightenment and of the modern state, within the jurisdictional system. A fine expression of this was William Paley's *Principles of Morals and Political Philosophy* (1785), in which he not only argued that the State had the right to choose which religion should be established, but suggested:

That a comprehensive national religion, guarded by a few articles of peace and conformity, together with a legal provision for the clergy of that religion; and with a *complete* toleration of all dissenters from the established church, without any other limitation or exception, than what arises from the conjunction of dangerous political dispositions with certain religious tenets, appears to be, not only the most just and liberal, but the wisest and safest system, which a state can adopt: inasmuch as it unites the several perfections which a religious constitution ought to aim at – liberty of conscience, with means of instruction; the progress of truth, with the peace of society; the right of private judgment, with the care of the public safety.[43]

The way in which Paley repackaged and at the same time fulfilled the requisites of the various traditions of toleration hardly needs spelling out.

Indeed it is entirely characteristic of enlightenment thinking upon toleration that it seeks to do this. As far as toleration is concerned the Enlightenment might best be viewed as a movement in which the thinkers sought to find ways of combining the various traditions of toleration in ways which allowed the development of toleration without releasing new opportunities for sectarian enthusiasm or popular fanaticism. If we return to the early Enlightenment period, we can see how the contributions of the three major thinkers on toleration of that time, Baruch Spinoza, Pierre Bayle and John Locke, relate to such concerns, and we can take the story on from there.

The most obvious thing to note about Spinoza, Bayle and Locke as thinkers is that they belonged to the British, Dutch and French (predominantly Huguenot) nexus of the early Enlightenment. This is not, however, to say that there was unanimity in their thinking or that they were part of a homogeneous movement. Indeed they were all distinctive in their ideas and solutions. Yet all in their different ways drew on the various traditions of toleration in the early-modern period. I shall only treat Spinoza briefly as he is discussed in some depth by Jonathan Israel. Suffice it to point out that he shows how Spinoza's arguments in his *Tractatus Theologico-Politicus* (1670) drew on the Arminian and Republican traditions. Spinoza's religious ideas however were regarded as deeply heretical, and even those who were influenced by him did not always acknowledge his influence. Moreover, the Huguenots in the United Provinces deliberately sought to marginalize his work. None the less, his influence in Germany was considerable, and his recommendation of civil religion would find sympathetic hearers.[44] It later found a powerful echo in the ideas of Jean-Jacques Rousseau. However, perhaps his most significant influence was upon arguments for freedom of thought, which would be taken up by Deists in Britain.

There is some irony in the fact that Pierre Bayle, who was so anxious to marginalize the influence of Spinoza,[45] found that the exiled Huguenot community in the United Provinces was anxious to marginalize him on not entirely dissimilar grounds. He was regarded as a dangerous thinker, who undermined orthodoxy and who was probably an atheist. He was also faulted because he refused to subscribe to Huguenot resistance theory. His quarrel with Louis XIV was over the king's intolerance not his absolute government. That is, he refused to relate his theory of toleration to a contractarian theory of government. This made him a powerful advocate of the rights of conscience,[46] a withering critic of the intolerance justified by proponents of the divine right theory of monarchy, notably Bishop Bossuet, and a devastating satirist of superstition. Combined with his deliberate cultivation of an enlightened republic of letters, Bayle made a powerful contribution to the way *philosophes* would wage war on intolerance and superstition, and the most radical arguments for complete toleration. Yet in some ways it was his reputation for destroying the argument that compulsion could be justified in matters of religious salvation, and his fearless speaking out against persecution, rather than the precise nature of his arguments which were influential.[47] *Philosophes* associated themselves with the memory of the great champion of tolerance and were anxious to have his works on their shelves. His influence was therefore impalpable. Yet there were flaws within his theory of toleration. He wrote largely from the standpoint of the single individual. Duty to obey one's conscience lay at the heart of his thinking. He therefore ruthlessly exposed the injustice and futility of Church and government intervening in an individual's relationship with God. Kamen goes so far as to suggest that his writings did not fully address the problems of religious toleration because 'they were written from the standpoint of complete theological indifference'.[48] The same criticism could be levelled at some of the writings of eighteenth-century *philosophes*. But more generally Enlightenment writers were interested in creating conditions for religious peace and in the relationship between religious affiliation and citizenship. On these issues Bayle provided no real guidance. Moreover, his ironic style tended to obscure his own position; he was and is viewed alternatively as an atheist, pyrrhonist and a fideist. Although he was very much in touch with the latest thinking, his instinct was to compartmentalize, to keep matters concerning morals apart from those concerning faith, natural philosophy apart from those concerning theology, religious toleration apart from those concerning political philosophy. He parted company with currents of thought leading into the Enlightenment which represented a concern to construct a sound philosophical basis for relating ideas to action, beliefs to behaviour, and which sought to retain an intimate relationship between religion and morality by reducing faith to essentials and subjecting morality to rational simplicities. Bayle agreed with the ethical dimension of the enterprise, but not the religious, for it led, he believed, in the direction of Socinianism.[49] He did not share the growing confidence instilled by the achievements of natural philosophers, which encouraged the belief that a unified body of truth could be constructed through reason and experience.[50] Indeed, he differed from the *libertin* stream of scepticism because he used reason not only to undermine confidence in sense experience and past history, but also to show its own limitations.[51]

Pierre Bayle and John Locke had a good deal in common. Locke knew what it was like to live the life of an exile. While staying in Holland from 1683 to 1689 he shared many friends with Bayle, including Philip van Limborch, to whom he addressed his *Epistola de tolerantia*, and Jean de Clerc. We do not know whether they met even though both attended the Lantern Club set up by Locke when staying with the Quaker, Benjamin Furly. Later, Locke was interested in Bayle's opinion of his *Essay Con-*

cerning Human Understanding.[52] Yet if they shared a belief in the limitations of reason and understanding, Locke was the more systematic thinker, and it was this which made his contribution to Enlightenment theories of toleration more compelling. Indeed, in shaping the intellectual climate of the Enlightenment, he would give commonplace ideas on toleration new significance. The great Reformation scholar, Roland Bainton, noted that John Locke's 'ideas on religious liberty were not original' but crucially he added, 'the case did need to be restated in terms pertinent to the immediate situation'.[53] That situation in political terms was one in which statesmen and politicians required assurance that the introduction of some measure of toleration would not be harmful to the state, and in which dissenters, for their part, were anxious to prove themselves worthy of toleration. Lockean-style ideas would provide a framework of thought within which individuals, dissenting communities *and* states could adjust their demands and some form of compromise could be reached. Religious minorities would try to show that their adherents were good and loyal citizens and so worthy of toleration, statesmen for their part saw the utilitarian value of allowing dissenters some measure of toleration, of mitigating the intolerance of established churches and of posing as champions of enlightened ideas. Locke's genius was to combine many aspects of the traditions of toleration in a way which was both cautious and pragmatic, and principled. Thus he accepted the natural rights of conscience but added the proviso that they had to be consonant with civil society. Atheists could not be accepted because atheism dissolves all bonds between men, Roman Catholicism could not be accepted because Catholics owed allegiance to an external authority, which claimed powers independent of the state, and which could dispense Catholics from moral and political obligations. Provided there was nothing in one's beliefs which would lead to conduct harmful to the state and society one could be tolerated. Active coercion of consciences was not to be contemplated, but the law could be used to proscribe alien belief systems. When combined with Locke's views on religion one can construct a picture in which Locke emphasized the reasonableness of Christianity, the harmony of reason with revelation, and the notion of a church as a voluntary society entered by freely enquiring individuals. The state protected the civil interests of citizens, their lives, liberties and properties, the magistrate did not take care of souls which were entrusted to the churches. From this it is possible to see Locke as, if not the progenitor of radical views of toleration, at least the systematizer of them. But this is to ignore the context of Locke's views and perhaps some of the devil in the detail. Locke remained a member of the established Church of England, clearly of the Latitudinarian wing, for whom comprehension and toleration were complementary. He did not favour toleration in order that there would be a proliferation of sects, although it appears that he came to view toleration as a prior condition for comprehension.[54] He accepted that individuals had the right to make up their own minds in religious matters, indeed they were conscientiously obliged to do so, but his argument in favour of freedom of thought, which one might think was the prerequisite for conscientious enquiry, was more muted. It was perhaps inevitable that, at a time when religious conflicts were also profoundly political, Locke's concern both for toleration and social and political stability would lead him to be less than dogmatic about the boundaries between Church and State, and between freedom of conscience, freedom of worship and freedom of speech.[55] Perhaps another reason for cautious elements in his thought lies in his scepticism about the control which individuals possessed over their own beliefs. Indeed, in his *Third Letter on Toleration* (1692) Locke endorsed the use of the power of the magistrate to enforce morals.[56]

These qualifications should not blind us to the power of Locke's ideas in criticizing institutionalized intolerance; Locke, himself, was dissatisfied with toleration in England even after the Act of Toleration of 1689.[57] Moreover, he combined radical and conservative traditions of toleration in such a way that his theory of toleration provided satisfactory elements for both. In Britain and America, and in the Netherlands in particular, his ideas were seen as radical, especially from the mid century.[58] This is in part a result of the latent radicalism in his thought which has enabled a recent commentator to describe Locke's vision as 'of a pluralist society, one where each individual is free to pursue his own salvation without hindrance and without civil penalties'.[59] But it also needs to be remembered that the English translation of his *Epistola de Tolerantia* by the Socinian, William Popple, included a bold preface by Popple, stating that

absolute liberty, just and true liberty, equal and impartial liberty upon the principle that neither single persons nor churches, nay nor commonwealths, have any just title to invade the civil rights and worldly goods of each other, upon pretence of religion, is the thing we stand in need of.[60]

Many thought that this was Locke's view. Yet even in those states where the pragmatic elements in Locke's ideas were emphasized, they created a new intellectual environment for thinking about toleration whether one interpreted his particular proposals in a radical or more conservative way. Locke was by no means the first to posit the notion that at birth the mind was like a *tabula rasa*, but he was the first to develop a coherent sensationalist epistemology, and this added a key dimension to eighteenth-century thinking on toleration.[61] It strengthened the tendencies already noted to evaluate claims for toleration on secular and factual bases, and highlighted the importance of creating an enlightened environment as a means of promoting toleration and good citizenship. Locke's influence on eighteenth-century thinking on toleration should be understood in the wider context of his impact as a liberal Christian political theorist, student of human nature and philosopher. In his discussion of Locke in letter thirteen of his *Lettres philosophiques*, Voltaire focused on the broader aspects of his philosophy, and did not refer specifically to his writings on toleration. He was fascinated by Locke's account of the origins of our knowledge, by his agnosticism on the question of whether 'a purely material being thinks or not' and by his lack of dogmatism and willingness to confess ignorance. If his readers proceeded to read Locke's *An Essay Concerning Human Understanding*, to which Voltaire referred although not by title, they would find significant arguments relating to toleration.[62] In discussing probable knowledge, Locke asserted,

And if the opinions and persuasions of others whom we know and think well of be a ground of assent, men have reason to be Heathens in *Japan*, Mahometans in *Turkey*, Papists in *Spain*, Protestants in *England*, and Lutherans in *Sweden*.

Although he argued that we would be mistaken so to found our judgement on the opinions of others, such were the difficulties and uncertainties in making sound judgements that we would do well to be charitable to others who hold opinions which differ from our own. Rather than 'constrain others' we should seek to 'inform ourselves'.[63] Voltaire was not, however, indifferent to the specific arguments of Locke's *Letter Concerning Toleration*. Translated into French in 1710, it was reprinted in 1732, he included it with one of the editions of his own *Treatise on Toleration* in 1764. In a powerful preface thought to be written by Voltaire, he recommended the contribution of the 'celebrated John Locke' for upholding the utility of universal tolerance, and hoped that 'the force and solidity' of its arguments would persuade his readers that it was not only in his time that intolerance was a horror to all those who were well-educated.[64]

In so many ways Locke became 'the starting point for the discussion on the problem of religious tolerance in the following centuries'.[65] He had created a flexible framework for testing qualifications for toleration. Many of the arguments and new legislation relating to toleration arose from the reappraisal of the value of dissenters of one sort another to the State, coupled with a growing acceptance amongst the educated that coercion in religious matters was undesirable and ineffective. Questions such as did they, dissenters, owe true allegiance to the State, and did they obey the moral law, that is, could they be trusted, were critical and, as the century wore on, as the State was seen in more secular terms, would they be good servants of the State, were they useful to the State? Prince Kaunitz's recommendations in 1777, concerning 'heretics' (Protestants) in Moravia, exemplified the new sort of emphasis. He suggested that a distinction should be made between law-abiding heretics and overt troublemakers; the former were to be left alone and allowed to worship privately; as regards the latter, he favoured the due course of the law and not special measures. Generally, he preferred the authorities to look the other way rather than stir up trouble. Fundamental to his outlook was his knowledge that heresy had existed in Moravia even before the Reformation, and all the efforts to extirpate it had proven futile. Toleration would be of benefit to the State and persuasion rather than repression might lead to the gradual elimination of heresy.[66] In Western Europe, the late eighteenth-century debate on toleration, in its attention to the question of what made a good citizen as a criterion for toleration, became associated with wider discussion of liberty and political rights. Joseph Priestley in England suggested what he considered to be a radicalization of Lockean theory. Yet his views were not totally dissimilar to those of Kaunitz in that he favoured toleration for all law-abiding citizens. He helped to effect a change in attitude amongst a crucial group of radicals previously marked by their fierce anti-Catholicism. Their influence was a minor factor in allowing the government to consider legislation which ultimately would allow Catholic Dissenters the same freedoms as Protestant Dissenters.[67] Yet as far as the government was concerned it was not a relaxation of Lockean criteria which led to toleration of Roman Catholics so much as their reappraisal. Thus although radicals of the late eighteenth century certainly pushed the argument further concerning toleration, it was really the growing feeling that the age was an enlightened age and that it was time to think again about religious discrimination which played a crucial role in widening toleration at that time. Dissenters appealed to the enlightened spirit of the time, and governments sought to demonstrate their enlightened credentials. One person was crucial in this change of atmosphere, and that was Voltaire.

Voltaire was responsible for setting up England as the model of toleration to be followed. In his *Lettres philosophiques*, the England he portrayed was largely free of sectarian strife; it was a 'land of sects' and yet one in which 'every man goes to heaven by whatever route he likes'. England was not such a liberal paradise as he portrayed.[68] But in contrast with France it was; and his purpose, anyway, was to draw the contrast as a means of exerting pressure for change. Voltaire, moreover, was not as radical as Locke; he rather favoured the limited toleration available in Britain. He qualified his opening statement of sectarian freedom by saying that the real religion in England was 'the one in which you get on in the world' namely the Anglican Church. Indeed he seemed to approve of the fact that membership of 'the Church' was a condition of holding public office. His sub-text was that the English were wise enough not to let religion matter too much. They might rail at each other in the pulpit, but the real indicator of their toleration of each other was the London Stock Exchange, where they were all prepared to trust each other, not only various Christians but also Jews and Mohammedans, not only Englishmen but men of all nations. And what was so admirable about this was that they were all gathered together 'for the utility of men'. It was this observation which preceded his famous remark that,

If there were only one religion in England there would be danger of despotism, if there were two they would cut each other's throats, but there are thirty, and they live in peace.[69]

In making his case that the English were a free and tolerant nation, Voltaire was prepared to gloss over the odd awkward fact such as the imprisonment of the Deist Thomas Woolston under the blasphemy laws. Yet, at the same time he was right in that the law was not the real indicator of the degree of toleration available in Britain.[70] He was also aware that the law in its operation offered far more protection to all British citizens than to French subjects. In particular he appreciated not only the equality before the law to which he had drawn attention in his *Lettres philosophiques*, but the openness of trials, the public reporting of criminal proceedings and the jury system. He knew well enough that injustices were not always righted by the force of public opinion as is evidenced by his ironic comment on the execution of Byng in *Candide*.[71] But he knew that with the jury system (not operative in Byng's case) and with a lively and uncensored press the chances of justice were greater than in contemporary France. Indeed, he was prepared to distort or gloss details in order to present the contrast. When he told the curious story of Elizabeth Canning, he did so to show how the force of public opinion could be brought to bear in order to right an injustice:

Fortunately, in England no trial is secret, since the punishment of crimes is designed as a public instruction to people, not as a private vengeance. All interrogations are made with open doors, and all interesting trials are printed in the newspapers.[72]

Voltaire's belief in the importance of free speech had been fortified many years earlier by his reading of Deist writings, including those of Locke's own pupil, the third Earl of Shaftesbury, which articulated convincingly the case for intellectual freedom,[73] and, as noted, he was prepared to exaggerate British freedoms in order to condemn by implication French limitations. It is perhaps fitting that his posthumous reputation for toleration rests in considerable measure upon a fabled statement of his own on the subject: 'I hate your opinions, but I would die to defend your right to express them.'

Voltaire's account of England can be faulted in detail, but England remained the exemplar of a society which had achieved open government and toleration. It was that combination which made England a more compelling example than Prussia, which was also seen, under Frederick the Great, as a haven of toleration. With the American Revolution, England lost its iconic status, yet it still remained something of a model as regards toleration. It was recognized that during the century it had become more tolerant of religious diversity and cautious steps were being taken towards complete religious toleration. For evidence, observers could cite the example of David Williams who established a Deist chapel at Margaret Street, London, without any fuss. Voltaire, who admired his Deist liturgy, wrote of the comfort that he experienced at the age of eighty-two to 'see the tolerance openly teach'd in your country'.[74] Indeed the chapel became a beacon, if short-lived, of enlightened tolerance with supporters amongst the great and good, including besides Voltaire, Benjamin Franklin, Jean-Jacques Rousseau and Frederick the Great.

From Voltaire's experience and knowledge of England one can see emerging the major themes concerning toleration in the Enlightenment: the focus upon good conduct as a prime consideration in the extension of toleration (toleration leads to good conduct; those who conduct themselves peaceably deserve toleration); the quality and the administration of the penal laws concerning religion; and the importance of free speech as a potential corrective to ill-considered judicial decisions. The question of religious toleration therefore began to embrace wider questions concerning toleration and tolerance within government and society. Such general considerations were uppermost in his mind rather than the principle of the rights of conscience and precise concerns about the status of dissenters. Indeed, he favoured religious toleration and freedom of worship but not civil equality (events happened the other way in France). He did so because he feared enthusiasm and fanaticism. To return to the example of David Williams, he attempted in microcosm the synthesis which Voltaire and other *philosophes* desired, namely a solution to sectarianism by the creation of a religion which was founded on the universal principles of morality with the Deity acknowledged as a first cause and worship designed to produce social cohesion.[75]

Voltaire had more in common with Williams than belief in a social Deistic religion. The synopsis which Williams provided of the great principle of the English constitution in his *The Nature and Extent of Intellectual Liberty* (1779) could have come from Voltaire: parliament's control of the money supply, trial by jury, the *habeas corpus* and 'the liberty of thinking, speaking and writing'.[76] None the less, as the translator of Voltaire's *Treatise on Toleration* (1764), Williams was critical of Voltaire's chapter on opinions which were not to be tolerated and pointed to an inconsistency in Voltaire's attitude.[77] Indeed, Voltaire was caught between, on the one hand, a Lockean concern for good citizenship and a desire not to tolerate the intolerant, and, on the other, enthusiasm for the free expression of opinions as the best means of creating an enlightened society. In his *Treatise*, Voltaire had a section in which he elided the belief that all opinions ought to be tolerated and one should only be punished for committing crimes, with the argument that since fanaticism leads to crimes, the fanatics should not be tolerated:

For a government not to have the right to punish the errors of men it is necessary that their errors should not be crimes; they are only crimes when they disturb society; they disturb society when they engender fanaticism; hence men should begin laying aside fanaticism in order to merit toleration.[78]

In this view it was permissible to suppress the Society of Jesus, whose regulations were 'contrary to the laws of the kingdom', and by similar reasoning any group which exhibited fanatical tendencies.

Williams countered that every state tolerates anti-social opinions but does not punish unless a criminal act occurs – he instanced stealing, robbery and murder. A state benefits from knowing the opinions of its citizens rather than repressing them. He noted, 'It is a common practice with the King of Prussia to order pasquinades, on his person and government, to be taken down for his perusal, and he never fails to put them up again.'[79] This led Williams on to his notorious assertion: 'I do not see, why thieves should not be allowed to preach the principles of theft; seducers of seduction; adulterers of adultery; and traitors of treason'.[80]

Williams was confident that the people were sufficiently rational and sensible not to be seduced by seducers. Faced with rival opinions they would choose the rational one. Such optimism was buttressed by his belief that moral and political principles were either self-evident or deduced from self-evident principles. No mathematician worried about those who maintained erroneous ideas – they could easily be convinced of their errors. Compulsion was not required. Indeed if compulsion were required it would be to make subjects declare their opinions, whatever they were, but punishment would only be meted out to those who behaved intolerantly and with a view to rectifying their misconduct. From Greek times on, there were instances of wars being waged on that principle, the most recent being Catherine the Great's intervention in Poland 'to oblige the Poles to tolerate the dissidents'. Although the immediate reason for Williams's outpouring on the issue of intellectual liberty was the relatively minor issue of freeing Dissenting ministers from the requirement to subscribe to the Thirty-nine Articles, he saw the matter as of great moment for Enlightenment. In his peroration, he declared, 'The whole world is interested in this question; for it is on an universal principle of legislation. From Kamtskatka (*sic*) to the banks of the Ohio, its influence will be felt. Let the remaining chains of liberty be broken.' He envisaged liberty taking a flying tour of the Enlightenment hotspots, from Catherine the Great's Russia, via Prussia, Vienna, Switzerland (pausing to shed a tear over Voltaire's urn at Ferney), France and across to America, returning at last, he hoped, to England, her native land.[81]

There was a considerable pedigree for Williams's views and even his rhetoric. He admired Voltaire's own stand for free speech, although as we have seen he disagreed with the Lockean-style constraints on toleration which Voltaire favoured. He understood the intimate connection between the struggle for religious toleration and that for free speech.[82] He also drew on the arguments for free enquiry and free speech favoured by the British Deists and freethinkers of the late seventeenth and early eighteenth centuries, men like the third Earl of Shaftesbury, Anthony Collins, Matthew Tindal, John Toland, John Trenchard and Thomas Gordon. They in turn had been influenced by Locke, Spinoza and Bayle.[83] But there were two important differences. The first is that despite advocating freedom of enquiry and freedom of speech, those in Britain in the early eighteenth century were cautious about exercising free speech themselves for fear of prosecution under the Blasphemy Act. The fate of Thomas Woolston demonstrates that these fears were not groundless. However, it encouraged the belief that there were certain opinions which should be confined to an enlightened coterie, notably of Freemasons. Toland distinguished between 'open and public', and 'private and secret doctrines'; the former was 'accommodated to popular prejudices and the establish'd religions', the latter was 'the real truth stript of all disguises' which could be taught to 'the few and capable'.[84] The second difference is that almost all the writers of Toland's generation were prepared to exclude Roman Catholics from toleration. Williams set his face firmly against esoterism despite its not inconsiderable appeal in the Enlightenment, and was not prepared to undermine his own arguments by the inconsistent exception of Roman Catholics from toleration. In this he was representative of the radicalism and the optimism of late enlightenment thinking on toleration. He was also indicative of that period to in linking arguments about toleration to more general arguments about civil and political liberty. Williams, however, differed from many of his radical contemporaries who favoured the separation of Church and State, for he recommended a public, established religion as a means of preserving public morality. That not only links him with the republican civil religionists of the seventeenth century but also more generally with continental European thinking, where established religions were generally more powerful than in Britain and where the idea of a civil non-dogmatic religion was seen as a means of developing more tolerant attitudes, and by emphasizing the common elements of morality, strengthening the social cement.

The radicalization of Lockean-style thinking occurred in France as well as in England and some French thinkers sympathized with the radical solution of complete separation of Church and State. The supreme model for this was the Act of the Virginia Assembly for Establishing Religious Freedom of 1786. Developments in the newly independent America as regards religious freedom had been closely watched in Europe. Turgot, who had since his youth favoured religious toleration and civil equality for dissenters, at the end of his life was critical of the constitutions of several American states for imposing religious tests on representatives. He believed in 'the absolute incompetency of civil government in matters of conscience'.[85] It was but a short step to regarding toleration as a matter of irrelevance, rather one should be concerned about natural rights. This was expressed pithily by Thomas Paine in Part I of the *Rights of Man*: 'Toleration is not the *opposite* of Intolerance, but is the *counterfeit* of it. Both are despotisms. The one assumes to itself the right of withholding Liberty of Conscience and the other of granting it.'[86]

But Paine was not unique. Mirabeau [the younger] (who had translated Richard Price's *Observations on the Importance of the American Revolution* (1784))[87] had already made the identical point in the debates in the National Assembly on framing the Declaration of the Rights of Man.[88] A natural right to toleration was really a contradiction in terms, and there was growing dissatisfaction with the whole notion of toleration in the late Enlightenment.[89] However, states would be reluctant to give up their claim to adjudicate upon such issues. Pragmatism and *raison d'état* did not abandon the field to natural rights. The Declaration of the Rights of Man (1789) was indicative that the Lockean framework had not been entirely abandoned and that rights of conscience would still be limited by concerns about the public good. Nonetheless, the debates about toleration had been transformed by the concern about free speech. The Virginia declaration had argued that all attempts by the civil power to curb intellectual freedom were harmful. Mirabeau argued that the existence of an authority that has the power to tolerate circumscribes the liberty of thought. Moreover whatever the compromises of the Declaration, religious toleration was in a sense subordinate to the concern for freedom of expression. It was referred to indirectly in Clause 10, which declared that no one should be troubled on account of their opinions, 'even religious opinions', provided that they did not disturb the public peace. I say in a sense, because there were political considerations which in part explain this rather covert recognition of tolerance. But one can at least see that freedom of opinion generally had greater support than religious toleration. It was enshrined in the following clause, which described freedom of thought and opinions as 'one of the most precious rights of man'.[90]

Toleration had thus become vitally bound up in questions relating to intellectual freedom, and of the enlightened challenge of daring to know in a public sense. The Voltaire remembered by so many is the Voltaire who declared so firmly for intellectual freedom. Yet Voltaire, who early in his career was imprisoned in the Bastille for slanderous remarks about the Regent, took some time to see the relevance of the principle in the wider sense.[91] When he declared, 'Can there be anything more splendid than to put the whole world into commotion by a few arguments', he had the ideas of Locke in mind.[92] Yet, in his chapter devoted to him in his *Lettres philosophiques,* Voltaire suggested that very few would read him, that those who did 'were not interested in upsetting the world', and that 'philosophers do not write for the people and are devoid of emotional fire'.[93] Generally this view would hold until the mid century, when the *philosophes* and their allies began to publish works considered subversive. Forming what amounted to a 'party' of the Enlightenment, they defended their right to publish and challenged the authorities who threatened that right. Perhaps the best example of the way in which the defence of publishing for the few had radical implications for the freedom of the many, and for the broad toleration of opinions, comes from the Netherlands where there was a lively argument over the publication of La Mettrie's *L'Homme machine* (1747) by a second generation Huguenot, pastor Elie Luzac.[94] Luzac at first defended publication on utilitarian grounds, but in response to fierce criticism from close associates – Pierre Roques, pastor at Basle, and Jean Henri Samuel Formey, a Huguenot minister and permanent secretary of the Berlin Academy of Sciences – he published a more rigorous defence of freedom of expression in his *Essai sur la liberté de produire ses sentimens* (1749). Dedicated to the English, the only nation which enjoyed 'unfettered freedom of expression', he argued the case for establishing such conditions in Europe.[95] Freedom of expression was not harmful to society; individuals had no right to limit the freedom of expression of other individuals, nor did sovereigns generally have the right to limit that of their subjects. Indeed, governments sought to curtail freedom of expression through fear of criticism. Only bad governments however were vulnerable to criticism, good governments had nothing to fear. He concluded with a ringing declaration:

It is therefore no more than a bad principle which brings people to curtail the freedom of expression. The good of society does not demand it. It is not done by right and it is useless. That, I believe, is sufficient to prove that everybody should be left entirely free to express their opinions.[96]

For all his confident assertiveness, Luzac represents a transitional phase in arguments for the free expression of opinion. He undoubtedly believed in the power of ideas, for 'to produce ideas is to act', yet thought that he was conducting his argument amongst an educated elite.[97] He did not realize that it was a feature of the *philosophes'* programmes to upset the world as they knew it. Later in 1782 he was shocked when his treatise was translated into Dutch and used against him by his Patriot opponents; similarly he turned against Locke whom he had earlier used, albeit selectively, in his defence of the Orangists.[98] Yet he did believe that in the religious sphere the free exchange of opinions would lead to the triumph of truth. He published La Mettrie *and* his own refutation of La Mettrie's mechanistic materialism. His view of the religious sphere was liberal for he included natural religion in his notion of religion. Indeed, he is indicative of the shift taking place in thinking about toleration; so that the questions relating to tolerance embraced morality (and especially the moral conscience) as well as revealed religion, and became enmeshed in arguments about the progress of knowledge in general.[99]

The crucial importance of open-minded truth-seeking was powerfully expounded in the most important history of philosophy available to the *philosophes*, namely Johann Jakob Brucker's *Historia critica philosophiae* (1742–4, 2nd edn 1766).[100] Brucker believed that, 'an indifference to rational inquiry ... obstructed the progress of knowledge'.[101] The heroes of modern philosophy for him were those who had been capable of thinking for themselves in an undogmatic way. He discussed a whole series of philosophers who had to a degree managed to throw off the yoke of scholasticism, but only those who had succeeded completely were entitled to be included in his hall of fame, and these he described as his modern eclectic philosophers. Such philosophers he divided into those who contributed to modern philosophy in specific areas and those who contributed more generally. They were tolerant and open-minded and did not claim unique truth for their 'school'. Such notions were reflected in a contemporary definition of 'eclectick' as applying 'to those philosophers who did not adhere to any particular, but picked out of all systems, that which they thought best, or approved and liked most'.[102] Brucker himself cited Grotius's view that 'as there never was any sect so enlightened as to see the whole truth, so there never was any sect so erroneous as to be entirely destitute of truth'.[103] Consequently the history of philosophy and the study of philosophy should be eclectic. It also required an open-minded, enquiring approach. Diderot followed Brucker in defining an eclectic as 'a philosopher who dares to think for himself'.[104] In his article on intolerance in the *Encylopédie*, Diderot made a simple distinction between ecclesiastical intolerance, the claim of Churches to be the sole possessors of truth, and civil intolerance, the persecution of those whose religious beliefs were different from one's own. Diderot knew well enough that his whole enterprise was endangered both by the ecclesiastical authorities and the Jansenists in the *parlement* of Paris, but he also knew that intolerance embraced philosophical as well as theological views. Enlightenment had developed, as Brucker had shown, by undermining the scholastic alliance of dogmatic theology and philosophy. Indeed, in the struggle to publish their views, the *philosophes* waged war on all the forces which impeded their right to think and criticize freely. Their attitude was unequivocally expressed in the well-known lines of the preface to the first edition of Kant's *Critique of Pure Reason* (1781):

Our age is, in especial degree, the age of criticism, and to criticism everything must submit. Religion through its sanctity, and law-giving through its majesty, may seek to exempt themselves from it. But they then awaken just suspicion, and cannot claim the sincere respect which reason accords only to that which has been able to sustain the test of free and open examination.[105]

Kant, however, had in mind critical debate in a civilized non-political public sphere. Such notions belonged to idealized views of the republic of letters and rested upon the assumption that dangerous and contentious knowledge was safe amongst an educated elite. This was undoubtedly the assumption of Luzac when writing boldly in favour of free speech in the mid century. As his historian has pointed out, he was 'writing about the exchange of opinions within a limited and highly educated elite . . . he was writing about the collective search for truth within an idealized Republic of Letters'.[106] But the defence of those ideals was controversial and the more one became involved in controversy, the more the nature of the debate changed, the more the republic of letters lost its civility and the more it came into conflict with authority.[107] Luzac later in life found his own work 'misused'. Similar fears were voiced in Germany where there was a vigorous debate at that time on 'What is enlightening'. Andreas Reim, the secretary of the Berlin Academy of Arts and Mechanical Science, in his controversial pamphlet *On Enlightenment* (1788) argued that it was beneficial to the State, religion and individuals alike. Yet, like Luzac, he believed 'unenlightened demagogues' had led the Dutch 'to the brink of the abyss'. Reim's career, however, demonstrated that it was not possible to sanitize the public sphere. He lost his position as pastor at the Friedrichshospital on account of his pamphlet and eventually, in 1793, was exiled from Prussia for his political writings.[108]

In France the *philosophes* were forced to defend themselves against repression and censorship and that helped to give them a sense of cohesion as Darnton noted. However, it would be simplistic to argue that they deliberately fostered the development of public opinion as a Davidic attempt to slay the monolithic Goliath of the confessional state. Certainly in campaigning for religious toleration they used pamphleteering in a more positive way to attack the authorities. But they were enormously assisted by the contestation of powers between the authorities. This meant that *philosophes* never came into a direct conflict with a single authority and perhaps more importantly that those rival authorities were themselves seeking to win over public opinion to their cause. Repression was still used as was deemed appropriate, but silence was no longer an option as it was in Louis XIV's reign. In Malesherbes, *directeur de la librairie* (1750–63), the *philosophes* had an invaluable ally.

In 1752 and again in 1759 he was able to protect the *Encyclopédie* from the more damaging attacks of the *parlement* of Paris; on both occasions he even kept Diderot's manuscripts in his care.[109] Malesherbes believed in a policy of tolerance for both pragmatic and idealistic reasons. It was necessary to prevent the process of censorship and control breaking down altogether and it was necessary for the progress of truth. He expounded his ideas in his *Mémoires sur la librairie* (1758/9) and *Mémoire sur la liberté de la presse* (1788). Similar ideas, at least as regards the progress of truth, were expressed by Diderot in his *Lettre sur le commerce de la librairie* (1763) written at the request of the Parisian printer–booksellers. Like Malesherbes's memoirs, it was not published until the nineteenth century. Both Malesherbes and Diderot wrote to advise and instruct the administration; both accepted control of the book trade and neither considered following the English model. As Roger Chartier has argued, Diderot thought that by defending printer's privilege he was also protecting the rights of professional authors.[110] Although Malesherbes was prepared to speculate that orthodox works of piety might do more harm than advanced heterodox works,[111] religion was one of the areas where he believed it was important to retain censorship.[112] Within a broadly tolerant approach, he weighed up rival considerations. He generally favoured granting tacit permission to Protestant works which would only be published and imported from abroad if they were not published in France, but in 1759, a time of religious and political crisis, he refused permission to a Calvinist Psalm Book even though it had been approved by a censor and was easily obtained in Paris. Besides contentious works he also repressed those which he thought were of poor quality, including a pious work dedicated to his father.[113]

One cannot help feeling that Malesherbes was an enlightened version of King Canute, but he was not alone in worrying that freedom of expression might well strike at the foundations of religion. Voltaire was the most notable of the *philosophes* who worried about the development of the professional scribblers and their corrosive and indiscriminate *libelles* on the established order. He describes them as *la canaille de la littérature*.[114] The cultivation of an audience was a crucial source of strength and power for the *philosophes* and one which could not be ignored so long as they had difficulties in publishing their works.[115] Yet this essential Enlightenment strategy caused them gnawing anxieties of the sort anticipated in Jean Barbeyrac's preface to his popular translation of Pufendorf's *Law of Nature and of Nations* in which he identified the prime obstacles to moral knowledge as 'the illusions of the heart and the tyranny established in the world in the realm of opinions'.[116] As that tyranny insensibly weakened and publishing became easier, it was even more vital that the illusions of the heart did not begin to rule unrestrained. If so, then the struggle for toleration would be all the more difficult. Indeed, many *philosophes* were unconvinced that dissenters were worthy of toleration unless they could rid themselves of those illusions. It did not require the Gordon Riots to remind the *philosophes* of the danger posed by a polity which was growing more enlightened, and a public still entrenched in prejudice. Thus the quest for toleration became subsumed in the wider enlightenment programme for civilizing mankind. In his *Système sociale* (1774), d'Holbach declared,

Human reason is not yet sufficiently exercised; the civilization of peoples is not yet complete; obstacles without number have hitherto opposed the progress of useful knowledge, the advance of which can alone contribute to perfecting our government, our laws, our education, our institutions, and our morals.[117]

The campaign for toleration, nonetheless, remained a crucial and distinct element in the civilizing process. It was also fraught with tactical difficulties. It was generally conceded that many of the problems relating to religious toleration would be solved if sects were susceptible to enlightened ideas. Part of the solution lay in the extension of tolerance, for it was constantly stressed that tolerance was not indifference, it was an active force. Hence Malesherbes believed that religious fanaticism was weakened by tolerance rather than repression.[118] Yet there remained considerable apprehension about emancipating those who lacked sufficient credentials for enlightenment. Many, like Malesherbes, lacked the confidence of more radical enlightened spirits that truth would prevail in any free contest, although there were all sorts of variations on that theme since a good deal depended upon what one meant by a free contest.[119] The dice at any rate needed to be loaded in its favour, not simply by covert assistance from enlightened authorities (by a 'sophisticated' use of the censor), but by taking the argument right into the heart of the enemy camp. The demolition of error was equally as vital as the propagation of truth. Hence the campaign cry, *écrasez l'infâme*.

It is perhaps appropriate that the motto, *écrasez l'infâme*, is almost untranslatable, it conveys the desire to rid the system of all that is pernicious. When the *philosophes* proclaimed that their politics was the politics of truth, it is important to bear in mind the purgative dimension of that notion. It was almost as if they were waging war on sin itself. The notion of crushing or overwhelming is less a sign of confidence than of the measure of the task and the resilience of the enemy. It was Voltaire who used the cry as a call to arms in his campaign to secure the posthumous rehabilitation of Jean Calas. On the very eve of succeeding (9 March, 1765), Voltaire wrote to his ally, the lawyer Elie de Beaumont, 'It is said that we are in the century of philosophy, but there are still a hundred fanatics against one philosophe.'[120] Indeed there was a constant juxtaposition between the belief that the march of reason was irresistible and the fear of unreason. Perhaps if one repeated often enough the belief that the triumph of enlightenment was inevitable it would become inevitable. At any rate, its cultivation was a duty. Just as the Stoics envisaged spreading circles of affection, from one's family and relations, to one's city and country, and then to the human race, so the *philosophes* envisaged the pursuit of truth not as a quest for personal happiness and amusement of the educated, but as vital for one's government and society. In so doing they imposed new terms on government. Public debate, and an enlarged public sphere were the means of ensuring the progress of knowledge.[121] The *philosophes* captured the Académie des Sciences which ceased to be an aristocrats' club, being at best an adornment to the state, but indifferent to the wider implications of the pursuit of knowledge. England, as ever, had provided an alternative model: the Royal Society of London had believed that the pursuit of knowledge was for the good of mankind, it provided the model for the diffusion of enlightenment, an example of tolerance and of cosmopolitan vistas.[122] The first ally of the *philosophes* to be elected to the Académie was quite explicit about the special role of the *philosophe*. In his reception address in January 1767, Antoine-Léonard Thomas declared:

Those who govern men cannot at the same time enlighten them. Busy with action, they are always on the move, and their souls do not have the time to reflect. A class of men has thus been established – and protected everywhere – whose état is to use their minds in peace, and whose duty is to activate those minds for the public good; men who . . . pull together the enlightenment of all countries and centuries, and whose ideas must . . . as it were, represent to the patrie the ideas of the whole human race.[123]

Who were to be so enlightened? Was this just the propaganda of the enlightened or did it seriously address the question of who were capable of enlightenment? Voltaire was among the most sceptical of the *philosophes* concerning the potential of the people for enlightenment. At the time of writing his *Lettres philosophiques*, he believed that philosophy was of consequence only to a small minority. He saw religion as the protector of the moral order and so was happy to leave its sway over ordinary people undisturbed. His later experience however inclined him to think that religion ought to be exposed to philosophical sentiment, at least as far as toleration and tolerance was concerned. In his *Treatise of Toleration*, he addressed a chapter to the question of whether it was better to maintain the people in superstition. Allowing that superstitious religion, as it was not murderous, was preferable to atheism, he defined superstition in memorable terms: 'Superstition is to religion what astrology is to astronomy, the truly mad daughter of a very wise mother.' And he added, 'These two daughters have long since dominated the earth.'[124]

Voltaire was prepared to be indifferent to, and amused by, many superstitions which did not do much harm, but could not be indifferent to those that led to persecution. The tolerant were required to challenge intolerance, fanaticism and superstition, because these were harmful to mankind.[125] The most dangerous of all superstitions was 'that of hating one's neighbour on account of his opinions'.[126] In Toulouse, Catholic hatred of the Huguenot community was deliberately cultivated by the annual celebration of the massacre of some 4,000 Huguenots in Toulouse in 1562. 1762 was the bicentenary of the massacre and Voltaire argued it contributed materially to the unjust but successful prosecution of Jean Calas for the murder of his son, Marc Antoine.[127]

Voltaire argued, as he had in *Letters on England*, that the remedy lay in tolerance: 'the more sects there are, the less danger in each'. Beyond his appeal for legislation introducing such tolerance, was a more fundamental one to reason:

The great means to reduce the number of fanatics . . . is to submit that disease of the mind to the treatment of reason, which slowly, but infallibly, enlightens men. Reason is gentle and humane. It inspires liberality, suppresses discord, and strengthens virtue; it has more power to make obedience to the laws attractive than force to compel it.[128]

Moreover, a rational religion is not one that sought to make converts so much as to pursue truth. Voltaire had been impressed by the English philosopher and theologian Dr Samuel Clarke. He believed him to be an Arian and therefore a heretic. Yet far from being fanatical, Clarke was 'a man of unswerving virtue and a gentle disposition, more interested in his opinions than excited about making converts'.[129] Quiet reasoning, however, required a noisier ally in the battle against enthusiasm and superstition, and that was found in ridicule. This was recommended by a contemporary of Clarke, the third Earl of Shaftesbury.[130] The saying attributed to him that 'ridicule is the test of truth', became a commonplace in enlightened circles. Voltaire, who was anyway a natural satirist, recommended ridicule as a means of dissipating prejudice. But there was a precondition for successful argument and satire, namely a robust public sphere. For all Voltaire's dislike of *libelles* his own technique was to 'mix it' with his opponents. This disconcerted his Victorian biographer John Morley who apologizes for the fact that Voltaire 'never rises from the ground into the region of the higher facts of religion'. While accepting that Voltaire's intelligence 'was practical rather than speculative' his main explanation was that 'it would have been controversially futile if he had done so'. 'Ordinary men' needed not abstract reasoning but the detailed confutation of the truths they had been taught. Morley apologizes for Voltaire's flippancy, triviality and 'gross irreverence', his combination of 'shallow mockery' and 'just objection'. In all this he sees Voltaire, correctly, as the direct descendant of Bayle: 'ridicule', he declared in his *Treatise on Toleration*, 'is a strong barrier to the extravagance of all sectarians'.[131] But it was more than ridicule that he used; he used every weapon available: reason, accurate information and ridicule, weapons that had been forged by Pierre Bayle. Voltaire might find Locke useful in his campaign, but he himself could never plead for toleration in his urbane general way. If he learnt from Locke the value of the empirical method for pursuing truth in an undogmatic way,[132] he made use of 'fact' in an almost unique way. The *philosophes* generally did not believe in the neutrality of fact but few used facts so effectively not only to persuade but to excite indignation against the *status quo*.[133] Of course Voltaire pulled all the strings he could to procure change, and it is true he addressed his *Treatise* to men of influence in the government, but he also used the treatise to arouse public opinion to convince the authorities that they had acted in a benighted way.[134]

Voltaire was not unaware of the hazards of the enterprise; he did his best to control the propaganda for the rehabilitation of Jean Calas, persuading Antoine Court de Gébelin to withdraw his anti-Catholic *Lettre Toulousaines* (1763) in which he claimed that the Protestants were more tolerant, civilized and prosperous than the Catholics.[135] But such control could not be for long maintained. Although the *philosophes* took some satisfaction in the expansion of their audience, and even Voltaire could write as if the progress of reason were inevitable, they were voyaging into the unknown. Not all would share their high-minded notions of public education through public debate. Public discussion might stoke the fires of prejudice rather than damp them through the influence of reason. In seeking to *écraser l'infâme* there was a real danger that one would revive it in new forms. In Britain and America where the public sphere was well-established and most developed, reformers worried about the consequences of free speech and a politically emancipated public. Turgot voiced his concern that the 'efforts of true philosophers and good Citizens' might be undermined by self-interested politicians allying with 'the prejudices of the multitude'.[136] This was not just the worry of an outsider. Rational Dissenters in England developed the doctrine of candour, which represented not simply intellectual honesty and sincerity, but the impartial exchange of views. Thomas Paine, despite his own strong opinions, stressed the social value of good temper which he associated with the absence of prejudice, and William Godwin stressed the need for calm sagacity in the pursuit of political justice.[137] Joseph Priestley was warned by William Enfield of the danger of 'rousing the sleeping lion' through his vigorous pamphleteering in the cause of wider toleration. It was a message which he largely ignored, and he paid the price in the Birmingham Riots of 1791.[138] In the long run *l'infâme* could only be tamed by a programme of public education, and it is significant that Thomas Jefferson, who had played a crucial role in framing the act of the Virginia Assembly, should spend so much of his subsequent career trying to implement his tripartite plan for elementary, grammar and university education.

When the dust had settled after the French Revolution, religious toleration, understood in terms of freedom of worship, was broadly conceded, but the intellectual freedom which had helped to bring this about remained contentious. In 1885 the Pope Leo XIII issued an encyclical which conceded somewhat reluctantly that states might grant a measure of toleration to non-Catholic forms of worship, but cautioned that, 'freedom of thinking and of writing whatever one likes, without restraint, is not of itself an advantage at which society may rightly rejoice, but on the contrary, a source of many evils'.[139] This was but a delayed reaction to the general trend of thinking in the late seventeenth and eighteenth centuries which broadened the debate on toleration and switched the focus away from exclusively religious concerns. As the confessional state came under attack, toleration became more a secular concern than a religious one. In effect, as Louisa Simonutti has remarked, 'The debate on toleration . . . developed above all in the direction of political problems relating to the running of society.'[140] Yet the framework of thought was not profoundly altered by secularization. Conscience came to embrace matters of secular morals and was universalized in Enlightenment thought, but it was still the individual conscience which claimed its right of judgement, of freedom of choice and expression of opinion.[141] The various declarations and constitutions which, in varying degrees, enshrined the rights of conscience which were introduced at the end of the eighteenth century and were copied by others in the nineteenth, represent not the reification of enlightenment individualism, but the victory of claims which can be traced back to the roots of European civilization. If the *philosophes* and their allies repackaged those claims and made them acceptable to the sovereign authorities, they were able to do so in part because they could draw on a rich heritage of tolerationist traditions. The Enlightenment movement did not succeed in solving the problems posed when society becomes freer and more tolerant, partly because the *philosophes* did not experience such a society. They saw far enough ahead to worry about some of its problems, but they could not foresee that crucial problems in the future would not solely be about rights of individuals *vis-à-vis* the Church/State but also of minority communities *vis-à-vis* the State/society. It is one of the paradoxes of history that at the heart of the claim of dissenting communities for toleration was that of right of the individual conscience. Enlightenment thinkers did not alter that way of thinking. Their solution combined an enlightened view of the relationship between religion and society with an extended notion of the rights of conscience which should be available to good, enlightened citizens. Critics of the Enlightenment today need to be reminded both of the immediate context of the Enlightenment and of the traditions which they updated. They are embodied in these lines written by Turgot at the time of the American Revolution which were soon to be highly applicable to Europe of the French Revolution:

The clergy are only dangerous when they exist as a distinct body in the State; and think themselves possessed of separate rights and interests and a religion established by law, as if some men had a right to regulate the consciences of other men, or could have an interest in doing this; as if an individual could sacrifice to civil society opinions on which he thinks his eternal salvation depends; as if, in short, mankind were to be saved or *damned* in *communities* – Where *true toleration, (that is where the absolute incompetency of civil government in matters of consciences is established); there the clergyman*, when admitted into the national assembly, becomes a *simple citizen*; but when excluded he becomes an *ecclesiastic*.[142]

Notes

1 In 1971 G. Gusdorf wrote, 'le siècle des Lumières, mieux connu, n'en demeure pas moins mal connu'. George Gusdorf, *Les principes de la pensée au siècle des lumières*, Paris, 1971: 17.

2 The varieties of national manifestations of the Enlightenment are illustrated in R. Porter and M. Teich (eds), *The Enlightenment in National Context*, Cambridge, 1981.

3 'Enlightenment and the Revolution: the Case of North America', *Seventh International Congress on the Enlightenment: Introductory Papers*, Oxford, 1987, cited by L.G. Crocker, in his introduction to J.W. Yolton *et al.* (eds), *The Blackwell Companion to the Enlightenment*, Oxford, 1991, 9 n.1; N. Hampson, *The Enlightenment*, Harmondsworth, 1968: 9–10. It should be noted Hampson does offer unifying themes in the Enlightenment, and in particular pinpoints them in his essay on 'The Enlightenment in France' in Porter and Teich (eds), *The Enlightenment in National Context*: 41–2; and also, *The Enlightenment*, 106 and 146–61.

4 P. Gay, *The Enlightenment: An Interpretation*, I, *The Rise of Modern Paganism*; II, *The Science of Freedom*, London, 1966 and 1969: I, x; II, xii and 3.

5 R. Darnton, 'George Washington's False Teeth', *New York Review of Books*, 27 March 1997: 34–8.

6 On this, see A. Goldgar, *Impolite Learning: Conduct and Community in the Republic of Letters, 1680–1750*, New Haven and London, 1995. The Huguenot diaspora of course spread to Prussia and Switzerland, as well as Ireland and the American Colonies.

7 A.M. Wilson, 'The Enlightenment Came First To England', in S. Baxter (ed.), *England's Rise to Greatness, 1600–1763*, Berkley and Los Angeles, 1983: 1–28. Many of Wilson's points apply more generally to Britain and the Netherlands.

8 R.R. Palmer, *The Age of the Democratic Revolution: A Political History of Europe and America*, I, *The Challenge*; II, *The Struggle*, Princeton, New Jersey, c.1959–1964, esp. I, Introduction.

9 See Franco Venturi, *Italy and the Enlightenment. Studies in a Cosmopolitan Century*, ed. with intro. Stuart Woolf, trans. Susan Corsi, London, 1972: 1–32. This essay on 'The European Enlightenment' explores the relationship between the Enlightenment in Western Europe and the rest of Europe.

10 Gay, *The Enlightenment: An Interpretation*, I, *The Rise of Modern Paganism*, II: citing Shaftesbury to John le Clerc, 6 March, 1706; Benjamin Rand (ed.), *Life, Unpublished Letters, and Philosophical Regimen of Anthony, Earl of Shaftesbury*, London, 1900: 353.

11 The *Lettres philosophiques* included an extra section devoted to Pascal. References will be to the English translation by Leonard Tancock: *Voltaire, Letters on England*, Harmondsworth, 1980. For the publishing details of the work, see, René Pomeau, *D'Arouet à Voltaire*, Oxford, 1985: 321–2.

12 D.O. Thomas (ed.), *Richard Price, 1727–1791: Political Writings*, Cambridge, 1991: 182.

13 *Ibid.*: 196.

14 For the view of *The Magic Flute* as the apotheosis of the Enlightenment, see E. Wangermann, *The Austrian Achievement, 1700–1800*, London, 1973: 149–55, cf. N. Till, *Mozart and the Enlightenment*, London and Boston, 1992: 270–319.

15 Birmingham Public Library, Timmins Collection MS 210679, 'Proposal for Printing by Subscription a Complete Edition of the Works of Voltaire Printed with the types of Baskerville, for the Literary and Topographical Society' [n. d.].

16 See Q. Skinner, *The Foundations of Modern Political Thought*, I, *The Renaissance*; II, *The Age of the Reformation*, 1978: II, 244–9.

17 On this tradition, see O.P. Grell, 'Introduction', and H.A. Oberman, 'The travail of tolerance: containing chaos in early modern Europe', in O.P. Grell and B. Scribner (eds), *Tolerance and Intolerance in the European Reformation*, Cambridge, 1996: 6–7; J. Tully (ed.), *Pufendorf. On the Duty of Man and Citizen*, Cambridge, 1991: xviii; K. Haakonssen, *Natural Law and Moral Philosophy. From Grotius to the Scottish Enlightenment*, Cambridge, 1996: 30.

18 See N. Keohane, *Philosophy and the State in France. The Renaissance to the Enlightenment*, Princeton, New Jersey, 1980: 98–115 and 135–50; on the complexities of the libertine tradition, see J.G. Turner, 'The Properties of Libertinism', in R.P. Maccubin (ed.), 'Unauthorized Sexual Behavior during the Enlightenment', *Eighteenth-Century Life Special Issue* (IX, n.s.) 3 May, 1995: 75–88. Turner notes (79–80) that although three separate movements may be identified, the religious, the philosophical and the sexual, it is possible, 'with due caution', to establish a maximalist conception of libertinism in which the three are associated.

19 When the Académie Française, in its first dictionary published in the late seventeenth century (1694), defined the *philosophe* it suggested three meanings: 1. A student of the sciences (in the language of the late seventeenth century this was the traditional meaning of philosopher as someone concerned with the nature of our being and understanding); 2. A wise man who lives a quiet life; 3. A man who by free thought puts himself above the ordinary duties and obligations of civil life. The precise meaning of the French is difficult to convey. The full original phrasing is: '*un homme, qui, par libertinage d'esprit, se met au dessus des devoirs et des obligations ordinaires de la vie civile et chrétienne. C'est un homme qui ne se refuse rien, qui ne se contraint sur rien, et qui mène une vie de Philosophe*'. Preserved Smith, *A History of Modern Culture*, II, *The Enlightenment*, 1934, repr. New York, 1963: 309–10; H.S. Commager, *The Empire of Reason. How Europe Imagined and America Realized the Enlightenment*, New York, 1977: App. 'The term philosophe', 236–45; D. Beales, 'Christians and *philosophes*: the case of the Austrian Enlightenment', in D. Beales and G. Best (eds), *History,*

Society and the Churches: Essays in Honour of Owen Chadwick, Cambridge, 1985: 169–70.

20 E. Gibbon, *The History of the Decline and Fall of the Roman Empire*, 9 vols., new edn S.A. and H. Oddy, London, 1809: I, 31. The thrust of the statement was actually closer to the sentiments of Frederick the Great of Prussia than of Gibbon. The latter portrayed the ancient pagans as more benign than modern sectarians for their beliefs had not been contaminated by 'theological rancour' and 'speculative systems', which made modern sects dangerous. He was especially anxious to protect the Church of England and was prepared to use the letter of the law against heretics like Joseph Priestley. See J.G.A. Pocock, 'Gibbon's Decline and Fall and the World-View of the Late Enlightenment', *Eighteenth-Century Studies*, X, 1977: 287–303; 'Superstition and Enthusiasm in Gibbon's History of Religion', *Eighteenth-Century Life*, VIII, n.s., 1982: 83–93; P. Turnbull, 'Gibbon's exchange with Joseph Priestley', *British Journal for Eighteenth-Century Studies*, 14, no. 3, Autumn 1991: 139–58.

21 See Grell, 'Introduction', in Grell and Scribner (eds), *Tolerance and Intolerance in the European Reformation*: 6–10.

22 A. Smith, *An Inquiry into the Nature and Causes of the Wealth of Nations*, ed. with intro. by E. Cannan, New York, 1994: Bk. IV, ch. 2, 482; Smith, following Hume, believed that sectarianism was harmful, but thought that a multiplication of sects dissipated the dangerous tendencies of sectarianism. He believed that in Pennsylvania where the law favoured no one sect, it was productive of 'the most philosophical good temper and moderation', and that generally equality of the sects would, if not be productive of such effects, on balance produce more good than harm. *Ibid.*: Bk V, ch. 1 pt. III, 850–53.

23 Montesquieu, *Persian Letters*, trans. with intro. and notes, C.J. Betts, Harmondsworth, 1973, Letter 85, 164–66. This letter is significant because Usbek is addressing the question of religious intolerance, not by reflecting on the French example, but by referring to the Persian situation. Montesquieu, in his *Cahiers*, suggested that the comments in the letters on religion should be understood not so much in a critical light as in terms of the wonder and puzzlement of the Persian witnesses of Catholic religion. This could not hold true of the comments on intolerance. The letters were published anonymously in Holland and went into ten editions within the year. See *Montesquieu, Cahiers 1716–1755, Textes recueillis et présentés par Bernard Grasset*, Paris, 1941: 197–8, 'Apologie de "Lettres persanes" '.

24 W. Doyle, *The Old European Order, 1660–1800*, Oxford, 1978: 156.

25 See D. Beales, *Joseph II. In the Shadow of Maria Theresa 1741–1780*, Cambridge, 1987: 253–4; F.A. Szabo, *Kaunitz and Enlightened Absolutism*, Cambridge, 1994: 256–7. The riots were cited by a Prussian Professor, Brunn, as evidence of how, in contrast with Prussia, freedom in England degenerated into licence. K. Epstein, *The Genesis of German Conservatism*, Princeton, New Jersey, 1966: 346–7.

26 Lord Acton, *Lectures on Modern History*, 1906, repr. London, 1960: 60, lecture on the 'Beginning of the Modern State'.

27 Rev. P. Furneaux, *Letters to the Honourable Mr. Justice Blackstone concerning His exposition of the Act of Toleration*, 2nd edn with additions, London, 1771: 278.

28 T.W. Davis (ed.), *Committees for the Repeal of the Test and Corporation Acts;*

Minutes 1786–90 and 1827–8, London Record Society Publications, XIV, 1978: 8–15.

29 Furneaux, in his *Letters to Blackstone*: 164–5, defined persecution as, 'an injury inflicted on a person for his religious principles or profession only'.

30 Kamen, *Rise of Toleration*: 216–17.

31 R.A. Jackson, *Vive le Roi! A History of the French Coronation from Charles V to Charles X*, Chapel Hill and London, 1984: 218.

32 See J. McManners, 'Jansenism and Politics in the Eighteenth Century', in D. Baker (ed.), *Church, Society and Politics: Studies in Church History*, XII, 1975 for the way in which persecution changed a religious and theological dispute into a political one.

33 The *locus classicus* for this was St Paul's Letter to the Romans, XIII, 1–5. It was elaborated on by Bishop Bossuet, in his *Politique Tirée des Propres Paroles de l'Écriture Sainte* in which he asserted that according to scripture one should obey unjust as well as good kings.

34 *Critique générale de l'histoire du calvinisme de M. Maimbourg*, Letter 1, sec. 4, cited by E.I. Perry, *From Theology to History: French Religious Controversy and the Revocation of the Edict of Nantes*, The Hague, 1973: 197, n.2. I am indebted to this work for my comments upon the role of history in debates upon toleration.

35 The literature on Hume is considerable. A useful guide is D.F. Norton (ed.), *The Cambridge Companion to Hume*, Cambridge, 1993.

36 Johann Lorenz von Mosheim, Chancellor of the University of Göttingen, was a latitudinarian in the Erasmian tradition. His great work, *An Ecclesiastical History, Ancient and Modern*, exemplifies E.I. Perry's argument that the history which contributed towards toleration was history which freed itself from confessional partisanship. Mosheim hated persecution, but sought to understand it. He also understood man's need for religious understanding and the way in which that was shaped by history. For example, he saw the tragedy of Servetus as a Greek tragedy rather than a simple battle between good and evil. From his respect for man's religious quest he derived his belief in the need for toleration of all forms of worship. J.L. Mosheim, *An Ecclesiastical History, Ancient and Modern, from the Birth of Christ, to the Beginning of the Eighteenth Century* (1755), trans. A. Maclaine, 2nd edn 6 vols, London, 1819: V, 503–6. See P.H. Reill, *The German Enlightenment and the Rise of Historicism*, Berkeley, Los Angeles, London, 1975: 161–5.

37 This theme is explored in J. Meyrick, 'Citizenship and Conscience in Eighteenth-Century France', *Eighteenth-Century Studies*, XXI, no.1, Fall 1987: 48–70.

38 L.W. Cowie (ed.), *The French Revolution. Documents and Debates*, Houndsmills and London, 1987: 32; J. Hardman (ed.), *The French Revolution. The Fall of the Ancien Regime to the Thermidorian Reaction 1785–1795*, London, 1981: 124–7.

39 W.R. Ward, *Religion and Society in England 1790–1850*, London, 1972: 1.

40 F. Furet, trans. A. Nevill, *Revolutionary France, 1770–1880*, Hachette, 1988, Oxford, 1992: 325.

41 See E. Wangermann, *The Austrian Achievement, 1700–1800*, London, 1973: 134–42. It was not only in absolutist states that the issues of toleration and freedom of thought were the source of anxiety. In England, William Paley, who advocated complete religious toleration, cautioned, 'I deem it no infringement of religious liberty to restrain the circulation of ridicule, invective and mockery upon religious

subjects.' See his, *The Principles of Morals and Political Philosophy*, 1785, 13th edn. in two vols., London, 1801: II, 344.

42 The distinction between a Separationist and Jurisdictional system of toleration is made by Francesco Ruffini, in his *Religious Liberty*, trans. J. Parker Hayes, with preface by J.B. Bury, 1912, and is discussed by J.B. Bury, *A History of Freedom of Thought*, London, 1913, 7th impression 1928: 125–6.

43 Paley, *Principles of Morals and Political Philosophy*, II: 310–12, 351–2. Paley's work was enormously influential in the Anglo-Saxon world. His influence on the continent is less clear. Book VI, in which toleration is discussed, attracted attention in France and two sets of extracts from the book were published in 1789 translated by 'M. Bertin'.

44 J. Israel, *The Dutch Republic. Its Rise, Greatness, and Fall 1477–1806*, Oxford, 1995: 931–3.

45 *Ibid.*: 924–5.

46 J. Plamenatz, *Man and Society*, I, London, 1963, 8th impression, 1974: 86; P. King, *Toleration*, London, 1976: 96, describes 'conscience' as being for Bayle 'the new religion'. Bayle's belief in the futility of persecution and his adherence to the duty to obey one's own conscience was informed by knowledge of the tragedy of persecution, including the loss of his own brother.

47 Thus the cautious Montesquieu, who came to disagree with Bayle's views on the impossibility of a society of true Christians and the possibility of one of virtuous atheists, revered his memory. See R. Shackleton, 'Bayle and Montesquieu', in P. Dibon (ed.), *Pierre Bayle. Le Philosophe de Rotterdam*, Paris, 1959: 142–9.

48 Kamen, *Rise of Toleration*: 239.

49 O. Kenshur, *Dilemmas of Enlightenment. Studies in the Rhetoric and Logic of Ideology*, Berkeley, Los Angeles, 1993: 85–6 and 94. In the work which provides Kenshur with evidence for Bayle's distaste for Socinianism, *Commentaire Philosophique sur ces paroles de Jésus Christ "Contrains-les-d'entrer"* (1686), he also argued vigorously for their toleration. See A.G. Tannenbaum, *Pierre Bayle's 'Philosophical Commentary'. A Modern Translation and Critical Interpretation*, New York, 1987, esp. The Second Part, ch. 8, 151–60.

50 See P. Casini, 'Newton's *Principia* and the Philosophers of the Enlightenment', *Notes and Records of the Royal Society*, XLII, no. 1 (January 1988): 36.

51 See R.H. Popkin, 'Pierre Bayle's place in 17th century scepticism', in Dibon (ed.), *Pierre Bayle. Le Philosophe de Rotterdam*: 1–19; also, Kenshur, 'Bayle's Theory of Toleration: The Politics of Certainty and Doubt', in his *Dilemmas of Enlightenment*: 77–111.

52 P.J.S. Whitmore, 'Bayle's Criticism of Locke', in Dibon (ed.), *Pierre Bayle. Le Philosophe de Rotterdam*: 84–90; M. Cranston, *John Locke a Biography*, Oxford and New York, 1985: 256–7, 455, note.

53 R.H. Bainton, *The Travail of Religious Liberty: Nine Biographical Studies*, Philadelphia, Westminster, 1951: 237; his views are cited in an important discussion of Locke on toleration by A.P.F. Sell, *John Locke and the Eighteenth-Century Divines*, Cardiff, 1997: 151.

54 M. Goldie, 'Locke, Proast and Religious Toleration 1688–1692', in J. Walsh, C. Haydon and S. Taylor (eds), *The Church of England c.1689–c.1833. From Toleration to Tractarianism*, Cambridge, 1993: 143–71; J. Marshall, *John Locke. Resist-*

ance, Religion and Responsibility, Cambridge, 1994: 368–70. A.P.F. Sell, *John Locke and the Eighteenth-Century Divines*: 157–62.

55 See J. Dunn, 'The claim to freedom of conscience: freedom of thought, freedom of speech, freedom of worship?' in O.P. Grell, J. Israel, N. Tyacke (eds), *From Persecution to Toleration: the Glorious Revolution and Religion in England*, Oxford, 1991: 171–93; cf. W. Walker, 'The Limits of Locke's toleration', *Studies on Voltaire and the Eighteenth Century*, 332 (1995): 133–54, esp. at 139. With the qualification suggested by Walker, it remains true that Locke offered a more coherent theory of toleration than Bayle. See the summary of their two positions in S. O'Cathasaigh, 'Bayle and Locke on Toleration', in M. Magdelaine, M-C. Pitassi, R. Whelan and A. McKenna, *De l'Humanisme aux Lumières, Bayle et le protestantisme. Mélanges en l'honneur d'Elisabeth Labrousse*, Paris and Oxford, 1996: 679–92.

56 Goldie, 'Locke, Proast and Religious Toleration 1688–1692', in Walsh *et al.* (eds), *The Church of England*: 167.

57 He wanted the abolition of the Test Act and especially the use of the sacrament as a Test. His views on this were echoed by Dissenters throughout the eighteenth century, and proved to be one of the main reasons for the Test and Corporations Acts eventually being repealed in 1828. Locke believed that the profane use of the sacrament encouraged irreligion and immorality; he, himself, favoured moral reformation. Goldie, 'Locke, Proast and religious toleration', in Walsh *et al. The Church of England*: 158–9; U. Henriques, *Religious Toleration in England 1787–1833*, London, 1961: 87–8.

58 C. Robbins, *The Eighteenth-Century Commonwealthman*, Cambridge, Mass., 1959, esp. ch. 9; S.M. Dworetz, *The Unvarnished Doctrine. Locke, liberalism, and the American Revolution*, Durham and London, 1990: 120–3; Israel, *The Dutch Republic*: 1074–5; I.L. Leeb, *The Ideological Origins of the Batavian Revolution. History and Politics in the Dutch Republic 1747–1800*, The Hague, 1973. In all three countries, ideas concerning toleration and religious liberty were increasingly an aspect of a more general concern for civil and political liberty.

59 W.M. Spellman, *John Locke*, London, 1997: 134; J.W. Gough also argues that 'intellectual liberty, or liberty of thought in general' was the logical outcome of Locke's argument for religious liberty and his belief in the value of applying reason to revelation. J. Locke, *'Epistola de Tolerantia;' A Letter on Toleration*, R. Klibansky (ed.), J.W. Gough trans. and intro., Oxford, 1968: 26.

60 W. Popple (1638–) was a merchant, of Socinian sympathies. At the time of the translation, he was not known to Locke, although they shared friends in the United Provinces, notably Jean Le Clerc and Benjamin Furly. Popple was also friendly with the Shaftesburys. Locke was not offended by the translation although he had not given permission for it. When Locke was appointed Commissioner of Trade and Plantations in May 1696, Popple became secretary to the Commission and they became firm friends. A second edition of his translation of Locke's *Epistola de Tolerantia* was published in 1765 sponsored by Thomas Hollis, the inveterate Whig publicist; J. Locke, *Epistola de Tolerantia*: 48–9; W.H. Bond, *Thomas Hollis of Lincoln's Inn. A Whig and His Books*, Cambridge, 1990: 121–2.

61 On this see, Whitmore, 'Bayle's Criticism of Locke', in Dibon (ed.), *Pierre Bayle. Le Philosophe de Rotterdam*: 83.

62 Tancock (ed.), *Voltaire, Letters on England*: 62–7.

63 J. Locke, *An Essay Concerning Human Understanding*, abr. and ed. by J.W. Yolton, London, new edn 1993, Bk. IV, chs. XV, XVI: 381–94.

64 J. Locke, *Epistola de Tolerantia*: xxix–xxx. Locke's *Epistle* was attached to only one of the many editions of Voltaire's treatise which appeared in 1763 and 1764.

65 J. Locke, *Epistola de Tolerantia*, preface by R. Klibansky: xxxv.

66 Kaunitz's recommendations were cautiously worded to gain Maria Theresa's approval, which she gave reluctantly in November 1777, Szabo, *Kaunitz and Enlightened Absolutism*: 252–5.

67 The group included both the libertine wing of radicalism led by Wilkes, and the Rational Dissenting element led on this issue by Priestley. Neither Priestley nor Wilkes backtracked on their support for the Catholic Relief Act (1778) following the Gordon Riots. See my 'Heretical Religion and Radical Politics', in E. Hellmuth (ed.), *The Transformation of Political Culture. England and Germany in the late Eighteenth Century*, Oxford, 1990: 356–7.

68 Voltaire underplayed the limitations on free speech. At the time of the publication of the fourth of the Deist Thomas Woolston's six *Discourses on the Miracles of our Saviour* (1727–9), Voltaire implied that it would be published with impunity, whereas it led to Woolston's trial and imprisonment in 1729. He died in 1733 while still in confinement. Nor did Voltaire pay much attention to the limitations of the Toleration Act (he seemed to have been unaware that Dissent was officially a crime until the Mansfield verdict of 1767) and of intolerance towards Roman Catholics, who in the 1720s were undergoing particularly hard times. Pomeau, *D'Arouet à Voltaire*: 253; C. Haydon, *Anti-Catholicism in Eighteenth-Century England. A Political and Social Study*, Manchester and New York, 1993: 121–4.

69 Tancock (ed.), *Voltaire, Letters on England*: 37–41. Voltaire returned to the Stock Exchange analogy in his article on *Tolérance* in his *Dictionnaire Philosophique* (1764).

70 As Colin Haydon has noted, 'the lead in such matters came from the top', and from a dynasty brought up in the tolerant court of Hanover. Voltaire would have sensed this atmosphere of tolerance amongst the elite. He also mistakenly believed that Thomas Woolston died at liberty, whereas he was under what we would call house arrest in the precinct of the King's Bench prison. Haydon, *Anti-Catholicism*: 124–6; J.M. Robertson, *A Short History of Free Thought*, 2 vols, London, 3rd edn 1915: II, 159.

71 Voltaire remarked that it was necessary from time to time to execute an admiral to 'encourage the others'. He had met the young Byng when he was in London in 1727. Pomeau, *D'Arouet à Voltaire*: 238.

72 In his *Histoire d'Élisabeth Canning et des Calas*, a work (completed in the summer of 1762) in which he contrasted the way in which an English girl, Elizabeth Canning, had been treated with that of Calas, Voltaire linked the English system with an enlightened notion of punishment, arguing very much as Montesquieu that punishment should be open and public. Elizabeth Canning, an English girl, had disappeared from her home for a month in 1753 and when she returned, undernourished and emaciated, a month later, she claimed that she had been abducted and forced into prostitution. Action was taken against those whom she accused, but after their trials the veracity of her testimony was publicly questioned. This led to a review of the case and to the convictions being overturned. In fact Voltaire turned the real, rather complicated story into a legend. He por-

trayed the girl as a villain, whereas her story is shrouded in mystery; only two, not nine, persons were initially convicted; and he attributed the re-opening of the case to the influence of one pamphlet by Allan Ramsay, the painter and philosopher, and not to the vigorous pamphlet war which was waged over her case. But, as Peter Gay has noted, his aim was to make the point that 'secrecy has pernicious and often irreparable consequences'. *Voltaire's Politics. The Poet as a Realist*, New Jersey and Oxford, 1959: 300–1. The case is examined in detail in J. Moore, *The Appearance of Truth. The Story of Elizabeth Canning and Eighteenth Century Narrative*, Newark, London and Toronto, 1994.

73 Voltaire does not mention leading English free-thinkers Anthony Collins, Matthew Tindal and John Toland in his *Lettres Philosophiques*, almost certainly for tactical reasons. Aldridge suggests that the section devoted to Pascal arose in part from reading the Deist thought of Shaftesbury, Collins and others. However, Collins's philosophical influence on Voltaire may be dated to the late 1730s. Tancock (ed.), *Voltaire, Letters on England*; XVI; A.O. Aldridge, *Voltaire and a Century of Light*, Princeton, New Jersey, 1975: 79; H. Mason, *Voltaire. A Biography*, London, 1981: 49.

74 Bodleian Library, Ms Autobiog. b10/197, Voltaire to David Williams, 3 September, 1776; *Correspondence and related documents*, ed. Th. Besterman, *Complete Works of Voltaire*: 85–235, Geneva, Banbury, Oxford, 1968–1976, Best.D20277. I owe this reference to Professor James Dybikowski; subsequent references are also indebted to him and to his paper, 'Voltaire and David Williams: Free-thinking and Toleration' in U. Kölving and C. Mervaud (eds), *Voltaire et ses combats*, 2 vols, Oxford, 1994: I, 601–12.

75 J. Dybikowski, *On Burning Ground: An Examination of the Ideas, Projects and Life of David Williams*, Oxford, 1993, *Studies on Voltaire and the Eighteenth Century*, v. 307, 61–105.

76 D. Williams, *The Nature and Extent of Intellectual Liberty*, London, 1779: 15, note. These principles were almost identical to those adopted by the London Revolution Society in 1788, but with the addition of the radical doctrines of popular sovereignty and the right of resistance. They in turn formed the basis of Richard Price's famous formulation of the principles of the Glorious Revolution in his discourse preached the following year, namely: 'First, The right to liberty of conscience in religious matters. Secondly, The right to resist power when abused. And, Thirdly, The right to chuse our own governors, to cashier them for misconduct; and to frame a government for ourselves'. *A Discourse on the Love of Our Country* (1789), in R. Price, *Political writings*, ed. D.O. Thomas, Cambridge, 1991: 189–90.

77 Williams, *Nature and Extent of Intellectual Liberty*, XXII; Williams's translation was published in an edition of the works of Voltaire published in 1780. The first English translation appeared in 1764. Dybikowski, *On Burning Ground*: 305.

78 J. Van den Heuvel (ed.), *L'Affaire Calas et Autres Affaires*, Paris, 1975: 165–6. Generally I shall follow McCabe's translation, except where, as in this case, he offers a rather free translation. Cf. Voltaire, *A Treatise on Toleration and Other Essays*, trans. J. McCabe, 1935 repr. New York, 1994: 202–3.

79 Williams, *Nature and Extent of Intellectual Liberty*: 31.

80 *Ibid.*: 31–2.

81 *Ibid.*: 38–40.

82 *Ibid.*: 15, note.
83 The literature on Spinoza and the radical Enlightenment is extensive; see M. Jacob, *The Radical Enlightenment; Pantheists, Freemasons and Republicans*, London, 1981: esp. 1–19 and 52–3; Whitmore, 'Bayle's Criticism of Locke', in Dibon (ed.), *Pierre Bayle. Le Philosophe de Rotterdam*: 93; R. Hamowy, 'Cato's Letters, John Locke, and the Republican paradigm', *History of Political Thought*, XVI, issue 2, 1990: 273–94.
84 J. Toland, *Tetradymus*, London, 1720, cited in D.M. Clarke, 'Locke and Toland on Toleration', in M. O'Dea and K. Whelan, *Nations and Nationalism: France, Britain, Ireland and the Eighteenth-century Context*, Oxford, 1995, *Studies on Voltaire and the Eighteenth Century*: vol. 335, 261–71, at 266; see also Dybikowski, *On Burning Ground*: 42–6.
85 B. Peach and D.O. Thomas (eds), *The Correspondence of Richard Price, 1748–1791*, 3 vols., Durham, N.C., Cardiff, 1983–94, II, D.O. Thomas (ed.): 3–19 (Turgot to Price), 22 March 1778; W.W. Stephens (ed.), *The Life and Writings of Turgot, Comptroller of France 1774–6*, 1895, New York, 1971: 210–18.
86 H. Collins (ed.), *Thomas Paine. Rights of Man*, Harmondsworth, 1969: 107.
87 Mirabeau published Price's work and his own translation of Turgot's letter of 1778 to Richard Price, together with his own comments under the title, *Considérations sur l'ordre de Cincinnatus*, London, 1784. Johnson published another edition in 1785. There were Dutch and American editions, and a Dutch translation in 1785. D.O. Thomas, J. Stephens and P.A.L. Jones, *Bibliography of Richard Price*, Aldershot, 1993: 119–20.
88 J. Godechot (ed.), *Les Constitutions de la France depuis 1789*, Paris, 1979, repr. 1994: 24. Mirabeau considered the word *tolérance* was restrictive: 'The most unlimited liberty of religion is in my eyes a right so sacred that the word tolerance, which aspires to express it, appears to me in some degree tyrannical itself, since the existence of an authority which has the power to tolerate circumscribes the liberty of thought, even that which it tolerates, and as well as that which it is not able to tolerate.'
89 Both Goethe and Schiller rejected the concept of toleration. See J. Whaley, chapter 9, this volume.
90 Godechot (ed.), *Les Constitutions de la France depuis 1789*: 24–5 and 33–5; M. Morabito and D. Bourmaud, *Histoire Constitutionelle et Politique de la France (1789–1958)*, Paris, 1993: 66.
91 Voltaire was imprisoned from May 1717 to April 1718 for libelling the regent Philippe d'Orleans in his *Puero Regnante*, in which he referred to 'the administration of a man notorious for poisonings and incests'. Aldridge, *Voltaire and a Century of Light*: 25; Pomeau, *d'Arouet à Voltaire*, 104–14.
92 K. Martin, *French Liberal Thought in the Eighteenth Century. A Study of Political Ideas from Bayle to Condorcet*, London, 1929, 3rd edn revis. 1962, repr. New York, 1963: 122.
93 Tancock (ed.), *Voltaire, Letters on England*: 67.
94 I have avoided categorizing the thinkers discussed here in terms of Orangist or Patriot affinities, since the intellectual cross-currents were considerable. Luzac, an Orangist, is perhaps as close as there can be to a representative figure. Leeb, *The Ideological Origins of the Batavian Revolution*: 2.

95 W.R.E. Velema, *Enlightenment and Conservatism in the Dutch Republic. The Political Thought of Elie Luzac (1721–1796)*, Assen/Maastricht, 1993: 6–22.

96 *Ibid.*: 19.

97 Leeb, *The Ideological Origins of the Batavian Revolution*: 73.

98 Velema, *Enlightenment and Conservatism*: 179; Leeb, *The Ideological Origins of the Batavian Revolution*: 68–73; Luzac leaned heavily on Locke for the theoretical discussion in his pamphlet, *The conduct of the Stadhtholder's party defended*, 1754.

99 Velema, *Enlightenment and Conservatism*: 11–12 and 15–19. J.H.S. Formey accused Luzac of separating morality and religion.

100 R. Tuck, 'The "Modern" Theory of Natural Law', in A. Pagden (ed.), *The Languages of Political Theory in Early-Modern Europe*, Cambridge, 1987: 99.

101 W. Enfield, *The History of Philosophy from the Earliest Period: Drawn up from Brucker's Historia Critica Philosophiac*, London, 1837: 576.

102 T. Dyche and W. Pardon (eds), *A New General English Dictionary*, 3rd edn, London, 1740.

103 Enfield, *History of Philosophy from the Earliest Period*: 624, citing *De Jure Belli ac Pacis* (1625); on this see Tuck, *op. cit.*: 100.

104 Brucker's synthesizing abilities and eclectic virtues were recognised by Denis Diderot who drew heavily on Brucker for his accounts in the *Encyclopédie* of the history of philosophy. See J.H. Mason and R. Wokler (eds), *Denis Diderot. Political Writings*, Cambridge, 1992: xiv, xxxi and 2.

105 *Critique of Pure Reason*, trans. N.K. Smith, London, 1958: A xi, note.

106 Velema, *Enlightenment and Conservatism*: 120.

107 *Ibid.*: 7. Luzac was ordered by the Walloon Consistory of Leiden to return all his copies of *L'Homme machine* and to promise never again 'to print or sell any book attacking Divinity, religion or good manners'. Luzac complied but refused to name the author of the work.

108 J. Schmidt (ed.), *What is Enlightenment? Eighteenth-Century Answers and Twentieth-Century Questions*, Berkeley, Los Angeles and London, 1996: 168–87 at 177. Reim was defending Prussian intervention against the Patriots in 1788.

109 R. Chartier, *The Cultural Origins of the French Revolution*, trans. L.G. Cochrane, Durham and London, 1991: 40–2. J. Lough, *The Encyclopédie*, Harlow, 1971: 21; P. Grosclaude, *Malesherbes. Témoin et Interprète de Son Temps*, Paris, 1961: 102–6. On 7 February, 1752 the Council of State condemned the first two volumes of the *Encyclopédie* for 'tending to destroy the royal authority, to establish the spirit of independence and revolt, and, in obscure and equivocal terms, to praise the foundations of error, the corruption of morals (*mœurs*), religion and unbelief'. In so doing it effectually protected the *Encyclopédie* from the censure of the Sorbonne and the *parlement* of Paris.

110 Chartier, *Cultural Origins*: 53–6.

111 A. Bachman, *Censorship in France from 1715 to 1750: Voltaire's Opposition*, New York, 1934: 76; Malesherbes wrote to the Duchesse of Agen, *'Il ne faut croire que les livres d'édification n'aient pas autant besoin d'examens que les livres profanes, ou comme on dit à présent Philosophiques. Peut-être les ouvrages du Père Quesnel ont-ils produit plus de mal dans le monde que ceux de Spinoza'* [8 August, 1758]. The choice of Quesnel, whose *Moral Reflections on the New Testament* led to the contentious Bull *Unigenitus*, leaves us uncertain

as to whether Malesherbes is really talking about the edification which the work produced or the political struggles it caused.

112 Chartier, *Cultural Origins*: 46.

113 E.P. Shaw, *Problems and Policies of Malesherbes as Directeur de la Librairie in France 1750–1763*, Albany, New York, 1966: 120–2.

114 Chartier, *Cultural Origins*: 58; R. Darnton, 'The High Enlightenment and the Low Life of Literature', in his *The Literary Underground of the Old Regime*, Cambridge, Mass., London, 1982: 1–40.

115 As late as 1785, Beaumarchais's complete edition of Voltaire's works was banned by a royal decree. W. Hanley, 'The Policing of Thought: Censorship in Eighteenth-century France', *Studies on Voltaire and the Eighteenth Century*, 183, 1980: 265–95 at 289.

116 Velema, *Enlightenment and Conservatism*: 7. Luzac used this as his title page motto for his *Essai sur la Liberté de produire se sentimens* (1749). Barbeyrac (1674–1744) was a Huguenot exile, his parents left France in 1686, and was Professor of Public Law in Groningen from 1717. His French translations of Pufendorf, Cumberland and Grotius with his own prefaces presented a coherent version of the seventeenth-century natural law tradition and gave it a 'strongly Lockean slant'. Haakonssen, *Natural Law and Moral Philosophy*: 58–9; Cranston, *Locke a Biography*: 163–4.

117 Baron d'Holbach, *Système sociale ou principes naturels de la morale politique*, London, 1774: III, 114, cited in N. Elias, *The Civilizing Process. The History of Manners*, trans. E. Jephcot, Oxford, 1978: 46–7; Elias notes how it was in the early 1770s the word 'civilization' came to be widely used by the *philosophes* with a generally understood meaning.

118 Bachman, *Censorship in France*: 76.

119 See J.P. Reid, *The Concept of Liberty in the Age of the American Revolution*, Chicago and London, 1988: 108–22. Reid cites, as a good example of ambiguity, Book IV of William Blackstone's influential *Commentaries on the Laws of England* in which he argued that 'The liberty of the press is indeed essential to the nature of a free state: but this consists in laying no *previous* restraints upon publications, and not in freedom from censure for criminal matter when published ... [T]o punish (as the law does at present) any dangerous or offensive writings, which, when published, shall on a fair and impartial trial be adjudged of a pernicious tendency, is necessary for the preservation of peace and good order, of government and religion, the only solid foundations of civil liberty.' This is some way from regarding liberty in terms of sacrosanct individual rights, a stance towards which some radicals were moving. The common denominator in European and Anglo-American attitudes was that liberty was viewed in terms of preservation from excesses seen, in varying degrees, in terms of those of arbitrary governments and licentious peoples. But it did not produce common solutions. Malesherbes read Blackstone when his work was translated into French, but although he admired him and drew on some of his ideas, he thought the French and English were too divided by their character and history for the approach of the one to be appropriate to the other. See, Grosclaude, *Malesherbes*: 400, 404, note and 406–7.

120 Voltaire to Elie de Beaumont, 27 February, 1765, *Oeuvres Complètes*, ed.

Beuchot, LII; *Correspondance Générale*, IX, 31; cited in M. Dommanget, *Le Curé Meslier. Athée. Communiste et Révolutionnaire sous Louis XIV*, Paris, 1965: 377.

121 For an important discussion of the development of the public sphere, see Chartier, *Cultural Origins of the French Revolution*: 20–37; S. Maza, *Private Lives and Public Affairs*, Berkeley, 1993: 27–33.

122 See G. Lamoine, 'L'Europe de L'Esprit ou The Royal Society de Londres', *Dix Huitième Siècle*, 25, 1993: 167–97, at 180–4. Lamoine argues that the first criterion for foreign members was individual merit, and that, '*Dans cette république multilingue des esprits, la tolérance semble le trait dominant*'. Lamoine notes that, between 1721 and 1770, 354 foreign members were elected. Although the list reads like a '*Who's Who*' of the Enlightenment, occasional blunders were made. Diderot was not elected in 1753 despite strong sponsorship, including D'Alembert, Buffon and Needham.

123 [A.L. Thomas], *Discours prononcé dans l'Académie françoise, le jeudi 22 janvier 1767, la reception de M. Thomas*, Paris, 1767: 4–54, cited in D. Goodman, *The Republic of Letters. A Cultural History of the French Enlightenment*, Ithaca and London, 1994: 46–7.

124 Van den Heuvel (ed.), *L'Affaire Calas*: 171.

125 'Homily on Superstition' in Voltaire, *A Treatise on Toleration and Other Essays*, trans. McCabe: 124. Peter Gay notes that Plutarch's essay *On Superstition*, cited by Bayle in his *Pensées Diverses sur la Comète*, in which he argued that superstition was 'a far greater calamity than atheism', was widely influential amongst the *philosophes*. Gay, *The Enlightenment. An Interpretation*: I, 152. Voltaire's fear of superstition and his worry that it would not necessarily be dispelled by education is discussed in H.C. Payne, *The Philosophes and the People*, New Haven and London, 1976: 65–116. Voltaire clung to one double truth, namely that the people should continue to be taught the doctrine of rewards and punishments.

126 Voltaire, *A Treatise on Toleration and Other Essays*, trans. McCabe: 209.

127 *Ibid.*: 147 and 149. Voltaire noted that the Toulousians celebrated the massacre 'like a floral festival'.

128 *Ibid.*: 166.

129 Tancock (ed.), *Voltaire, Letters on England*: 42.

130 Shaftesbury wrote in his 'A letter Concerning Enthusiasm' in his *Characteristicks*, 'How comes it to pass, then, that we appear such cowards in reasoning, and are so afraid to stand the test of ridicule?' There were many English editions of *Characteristicks*, a French translation in 1769 and a German translation of the letter in 1768.

131 J. Morley, *Voltaire*, London, 1885, 1900 printing: 248–59; Voltaire, *A Treatise on Toleration and Other Essays*, trans. McCabe: 166; Bayle's influence on Voltaire varied over his long career. For a discussion of the chronology of his influence see I.O. Wade, *The Intellectual Development of Voltaire*, Princeton, New Jersey, 1969: 632–51; and H. Mason, *Voltaire and Bayle*, Oxford, 1963: 1–24.

132 This was an enduring theme in his life. In old age, Voltaire observed to D'Alembert, 'It is never by means of metaphysics that you will succeed in delivering men from error; you must prove the truth by facts.' *Corr, 1773, Oeuvres*, 75 vols, Badouin, 1826: lxxv and 614, cited in Morley, *Voltaire*: 250.

133 Diderot wrote to Voltaire, 'Other historians tell us the facts in order to teach us

the facts. You do it in order to excite in the depth of our souls a strong indignation against mendacity, ignorance, hypocrisy, superstition, fanaticism, tyranny;
and that indignation remains in the memory when the facts have gone.' *Correspondance*, III, 275, 18 November, 1760; cited in Gay, *The Enlightenment. An
Interpretation*: I, 188.

134 For a summary of Voltaire's programme, see Wade, *Intellectual Development*:
765–77.

135 G. Adams, *The Huguenots and French Opinion, 1685–1787. The Enlightenment
Debate on Toleration*, Waterloo, Ontario, 1991: 217–18.

136 D.O. Thomas (ed.), *The Correspondence of Richard Price, 1748–1791*: II, 17,
Turgot to Price, 22 March, 1778.

137 J. Fruchtman Jr, 'Paine's *Common Sense*', *History of Political Thought*, X, no.3,
1989: 434–5; M. Philp (general ed.), *Political and Philosophical Writings of
William Godwin*, 7 vols., London, 1993: III, Mark Philp (ed.), Austin Ghee
(researcher), *An Enquiry Concerning Political Justice*: 111 and 121–2.

138 M. Fitzpatrick, *'Rousing the Sleeping Lion': Joseph Priestley and the Constitution in Church and State*, Occasional Publications of the Leeds Library, no.3,
1993: 1–21.

139 G. K. Clark, *The Kingdom of Free Men*, Cambridge, 1957: 131. See also Fitzpatrick, *'Rousing the Sleeping Lion'*: 1–21.

140 L. Simonutti, 'Between Political Loyalty and Religious Liberty: Political Theory
and Toleration in Huguenot Thought in the Epoch of Bayle', *History of Political
Thought*, XVII, no.4, 1996: 523–54 at 554.

141 I have discussed such matters in, 'Enlightenment and Conscience', in J. McLaren
and H. Coward (eds), *Religious Conscience, the State and the Law: Historical
Contexts and Contemporary Significance*, Albany, 1999: 46–61. See also L.
Simonutti, 'Between Political Loyalty and Religious Liberty', *op. cit.*: 523–54,
esp. 553.

142 D.O. Thomas (ed.), *The Correspondence of Richard Price*, 1748–1791, II, 17,
Turgot to Price, 22 March, 1778. The translation is by Mirabeau who rendered
en commun as 'in communities'.

3.   Multiculturalism and Ethnic Cleansing in the Enlightenment

Robert Wokler

If the meaning of words were accessible only to those who actually employed them, neither *multiculturalism* nor *ethnic cleansing* could have been intelligible to anyone in the age of Enlightenment. In addressing themselves to what is always local and peculiar, historians must be specially attentive to their use of words, alert to anachronisms and the perils of ascribing timeless significance to ideas plucked out of context like magician's rabbits from a bottomless hat. *Multiculturalism* and *ethnic cleansing* are terms which pertain to the political world of the late twentieth century, in one case predominantly with respect to notions of community generated in North America, in the other with respect to the conduct of a civil war in Bosnia. My choice of title here is deliberately anachronistic, not because I believe that our current political vocabularies would have had the same resonance 200 years ago but, rather, because I am convinced that certain features of the discourse of the civic and religious life of the seventeenth and eighteenth centuries have persisted and thus remain strikingly familiar, rather than alien, in our time.

The allegedly Eurocentric or, alternatively, gendered nature of Enlightenment philosophy is often identified as underpinning the most blameworthy practices of intolerance today, and in the light of the Holocaust – made possible according to some commentators by the self-destructive tendencies of Enlightenment notions of science and reason – it has come to be maintained that 'the fallen nature of modern man cannot be separated from social progress'.[1] Implicit in such claims are certain assumptions about the practical influence of ideas over long epochs and across different cultures, and while those assumptions may themselves be characteristic of much philosophy of history cast in an Enlightenment mould,[2] they may not be so congenial to modern historians who are less convinced of the unity of theory and practice than were the *philosophes* of the eighteenth century. I make no claims here with regard to the power or impotence of seminal ideas. By way of commenting on ethnic cleansing and multiculturalism with respect to eighteenth-century principles of toleration, I do, however, mean to show that any suggestion to the effect that the philosophy of the Enlightenment somehow culminated in the ideology of Joseph Goebbels or was executed with the clinical precision of Adolf Eichmann must be false.

The juxtaposition of a so-called 'Enlightenment Project' with the Holocaust and other twentieth-century crimes against humanity has been unfortunately all too common in modern and post-modern social science and philosophy since the publication of Max Horkheimer's and Theodor Adorno's *Dialektik der Aufklärung* in 1947.[3] When, in *Modernity and the Holocaust*, Zygmunt Bauman claims that 'at no point in its long and tortuous execution did the Holocaust come in conflict with the principles of rationality',[4] he too implies that the darkest episode of modern history was compatible with the Age of Reason's love of order and efficient government, which by way of German cameralist and French physiocratic and English utilitarian programmes of the scientific management of public affairs may be understood as having given rise to modern bureaucracy. In confronting those who believe that the Holocaust fulfilled rather than abandoned Enlightenment principles and thus bears testimony to the barbarism that lies at the very heart of civilization, it is not enough to protest against anachronism. It is not enough for eighteenth-century scholars to complain that the term 'Enlightenment Project' was invented by Alasdair MacIntyre[5] some thirty years after the world had first learnt of the 'Manhattan Project' and more than seventy years after the first mention of a 'Scottish Enlightenment', similarly unknown in the period to which it applies. It is also incumbent upon us to show as best we can that barbarism is not a deformed fruit of civilization but its enemy.

Allowing that the term 'Enlightenment', in so far as it encapsulates the main intellectual currents of the eighteenth century, was itself unknown then,[6] it still seems to me plain that the literary salons, academies, moral weeklies and journals of that age all lend warrant to the notion of shared principles, a campaign, an international society of the republic of letters, 'a party of humanity' as Peter Gay, following Hume, describes it.[7] What is most needed in combating the misattribution of blame for peculiarly modern forms of bigotry to the Enlightenment is an appreciation of the fundamental commitment to ideals of toleration of leading Enlightenment thinkers themselves. To my mind, Voltaire's battlecry, *écrasez l'infâme*, is scarcely less pertinent to the ethnic cleansing of Bosnia today than to the Catholic purification of France in the eighteenth century. Much the same issues of freedom of worship for religious minorities apply in both cases. No issues of alleged racial purity or miscegenation arise. If the spirit of Enlightenment had indeed triumphed in the twentieth century, we might actually have averted the Holocaust and been thereby spared the need to invent such a term to express it; if after its failure in the Second World War it could at least have been resurrected in the collective memory of both Eastern and Western Europe, our slogan 'Never again!' which recalls it might have served to extinguish the spark of ethnic cleansing in Bosnia before it was fanned into a fresh conflagration.

My chief aim here will be to explain how the anachronisms which inform contemporary criticism of a so-called 'Enlightenment Project' are fundamentally flawed on two counts, even if we grant that project, supposing that there was one at all, the specious coherence ascribed to it by its opponents. On the one hand, I shall try to show that in their hostility to religious orthodoxy the *philosophes* did not just replace dogmatic faith with dogmatic reason. On the other hand, I shall argue that however much they were committed to the uniformity of scientific truth, they characteristically attached no less importance to cultural diversity or pluralism. On both counts I mean to emphasize eighteenth-century thinkers' appreciation of human variety and difference – which their post-modernist critics in particular have charged they ignored. I shall claim that their views on religious toleration and cultural pluralism have no less to commend them today than in the eighteenth century, and that we accordingly ought to press as hard as ever for the realization of what its critics continually decry as the 'Enlightenment Project'.

It may be as difficult now as it was 200 years ago for admirers of either Rousseau or Voltaire to praise the other without whistling through clenched teeth. And yet a manifest and deep felt principle of toleration, whose abuse in practice each man suffered personally, drew these two enemies together in common defiance of all that passed in their day for revelation, superstition and priestcraft. When, in the British general election of 1997, I canvassed for the BBC broadcaster, Martin Bell, in the Tatton constituency which he won from the Conservative incumbent, Neil Hamilton, it was mainly because of his outspoken stand with regard to Bosnia, which struck me as engaged and enlightened. But I confess it was also because Mr Hamilton's predecessor, Sir Walter Bromley Davenport, had been a direct descendant of Richard Davenport, who had befriended Jean-Jacques Rousseau 235 years ago, and in whose cottage on the Staffordshire borders Rousseau had drafted a good part of his *Confessions*. Unlike Mr Bell I bear no scars of any shrapnel wounds, but I am proud of the trouser leg torn from me in Alderley Edge on polling day by what must have been one of the last hounds of the Baskervilles when I trundled up an exceedingly long driveway sporting the wrong rosette. Hardly a red badge of courage, though as I address the Enlightenment here I make no apology for sometimes having the recent history of Bosnia and Kosovo in mind as well. The refinement of Enlightenment notions of science in Western cultures may indeed have served fascist ends. But, to my mind, had belief in Enlightenment principles of toleration been sufficiently widespread, it would not have been possible for our governments to disregard first genocide and then ethnic cleansing on European soil, and we just might have come to be as dedicated to the prevention of war crimes as, belatedly, we seem determined to secure the prosecution of war criminals.

Of course a commitment to toleration, and particularly religious toleration, has always been recognized as central to the Enlightenment conceived as an intellectual movement or project. In France, the inception of that movement as a whole may be dated from 1685,[8] when the Revocation of the Edict of Nantes by Louis XIV, and subsequently his acceptance of the Bull *Unigenitus* of 1713, inaugurated a century-long quarrel between Catholic assenters and recusants, and between ultramontane monarchists, on the one hand, and Gallican clerics and parliamentarians, on the other, which was to issue in the remonstrances of the *parlements* and their expulsion by Louis XV, followed by the suppression of the Jesuits and ultimately Louis XVI's convocation of the Assembly of Notables in 1787, succeeded by the Revolution of 1789.[9] That history of the institutionalization of political and theological intolerance in eighteenth-century France coincides with the history of the French Enlightenment itself, and opposition to it united *philosophes* of all denominations – atheists, Deists and those among them who were Pietists, alike. From Montesquieu's *Lettres persanes* to Diderot's *Supplément au voyage de Bougainville*, sceptics in France railed against theological controversy and the persecution of heretics, often denouncing, like Rousseau in the *Contrat social* or Voltaire in his *Traité sur la tolérance*, the refusal of French Catholic priests to administer the sacraments to Protestants, which thereby disenfranchised them of all their civil rights.[10]

Enlightened thinkers in France did not all feel inclined to support a Gallican Church against the universalist pretensions of the papacy. On the contrary, they sometimes took the side of Jesuits against Jansenists, in supposing, from the point of view of religious toleration, that it would be better to 'lengthen the creed and shorten the decalogue'.[11] Even in commenting on *Unigenitus* they often welcomed the intrusion of Italians into French political life, hoping with Rousseau or d'Alembert that the spirit of ancient republicanism, wafting into France from southern Europe, might help to rein in the imperial powers of that gothic state. But there can be little doubt that the toleration of religious minorities in a nation governed, both politically and theologically, by the dogmas of an overwrought and supersaturated religious faith was of paramount importance to them, and if we are to identify the *philosophes* as contributors to one great 'Enlightenment Project', I can think of no other principle that might more plausibly describe the commitment they shared than that of toleration.

Religious dissenters under the reign of a Catholic king in England fared little better in the 1680s than did Protestants in France, and it is as much with reference to the same issue – either by way of Locke's *Letter Concerning Toleration*, or William and Mary's *Act of Toleration*, both dating from 1689 – that the English Enlightenment may be said to have been inaugurated as well, allowing that, in each case, toleration was to be limited so as to ensure that public office could not be held by subscribers to all faiths. In other domains, of course, it was Locke's *Essay Concerning Human Understanding* or even his *Two Treatises of Government* of the following year which could be said to serve this purpose, but the idea of toleration lies at the heart of his philosophy in virtually all the domains which engaged his attention, and it was through embracing that idea and the civic culture which gave rise to it that enlightened *philosophes* in France who described themselves as lovers of freedom emulated both Locke's achievement and England's success. At the beginning of the eighteenth century, the English Enlightenment had thus already taken a political form, whereas in France it was to remain more radical, because disenfranchised from the prevalent institutions of both the State and the Church. By virtue of already established principles of toleration, England's Enlightenment, that is, proceeded as if the requisite infrastructure for high speed travel by rail had been laid on the Dover side of the Channel first, giving rise to the claim that if France had been able to enjoy a similar bloodless revolution around the same time, the minds of Frenchmen might have been changed without it proving necessary to cut off their heads.

No major eighteenth-century thinker was more convinced of the indispensability of a spirit of religious toleration for the advance of civilization as a whole than Voltaire, who had found refuge in England after having been unjustly imprisoned in the Bastille, and was to see the achievements of English philosophy and science as in large measure due to the liberty of conscience which prevailed there.[12] Voltaire's anglomania was to prove fashionable in France, and after the 1730s it would come to lend a decidedly English flavour to much of the French Enlightenment as well. But in Scotland his virtually boundless love of perfidious Albion never really took root, least of all among those admirers of Scotland's national identity, religious traditions and indigenous culture, convinced that its true age of Enlightenment was brought to an untimely end through its affliction by the secular cosmopolitanism of a renegade David Hume. Alasdair MacIntyre's criticism of the 'Enlightenment Project' which not only failed but had to fail[13] sometimes strikes me as having been inspired by a Scottish Nationalist Party broadcast of the songs of Ossian, and I am inclined to believe that if it had not existed it would have had to be invented, if only to lend warrant to the most celebrated of all tributes to the principle of toleration produced in the Enlightenment. By this I of course mean Voltaire's treatment of the Presbyterians in his *Letters Concerning the English Nation*, where he remarks upon the peaceable assembly of the representatives of all mankind in the London Stock Exchange, each a follower of his church, but jointly, in their transactions with one another, professing the same religion, giving the name of 'Infidel' merely to those who go bankrupt. In such circumstances do Jews, Muslims and Christians trust one another and even Presbyterians are at ease with Anabaptists. Only in Scotland, where they are supreme, concludes Voltaire, do Presbyterians affect a solemn bearing, behave like pedants and preach through their nose.[14]

If Paris was indisputably the capital of the European Enlightenment throughout the eighteenth century, its prominence was due as much to its successful importation, distillation and then re-export of seminal works initially produced for smaller markets abroad as it was to the richness of the material generated by its own literary elites. With respect to ideas of religious toleration, the influence of tracts and treatises emanating from Italy and England, often given fresh impetus by Swiss or German writers who had come to Paris to launch their literary careers, may have been more striking than the works produced by French Jansenists and Jesuits, or by disciples of Bossuet or Jurieu with regard to the divine right of kings, or than jurisprudential texts emanating from the *parlements*. But with respect to the Revocation of the Edict of Nantes, the most important writings of all were those of French Protestants who either fled from France for their safety or, like Pierre Bayle, had been victims of the dissolution of Huguenot academies and other centres of learning already achieved by Louis XIV prior to 1685.

It was in Holland that Spinoza put his case for the liberty of judgment and opinion and for the civic harmony which was to be gained by the unfettered circulation of ideas.[15] It was in Holland, while in exile, that Locke drafted his own account of the need for freedom of conscience, the right of religious disagreement and the silence of the civil powers in matters of belief; and from Holland that England's new king and queen, committed to religious toleration above all else, would descend. It was by way of Huguenot publishers in Holland that many of the most notable French-language pleas for toleration in the eighteenth century were produced, sometimes coming to be impounded at their ports of arrival in France and then, as often as not, distributed surreptitiously. The ethnic cleansing of the French nation after 1685 did not take the form of the St Bartholomew's Day massacre more than 100 years earlier, nor was it pursued by way of the terrorist tactics employed in Bosnia three centuries later. The violence it provoked was directed more against individuals or families than against whole communities, and a larger proportion of its immediate victims survived. But like all campaigns of ethnic cleansing as distinct from genocide it gave rise to a diaspora, to a brain drain and an outcast culture which abroad fermented more richly than it had managed under relative tranquillity at home. As much as from any other philosophical, political or economic source, it was from the precipitation of that brain drain, and the depth of the reaction to it among intellectuals in France, that the French Enlightenment of the eighteenth century was formed. Religious intolerance, and the ethnic cleansing of a nation that issued from it, kindled the 'Enlightenment Project'.

If either Voltaire or Diderot could claim to be the godfathers of that Project, its patron saint, in each instance, was Bayle. It was from Bayle above all other thinkers that French *philosophes* learnt what was to become the central premise of their literary campaigns – that the chief obstacle to rational judgment is not ignorance but prejudice. It was especially from Bayle that they came to be persuaded that silencing opposition fails to put an end either to conviction or error and that God could be expected to find a multiplicity of faiths, like a choir of many voices, more pleasing than just one. Bayle thought God innocent of all responsibility for human suffering but not blameless for the wastefulness of an act of Creation out of which had arisen so many wretched and tormented lives, and in appreciation of his highly personal manner of putting such claims it was most particularly from their reading of Bayle's work, rather than Spinoza or Locke, that the *philosophes* of the French Enlightenment acquired and then fanned their irreverence.[16]

Seventeenth- and eighteenth-century arguments for toleration were of course developed from many Reformation and humanist sources as well, and most of the principles articulated at the dawn of the age of Enlightenment by Spinoza, Locke or Bayle had been espoused earlier by Socinians, Anabaptists and Erasmians.[17] The claim that belief is not subject to compulsion which figures in virtually all Enlightenment pleas for toleration has theological roots which long predate the Reformation itself, and both the Edict of Nantes of 1598 and its Revocation almost a century later owe their origins to features of the social and political fabric of early-modern Europe which extend well beyond matters of dogmatic faith. However, in the Enlightenment the case for toleration was advanced by its proponents in fresh idioms, with new weapons and a new vitality. It was put forward in campaigns to reform the criminal law and secure the abolition of torture. It began to figure within theories of human perfectibility, whose advocates identified the acceptance of theological dogmas, not as belief but as superstition.

In the eighteenth century, religious conviction came to be denounced as blind faith, at once barbarous and irrational. Even when they acted dutifully in accord with their own Christian scruples, Europe's leading *philosophes* could suppose, contrary not only to Hobbes and Mandeville but also to Scripture, that human nature was fundamentally good. Alternatively, they could be persuaded that it was selfish but sociable, or, when they succumbed to the Pelagian heresy, that it was made of a pliant clay which could be cast in infinitely perfectible ways. What they could not accept, because it was no longer philosophically correct to do so, was the theological doctrine of mankind's original sin, now regarded as a myth invented by clerics to regulate

the salvation of gullible souls. At the heart of their commitment to the progressive education of mankind lay a crusade against all the dark forces of
idolatry. 'Civilization', a term which first acquired its current meaning around
1750, came progressively in the eighteenth century to be identified with the
abandonment of the trappings of arcane religions, whose gospels, shrouded
in mysteries and revelations, only obscured the truth.[18] It was in reason's light
that philosophers of every denomination now sought to dispel the shadows in
which their adversaries lurked. Voltaire, Diderot, Turgot, d'Alembert and
Condorcet joined Helvétius, d'Holbach and other materialists in their perception of the whole of human history as just one great struggle between the
friends and enemies of enlightenment – between nefarious tyrants, priests
and barbarians, on the one hand, and civilized, educated, and thus liberated
men of science and letters, on the other. Through the *Encyclopédie* and the
book trade as a whole, progressive thinkers of the age of Enlightenment
sought to build an eighteenth-century Crystal Palace of the human mind,
accessible to readers of all vernacular languages, as transparent as the open
book of nature. By contrast, they held the arcane dogmas of Christian theology responsible for fanaticism and hypocrisy throughout human history –
for wars of religion, for the Inquisition, for bigotry everywhere. In promoting
their multifarious schemes of popular instruction, *philosophes* who espoused
the 'Enlightenment Project' sought to overcome mankind's enthralment to
gospels which stood in the way of each person's attainment of worldly knowledge of the good and a desire to practise it.

All these familiar themes bear repetition in a volume addressed to notions
of toleration in the age of Enlightenment only because no trace of them will
be found in any of those critiques of eighteenth-century philosophy which
portray its ideals as if they comprised the conceptual underpinnings of either
the most dreadful crimes, or alternatively the most empty desolation, of modernity. While such charges are characteristically made with respect to much
the same features of Enlightenment thought – indeed the same doctrines or
ideas – they need to be distinguished, since they concentrate upon quite different terrors of the modern world: on the one hand the totalitarian regimes
of Nazi Germany and Communist Russia and most particularly the destruction of European Jewry in the Holocaust; on the other the vacuous morality
of atomistic individualism prevalent in Western liberal societies and most
especially the United States of America.

How such features of twentieth-century civilization might be supposed to
bear the still traceable imprint of Enlightenment philosophy is a matter of
bewildering complexity which I dare not pause to contemplate here, except
perhaps to suggest that in disposing of original sin philosophers of the eighteenth century must have unwittingly committed it. But it is, to my mind,
important to keep apart these two lines of criticism of the 'Enlightenment

Project', since their authors have wholly disparate objectives, those who complain of the Enlightenment's totalitarian tendencies having scant quarrel with its individualism, which they would no doubt have found congenial, had they only been able to locate it. On the one side, I have in mind critics of the 'Enlightenment Project', such as Jacob Talmon or Lester Crocker,[19] who claim that its attempts to recast human nature have given rise to social engineering on a vast scale, as well as Horkheimer, Adorno and Bauman, who have argued that the virtual extermination of European Jewry, planned and executed in the most methodical manner, constituted a dreadful expression of the instrumental notion of scientific rationality to which Enlightenment thinkers subscribed. On the other side, I identify Charles Taylor, Michael Sandel and their disciples, who perceive Enlightenment notions of subjectivity and impartiality as purely formal, because abstracted from the communities which individuals actually inhabit, as well as certain so-called postmodernist writers, Michel Foucault and Jean-François Lyotard foremost among them, who point to the uniformitarian principles of Enlightenment science as hostile to human diversity, complexity and difference.[20]

I suppose that the first set of objections to the 'Enlightenment Project' may be crudely described as liberal and the second as communitarian, but my aim here is to address them only with respect to Enlightenment principles of toleration and to show, if I can, how such principles in each case overcome those objections. With respect to the idea of toleration, critics of the 'Enlightenment Project' are usually agreed only that no genuine expression of it can be found in the political doctrines of the major authors to whom it has been ascribed. Locke was unwilling to tolerate either Catholics or Atheists; Voltaire was apparently contemptuous of the people as a whole and displayed particular disdain for Jews; and Rousseau, when he was not forcing men to be free in Wormwood Scrubs or Broadmoor, was contriving to put citizens to death for refusing to obey the general will, or, rather, as Bonaparte imagined, the general's will. What sorts of pleas for toleration survive such intolerance?

My answer to these charges is quite simple and makes no recourse to excuses based on the prevailing doctrines or prejudices of the age of Enlightenment, since the case I make here for anachronisms prohibits just such a defence. Voltaire mistrusted Jews on two counts. On the one hand, as he remarked about a money-lender whom he suspected of complicity with France's enemies, 'a Jew, being of no country apart from that in which he makes his money, may as easily betray the king for the emperor as the emperor for the king'.[21] On the other hand, he held the Jewish religion to be more primitive, more theologically absurd, than Christianity, insofar as it was so reliant upon an unforgiving, vengeful, god. These are not such sentiments as would come to inform the policies of Goebbels or Eichmann. Voltaire sympathized with the Jewish people for the persecution it had endured and politely expressed the hope that one of his Jewish critics might also be a philosopher. His mockery of the Old Testament was inspired above all by a Deist's contempt for revealed religions in general and for miraculous truths in particular. Assimilationist Jews have often expressed the same opinions, but in the eighteenth century it was, of course, impossible for Jews to be assimilated at all, and in the twentieth century their successful assimilation afforded them precious little protection against genocide. Perhaps Voltaire should be faulted for neglecting to campaign on behalf of the political enfranchisement of Jews, along the lines he was to pursue so famously on behalf of disenfranchised Protestants. But he seldom turned his acerbic wit upon any individual Jew, and he was conspicuously much less kind to Rousseau.

With respect to the intolerance of Catholics and Atheists shown by Locke, and of individuals who betray their civil oath by Rousseau, I note only the importance which both men attached to the pledge of allegiance required to establish a social contract state, from which it followed, for Rousseau, that persons who swear falsely, and for Locke, that individuals in awe of no God at all or members of a church beholden to a foreign prince, could not be trusted to keep their word. The central issue here in each case is not impiety but sedition, with the further implication that governments cannot tolerate persons whose intolerance of others must inevitably threaten the very fabric of society. Rousseau's aversion to Catholicism was in most respects as great as Locke's, but at the bosom of his beloved Madame de Warens he converted to it more than once in his life and thereby automatically forfeited his Genevan citizenship, even before he was deprived of it by his compatriots. Locke and Rousseau were by and large in agreement that Protestantism was the most peaceful form of Christianity, above all, because it permits the rule of law and the authority of the civil power to prevail. Bearing in mind Rousseau's remark that even the liberty of the whole of humanity could not justify shedding the blood of a single man, it is quite impossible to derive *Arbeit macht frei* and all its attendant implications from his expression 'Forced to be free'.

According not only to MacIntyre, Horkheimer and Adorno, however, but also to post-modernists, feminists and deconstructivists of virtually all denominations, modernity has been both shaped and scarred by the totalitarian doctrines of the eighteenth-century *philosophes*, who are taken to have embraced all that was worst in the Christian civilization they deplored while disgorging all that was best. In subscribing to the 'Enlightenment Project', its true believers just sought earthly happiness instead of the unworldly salvation of their souls, thereby recasting a secular world within an ideological mould which merely turned Christianity inside out, in the service of absolutist principles of another sort. That is the central thesis of a book, elegantly written, light-hearted and urbane, but to my mind sinister in its influence, which first appeared in 1932 and has since been published in more editions and in more languages than any other study of eighteenth-century thought I know. The book I refer to is Carl Becker's *Heavenly City of the Eighteenth-Century Philosophers*.[22] According to Becker, the *philosophes* demolished the city of God only to rebuild it upon the terrestrial plain. The Enlightenment thus loved the thing it killed and took on its mantle in the very act of destroying it, by substituting a rationalist form of arcane dogmatism for another, based on faith and shrouded in incense.

It is, of course, not necessarily absurd to suppose that adherents to an intellectual movement only put an end to it by taking on its character themselves. It is not inconceivable that apostate *philosophes*, in seeking to ensure their own succession, recast their scientific alternative to Christianity within the same apostolic mould. What is so fundamentally wrong with most critiques of Enlightenment totalitarianism is that they betray virtually everything in particular that we have come to learn about it in order to show how the 'Enlightenment Project' had to betray itself. Leaving aside the fact that their short cut from the eighteenth century to the twentieth skips through European history rather in the way that Marx supposed would be possible for Russia if it passed directly from feudalism to communism, they construct an 'Enlightenment Project' shorn of its central thrust following the Revocation of the Edict of Nantes. If a spirit of toleration was not at the heart of that Project, then it was nothing. And if from a spirit of toleration intolerance invariably springs, then toleration has no meaning either and ethnic cleansing or genocide lurk everywhere, like a deadly vapour swelling through the air we breathe. Ernst Cassirer's *Die Philosophie der Aufklärung* was also first published in 1932, and is, in my opinion, a much finer treatment of the Enlightenment than Carl Becker's book, which expresses the noble lament of the Enlightenment in the face of the gathering storm that would soon lay Europe to waste.[23]

Cassirer's work, drafted hastily in a period of a few months in the spring and summer of that year, was written by a man soon destined to become a refugee from fascism. While in it he followed the model of d'Alembert's *Discours préliminaire* to the *Encyclopédie* in providing a bright clear mirror of the mind of the European Enlightenment itself, he attempted to show as well how German philosophy and poetry had, by way of Leibniz, Herder, Baumgarten and Goethe contributed to the apotheosis of that intellectual movement, rather than to its nationalist destruction. But dusk had already settled on his world when Cassirer took up his defence of it in this way. At the beginning of June 1932, President Hindenburg dissolved the *Reichstag*, and at the end of January 1933 Adolf Hitler was made Chancellor of Germany; a few months later the Republic itself was obliterated, and with this, Bertolt Brecht, Albert Einstein, Walter Gropius, Wassily Kandinsky, Thomas Mann, Paul Tillich, Bruno Walter and many other luminaries of twentieth-century science and culture, as well as Cassirer, went into exile.[24]

How has it been possible for contemporary social philosophers to abandon these orphans of the 'Enlightenment Project' and to nominate Goebbels and Eichmann in their stead? In the year 1932, *Die Philosophie der Aufklärung* stood in much the same relation to the Weimar Republic as had Hegel's *Phänomenologie des Geistes* with respect to the survival of the city of Jena in 1806 when it was bombarded by Napoleon. It formed the expression of a civilization besieged by the armed World Spirit of an alternative culture, in effect constituting what might be termed the last will and testament of this civilization. To my mind, the claim of Becker and his post-modernist followers that the Enlightenment loved the thing it killed is categorically false, but I believe that Cassirer's work, more than any other text produced in this benighted century scourged by waves of ethnic cleansing and genocide, bears witness to the fact that modernity has endeavoured to kill the thing it loved. If, in assessing the influence of the 'Enlightenment Project' as I have defined it here, we may not yet have reached our verdict, on balance, so far from having triumphed by virtue of embracing the thing it killed, I believe it has instead proved our God that failed.

I turn, finally, to the question of cultural diversity or pluralism in the Enlightenment, addressed here mainly with respect to what I have termed the 'communitarian' and 'post-modernist' critiques of Enlightenment philosophy. Here I have in mind a collection of charges against its allegedly atomistic notion of subjectivity, its abstract account of the self in disregarding the concrete circumstances that actually shape the human will, its attachment to universal rules legislated in the light of reason, its Eurocentric perspective upon human nature in general and its essentially cosmopolitan indifference to difference. At least some of these charges may be traced to the Hegelian critique of Kant in his *Philosophie des Rechts* and elsewhere,[25] and they underpin both his view, and subsequently that of Marx, to the effect that vacuous notions of autonomy, and of social relations constructed by acts of will and the exchange of rights, form the main contribution of eighteenth-century thinkers to the history of the human sciences. Much of twentieth-century scholarship on Adam Smith and other Scottish Enlightenment thinkers has sought to show that their writings embraced no such themes, but readings of this kind continue to colour many critical treatments of the Enlightenment Project's putative failure, as well as of the attendant moral bankruptcy of Western liberalism as a whole.

The predominant Eurocentric perspective of Enlightenment philosophy and social thought is undeniable, though to my mind scarcely more conspicuous in the eighteenth century than in any previous age. Our very notion of the passage from savagery and barbarism to civilization embraces a Eurocentric outlook on human values, no doubt to the detriment of non-European cultures and species. A native American Indian in the eighteenth century would not have been pleased to read the passage in Lord Kames's *Sketches of the History of Man* in which he explains the retarded development of the people of that continent by virtue of their sexual shortcomings – that is, their feeble organs of generation – giving insufficient rise to the matings necessary for population growth, such as had subjected the hunting peoples of the Old World to find more ample sustenance first through livestock and then agriculture, thereby ensuring the advance of European culture and society.[26] A grizzly bear in the Rocky Mountains, on the other hand, might well have taken delight from Buffon's *Histoire naturelle*, where he also identified all the weaker and smaller varieties of the animal kingdom in the New World by contrast with the Old, since it was partly out of frustration with his account of the diminutive species of America that the Lewis and Clarke expedition to the Northwest of 1804 included a naturalist charged with the task of locating larger bears and taller trees, which he duly did, to their eternal detriment.[27]

But just as a principle of toleration must not be confused with the dogmatic theology it seeks to undermine, neither should we suppose that the *philosophes* imitated the Christian faith which they decried by adopting its ecumenical ideals in a fresh idiom. The pursuit of scientific truth in the Enlightenment did not take the form of belief in the one and only true religion by another name. Of all major eighteenth-century thinkers, Montesquieu was perhaps the most tenacious supporter of the proposition that the laws of nature and the operations of the human mind must be understood in the same way. No one in the Enlightenment subscribed more plainly to physicalist explanations of social behaviour and culture, and Richard Rorty's account of mind as Nature's mirror in fact describes the central thrust of Montesquieu's philosophy perfectly.[28] And yet from that monolithic perspective on both the natural and human sciences, there springs no universalism, no cosmopolitanism, of any kind. Above all his contemporaries, Montesquieu was specially sensitive to the local variety, specificity and uniqueness of social institutions, customs and mores. His *Esprit des lois* might well have been subtitled 'A Study of Difference'. His *Lettres persanes* ought to be required reading in any course of French or comparative literature devoted to the subject of 'Otherness', as indeed should be Swift's *Gulliver's Travels* and Voltaire's *Candide*. Montesquieu, in particular, was at once the Jacques Derrida and Julia Kristeva of the eighteenth century, and his work the epitome of the philosophy of post-modernism in the Enlightenment.

The deconstruction of Christian dogmas by way of critical theory aptly describes the whole of the Enlightenment, no less than do its principles of religious toleration. In the intellectual history of Europe, the advent of that fresh approach is marked as much by the passage from Bossuet's *Histoire universelle* to Fontenelle's *Pluralité des mondes* as by the Revocation of the Edict of Nantes. No one who read the voyages assembled by the Abbé Prévost in his collection, so much enlarging that produced by Samuel Purchas in the previous century, could fail to notice how disparate were the cultures of mankind throughout the world, and how diverse their social institutions.[29] No one who read about the Egyptian or Hebrew chants in Burney's *General History of Music* or about Persian or Chinese tunes in Rousseau's *Dictionnaire de musique* could any longer be persuaded that the Western scale and its harmonies were universally appreciated.

Accounts relating real or imaginary journeys to exotic worlds, or which sang the praises of a primitive golden age, circulated as widely, and often to the same readers, as did Enlightenment treatises on the natural sciences and on the progress of civilization. Europe's spiritual and political hegemony over the rest of the world was not appreciated at all but in fact fiercely opposed in a great many anti-colonialist classic works of eighteenth-century philosophy and anthropology, from Rousseau's *Discours sur l'inégalité*, to Diderot's *Supplément au voyage de Bougainville*, to the Abbé Raynal's *Histoire des deux Indes*.[30] Even while expressing optimism with respect to the increasingly secular development of the human race as it rose from barbarism to civilization, the proponents of the Enlightenment Project characteristically displayed a profound pessimism about the imperialist nature of Western Christendom. Instead of denouncing its rationalist and universalist pretensions, its current communitarian and post-modernist critics would do better to investigate the sceptical empiricism which informed the doctrines of its leading advocates, from Bayle to La Mettrie and d'Holbach, who framed fundamentally liberal objections to the bigotry of sacred truth and the universalism of blind faith. Supposing even that the Enlightenment Project failed, or indeed had to fail, we do not correctly describe the trajectory of its conceptual demise by retracing the worst horrors of modernity to its seminal principles.

In seeking to exculpate the *philosophes* from such blame, it is not for me, in a concluding paragraph, to identify modernity's true roots. With respect to genocide I feel inclined to add a peculiarly French dimension to German antisemitism, in lamenting the confusion, by the revolutionaries of 1789, of the rights of man with the rights of the citizen in their establishment of the first genuinely modern nation-state. In so far as they linked the rights of man to the sovereignty of the nation, the legislators of the National Assembly defined those rights in such a way that only the State could enforce them and only members of the nation could enjoy them, thereby ensuring that only persons comprising nations which formed states could have rights. In the modern world, that is to say, whole peoples which comprise nations without states have found themselves comprehensively shorn of rights they might have supposed they possessed by virtue of their humanity. This legacy of the French Revolution, it seems to me, has special bearing upon the problem of genocide in the modern world, because it defines the limits of state intervention with respect to the prevention of war crimes which most governments of the twentieth century have been reluctant to transgress. The French *Déclaration des droits de l'homme* may in effect be invoked to sanction the appeasement of crimes committed abroad.[31]

That is of course another matter, but in this context I must not fail to note that the term 'appeasement' more or less accurately describes the opposite of the 'Enlightenment Project' as I have portrayed it here. Political modernity since the French Revolution, particularly in the forms most virulent in the twentieth century, has by and large escaped the influence of Enlightenment principles of toleration, and if they could comment upon it, the *philosophes* might well wonder how later generations, by abandoning such principles, permitted the resurgence of worse forms of barbarism than they ever dared contemplate. Since our faults lie in ourselves and not our stars, there is nothing in the history of human affairs, including the Holocaust, that was not avertible. Such is the burden of guilt which those who fail to act must always carry. It is also perhaps the chief lesson that we have still to learn from the *engagés volontaires* of the age of Enlightenment, the International Brigade of the eighteenth-century republic of letters whose members, unlike most of us, were convinced that they were charged with the duty to *écraser l'infâme*.

Notes

1 Max Horkheimer and Theodor Adorno, *Dialectic of Enlightenment*, trans. J. Cumming, London, 1997: Introduction, xiv.
2 The principal English-language treatments of this subject are J.B. Bury, *The Idea of Progress*, London, 1920; R. Nisbet, *History of the Idea of Progress*, London, 1980; and J. Passmore, *The Perfectibility of Man*, London, 1970
3 Published by Querido of Amsterdam in 1947, although the text, under the title *Philosophische Fragmente*, was already available since 1944, circulated as a mimeographed typescript by the Institute for Social Research.
4 *Modernity and the Holocaust*, first published in 1989, Oxford, 1996: 17.
5 A. MacIntyre, *After Virtue*, London, 1981.
6 The early history of the English expression 'the Enlightenment' has still to be written, as the *Oxford English Dictionary*, by way of illustrations drawn from late nineteenth-century idealism, only offers examples of the term without the definite article. For a history of the late eighteenth-century German debate on the meaning of *Aufklärung*, see especially E. Bahr (ed.), *Was ist Aufklärung? Thesen und Definitionen*, Stuttgart, 1974 and J. Schmidt (ed.), *What is Enlightenment? Eighteenth-Century Answers and Twentieth-Century Questions*, Berkeley, 1996.

7 P. Gay, *The Party of Humanity: Studies in the French Enlightenment*, London, 1964.

8 See, for instance, P. Hazard, *La crise de la conscience européenne (1680–1715)*, Paris, 1935.

9 See. G. Adams, *The Huguenots and French Opinion, 1685–1787: The Enlightenment Debate on Toleration*, Waterloo, Ontario, 1991; B.C. Poland, *French Protestantism and the French Revolution: A Study in Church and State; Thought and Religion, 1685–1815*, Princeton, 1957; W. Rex, *Essays on Pierre Bayle and Religious Controversy*, The Hague, 1965; and B. Stone, *The French Parlements and the Crisis of the Old Regime*, Chapel Hill, 1986.

10 With respect to the juridical status of Protestants following the Revocation of the Edict of Nantes, and particularly the denial to them of the sacrament of marriage, see especially H. Anger, *De la condition juridique des Protestants après la Révocation de l'Edit de Nantes*, Paris, 1903.

11 See K. Martin, *French Liberal Thought in the Eighteenth Century*, London, 1962: 37.

12 On Voltaire and toleration, see especially G. Gargett, *Voltaire and Protestantism, Studies on Voltaire and the Eighteenth Century*, vol. 188, Oxford, 1980.

13 A. MacIntyre, *After Virtue*: 35–75.

14 See Voltaire, *Letters Concerning the English Nation*, London, 1733: Letter VI ('On the Presbyterians'): 41–5.

15 On Spinoza and toleration, see especially J. Israel, this volume: 102–13.

16 On Bayle and toleration, see Rex, *Essays on Pierre Bayle and Religious Controversy*; R. Popkin, *The High Road to Pyrrhonism*, San Diego, 1980; H. Bost, *Pierre Bayle et la religion*, Paris, 1994; J. Kilcullen, *Sincerity and Truth: Essays on Arnauld, Bayle and Toleration*, Oxford, 1988; and M. Magdelaine *et al.* (eds), *De l'humanisme aux lumières: Bayle et le protestantisme*, Oxford, 1996.

17 See O.P. Grell and B. Scribner (eds), *Tolerance and Intolerance in the European Reformation*, Cambridge, 1996; and S.E. Ozmont, *Mysticism and Dissent: Religious Ideology and Social Protest in the Sixteenth Century*, New Haven, 1973.

18 See J. Starobinski, 'Le mot *civilisation*' in *Le remède dans le mal*, Paris, 1989.

19 See J.L. Talmon, *The Origins of Totalitarian Democracy*, London, 1955; and L. Crocker, *An Age of Crisis: Man and World in Eighteenth-Century French Thought*, Baltimore, 1959.

20 See J. Tully (ed.), *Philosophy in an Age of Pluralism: the Philosophy of Charles Taylor in Question*, Cambridge, 1994; M. Sandel, *Liberalism and the Limits of Justice*, Cambridge, 1982; W. Kymlicka, *Liberalism, Community, and Culture*, Oxford, 1989; P. Rabinow (ed.), *The Foucault Reader*, London, 1984; J.-F. Lyotard, *Le postmoderne expliqué aux enfants*, Paris, 1986; K. Racevskis, *Postmodernism and the Search for Enlightenment*, Charlottesville, 1993. I have addressed these themes in 'The Enlightenment Project and its Critics', in S.-E. Liedman (ed.), *The Postmodernist Critique of the Project of Enlightenment, Poznań Studies in the Philosophy of the Sciences and the Humanities*, 58, 1997: 13–30.

21 Voltaire to Cardinal Guillaume Dubois, 28 May, 1722, in *The Complete Works of Voltaire*, vol. 85, *Correspondence*, definitive edition by T. Besterman, Geneva, 1968.

22 Published in New Haven by the Yale University Press.

23 Published in Tübingen by J.C.B. Mohr (Paul Siebeck). In English, as *The Philo-*

sophy of the Enlightenment, it was published by the Princeton University Press in 1951.

24 See P. Gay, *Weimar Culture: The Outsider as Insider*, London, 1969.

25 On the Hegelian critique of Kant, see especially N. Rotenstreich, *Reason and its Manifestations: a Study on Hegel and Kant*, Stuttgart, 1996; and C. Taylor, *Hegel and Modern Society*, Cambridge, 1979.

26 On this subject, see my 'Apes and Races in the Scottish Enlightenment: Monboddo and Kames on the Nature of Man', in P. Jones (ed.), *Philosophy and Science in the Scottish Enlightenment*, Edinburgh, 1988.

27 Buffon's denigration of the flora and fauna of the New World in comparison with similar species of the Old is studied in minute detail by Antonello Gerbi in *La Disputa del Nuovo Mondo: Storia di una polemica, 1750–1900*, Milan, 1955.

28 See R. Rorty, *Philosophy and the Mirror of Nature*, Oxford, 1980, and Book I of Montesquieu's *Esprit des lois*.

29 A.-F. Prévost's collection of the *Histoire générale des voyages* was published in Paris in twenty volumes between 1746 and 1789. The classic treatment of Enlightenment voyages of exploration is M. Duchet's *Anthropologie et Histoire au siècle des lumières*, Paris, 1971.

30 See the introduction to my edition, with J. Hope Mason, of *Diderot: Political Writings*, Cambridge, 1992.

31 On the composition of the *Déclaration des droits de l'homme*, see especially M. Gauchet, *La Révolution des droits de l'homme*, Paris, 1989; S. Rials, *La Déclaration des droits de l'homme et du citoyen*, Paris, 1988; and Chapters 4 and 5, by K.M. Baker and J.K. Wright, in D. van Kley (ed.), *The French Idea of Freedom: The Old Regime and the Declaration of Rights of 1789*, Stanford, 1994. I have pursued the theme of this paragraph at greater length in other publications, including 'The Enlightenment and the French Revolutionary birth pangs of modernity', in J. Heilbron, L. Magnusson and B. Wittrock (eds), *The Rise of the Social Sciences and the Formation of Modernity: Conceptual Change in Context, 1750–1850, Sociology of the Sciences Yearbook 1996*, Dordrecht, 1998.

4.   Intolerance, the Virtue of Princes and Radicals

Sylvana Tomaselli

Toleration is often taken to be a virtue, both in a loose and a strict sense. It has been said to be the 'liberal virtue *par excellence*'.[1] Modernity is likewise generally considered its temporal birthplace. Whether toleration is in fact a trait which one ought to cultivate in oneself and encourage in others is a philosophically taxing question. It may appear to be more complex at the end of the twentieth century than at any other time, but one should be wary of that assumption. Reading through the body of European literature, including that produced in the seventeenth and eighteenth centuries, it is clear that toleration was the subject of considerable intellectual scrutiny, particularly by those critical of it as an idea or a policy. Amongst its advocates, who, as is well known, were primarily concerned with religious toleration, it was by no means always a simple or indeed lucid idea. Notable within Enlightenment writings on toleration is the relative paucity of arguments in its favour founded on the conception of toleration as a virtue. Even its proponents presented it mostly as a means to an end or as commanded by the exigencies of logical consistency. Often the arguments for toleration made toleration itself entirely redundant as they belittled what was to be tolerated into sheer insignificance.

Voltaire and Rousseau led their readers to endorse religious toleration, or see that a true social contract would endorse it, by dint of disputation which did not rest on the goodness of acts of toleration or the fact that tolerance is morally edifying, an enhancement of one's moral character or persona. In the works of Montesquieu as well as others, religious toleration can also be seen to have been presented less as an end, than as a path to political stability, peace and prosperity. Generally speaking, for the case obviously admits exceptions, toleration was not depicted within Enlightenment debates as a neglected, or newly discovered virtue, a good in itself; individuals were not encouraged to develop a forbearance of differences because it would make them better human beings. Toleration, or more accurately the end of intolerance, it was thought, would make for a better world, one with less pain and civil as well as intellectual disorder. These were to be real benefits certainly; in fact, it was these very tangible consequences which were stressed above all else. One may venture to say, furthermore, that Enlightenment advocacy of toleration is rarely moving; the texts concerned with the topic are an unlikely source of greater resolve to work towards its increase, except insofar as it would secure some other good; although they may present a hazard for would-be perse-cutors, they can be safely read by those clinging to intolerance, provided the latter have little care for those goods which the *philosophes* claimed to be closely tied to toleration.

While there may appear to be obvious rhetorical reasons for the want of enthusiasm for toleration as an attractive feature of human personality, they merit re-examination in the context of the history of the idea of toleration, not least to ascertain whether this aspect of the liberal intellectual edifice, one that is deemed so integral to it, is as wanting in its foundation as the contemporary secular language of rights,[2] or to be somewhat less contentious, to determine whether there is as much continuity in Western thought on toleration as might be expected. From a purely historical point of view, it is important that the sheer ubiquity of appeals for toleration in Enlightenment social and political deliberations does not hinder understanding of the true nature of these appeals. It may well be that the Enlightenment proves to be first and foremost a movement calling for good government and well-policed countries, and that pleas for toleration are to be considered, and hence judged, primarily in that context. Certainly, the web of contention around toleration is not easily unravelled, but the fact that toleration was conceived first and foremost as *religious* toleration and that its promoters often chose to further their cause by undermining religious belief in one way or another directed the entire debate away from the language of moral virtue. Focusing on the material gains to be had from a policy of toleration did likewise.

Istvan Bejczy has reminded us that, contrary to facile assumptions about modernity, tolerance was in fact a medieval concept, which elaborated in canon law a classical and early Christian notion of tolerance as a 'bearing of difficulties which strike human beings personally'.[3] As a judicial notion in canon law from the twelfth century onwards it applied to evil deeds or prac-tices which were not actively prevented because to do so would cause a greater evil. Thus prostitution was tolerated in that sense. As a quality of a legal or political system or policy, being tolerant shifted from being a charac-ter trait of an individual learning to live with some personal affliction to become a feature of a community or polity similarly learning to live with a social phenomenon or a group of people which, all things being equal, they would not abide.

In neither case was the idea of toleration compatible with the idea of indif-ference or ambivalence to, or uncertainty about, the thing, practice, person or persons being tolerated: the object of toleration had to be an ill or be wrong either morally or epistemologically. This conceptual feature of toleration survives to this day, especially in the verb form, to tolerate, although it does so along with other aspects the idea has acquired over time, several of which are analytically antithetical to it. Whether tolerance was in either case a clear-cut virtue is questionable; it may have been so only to the extent that it was part and parcel of the process of individual self-restraint and self-denial; at the social and political level it seems to have been presented mostly as a necessity, a means to prevent greater evil.

If certainty on the part of those tolerating is at the core of the notion of toleration which was developed and predominated in early Western intellectual history, then the intellectual ravages caused by the moral and epistemological scepticism of the seventeenth century can be fully assessed in the *de rigueur* quotation on the subject of toleration in German, French, Italian and English contemporary literature, that is, the opening words of Voltaire's entry 'Toleration' in his *Philosophical Dictionary* (1764–9):

What is toleration? It is the endowment of humanity. We are all steeped in weaknesses and errors; let us forgive each other our follies; that is the first law of nature.[4]

Written in much the same tone as Voltaire's article, the *Encyclopédie* entry, 'Tolérance', is also striking for its depiction of human beings as weak and erring creatures, and for its implied epistemological scepticism. One of the most prominent texts of the period on the subject, the entry came closest to addressing the issue of toleration as a worthy trait in itself. This may be due to the fact that its declared author, Jean-Edmé Romilly (1714–96), was a Calvinist pastor, not unaccustomed to preaching. Even so, it is far from morally uplifting, beginning as it does with a definition of tolerance as 'being generally the virtue of any weak being, destined to live with beings which resemble it'.[5] While it refers to toleration as a virtue, and what is more, speaks of the 'sweet and conciliating virtues' which past centuries had 'proscribed', the first part of the piece proceeds negatively by emphasizing the limits of human reason and the difficulty of establishing truth as grounds for toleration. There are momentary glimpses of toleration as a positive human attribute, but in so far as toleration is seen to be alluring, it is mostly in consequential terms, through the peace and prosperity which the end of intolerance would bring, and the misery and discord which will continue to flow from its presence.

Intellectual fallibility was unquestionably already at the heart of the writings of the *philosophes'* great forerunners on the subject of toleration, not least those of Pierre Bayle, whose *Historical and Critical Dictionary* (published in 1697, 1702 and 1704–6) was so influential in the eighteenth century. Although philosophical commentators such as John Kilcullen have sought to distance Bayle's fallibilism from outright scepticism, their case is not entirely convincing, since by their very nature these epistemological positions blend into one another.[6] Be this as it may in Bayle's or other individual cases, the first increasingly led to, or was intermingled with, the second in philosophical circles in the eighteenth century, especially in France and concerning religious belief.

To emphasize the extent to which doubt (even if only of the tongue-in-cheek variety) and utility were, by the middle of the eighteenth century, being given as motives for toleration, is not to deny that other lines of contention – derived from some of the earlier debates, most famously associated with Thomas Hobbes and John Locke, continued to be deployed. Some of these, which sought to reduce Christian faith to a small set of beliefs consisting of those in the existence of God, in Christ as the Saviour and in the New Testament as divine revelation, had made indifference, especially to varying ways of worshipping, the prime reason for toleration, at least of those religions which the sovereign deemed not to threaten the peace. A toleration which has uncertainty and indifference as its principal motivations is, however, self-evidently an entirely different mental disposition or characteristic of a social or legal system from the notion depicted earlier as being the predominant medieval conception. That conception had been firmly anchored in faith and an intellectual confidence which in this particular context at least the *philosophes* did not have or pretended not to have. Yet, between doubt and indifference, the overt preference in the Enlightenment seems to have been for doubt. Here it must be noted that indifference was a stance which was not always openly embraced by eighteenth-century campaigners and a degree of opprobrium clearly remained attached to it; thus, the author of the *Encyclopédie*'s 'Tolérance' was most eager in his concluding paragraph (one that refers readers to Bayle for a deeper analysis of the subject) to distance what he saw as his call for a charitable and humane response to those who labour under error from 'this culpable indifference, which leads us to consider all human opinions in the same light'.[7]

Other grounds for toleration besides uncertainty, indifference and utility were, of course, proffered in the period. Among them was the view of toleration as a matter of theological coherence internal to Christian doctrine, or as a matter of moral consistency, insisting, for instance, on reciprocity and its implications in the spirit of 'do unto others as you would have them do unto you', both of which were woven into the fabric of the *Encyclopédie*'s 'Tolérance', 'Intolérance' and related articles. Most, if not all, had already been voiced in Locke's *A Letter concerning Toleration* (1689). Perhaps the most distinctly Lockean argument was the one based on the nature of belief, that is, that, unlike outward behaviour, belief is not by its very nature responsive to force. This, and most other points in Locke's *Letter*, were in truth made *against* persecution, rather than *for* toleration. No scriptural evidence, Locke contended, could be found which showed persecution to have been prescribed by Jesus, nor could it possibly be shown to be compatible with those virtues he enjoined his followers to acquire, namely charity and meekness. Moreover, Locke pointed to the ineffectiveness of persecution in inculcating faith, and writers throughout the eighteenth century repeated or were inspired by his argument. They followed him also, and this brings us back to the subject of utility, when they contended that it was not toleration, but intolerance which had brought about civil disorder and the miseries and atrocities of civil wars. Thus Voltaire insisted time and again that clemency and moderation were not the cause of social and political unrest. On the contrary, as he saw it,

The hands of government are every where strengthened, while manners have grown everywhere more gentle and humane. Besides this, the general police of nations, maintained by numerous armies constantly kept up, remove all apprehension of seeing again those times of anarchy and confusion, wherein Calvinist fought against Catholic, both raw and undisciplined peasants, trained only to war from seed-time to harvest.[8]

A prince or legislator contemplating easing restrictions on religious practices would have been comforted to read that:

The Turkish empire is filled with Jacobins, Nestorians, Christians of St John, Jews, Gebers, Banyans and various others; and yet their annals make no mention of any revolt excited by the toleration of all these different religions.

Go into India, Persia or Tartary, and you will there find the same religious toleration and civil tranquility. Peter the Great countenanced every kind of religious worship throughout his extensive empire, in consequence of which commerce and agriculture flourished, nor did the body politic suffer.[9]

Such a prince or legislator might have been persuaded that 'toleration hath never been the cause of a civil war; while, on the contrary, persecution hath covered the earth with blood and carnage'.[10] Although he might equally have been led to conclude that the author, the historiographer royal, was true to form in his creative use of evidence or that, properly implemented, a regime of persecution would have the opposite results from those conjured up by the enlightened party. He might have thought, what is more, that toleration was all well and good for heathen princes and legislators to contemplate, but not for a true believer, answerable only to God and his representative on earth. Here he, or she, would have been reminded by Voltaire that he was speaking of toleration 'only in a political sense, and, with all due deference to theologists, as it regards the civil interests of society'.[11]

Turning princes away from what were said to be purely theological issues and focusing their attention on what were defined as matters of state, as if these two were self-evidently entirely distinct spheres, was a common procedure in writings on toleration, including the *Encyclopédie*'s 'Intolérance', which told princes that they were fathers to all their subjects, and had a duty to make each and every one of them happy. To be an intolerant prince was to be no more than an executioner in a priest's pocket.[12]

The necessity of separating the State from the Church, of keeping Caesar to his legitimate responsibility over civil matters and leaving God's business well alone, had clearly been central to seventeenth-century political debates and can be found even in the works of so-called absolutists, including those not readily associated with toleration, such as the Grand Dauphin's tutor, Bossuet. The various calls made for the division of civil and ecclesiastical powers were differently motivated, but they were used to provide the keystone for arguments against intolerance in the eighteenth century. Addressed to heads of states or legislators, as most political writing was, the long-term effect of arguments insistent on distancing princes from ecclesiastical and religious matters was to lessen the opportunities as well as the need to ponder over the virtuousness of toleration. The case for religious toleration thus undercut its own subject almost from the start. That religious persecution was morally evil, psychologically ineffective, not a legitimate task of magistrates, was made abundantly clear by the *philosophes*. That religious toleration did not lead to disutility was also repeatedly emphasized. This was, however, not the case for toleration as something to cultivate in oneself, in order to become a better person, a more glorious prince.

Aside from the analytical and conceptual causes already mentioned which, whether deployed together or separately, gave a particular orientation to the polemic surrounding toleration, there are a number of stylistic reasons why discussions of the idea as a virtue are thin on the ground in the eighteenth century. One of them is the frequency with which writers, and particularly Voltaire, used ridicule to promote the cause of toleration. The intolerant (be they Catholics, Muslims or Calvinists) were, more often than not, dismissed as beasts, and their views were therefore rarely assessed with even a modicum of respect; the beliefs of those to be tolerated (especially those of the Jews) were trivialized, thereby rendering not only intolerance, but even tolerance, an absurd response to them. Much of the rhetoric and style of the pleas for toleration or attacks on intolerance was dictated by events. Thus, as Marisa Linton shows in her discussion of Voltaire's involvement in the Calas affair in this volume, the innocence of the persecuted and the crime of the persecutors were magnified by demonstrating that Protestants were, if anything, as dutiful fathers and subjects as Catholics. Such circumstances pushed the debate away from expounding on the merits of being tolerant to showing all the injustices involved in any given act of persecution.

Crossing the Channel briefly, and moving to the latter part of the eighteenth century to consider a philosopher who meticulously weighed the pros and cons of toleration, not only concerning religion, but also sexuality and pecuniary dealings, when he painstakingly argued that neither pederasty, as he called it, nor usury would lessen the level of general happiness, we find Jeremy Bentham writing to George Wilson in December 1786: 'You know it is an old maxim of mine, that interest, as love and religion, and so many other pretty things, should be free.'[13]

Although Bentham's thought is obviously not to be wrenched from its intellectual and political context, his treatment of toleration was rather less prey to the vicissitudes of polemical exigencies than that of his counterparts in the French intellectual world. It is possible to show moreover, as Lea Campos Boralevi has done, that Bentham's reflections on the topic were also more immune to his own prejudices than the views of other thinkers were to their presuppositions. He was sympathetic to homosexuals, though reluctant to part with his writings on the subject for fear of being presumed one himself, but that was effectively irrelevant; for in their case, as in the case of people he did not particularly care for, that is, Jews and Catholics, or in the case of usury, the emancipation of women or the extension of the franchise to all adults, he followed the logic of his utilitarianism.[14] If everyone counted as one, then they did just that, count as one, each and every one of them in any social reckoning. The same was true of his insistence that individuals were best placed to know wherein their self-interest lay and could assess outcomes, albeit after their minds had been cleared of all 'non-sense on stilts', such as notions of natural rights and original social contracts. Bentham was true to his philosophy and followed it to its logical conclusions, be they democratic or feminist, though he was neither at the outset of his jurisprudential enterprise.

Princes and legislators could find intellectual rigour in his writings; his arguments were sound (given the initial set of premises) and there was much in them to encourage them to be tolerant, although needless to say, the arguments were entirely consequentialist in nature. In following him, they would not risk demographic plunges even when tolerating homosexuality, for he took care to show that sexual vice – and vice he did not attempt to deny it was – did not adversely affect population levels. Bentham did not shame intellectually or morally, nor did he appeal to the kind-heartedness or moral sentiments of would-be reformers and enlightened despots and legislators. He spoke only to their self-interest: being tolerant made good political sense. It could lead to glory, not by entering the annals of history as a great tolerant prince *per se*, but for having maximized the happiness of the majority and increased that very majority, which was in itself an index of national bliss, given Bentham's very eighteenth-century belief that population growth is the true measure of a people's happiness.[15]

Among the various enticements for princes to espouse a *Toleranzpolitik* was one Voltaire advanced, which tied it to the idea of modernity and played on the vanity of rulers. 'New times, new manners', he had written.[16] A prince who fancied himself in keeping with his time, never mind ahead of it, had to be tolerant. Conversely, those who persecuted or incited others to persecute, e.g. the Jesuits, Le Tellier and Doucin, who were the forces behind the Bull *Unigenitus*, laboured under a misapprehension about the period they lived in.[17] They were retrograde, although it was not entirely clear how Voltaire perceived this to be consistent with his use of ancient history to strengthen his case for toleration. Even the Biblical Jews, whose faith and customs he so ridiculed in his essay about them, not to mention the Greeks and Romans, had, he claimed, been tolerant: if we examine narrowly into Judaism, we shall be astonished to find the most unlimited Toleration amidst the horrors of the greatest barbarity'.[18] Not shying from appeals to authority in this case, he further declared that, 'Our histories, orations, sermons, our works of morality, our catechism, all teach us the sacred duty of indulgence and toleration.'[19] Thus to be modern as well as in keeping with the whole of Western history, ancient and beyond, one had to be tolerant.

Attractive though this prospect might be, more cogent lines of argument were afforded by demographic and economic considerations of the kind briefly mentioned in relation to Bentham. Voltaire gave reason of state as an argument for allowing the emigrants to return to France, just as Locke had urged his compatriots to endure Huguenots by focusing their minds very sharply on the assets they would bring to England.[20] Drawing on the experience of other nations, Holland and England and, somewhat surprisingly, despotic oriental states, Voltaire wrote:

I will venture to suppose, that some spirited and enlightened minister, some humane and provident prelate, or some prince who knows that his interest consists in the multitude of his subjects, and his glory in their happiness, may deign to cast his eyes over this crude and imperfect work; the defects of which his own abilities will supply: in which case, he will naturally say to himself, 'What risk can I run, in seeing my lands well-cultivated and inhabited by more numerous labourers, in seeing my revenues augmented, and my states rendered more flourishing?'[21]

As we have seen with Bentham later in the century, what Voltaire had to offer was a low, indeed, no risk, yet productive public policy. He had already sought to establish a close, indeed necessary, connection between toleration and a prospering nation, with a growing population, flourishing scientific and philosophical culture, and thriving commerce, when praising England in his very influential *Lettres philosophiques* (1733).

Montesquieu was to follow suit in *L'Esprit des lois* (1748), although given the complexity of his overall endeavour in that text, isolating his position on toleration in it is not entirely straightforward. He had written on the subject in his earlier works, especially in his *Dissertation sur la politique des Romains dans la religion*, which he presented to the *Académie de Bordeaux* in 1716. In what was a careful analysis of the relationship between religion, morality and the State in ancient Rome with didactic implications for modern France, Montesquieu claimed that its priestly hierarchy was subordinate to the civil authorities, that religion was established in that great city-state as an instrument of social control, but that its elite's manipulation of religion for political purposes did not entail its being devoid of faith. Enlightened Romans were theists. As the Romans, generally speaking, regarded the manner of worship as a matter of indifference, they were a tolerant people who considered all theologies, all religions 'as equally good'.[22] They were intolerant only of inherently intolerant religions.

One of the more subtle commentators on the subject of religious toleration, Montesquieu was to find a place for it in all his political and social writings, and employ arguments already mentioned above, including, as we have just seen, that of indifference to forms of worship. Like many of the *philosophes* subsequently, Montesquieu's case *for* toleration rested on an attack on intolerance. In his *Lettres persanes* (1721), he spoke of it as an epidemic illness and the eclipse of human reason.[23] In that and other works, he argued that it violated not only the eternal laws of natural justice (which he regarded as emanating as a matter of necessity from God's nature, yet would exist even in a godless universe), but sound politics as it deprived a nation of the skills and knowledge which were often specific to a particular religious community, thus echoing Locke on the subject of skilled minorities. Describing the demise of the Roman empire in the East in *Sur les causes de la grandeur des romains et de leur décadence* (1734), Montesquieu made much of Justinian's and his successors' religious intolerance, claiming that it was the inability to recognize the proper limits of ecclesiastical and secular powers which had been the greatest source of the Eastern empire's afflictions. 'This great distinction', he explained, 'which is the basis of the tranquillity of peoples, is founded not only in religion, but also in reason and nature, which dictate that entirely separate things, which can only subsist separately, never be confounded.'[24]

Partly because of the subject matter of *L'Esprit des lois* and, in particular, Montesquieu's discussion of the support which religion could and did lend morality and civil law, toleration is mostly treated in an instrumental manner in that work. Nevertheless, it is notable that the *parlementaire* had either very limited expectations of human nature becoming more tolerant, or that he thought the progress of civilization through the spread of commerce would pre-empt the issue, for it is material self-interest which is conspicuous in his assessment of the causes of diminishing persecution. As he put it in concluding a survey of the treatment of the Jews in Europe, whose woes seemed to be lessening,

It is a blessing for men that they find themselves in a situation in which, while their passions inspire in them the thought of being evil, it is nevertheless in their interest not to be so.[25]

What is more, Montesquieu went out of his way in the brief chapters he specifically devoted to toleration (as opposed to his less overt treatment of the topic in his examination of the impact of commerce and politeness in modern monarchies) to say that were a prince in a position to welcome in his state a new religion, he should refrain from doing so, although once established a new religion should be tolerated.[26] He also recommended that princes should not change religion as it was likely to result in either a revolution or a lessening of respect for authority and the laws. He enjoined them not to persecute on the grounds that history demonstrated that it led only to destruction,[27] and remonstrated against persecution through the voice of a fictitious Jew writing after an eighteen-year-old Jewish girl had been burnt at the stake in Lisbon. The harangue deployed a number of familiar arguments, including the inconsistency of persecution with the Christian doctrine and the fact that this was the most enlightened age in which persecution could only be a vestige of former barbarism.[28] In sum, while there was neither lack of interest in the subject on Montesquieu's part, nor any reluctance to tell princes what they ought to seek to be and do, we find him critical of persecutors on the grounds of intellectual or theological consistency or because they are being impolitic, but not lecturing on the virtue of being tolerant.

At the very end of the preceding century, Fénelon's *Télémaque* (1699) had provided a mirror to a prince, the Duc de Bourgogne, which contained a claim that the truly great commercial centres of the world were devoid of any specific religious or national identity. Describing Tyre in all its one-time splendour, Fénelon wrote:

That great city seems to float on the surface of the waters, and to be queen of the sea. Merchants from all parts of the world resort to it, nor are there any more renowned in the universe than its own inhabitants. When one enters that city, one at first believes that it is a city that belongs not to one people in particular, but to all nations in general, and the centre of their commerce.[29]

It is perhaps not surprising that the Stock Exchange in Voltaire's *Lettres* and the commercial harbours of antiquity seemed to have been the predominant images of tolerance, or, perhaps more accurately, civil equality and fluidity between people of different cultures. The proper method of establishing commerce on his return to Ithaca, it was explained to an enquiring Telemachus, was in the first instance to 'give a ready and kind reception to all strangers; let them', the passage continues,

find in your havens security, convenience, and entire liberty; never suffer yourself to be blinded by avarice or pride . . . Endeavour to gain the love of all strangers: even overlook some misbehaviour on their part . . . Steadily observe the rules of commerce, and see that they be simple and explicit: accustom your people to adhere to them invariably . . . But above all things beware of cramping trade in order to make it favour your views. Princes ought not to be concerned in trade, but leave the whole profits of it to their subjects, who take all the pains; by acting otherwise they will discourage them.[30]

Fénelon's prescription to his Prince throughout the tale was detachment and retirement. The least involvement, especially in matters of detail, the better. The selfless and reluctant Guardians of Plato's *Republic* come to mind when reading what was to be one of the most influential works in the eighteenth century on both sides of the Channel. This distancing and disengagement which culminated in the economic theory of *laissez-faire* is the backdrop for much of the writing on toleration. Again, this could hardly be further from the medieval concept, and indeed spirit, of toleration. The redefinition which the State underwent in the Enlightenment period, at least on the theoretical plane, lessened or sought to lessen the legitimate field of governmental activity for pragmatic reasons, such as those found in the economic works of David Hume and Adam Smith, or moral ones, as put forward in the writings of Immanuel Kant and William Godwin. In reducing the scope of government, political theorists might have made for greater levels of toleration, but this was more by default than positive action. Were an enlightened despot or legislator to make his or her way through an eighteenth-century library, he, say, Frederick the Great, or she, say, Catherine the Great, would have found themselves being told from one end of it to the other, from Fénelon, Smith, Godwin and Kant, to leave commerce, the church and consciences, moral and religious, well alone. Whereas their forebears had only recently been told by the nascent political economy, most notably in Antoine de Montchrétien's (*c.* 1575–1621) seminal *Traicté de l'oeconomie politique* (1615), to realize that their responsibilities extended to the smooth operation of the market place, they were now being told that, on the contrary, it was their duty not to interfere in it, for to do so would necessarily be prejudicial to some of their subjects. As they had an equal duty to all, and given that only God could know all future outcomes, the prince ought to retire as best and as soon as he could from the market. He was being told the same in relation to religion and morals, with the resultant consequences for the question of toleration. We need only listen again to the tone of Kant's oft-quoted remark to hear the retreat:

It is now asked whether we at present live in an *enlightened* age, the answer is: No, but we live in an age of *enlightenment*. As things are at present, we still have a long way to go before men as a whole can be in a position (or even be put into a position) of using their own understanding confidently and well in religious matters, without outside guidance . . .

A prince who does not regard it as beneath him to say that he considers it his duty, in religious matters, not to prescribe anything to his people, but to allow them complete freedom, a prince who thus even declines to accept the presumptuous title of *tolerant*, is himself enlightened.[31]

Do not aspire, the works of Enlightenment princely advisers are saying, to be charitable or tolerant; the market will be a more effective means of distributing justice; a system of rights will render the notion of toleration obsolete. As Thomas Paine put it in his point by point rebuttal of Burke: 'The French Constitution hath abolished or renounced *toleration* and *intoleration* also, and hath established UNIVERSAL RIGHT OF CONSCIENCE.'[32]

If, as Peter Nicholson defined it, 'toleration is the virtue of refraining from exercising one's power with regard to another's opinion or action although that deviates from one's own over something important, and although one morally disapproves of it',[33] a definition, one might add, which seems to have captured the imagination of contemporary philosophers and historians, then the Enlightenment was not the birthplace of toleration, nor even its cradle. Nor was it an age which ostensibly fostered the view that toleration is the virtue of endeavouring to maintain a state of mind and character such as to be able to have a degree of sympathetic understanding of the beliefs and faith of others even when one is a committed believer oneself, or morally disapproving of those beliefs and the actions which follow from them. The Enlightenment did not produce any new argument of note, not even for toleration as a means to an end. To the extent that it reproduced seventeenth-century arguments, which were in any event not always as self-evident as they were and are taken to be, e.g. that the Church is a voluntary institution or that belief is not responsive to coercion, it did so almost mindlessly, sometimes incompetently, especially in its most famous works on the topic, as these tended to be produced in the thick of political and judicial events. To the degree that it did continue to advance the cause of toleration, it did so by holding out commerce, prosperity and population growth as its rewards. Above all, by restricting the legitimate power of the State, it also narrowed its moral domain. In asking princes to abjure the title of 'tolerant', the Enlightenment furthermore helped to undermine the moral language used to think and speak about the wrongs of persecution and intolerance. Some of the most acute insights into the idea of toleration, it might be added, came from the pen of those whom we have seen dismiss the notion entirely.

Naturally, given the volume of works produced in the Enlightenment on toleration and related subjects, these comments cannot but be vast generalizations. A fairer assessment would require both a much broader and more detailed examination of texts and intellectual circles beyond those mentioned. It would have to be nuanced to incorporate educational literature, works on politeness, conduct manuals, essays on civility and so forth. As a qualification for the identification of the Enlightenment as an intellectual movement in which toleration held, if not pride of place, then a central one, it may not be entirely amiss to draw attention to the fact that there is little in the mainstream literature of the period recommending to readers that they cultivate the spirit of toleration, that they make it a virtue, although there is much to seek to lessen their fears of Jews, Catholics, Protestants and atheists, by, for instance, showing these to be good and trustworthy subjects despite their beliefs or lack of them. Anxieties concerning usury, prostitution and other practices deemed immoral were tackled likewise. Yet, it remains surprising that in a period in which the mechanisms of moral sympathy received arguably the best intellectual treatment to date, most clearly so by David Hume and Adam Smith, there should be so little on the psychology and philosophy of toleration except in the terms outlined above.

Certainly, there were many works which exhibited toleration and mental dispositions related to it on the part of their authors. Lady Mary Wortley Montagu's *Embassy Letters* (posthumous, 1763) are almost without equal in that respect. She was not only sufficiently open-minded to investigate the practice of inoculation against smallpox and to introduce it to England from the East, but had such first-hand knowledge of life behind the veil that she wrote authoritatively about the freedom it afforded women in crowded bazaars. Wonderful though her writings undeniably are, they are neither those of the 'party of humanity', nor philosophically probing into the virtues they so brilliantly display their author as having to an exceptional degree.

If little would have been lost had Enlightenment pleas for toleration been destroyed by, say, the French Revolution, it seems also the case, judging by several of the chapters in this volume, that these works were by and large irrelevant to the legal and social changes that did take place in eighteenth-century Europe. *Realpolitik*, not economic and demographic considerations, commanded the terms and limits of toleration. Moreover, one virtue which princes and legislators were exhorted to acquire and prepare themselves to exercise was, in fact, intolerance. For in all likelihood, they would have to deal in the course of their reign or term of rule with those whom no one argued should be tolerated, the intolerant. As the Comte de Mirabeau put it in *Sur Mendelssohn sur la réforme politique des Juifs*, published in London in 1787:

To deprive government of a right to punish the errors of men, it is necessary that those errors should not be criminal: now they are criminal, when they disturb the peace of society; and they trouble that society, when they inspire fanaticism; it is therefore necessary that men should not be fanatics, to be entitled to the privilege of toleration.[34]

Retiring though rulers might be told to be from economic activity and meddling with consciences, they still had to decide what threatened the peace of the realm and how best to deal with it. Thus William Godwin argued in 1798,

It is not the business of government, as will more fully appear in the sequel, to become the preceptor of its subjects. Its office is not to inspire our virtues, that would be a hopeless task; it is merely to check those excesses which threaten the general security.[35]

His fundamental principle, we recall, was that 'government is little capable of affording benefit of the first importance to mankind', and he wrote to 'induce us to lament, not the apathy and indifference, but the inauspicious activity of government'.[36] He addressed the issue of how 'governors, and the friends of public tranquility, [ought] to conduct themselves in this momentous crisis', as he called the struggle between false opinion and enquiry erupting around him, and referred to contemporary discussions of the levels of violence which could be inflicted in such circumstances. He sympathized with those faced with these difficult decisions.

The reflections of Mary Wollstonecraft, his wife, might, however, be particularly suitable for a conclusion. She was not the most tolerant of persons, not just because she ridiculed Papists, and despised the French, amongst others, for much of her short life, but also because she loathed the women of her day, and sought to change the world so as to change them entirely. Her idea of the emancipation of women was through assimilation: they should become rational, God-fearing, educated, selfless creatures. So should men. This said, she undermines one of my early contentions. She could move one to reflect on toleration as a personal quality; she could be morally edifying. In each of two of her translations, one of Christian Gotthilf Salzmann's *Moralisches Elementarbuch* (1782), the other of Maria Geertruida van de Werken de Cambon's *De Kleine Grandison* (1786), there is a passage shaming Christians for their prejudices against Jews and prescribing unquestionable moral uprightness in all their relations to them.[37] In *Mary, A Fiction* (1788), Mary reflects on how her reading of Joseph Butler's *Analogy of Religion, Natural and Revealed, to the Constitution and Course of Nature* (1736)

made her a Christian from conviction, and she learned charity, particularly with respect to sectaries; saw that apparently good and solid arguments might take their rise from different points of view; and she rejoiced to find that those she should not concur with had some reason on their side.[38]

These thoughts occur in fiction. Perhaps it is to the fictional writings of the period, its highly didactic novels in particular, not its more vocal advocates of toleration, that we need to look for the portrayal of toleration as a virtue.

There remains another translation of Wollstonecraft's, one devoid of instructive and uplifting tales for little children or fictitious characters, but one into which, like the other translations already mentioned, she poured so much of her own eloquence that the work is to some extent also hers, namely,

Jacques Necker's *Of the Importance of Religious Opinions*. Both the French and the English texts appeared in 1788. As its title leads one to expect, the book does examine the 'operation of the mind', the effect of emotions on reason, and the shaping of opinions in response to rhetoric and knowledge. In this context, a few pages are devoted to the issue of toleration. The relative brevity of the discussion is partly explained by the fact that its author(s) found that 'there is nothing more to be said on intolerance when we consider it in its excess'.[39] Everyone knew, they wrote, what to think of persecution and inhumanity and their inconsistency with Christ's teachings and injunction to forgive. The absurdity of the 'attempt to inspire faith by acts of rigour and severity, has been so often and so ably combated' that there was no further need to dwell on what had become common sense.[40] 'But', the piece went on,

as it is only by spreading knowledge and diffusing wholesome precepts that we can hope to cure enthusiasm and intolerance; we ought to be on our guard against the dangerous spirit of indifference, otherwise one evil will be removed only to introduce another equally fatal; when trying to divert men from fanaticism, we destroy the ideas which served as a foundation for religion . . .

Let us loudly acknowledge the benefits which we have received from distinguished writers, who have defended with zeal and energy the cause of toleration; it is an obligation, added to many others, which it is just to acknowledge, that we have received from genius and talents united: but permit us to observe, that several of those writers have lost part of the applause due to them, by seeking to depress religion, in order to succeed in their attempt; such a proceeding was unworthy of enlightened philosophers, who more than others ought [not] to assign limits to reason, and never despair of its influence . . . What should we think, if, amongst those who justly attack the tyranny exercised over conscience, there were some intolerant in the defence of toleration; and if we had reason to reproach them with despising, and sometimes hating those who do not concur with them; and by inconsiderate imputation or pusil-lanimity or hypocrisy, make the characters and intentions of those who do not adopt their sentiments appear suspicious?[41]

Notes

1 R.A. Leigh, *Rousseau and the Problem of Tolerance in the Eighteenth Century*, Oxford, 1979: 2.
2 See the works of John Dunn on this subject, esp. *Western Political Theory in the Face of the Future*, Cambridge, 1979.
3 I. Bejczy, '*Tolerantia*: a Medieval Concept', *Journal of the History of Ideas*, 58, no.3, July 1997: 365–84.
4 P. Gay (ed.), *The Philosophical Dictionary*, New York, 1962: 482.
5 *Encyclopédie*, XVI, 1765: 390a. The article is by M. Romilly le fils.
6 J. Kilcullen, *Sincerity and Truth: Essays on Arnauld, Bayle, and Toleration*, Oxford, 1988.
7 'Tolérance', *Encyclopédie*: 395a.

8 F.M.A. de Voltaire, *A Treatise on religious Toleration, occasioned by the Execution of the Unfortunate John Calas; unjustly condemned and broken upon the Wheel at Toulouse, for the supposed Murder of his own Son*, London, 1764: 35.

9 *Ibid.*: 42.

10 *Ibid.*: 47.

11 *Ibid.*

12 'Intolérance', *Encyclopédie*, VIII, 1765: 844a.

13 Quoted in L.C. Boralevi, *Bentham and the Oppressed*, Berlin and New York, 1984: 38.

14 See T.R. Harrison's, *Bentham*, London, 1983.

15 See S. Tomaselli, 'Moral Philosophy and Population Questions in Eighteenth-Century Europe' in M.S. Teitelbaum and J.M. Winter (eds), *Population and Resources in Western Intellectual Traditions*, Cambridge, 1989: 7–29.

16 Voltaire, *A Treatise on religious Toleration*: 36.

17 *Ibid.*: 53.

18 *Ibid.*: 165.

19 *Ibid.*: 183.

20 M. Cranston, 'John Locke and the Case for Toleration', in S. Mendus and D. Edwards (eds), *On Toleration*, Oxford, 1987: 114ff.

21 Voltaire, *A Treatise on religious Toleration*: 49.

22 *Oeuvres Complètes*, Paris, 1964: 41.

23 *Ibid.*, see esp. Lettre lxxxv.

24 *Ibid.*: ch. XXII: 483.

25 *Ibid.*: Bk XXI: ch. 20, 673.

26 *Ibid.*: Bk XXV: ch. 10, 708.

27 *Ibid.*: Bk XXV: ch. 12, 708.

28 *Ibid.*: Bk XXV: ch. 13, 709.

29 *Telemachus*, trans. and ed. Patrick Riley, Cambridge, 1994: 36.

30 *Ibid.*: 37.

31 I. Kant, *Political Writings*, H. Reiss (ed.), Cambridge, 1971: 58.

32 T. Paine, *The Rights of Man*, A. Seldon (ed.), London, 1969: 65.

33 Quoted in M. Warnock, 'The Limits of Toleration', in Mendus and Edwards (eds), *On Toleration*: 125.

34 *Ibid.*: 197.

35 W. Godwin, *Enquiry concerning Political Justice and its Influence on Modern Morals and Happiness*, I. Kramnick (ed.), Harmondsworth, 1976: 557.

36 *Ibid.*: 568.

37 J. Todd and M. Butler (eds), *The Works of Mary Wollstonecraft*, London, 1989: II, 149–50 and 330.

38 *Ibid.*: I, 29.

39 *Ibid.*: III, 154.

40 *Ibid.*: 154–5.

41 *Ibid.*: 155–6.

5. Spinoza, Locke and the Enlightenment Battle for Toleration

Jonathan I. Israel

Of the two principal traditions of toleration theory in seventeenth-century Europe, what have been termed the 'Arminian' and the 'republican', the first culminates in Locke and the second in Spinoza.[1] Both theories were products of the late seventeenth-century European intellectual ferment, both were deployed in England during the public debate about toleration in the aftermath of the Glorious Revolution,[2] and both were destined to exert a pervasive influence in intellectual debate throughout Protestant and Catholic Europe during the eighteenth century. Yet an immense philosophical and ideological gulf separates the two – one might almost say *rival* – conceptions of toleration, a gulf which becomes greater the more it is considered. For if 'we should be wary', as Dr Davidson observes in chapter 12 of this volume, 'of equating a call for religious toleration too easily with a call for unlimited freedom of belief' it was generally true of Enlightenment Europe that religious toleration in the sense expounded by Le Clerc, Van Limborch and Locke, or at least something approaching it, gained much wider acceptance than did freedom of thought and expression in Spinoza's sense and that of the radical Deists. What was deemed the acceptable face of toleration, the toleration of Locke and Le Clerc, was aptly characterized by the Venetian theologian, Daniel Concina, in 1754, in a work identifying Spinoza and Spinozism as the backbone of the Deist threat to Christianity, as in essence a *'tollerantismo* between the Christian churches'.[3] What the vast majority of eighteenth-century writers were utterly unwilling to countenance was a toleration of ideas which deviate from the core tenets of revealed religion.

Although some of the more extreme of Locke's English opponents, endeavouring to sink him by tying him to Spinoza, professed to think that Locke's toleration reached as far as Spinoza's, few contemporaries agreed with this view. Thus, the Irish Anglican William Carroll in his *A Letter to the Reverend Dr Benjamin Prat* (1707), having charged Spinoza, 'the most celebrated patron of atheism in our time', with subverting all religion and morality, and quoted several propositions from the *Ethics* verbatim, directly equates Locke's and Spinoza's 'principles of universal toleration in matters of religion' founded on their allegedly common conviction, and that of 'their few scholars', that human reason stands above 'divine revelation and faith'.[4] But in reality the two conceptions were quite different. Locke's was not a 'universal toleration' in the sense that Spinoza's was, and the gap remained crucial to the antagonism, continuing throughout the eighteenth century, between the 'moderate' and the 'radical' Enlightenment.

Locke's is at bottom a theological notion of toleration rooted in the idea that it is for each and every individual believer not just to be personally responsible for seeking the salvation of his or her soul but, as Episcopius and Van Limborch argued before him,[5] to perform openly that form of worship by which he or she seeks salvation.[6] Locke's toleration thus stresses above all freedom of worship, as an extension of freedom of conscience, putting less emphasis on freedom of thought, speech and persuasion.[7] Spinoza's toleration, by contrast, is anti-theological and republican. Freedom of thought and speech, what he calls *libertas philosophandi*, is its central concern and the saving of souls plays no part either in his theory of toleration as such or in the limits to toleration which he concedes may be necessary in a given society.

Because Locke's theory of toleration is inherently theological, and Christian in a distinctly Protestant sense, it is, on doctrinal grounds, somewhat grudging about extending toleration to certain groups and emphatic in excluding others from toleration.[8] Three limitations to toleration are especially fundamental in Locke. Firstly, because his toleration is essentially what John Dunn has called a 'privilege', and 'immunity' from the form of worship otherwise generally prescribed through crown and Parliament for the people as a whole through the State Church – the Church of England, toleration can only clearly and explicitly apply to groups who have an organized, publicly constituted, form of worship for which exemption can be claimed, be they Protestant dissenters, Catholics, Jews or Mohammedans.[9] Those who subscribe to no organized religion, be they agnostics, Deists or *indifferenti*, in confessional matters while not explicitly excluded are left in a vague limbo without any clear status or guaranteed freedom. The exemption from what generally applies which Locke's toleration allows to dissenters, Jews and so forth, is chiefly justified by Locke, as by Episcopius and Van Limborch before him, on the grounds of the priority over all other concerns of the individual's religious duties, obligations and needs. Saving one's soul has priority over everything else and the properly ordered state must acknowledge that this theological requirement overrides all other considerations. But if a particular individual's spiritual condition is such that no alternative form of worship, or exemption, can be specified, or allowed, it becomes unclear, in that case, what precisely the justification for toleration is.

A second main limitation of Locke's theory is the well-known equivocation in relation to Catholics. In broad terms, as an acknowledged confession with a defined form of worship, there ought to be no difficulty about extending toleration to Catholics and Episcopius – and at a later stage also Uyttenbogaert – do so explicitly.[10] But in Locke this is left in doubt. For the magistrate in the *Epistola* does not have to tolerate churches which claim an authority which can be said to undermine civil peace and the sovereignty of the state, as do the Catholics who claim that the Pope can dispense them from oaths of allegiance, depose rulers, and release them from keeping faith with, and oaths to, 'heretics'.[11] The tendency in Locke is clearly to deny toleration to Catholics.

A third important limitation of Locke's toleration is his explicit and absolute exclusion of atheists. Since they do not believe in a providential God and own to no recognized form of worship, and are not seeking to save their souls, by definition they are not entitled to toleration.[12] Since Locke's toleration is based on the principle that

every man has an immortal soul, capable of eternal happiness or misery; whose happiness depends upon his believing and doing those things in this life which are necessary to the obtaining of God's favour, and are prescribed by God to that end. It follows from thence, first, that the observance of these things is the highest obligation that lies upon mankind, and that our utmost care, application, and diligence ought to be exercised in the search and performance of them, because there is nothing in this world that is of any consideration in comparison with eternity.[13]

Atheists could have no part in it. Locke holds that 'those are not at all to be tolerated who deny the being of a God' not least because 'promises, covenants, and oaths, which are the bonds of human society, can have no hold upon an atheist'. In Locke's view, the 'taking away of God, though but even in thought, dissolves all'.[14]

In dramatic contrast to Locke, freedom of worship in Spinoza is not part of a system of exemptions from any overarching, dominant public Church, and, in any case, is not the chief focus of toleration but, on the contrary, very much a secondary issue. Indeed, freedom of exercise of one or another religion is not discussed at all in the *Tractatus Theologico-Politicus*, the text in which Spinoza chiefly sets out his views on the place of religion, and theological doctrines, in society and politics, including the main lines of his theory of toleration, because, as he remarked later, he saw it as outside the scope of that work.[15] However, he does discuss the matter briefly in his later work, the *Tractatus Politicus*, which was left unfinished at his death, in the context of the aristocratic republic which he says is a better, and more absolute, form of government than monarchy and more 'suitable for the preservation of freedom'.[16]

As always in Spinoza, toleration is chiefly about individual freedom and decidedly not the freedom of large ecclesiastical structures to impose themselves on society. He says in the *Tractatus Politicus* that everyone should have the freedom to express their beliefs whatever religion they may incline to, but that large congregations should be forbidden unless they belong to the state religion which in Spinoza, like Rousseau, is an idealized philosophical religion, not Christianity but what he calls a 'very simple, universal faith' in which Christ plays no role and in which *'cultum Dei ejusque obedientiam in sola justitia et charitate sive amore proximum consistere'* (worship of God and obedience to him consists solely in justice and charity, or love, towards one's neighbour).[17] 'While dissenters should be allowed to build as many churches as they wish, these churches must be small, of fixed dimensions, and situated some distance apart. On the other hand', he continues, 'it is most important that churches dedicated to the state religion should be large and magnificent and that only patricians or senators should be permitted to perform its principal rites'. He concludes by remarking that only the patricians who govern the republic should be 'ministers of churches and the guardians and interpreters of the state religion'.[18] This last stems from Spinoza's intensely republican conviction that it is ruinous in a state to have a clergy whom most people regard as an alternative, and higher, form of authority than those who rule the state. But toleration is necessary to the State also in a well-ordered monarchy where similarly, Spinoza asserts, 'laws should not be passed prohibiting religious beliefs unless they are seditious and destroy the foundations of the state'.[19]

The most striking difference between Spinoza's and Locke's theory of toleration lies precisely in the subordination of freedom of worship and conscience in the Dutch thinker's schema and the emphasis on preventing the emergence of powerful church hierarchies.[20] What above all lends unity and cohesion to the seventeenth-century republican tradition of toleration is precisely this drastic weakening of ecclesiastical authority and the merging of it as far as possible into the political sovereign. This feature is indeed very marked in the writings of Lambert van Velthuysen, Johan and Pieter de la Court, Franciscus van den Enden and Petrus Valkenier as well as Spinoza.[21] By contrast, in Locke toleration necessarily involves a measure of retreat of the State from the ecclesiastical sphere once the liberty and autonomy of a variety of ecclesiastical structures within society is acknowledged.

It is essential to Spinoza's purpose that the patricians who run the aristocratic republic should be prevented from splitting up into sects and supporting rival priesthoods and doctrines. This is not only because such dissension is bound to damage the state by inflating the influence of rival church hierarchies, and aggravating the divisions among the ruling elite, but also because the more ruling patricians become a prey for 'superstition' – Spinoza's shorthand for subservient to ecclesiastical power and theological doctrines – the more both they and their rivals will encourage churchmen to extend their leverage over the people and therefore will seek to 'deprive their subjects of the freedom to express their beliefs'.[22] In other words in Spinoza there is an inverse relationship between the measure of power ecclesiastical structures achieve within society, where these are separate from the ruling elite, and the measure of liberty which individuals enjoy to express their beliefs. The implication is the less he or she is influenced by the doctrines of an organized church the freer that individual is.

In the Spinozan republic it is not the need for every individual to seek the salvation of the soul which propels the drive to toleration, as in Locke, but rather the need to ensure liberty of individual thought, belief and expression whether one's thoughts are religious or 'philosophical' in the special sense intended by Spinoza – and indeed Blount, Van Den Enden, Lodewijk Meijer and more generally the Spinozists and English Deists.

Since an individual's thoughts which are 'philosophical' in the sense of guided by Blount's 'natural reason', and not by theological doctrines, have a higher status and are of greater benefit to society, in the view of Spinoza and his followers, than do beliefs shaped by religious doctrines, Spinoza's toleration theory implies and in places expressly asserts, the use of the law, and of political power, to weaken, or remove, the force of theological concepts from broad areas of social, cultural and economic life. Obviously, under this schema, toleration is extended when ecclesiastical leverage over education is reduced, and diminished when it is allowed to expand. One specific area where Spinoza presses for ending the primacy of theological concepts was in the taking of oaths and curtailing of perjury before the law. Locke excludes atheists from his toleration in part because 'promises, covenants and oaths which are the bonds of human society can have no hold upon an atheist'.[23] By the same token, upholding oaths in law-courts and curtailing perjury where toleration is being extended must, in Locke's scheme, lead to the introduction of Jewish, Mohammedan, dissenting, and other confessional oaths, while at the same time agnostics and *indifferenti* are placed in a highly ambiguous position. By contrast Spinoza is determined there should be no weakening of the force of law, or encouragement to perjury, resulting from extension of toleration to, and propagation by philosophy of, philosophical atheists, Deists and agnostics, and accordingly stipulates that

those whom the law compels to take an oath will be much more careful to avoid perjury if they are told to swear by the safety and freedom of their country, and by its supreme council, than if they are told to swear by God; for he who swears by God interposes a private possession of which he is the judge, i.e. his idea of God, but he who swears by the freedom and safety of his country, swears by the common good of all, of which he is not the judge.[24]

In Spinoza's main discussion of freedom of thought, in the last chapter of the *Tractatus Theologico-Politicus*, the individual's right to freedom of thought is based partly on Spinoza's conception of political power and partly on his conception of the State. Because, in Spinoza, the right of the State is equivalent to the power of the State, it is essentially because it is impossible to control men's minds that it is outside the proper sphere of the State to try to do so:

If no man, then, can give up his freedom to judge and think as he pleases, and everyone is by absolute natural right the master of his own thoughts it follows that utter failure will attend any attempt in a commonwealth to force men to speak only as prescribed by the sovereign despite their different and opposing opinions.[25]

In any case, whatever abuses of political power actually occur, the ultimate purpose of the State, Spinoza reminds his readers, 'is, in reality, freedom'. (*Finis ergo reipublicae revera libertas est.*[26]) In the forming of political power and the making of the State, each individual surrenders his right to act just as he thinks fit but not his right to reason and to judge for himself. And since it is everyone's right to think and judge for themselves it follows, according to Spinoza, that everyone has the right to speak freely and express their opinion without this in any way harming the State. From this Spinoza deduces that holding and expressing political views or views about this or that piece of legislation or policy, can only be seditious if it directly implies obstruction or contravention of decrees and laws made by the sovereign. A good commonwealth then, according to Spinoza, 'grants to every man the same freedom to philosophize as I have shown to be permitted by religious faith'.[27] Here Spinoza is referring back to the amazing passage, in chapter fourteen of the *Tractatus Theologico-Politicus*, where he sets out the seven articles of his ideal philosophical state religion and then says that it does not matter what conclusions the individual comes to about how to understand the meaning of these articles:

Nor does it matter whether God is believed to be omnipresent actually or potentially, to govern things freely or by natural necessity; to lay down laws as a ruler or to teach them as eternal truths: whether man is held to obey God from free will or by the necessity of the divine decree; or, finally whether the reward of the good and the punishment of the wicked is regarded as natural or supernatural. (*Deinde nihil etiam ad fidem si quis credat quod Deus secundum essentiam vel secundum potentiam ubique sit; quod res dirigit ex libertate, vel necessitate naturae; quod leges tanquam princeps praescribat, vel tanquam aeternas veritates doceat; quod homo ex arbitrii libertate, vel ex necessitate divini decreti Deo obediat; quodque denique praemium bonorum et poena malorum naturalis vel supranaturalis sit.*)[28]

In short, Spinoza is effectively denying that faith and religious doctrines contain any truths at all. Their only purpose is to instil good conduct, charity and obedience, and faith is to be measured only in terms of good conduct and obedience: 'in fact, as I have already said above, everyone must adapt these dogmas of faith to his own understanding, and interpret them for himself in whatever way he thinks will best enable him to embrace them unreservedly and with complete conviction . . .'[29] Truth then can only be striven for, and grasped, individually and philosophically and cannot be expressed in the form of theological doctrines. It is for this reason that freedom of thought and speech, and not freedom of conscience and worship, is the true core of toleration in Spinoza's philosophy.

To control men's beliefs and their minds might be impossible but it nevertheless constantly happens that laws are enacted, or were in Locke's and Spinoza's day, against beliefs of one sort or another. No doubt Spinoza has in mind here the various kinds of anti-heresy laws which existed in all the countries of Europe at the time and especially the 1653 anti-Socinian legislation of the States of Holland which remained the basis of theological and philosophical book censorship in the United Provinces for the rest of the seventeenth century, and beyond, and which posed a major problem for Spinoza himself with regard to publication of his own works.[30] Such laws could not be fully effective and, in Spinoza's view, they could not be enforced without great danger to the State. The reason Spinoza gives for some men seeking to enlist the law behind the suppression of certain beliefs and doctrines was so that they could, by this means, triumph over their rivals, winning the applause of the multitude and also gain office. Such laws were engineered for personal advantage but, Spinoza insists, at great cost to the public: for when the state intervenes to ban beliefs it thereby encourages and intensifies doctrinal disputes. He asserts that,

Laws of this kind, prescribing what everyone must believe, and prohibiting the saying or writing of anything that opposes this or that opinion, have often been enacted to pander, or rather to surrender, to the anger of those who cannot endure enlightened minds, men who, by the exercise of a stern authority, can easily turn the devotion of the unruly masses into a rage, inciting them against whomsoever they will.[31]

'What greater misfortune can be imagined for a state than that honourable men should be exiled as miscreants because their opinions are at variance with authority and they cannot disguise the fact?'[32] No doubt Spinoza here partly has in mind the exile of Grotius, Uyttenbogaert and Episcopius after the downfall of Oldenbarnevelt and the Synod of Dordrecht. 'Therefore', he concludes,

if honesty is to be prized rather than obsequiousness and if sovereigns are to retain full control and not to be forced to surrender to agitators, it is imperative to grant freedom of judgment and to govern men in such a way that the different and conflicting views they openly proclaim do not debar them from living together in peace.

'This system of government', he argues, 'is undoubtedly the best and its disadvantages are fewer because it is in closest accord with human nature'.[33] By placing the main stress on individual freedom of thought rather than on freedom of conscience and worship in the manner of Locke and the Arminians, Spinoza is patently clearing a much wider space for freedom of speech and expression than is provided for by other theories of toleration. For freedom of conscience, even at its greater extent, does not necessarily include unimpeded access to all arguments and points of view and especially not philosophical views which conflict with the essentials, however one defines them, of revealed religion whether Christian or non-Christian. Spinoza's insistence that the 'less freedom of judgment is conceded to men, the further their distance from the most natural state, and consequently the more oppressive the regime'[34] both directly implies freedom of access to all ideas and provides a way of measuring the degree of freedom provided by any given State.

At this point, close to the end of the *Tractatus Theologico-Politicus* Spinoza proceeds to discuss what for him was undoubtedly one of the chief elements in the entire debate about toleration – the freedom to publish views however much these may be disliked by large sections of society. No other seventeenth-century theory of toleration does in fact inherently champion freedom to publish, neither the toleration of Bayle nor that of Locke and the Arminians. It is also one of the points where Spinoza's political thought diverges most sharply from that of Hobbes with which, as has often been pointed out, it shares some common features. For Hobbes held that

it is annexed to the Soveraignty, to be Judge of what Opinions and Doctrines are averse, and what conducing to Peace; and consequently, on what occasion, how farre, and what men are to be trusted withall, in speaking to Multitudes of people; and who shall examine the Doctrines of all bookes before they be published.[35]

For Hobbes argues that the 'Actions of men proceed from their Opinions; and in the well governing of Opinions, consisteth the well governing of mens Actions, in order to their Peace and Concord.'[36] But here Spinoza is in complete contradiction with him: the individual must submit to government – or rather the law – as regards his actions but should be, and is, free in his judgment.

Spinoza's vigorous advocacy of the unrestricted right to publish is no doubt closely connected with his own difficulties in publishing his works in Holland and those of his friends and allies and not least Adriaen Koerbagh who was tried and imprisoned in the Amsterdam *Rasphuis* (where, in 1669, he died), for writing and publishing 'blasphemous' books in contravention of the anti-Socinian legislation of 1653. All attempts, Spinoza warns, to restrict expression of views, and publishing those views in books, not only restricts justified freedom, but is dangerous to the State. The conflict between the Remonstrants and the Counter-Remonstrants, he maintains, makes it clearer than the sun at noon that the real schismatics are those who condemn the writings of others and seditiously incite the quarrelsome mob against the writers, rather than the authors themselves, who usually write only for scholars and appeal to reason alone; and that, finally, the real disturbers of peace are those who in a free commonwealth, vainly seek to abolish freedom of judgment, which cannot be suppressed.[37]

In recapitulating at the end of the *Tractatus Theologico-Politicus*, Spinoza restates his axiom that the

state can pursue no safer course than to regard piety and religion as consisting solely in the exercise of charity and just dealing and that the right of the sovereign, both in religious and secular spheres, should be restricted to men's actions, with everyone being allowed to think what he will and to say what he thinks.[38]

To try to suppress or restrict the beliefs of dissenters is equivalent to the sovereign abdicating government to those who have converted the rulers to their creed, and who are regarded as its interpreters. Here, plainly revealed, is the radical secularizing tendency which underlies Spinoza's toleration theory – as it does much of the rest of his thought – and confirmation of how drastically it diverges from the toleration of Locke and the Arminians. Ultimately what Spinoza means by *libertas philosophandi* is the right to argue against, and eventually overthrow, the prevailing structures of theological and ecclesiastical authority, 'philosophy' here denoting what it implied later for the more radical sections of the Enlightenment, thought opposed to the structures of authority based on the theologies of revealed religion. It is in some degree incorrect, therefore, to maintain that Spinoza held 'extremely negative views on revolution' or denied that revolutions 'are ever effective . . . in the sense of leading to a genuine amelioration of the human condition'.[39] What Spinoza opposes is revolution rooted in agitation, violence and the passions and prejudices of the multitude. The importance he assigns to freedom to publish books which 'appeal to reason alone' is precisely that the ideas contained in such books can instigate the kind of revolution which does ameliorate the human condition.

By contrast, Locke not only put forward a limited toleration but subsequently had to defend his conception in particular against Jonas Proast's charge that his 'universal toleration of religions', by weakening respect for the established Church and widening freedom of expression, not only inevitably encourages the spread of fringe sects 'even the wildest and most absurd', the 'multiplying of sects and divisions' and even the 'promoting of scepticism in religion among us' but goes further – promoting the spread of 'even Epicurism and atheism'.[40] In reply, Locke could only question 'as to atheism and Epicurism, whether they more spread under toleration, or national religions, establish'd by moderate penal laws', challenging Proast to 'shew us the countries where fair trial hath been made of both, that we may compare them together'.[41] As part of his defence, Locke again flatly denies 'atheism (which takes away all religion) to have any right to toleration at all'.[42]

Of course Locke's position could be radicalized up to a point. But only by 'Christian' Deists, like Thomas Woolston, whose thinking retains a basically theological framework. In the late 1720s, Woolston, who was afterwards prosecuted himself for blasphemy and put in prison where he died, argues passionately for a 'liberty of thinking, writing and judging for our selves in religion', calling this a 'natural, a Christian, and a protestant right'.[43] The only way, he insists, finally to eradicate all oppression 'by an ignorant and tyrannical priesthood' is to put an end to prosecution for 'infidelity and blasphemy'. What Woolston lacked, and what he demanded, was freedom to express his views on Christ's miracles and the 'Messiahship of the Holy Jesus, to whom be glory for ever'.[44]

But there was no way Locke's toleration could be stretched to cover the needs of philosophical Deists who rejected revelation and divine providence, or pantheists such as Toland. These men, as has been noted, 'sought a freedom from any embargo upon ideas', a 'free trade in books' and a comprehensive liberty of the press.[45] But finding a cogent philosophical basis for such full liberty of thought and expression meant that one had to look elsewhere than Locke, as, for example, Mandeville does in his *Free Thoughts on Religion* (1720). Mandeville, born and raised in Holland, studied in the early 1680s at Leiden where he was taught in particular by that remarkable scholar Burchardus de Volder (1643–1709) who had known Spinoza and was widely suspected of being a crypto-Spinozist.[46] Mandeville, as has been observed, was strongly influenced by Bayle who may indeed have taught him, as a youth, in his native city of Rotterdam.[47] But Spinoza too, and no less so than Bayle, was a crucial influence on Mandeville, and not least on his conception of religion and toleration. Thus, Mandeville's insistence that Gospel is essentially something which 'teaches us obedience to superiors and charity to all men' has an unmistakably Spinozist ring to it, as does his contention that the only proper limit to toleration is the exclusion from it of such ecclesiastics who refuse to 'own the government to be the supream authority upon earth, both in church and state'.[48] Otherwise, concludes Mandeville in a style typical of the republican, philosophical Deists, since 'it is evident . . . there is no characteristick to distinguish and know a true church from a false one' that the 'greatest argument for tolleration is, that differences in opinion can do no hurt, if all clergy-men are kept in awe, and no more independent on the state than the laity'.[49]

Notes

1 On the evolution of the two traditions of Dutch and English toleration theory, see J. Israel, 'Toleration in seventeenth-century Dutch and English Thought', in S.

Groenveld and M. Wintle (eds), *Religion, Scholarship and Art in Anglo-Dutch Relations in the Seventeenth Century*, Britain and the Netherlands, XI, Zutphen, 1994: 13–30; J. Israel, 'The Intellectual Debate about Toleration in the Dutch Republic', in C. Berkvens-Stevelinck, J. Israel and G.H.M. Posthumus Meyjes (eds), *The Emergence of Tolerance in the Dutch Republic*, Leiden, 1997: 3–36; J. Israel, *The Dutch Republic. Its Greatness and Fall, 1477–1806*, Oxford, 1995: 637–45, 952–6 and 501–5.

2 On the deployment of Spinoza in Britain in 1688–9, see R.L. Colie, 'Spinoza and the early English Deists', *Journal of the History of Ideas*, XX, 1959: 30–4; R.H. Popkin, 'The Deist Challenge' in O.P. Grell, J. Israel and N. Tyacke (eds), *From Persecution to Toleration, The Glorious Revolution and Religion in England*, Oxford, 1991: 206–7.

3 D. Concina, *Della Religione Rivelata contra gli Ateisti, Deisti, Materialisti Indifferentisti, che negano la Verità de i Misteri*, 2 vols, Venice, 1754: ii and 362; see also J. Dunn, *Locke*, Oxford, 1984: 17.

4 W. Carroll, *A Letter To The Reverend Dr Benjamin Prat*, London, 1707: 16; see also W. Carroll, *Remarks upon Mr Clarke's Sermons Preached at St Paul's Against Hobbs, Spinoza, and other Atheists*, London, 1705: 3 and 9.

5 S. Episcopius, *Vrije Godesdienst*, n.p. 1627: 37–47; P.J. Barnouw, *Philippus van Limborch*, The Hague, 1963: 18 and 41–4; Israel, 'Toleration', 20–1.

6 J. Dunn, 'The Claim to Freedom of Conscience: Freedom of Speech, Freedom of Thought, Freedom of Worship?' in Grell, Israel and Tyacke, *From Persecution to Toleration*: 174–8; I. Harris, *The Mind of John Locke*, Cambridge, 1994: 185–6.

7 Dunn, 'Claim to Freedom': 174; M. Sina, *L'avvento della ragione. 'Reason' e 'above Reason' dal razionalismo teologico inglese al deismo*, Milan, 1976: 344–7.

8 See D. Wootton, 'Introduction' to *John Locke. Political Writings*, Harmondsworth, 1993: 104–5.

9 Dunn, 'Claim to Freedom': 177–9; J. Marshall, *John Locke. Resistance, Religion and Responsibility*, Cambridge, 1994: 367–9.

10 Episcopius, *Vrye Godesdienst*: 44; Israel, 'Toleration': 21.

11 Wootton, 'Introduction': 95; Harris, *Mind of John Locke*: 189; in the *Epistola*, Locke alludes to the Catholics, without naming them specifically, as suspect and liable to exclusion from toleration, Wootton, *John Locke. Political Writings*: 425–6.

12 Dunn, 'Claim to Freedom': 180–2; Harris, *Mind of John Locke*: 189.

13 Wootton, *John Locke. Political Writings*: 421.

14 *Ibid.*: 426.

15 Benedict de Spinoza, *The Political Works*, ed. A.G. Wernham, Oxford, 1958: 410–11.

16 *Ibid.*: 366–7.

17 *Ibid.*: 411; Spinoza, *Tractatus Theologico-Politicus* (Gebhardt edition 1925), trans. S. Shirley, Leiden, 1989: 224; C. Gebhardt (ed.), *Spinoza Opera*, 5 vols., Heidelberg, 1925: III, 177.

18 Spinoza, *The Political Works*: 411.

19 *Ibid.*: 333.

20 Spinoza's justification for this subordination is that the outward forms of religion, its public exercise and observance are above all the concern of the State since they affect the peace, stability and other vital interests of the State, see P.F. Moreau, 'Spinoza et le *Jus Circa Sacra*', *Studia Spinozana*, I, 1985: 336.

21 Israel, 'Intellectual Debate', 27–8; for an English example, see Matthew Tindal, *The Rights of the Christian Church Asserted*, London, 1706: 10 and 224.
22 Spinoza, *The Political Works*: 411.
23 Wootton, *John Locke. The Political Writings*: 426.
24 Spinoza, *The Political Works*: 412–13.
25 Spinoza, *Tractatus Theologico-Politicus*: 292.
26 Gebhardt, *Spinoza Opera*: III, 241.
27 Spinoza, *Tractatus Theologico-Politicus*: 295.
28 *Ibid.*: 225–6; Gebhardt, *Spinoza Opera*: III, 178.
29 Spinoza, *Tractatus Theologico-Politicus*: 225.
30 On Spinoza's problems with the Dutch censorship, see J. Israel, 'The Banning of Spinoza's Works in the Dutch Republic (1670–1678)' in W. van Bunge and W. Klever (eds), *Disguised and Overt Spinozism around 1700*, Leiden, 1996: 3–14.
31 Spinoza, *Tractatus Theologico-Politicus*: 296.
32 *Ibid.*: 297.
33 *Ibid.*
34 *Ibid.*
35 Hobbes, *Leviathan* chap. XVIII, sixth 'right' of the sovereign; E. Curley, 'Kissinger, Spinoza and Genghis Khan' in D. Garrett (ed.), *The Cambridge Companion to Spinoza*, Cambridge, 1996: 318.
36 Hobbes, *loc. cit.*
37 Spinoza, *Tractatus Theologico-Politicus*: 298.
38 *Ibid.*: 299.
39 For this assertion, see H.E. Allison, *Benedict de Spinoza: an Introduction*, revised edn New Haven, Conn., 1987: 195.
40 J. Proast, *A Third Letter Concerning Toleration in Defence of The Argument of the Letter Concerning Toleration*, Oxford, 1691: 34–5; Marshall, *John Locke*: 379.
41 J. Locke, *A Third Letter for Toleration, To the Author of the Third Letter Concerning Toleration*, London, 1692: 236.
42 *Ibid.*
43 T. Woolston, *A Fourth Discourse On The Miracles Of Our Saviour*, London, 1728: 70.
44 *Ibid.*: 71; significantly Woolston described his ideal regarding toleration as 'an universal and unbounded Toleration of Religion, without any Restrictions or Impositions on Men's Consciences, for which Design the Clergy will hate and defame me', see T. Woolston, *Mr Woolston's Defence Of His Discourses On The Miracles Of Our Saviour*, London, 1729: 20–1.
45 See J. Redwood, *Reason, Ridicule and Religion. The Age of Enlightenment in England, 1660–1750*, London, 1976: 81–3.
46 On Mandeville's Spinozism, see my forthcoming book on the *Early Radical Enlightenment*.
47 Redwood, *Reason, Ridicule and Religion*: 88 and 91; M. Wielema, *Filosofen aan de Maas*, Baarn, 1991: 61 and 69–70.
48 B. Mandeville, *Free Thoughts On Religion, The Church and National Happiness*, London, 1720: 241 and 246.
49 *Ibid.*: 234, 241.

6. Toleration and Enlightenment in the Dutch Republic

Ernestine van der Wall

The eighteenth-century Dutch toleration debate can only be understood in the specific context of the Enlightenment. The arguments for toleration in the eighteenth century were quite similar to those of earlier decades, but the religious context had changed significantly: a new intellectual force, going under the name of Enlightenment, affecting the status of Christianity, made itself felt in the Dutch Republic like elsewhere in Europe. It was this change in context which occasioned a series of bitter controversies about toleration in the United Provinces from about 1740 onwards.

The eighteenth-century Dutch toleration debate was not a matter of an intellectual elite as it had been during the early Enlightenment, when Spinoza and Philippus van Limborch, John Locke and Pierre Bayle, Gerard Noodt, Jean Barbeyrac and Jean Le Clerc, published their essential writings on tolerance in the Dutch Republic.[1] The religious and political climate in the Republic was characterized by a limited toleration which, however, was wider than in most other European nations. Such an atmosphere inspired those at home and abroad who were engaged in a campaign in favour of toleration. Native and foreign traditions advocating toleration went hand-in-hand in order to promote their ideal throughout Europe through learned treatises and, in particular, periodicals.[2]

The Dutch context in which Locke came to write his standard work on tolerance was marked by his friendship with Van Limborch who, as a true Remonstrant in the line of that great propagator of toleration, Episcopius, strongly argued for toleration.[3] Anticipating the Revocation of the Edict of Nantes, Bayle arrived in the Republic where, from Rotterdam, he launched scathing attacks on orthodox rigid notions of tolerance. He doubted whether ecclesiastical tolerance could ever be realised. Yet, like Locke and other liberal contemporaries, he hoped that at least civil (political) tolerance might be achieved: dissenters should be tolerated, on condition that no harm was done to the State. His scepticism made him wonder whether anyone could ever know the truth. So nobody, the monarch included, should enforce his religious opinions on his fellow men.[4] More than any other contemporary theorists of toleration, Locke and Bayle set the tone for the great toleration debate in the eighteenth century.

Although everything that could be said about religious tolerance – both civil and ecclesiastical – had indeed been said by the middle of the eighteenth century, this did not hinder the Dutch in making tolerance a key issue in a nationwide discussion which started in the 1740s. Apparently the practice of toleration lagged behind theoretical expositions. The participants of this discussion came from various professional and denominational backgrounds. In order to spread their ideas they made use of a variety of means: spectatorial magazines and literary journals, pamphlets and broadsheets, satirical writings, poems, book reviews and, of course, the usual academic treatises. They did not write in Latin or French – as in the early Enlightenment – but in the vernacular.

Dutch advocates of toleration joined enlightened intellectuals from England, France and Germany in proclaiming the universality of religion, repudiating dogmatic systems and strict subscription to confessions. Such Enlightenment attitudes towards religious matters went hand-in-hand with a strong plea for unlimited tolerance. Thus tolerance became a key word in the discussions. However, gradually it dawned upon these advocates of toleration that while toleration was a laudable aim, it was not enough. Toleration implied a dominant party which tolerated a non-dominant minority. Or, in the words of Thomas Paine:

Toleration is not the *opposite* of Intolerance, but is the *counterfeit* of it. Both are despotisms. The one assumes to itself the right of withholding Liberty of Conscience, and the other of granting it. The one is the pope armed with fire and faggot, and the other is the pope selling or granting indulgences. The former is church and State, and the latter is church and traffic.[5]

In the last decades of the eighteenth century a significant change occurred in the Netherlands: advocates of toleration turned into advocates of equality. They pleaded for religious and civil equality of all Dutch citizens, regardless of their denominational background. The relationship between the various confessional blocks should become a matter of what might be called 'mutual toleration'; and so the ideal of tolerance was transformed into an ideal of equality.

Such pleas for tolerance and equality met with resistance in the United Provinces. Why? The reason was simply that, particularly in the second half of the eighteenth century, the opponents of tolerance perceived these pleas as an apt expression of a novel intellectual and religious tendency: they regarded this issue in the perspective of the Enlightenment. To their mind Enlightenment stood for such detestable notions as Deism and Remonstrantism – two concepts which were often equated by orthodox Protestant divines. Enlightenment implied a different view on such importants topics as the relationship between Church and State and the natural rights of man; both issues directly affected the toleration debate. Moreover, although the debate on toleration had already started in the sixteenth century, toleration was seen as representing a key notion among enlightened ideas. More toleration implied more enlightenment; a matter which would not enthuse every Dutch divine.

This perception of a close connection between Deist, Remonstrant notions and the ideal of toleration led to heated discussions about the limits of toleration, culminating in the late 1760s in a vehement polemical debate which contemporaries labelled the 'Socratic War'. This 'war', to which I shall return later in this discussion, perfectly illustrates the religio–political nature of the toleration debate. Political and religious motives were closely intertwined as the battle between Patriots and Orangists in the 1780s abundantly showed. In general the first were fierce defenders of the toleration ideal and came to strive after equality for all religious denominations, while the latter did everything to maintain the privileges of the Dutch Reformed Church.

Eventually the enlightened toleration party would win: in 1795 all religio–political privileges were abolished in the Netherlands. In the wake of the Batavian Revolution the separation between Church and State was officially proclaimed (August 1796) in a decree which stated that 'the principles of liberty, equality and fraternity do not allow for a privileged church' and that 'all placards and resolutions of the former States General, born of the late union of Church and State, should be abolished'. The separation of Church and State implied the equality of all Protestant and Roman-Catholic citizens in the United Provinces. The Jews were granted civil rights only shortly afterwards, in September 1796.[6]

The Protestant Dutch Enlightenment is usually characterized as 'moderate' and 'Christian'.[7] Instead of anticlericalism or attacks on Christianity as such, there was a quest for a harmonious relationship between reason and revelation, theology and philosophy. However, this picture has been challenged in recent years. Both the early Dutch Enlightenment and the last stage of the Dutch Enlightenment show radical tendencies of an anti-Christian nature. First Spinoza and Spinozistic thinkers, next – in the last decades of the century – English radical dissenters such as Joseph Priestley and Thomas Paine seem to have found avid readers in the Dutch Republic.[8] Obviously such radical tendencies need to be investigated more thoroughly, which, it might be added, also holds true for religious aspects of the Dutch Enlightenment in general.[9] For the time being the main features of the Dutch Enlightenment appear to be moderation and a pro-Christian attitude. The Dutch seem to have preferred a *via media* between the extremes of unbelief and fanaticism. It is a peaceful picture, if not soporific.

Some groups in the Netherlands showed themselves to be open-minded towards the novel intellectual movement which manifested itself in contemporary Europe: the Protestant dissenters, Mennonites, Lutherans and Remonstrants strove to incorporate enlightened thinking in their religious, scientific and political views.[10] It will come as no surprise that they strongly favoured toleration and participated actively in the toleration debate. Apparently they drew on contemporary enlightened ideas about toleration, but their pleas also received a strong impetus from their own status as tolerated minorities.

To grasp the vehemence of the toleration debate in the eighteenth century we must take into account the different status of Reformed and non-Reformed citizens in the Dutch Republic. The United Provinces had proclaimed in its founding charter, the Union of Utrecht (1579), that any individual should be free to choose his religion and that nobody should be persecuted because of his religion. The measure of civil toleration could, and did, vary locally and regionally in the Republic; ecclesiastical tolerance was hard to find. From the mid-seventeenth century onwards the privileged status of the Dutch Reformed Church as the ruling church was officially confirmed in the declaration issued in 1651 by the *Grote Vergadering* at The Hague.[11] The Reformed Church maintained the 'true Christian Reformed religion', i.e., the anti-Remonstrant kind of religion which had been proclaimed by the national Synod of Dort in 1619. It was explicitly stated that other Protestant denominations – or 'sects' as they were called – were only tolerated and should remain inconspicuous, being granted a restricted freedom to worship, while it was also emphasized that the anti-Catholic placards remained in force. The Reformed Church was not a state church in the strict sense. Yet it was greatly privileged, enjoying the backing of the civic authorities. Its ministers were paid by the State, while preachers of non-Reformed denominations were paid by their own flock; a flock which, moreover, had also to contribute to the salary of the Reformed ministers. The Reformed synods were paid for by the magistrate. The Reformed preachers were allowed to wear their bands and cassocks in public, which was forbidden to other denominations.

Besides such ecclesiastical privileges Reformed citizens also enjoyed civil privileges: one ought to be a member of the Reformed Church in order to hold a job in public service. In the eighteenth century, some Protestant dissenters became members of the Dutch Reformed Church through sheer political ambition.[12] As to their political attitudes, generally speaking, Reformed citizens were adherents of the *Stadholder*, while non-Reformed citizens often moved in anti-Orangist circles. This difference in political attitude is clearly reflected in the 1780s and 1790s when Reformed Orangists and non-Reformed Patriots fought each other. So the existence of a ruling Church had far-reaching consequences in both the ecclesiastical and civil spheres. In short, the Dutch Republic was a class society, consisting of an ecclesiastical and civil Reformed elite and a non-Reformed non-elite.

The Reformed church encompassed a remarkable variety of movements, from liberal to strictly orthodox. It goes without saying that the liberal Reformed wing, which shared the growing dislike of theological controversies and pleaded for a wider toleration, often joined the non-Reformed in their struggle against Reformed privileges.

There had been a struggle indeed; a struggle which expressed itself in a continuous debate about toleration in the United Provinces from 1740 until 1795. At times the official authorities interfered and issued decrees to stop the discussions – but Dutch discussants were not to be stopped by official decrees. From the beginning of the Calvinist Reformation, civic authorities had generally been more liberal-minded than orthodox divines, which created a tension between the mild Protestantism of the first and the rigid form propagated by the latter.

The paradox that the issue of toleration is capable of evoking intolerant attitudes also presents itself when we take a look at the Dutch discussions. These revolved around such topics as full freedom of worship for non-Reformed denominations; toleration of latitudinarian (Remonstrant) sentiments within the Dutch Reformed Church; the role of natural law; the relationship between virtue and revelation; and the attitude towards non-Christian religions.

It started in 1740 with the so-called 'Stinstra-affair' occasioned by the plea for freedom of conscience addressed to the Frisian States. The Mennonite minister Johannes Stinstra had had a great hand in this plea, the so-called *Deductie*, referring to such tolerationists as Barbeyrac and Noodt, as well as to the Union of Utrecht. His plea for toleration, together with an accusation of Socinianism, led to his being suspended from the ministry for fifteen years – a suspension achieved by Reformed intervention. The victim took the opportunity to translate English literature during his imposed sabbatical.[13] In 1741, C.H. Trotz, professor of law at the University of Franeker, devoted his inaugural lecture to the freedom of religion as a universal right.[14] A quarter of a century later the de Cock affair showed that tolerance still could occasion great unrest in Friesland: several weeks after the Frisian States had banned a Dutch translation of Voltaire's *Traité sur la tolérance* which had appeared in Leeuwarden in September 1764,[15] a minister of the Reformed Church, Gerardus Theodorus de Cock, saw it as his duty to deliver a sermon in Leeuwarden on universal Christian love which implied universal tolerance. The 'tolerants' applauded the sermon, but the 'zealots' thought it spread 'an odour of heterodoxy' and required his suspension. Thanks to the intervention of the Frisian States and of *Stadholaer* Willem V this did not happen.[16]

In the 1740s toleration was also pleaded for by a prominent Lutheran dissenter, the Amsterdam lawyer Herman Noordkerk, who cried out in an address which was soon to bring him fame:

Persecution is persecution, whether it stems from Rome, Augsburg, Geneva or Dordt! . . . Orthodoxy is a kind of lottery – it is the sentiment of the ruling party. Today your orthodoxy is in power, and, if the tables will be turned, mine will be tomorrow: then today's orthodoxy will have become heresy and awaits persecution just as much![17]

Within the Reformed church professional theologians such as the Franeker professor, Herman Venema, and the Leiden professor Joan van den Honert argued for toleration. The first was one of the very few Reformed supporters of Stinstra; the latter preached mutual tolerance which, however, was not intended to include Roman Catholics.[18]

Thus the 1740s saw the beginning of the polemics about the limits of toleration. These debates set the tone for the controversies in the next decades. In the early 1750s a Reformed minister at Zwolle (Overijssel), Antoni van der Os, caused a great stir with his plea for ecclesiastical tolerance; after being suspended in 1755, he eventually went over to the Mennonite community.[19] The case of Van der Os was one of the factors which led two staunch defenders of Calvinist orthodoxy, Nicolaus Holtius and Alexander Comrie, to detect a Remonstrant conspiracy within their own church. The popularity of Remonstrantism among their co-religionists was put down to the Academy of Saumur, that French bastion of rationalism and Arminianism. It was feared that the schism of 1619 would finally be healed in favour of the Remonstrants. The widely read serial publication by Holtius and Comrie, entitled *An Investigation into a Sketch of Toleration*, consisted of a dialogue between five persons, bearing such telling names as 'Orthodoxus', 'Philalethes' and 'Adiaphorus'.[20] According to the authors, the source of all contemporary problems were those flattering concepts 'love' and 'toleration', which guided people away from the pureness of the Gospel. In their attempt to stem the novel Remonstrant tide, these Calvinists turned to early seventeenth-century Dutch religio–political history, which in 1618–19 culminated in the Calvinist victory at Dort. Their country's past provided Holtius and Comrie with a whole range of arguments. But they were not alone in this; their liberal opponents also used national history as a storehouse of weapons. The history of the Dutch Revolt and the Remonstrant quibbles enjoyed great popularity in the eighteenth century. While the orthodox greeted Prince Maurits as their hero, the others regarded Oldenbarneveld and Hugo Grotius as symbols of freedom and tolerance. Both parties had their statues, bone china services and plaques (some made by Josiah Wedgwood) commemorating their heroes.[21]

From the 1760s onwards the discussion became more vehement than ever before, which was undoubtedly due to the progress of Deism. Steps were taken to have enlightened writings banned. For example, Voltaire's *Dictionnaire portatif*, his *Philosophie de l'histoire* and *Traité sur la tolérance* were put on the list of forbidden books. Voltaire's plea for toleration did not go down well with the Utrecht professor of theology, Gisbertus Bonnet, nor with his Leiden colleague, Didericus van der Kemp, who both spoke out fiercely against ecclesiastical tolerance in 1766.[22]

The defenders of Calvinist orthodoxy were particularly shocked by the fact that the attacks on the Christian faith were no longer a matter of an intellectual coterie, but came from a broad spectrum of society as a whole. They felt uneasy about the fact that journals, pamphlets and broadsheets, which were available to any interested reader, spread enlightened ideas freely. This process of 'enlightenment of the common people', which was rightly regarded as a new phenomenon, changed the religious atmosphere significantly. The possibility that the man and woman in the street might be influenced by anti-Christian ideas of the intellectual elite, which often went hand-in-hand with pleas for tolerance, was regarded as a great danger by the upholders of the religious and political *status quo*. No wonder that these conservatives acted immediately when international anti-Christian publications were translated into the vernacular.

Understandably, the non-Reformed participants of the toleration debate were motivated by their own status as tolerated minorities. Referring to natural law as well as to the national past, they launched an attack on the civil and religious privileges of the Reformed citizens. They were often joined in this by the liberal Reformed; united they strove for mutual toleration.

A good illustration of the change in context which occurred in the 1760s is the 'Socratic War'. This nationwide debate started in 1769 and lasted until around 1780. The participants belonged to various denominations and professions, including lawyers, professors, preachers, poets, writers and architects.[23]

How did Socrates become involved in the Dutch toleration debate? He appeared on the scene in connection with the first main theme of this controversy: the salvation of virtuous pagans. This issue was suddenly to be found high up on the religious and literary agenda when a French novel, entitled *Bélisaire*, became widely known in the Dutch Republic. In 1768 a Dutch translation of this novel came from the press in Amsterdam (entitled simply *Belisarius*) and was soon reprinted twice. The author was a well-known French writer and historian, Jean François Marmontel, who had written his novel at the instigation of his good friend Voltaire. The *Bélisaire* caused much uproar among the theologians of the Sorbonne. The novel, which appeared only a few years after Voltaire's *Traité sur la tolérance*, proclaimed similar ideals to those of Voltaire, who wrote some pieces in support of Marmontel.[24]

The protagonist Belisarius, the renowned general of the Byzantine emperor Justinian, was depicted by Marmontel as a deeply virtuous man who pleaded wholeheartedly for civil and religious toleration. Like other advocates of toleration before him, the French writer referred to man's fundamental inability to know whether he is right or wrong.[25] Princes should not wield their power in order to impose their own faith upon their people. 'Alas!', Marmontel cries out, 'why is man so arrogant as to set up his own religious creed as a law to others? . . . Truth shines with its own pure genuine lustre, and the understandings of men are not enlightened by burning the faggots of persecution.'[26] A prince can serve the interests of religion by making the soundness of his faith appear from the purity of his morals.[27]

In this context, Belisarius shows himself to believe in the salvation of virtuous pagans. The heavenly court will be filled with Roman emperors: the Tituses, the Trajans and the Antoninuses, 'those delights of mankind'. 'It is in their company, and that of the virtuous of all ages and of all countries, that the poor blind Belisarius will glow with purest fire before the throne of a good and equitable God.'[28]

Why did Marmontel's ideas cause such a stir? While the issue of the salvation of virtuous pagans might have been very popular among the enlightened *philosophes*, it was certainly not invented by them – it dated from the early Church and also enjoyed popularity in pre-Enlightenment times (Zwingli). So why was there 'a *Bélisaire* affair' in France as well as in the United Provinces? Because the issue of the virtuous pagans came to be seen in the perspective of enlightened attitudes towards the Christian revelation. If virtue was sufficient to enter heaven, then obviously a particular revelation was superfluous. This view was fully in line with contemporary Deist ideas about religion. The emphasis upon virtue underlined the typical eighteenth-century shift from the dogmatic to the ethical aspects of religion.

While in Catholic France the *Bélisaire* affair was brief, in the Protestant Dutch Republic Marmontel's novel caused a long-lasting controversy, the Socratic War, a debate in which toleration was the central issue.

Marmontel's *Bélisaire* seems to have been the most popular foreign book in the Dutch Republic between 1760 and 1800.[29] Yet, unlike Voltaire's and Rousseau's works to which it was so similar, it was not forbidden by the official authorities, despite attempts by the orthodox Calvinist clergy to have it banned. One of the most prominent representatives of these Calvinists was a Rotterdam minister, Petrus Hofstede, whose critique of Marmontel's novel, entitled *The Belisarius Judged*, published in 1769, gave the initial impetus to the Socratic War. Hofstede was a learned theologian and, due to his multi-faceted interests, a prominent member of various learned societies.[30] In 1770 he was appointed professor of Church History at the Academy of Rotterdam; the same institution where Pierre Bayle had held a chair almost a century earlier – but there the similarity between them ends. Because of his extensive admiration for the House of Orange, Hofstede was a popular subject of derision in journals and cartoons in the 1780s. The mixture of staunch Reformed orthodoxy and a firm pro-*Stadholder* attitude led to a kind of 'Reformed Orangist belief', which shows indeed the close relationship between religion and politics in the final decades of the Dutch Republic. Hofstede was the embodiment *par excellence* of this religio–political complex.

In his refutation of Marmontel's *Belisarius*, Hofstede focused upon the supposed virtues of Marmontel's pagan friends. He argued that those pagans were not virtuous at all, drawing up an impressive list of pagan philosophers – from classical antiquity as well as Eastern religions – whom he barred from heaven; the lives of these so-called heroes were not marked by virtues but by vices. This was true of Socrates, Plato, Aristotle, Cicero and Seneca; of Zoroaster, of Chaldean and Chinese religious leaders and so forth. To Hofstede's mind, Marmontel could not be classified among the atheists – as some French theologians had done – but among those detestable 'pelagian naturalists'. In his final conclusion Hofstede stated that it was his sincere wish that many pagans would be saved on the Day of Judgement, but that he, Hofstede, did not know in what way God would be handling that.[31]

In his attempt to show that other religions were far from inspiring virtue but merely led to immoral behaviour, Hofstede needed to explore these religions. He compared them with his own religion, and, though he might not have been aware of it, he made his own contribution to the very thing he feared – the undermining of the uniqueness of the Christian faith. The principle of comparison of religions need not have led to a relativism of Christianity, but it somehow did. Of course in Hofstede's day it was no 'neutral' matter: Christianity remained the criterion by which to judge other religions. But the sheer fact that it could be compared with other religions brought about a change in climate, the effects of which were only to be felt later. Thus, in the second half of the eighteenth century, we see a slow but definitive development leading to a new, nineteenth-century discipline: comparative religion.

While he attacked Marmontel's notions about the salvation of virtuous pagans, Hofstede agreed with most of his ideas on civil toleration: a ruler ought not to enforce religion upon his subjects, Hofstede remarks, referring remarkably enough to such non-Calvinist authorities as the renowned spiritualist and propagator of toleration Dirk Volckertsz Coornhert and prominent

Remonstrant theologians such as Etienne de Courcelles and Gerard Brandt.[32] However, it was quite another matter to tolerate that virtuous pagans could enter heaven freely – the more so when this ideal was defended by members of tolerated minorities, as soon would be the case.

Marmontel had not mentioned Socrates in his novel, yet this hero of classical antiquity became the centre of the debate caused by the French novel. One of Hofstede's opponents took upon him the task of defending Socrates's honour. It was a Remonstrant minister of Rotterdam, Cornelis Nozeman, who tried to exempt Socrates from the accusations of ambition as well as homosexuality.[33] He did not shrink from filling many pages with his interpretations of classical witnesses on Socrates' character and behaviour, all of which showed that Socrates had led an impeccable life. For example, Socrates's love for a beautiful young man like Alcibiades was only to be understood in a platonic sense, Socrates had loved the beauty of his soul, not his body. Beautiful souls are present in beautiful bodies, thus one has to perceive Socrates' preference for beautiful young men. This argument made Hofstede wonder how the soul of Socrates had looked, in view of the philosopher's ugly body. Nozeman also pointed to the weakness of the argument founded on moral behaviour: did biblical heroes live such morally respectable lives? He accused Hofstede of playing into the hands of the Naturalists and Deists by using this argument.[34] He argued that the virtuous pagans will be rewarded by God to the extent of His mercy.

Due to this lengthy defence of Socrates the polemical debate soon came to be known as the 'Socratic War'. Perhaps it is no surprise that Socrates became the centre of this dispute. We know that the Greek philosopher was very popular in the eighteenth century; he was often compared to Jesus and depicted as a Christian 'avant la lettre'. We need only bring to mind Rousseau's *Profession de foi du vicaire Savoyard*, Voltaire's *Traité sur la tolérance*, or Priestley's treatise *Socrates and Jesus compared*.[35]

Other Remonstrants entered the battlefield, among them Abraham van der Meersch, professor at the Remonstrant Seminary (Amsterdam). He was a well-known scholar, a typical specimen of the Dutch enlightened milieu. Like Nozeman and other Remonstrants, Van der Meersch was greatly interested in English theology and literature. Among his English correspondents was William Warburton, bishop of Gloucester, who confessed to him that he had a predilection for the 'Arminian Church' since it was founded on the true principles of Christian liberty by a succession of heroes.[36]

Using the pseudonym Philalethes Aretophilus, Van der Meersch published *Vier brieven* ('Four letters', 1770) in which he, among other things, showed that the debate about Socrates's moral standing did not have any implications for the battle about Deism. This did not prevent him from clearing the Greek philosopher of the charges made by Hofstede. His Dutch translation of War-burton's *Divine Legation of Moses* (1761–71) got Van der Meersch into trouble when, in the preface to the fifth volume, he launched a sharp attack on Calvinist divines, accusing them of pride and prejudice. It was this preface which led to the famous decree by the States of Holland issued in May 1773 in an attempt to put an end to the Socratic War; in vain, as it turned out, since the dispute continued up till about 1780.

Van der Meersch was a great spokesman for toleration, in his own works as well as through editions and translations of foreign pro-toleration publica-tions. In 1774 he edited a volume in Dutch of key texts on toleration, entitled *De vrijheid van godsdienst in de burgerlyke maatschappy betoogd en verdee-digd uit het regt der nature en der volken en uit de nature van den kristelyken godsdienst* ('A defence of freedom of religion in civil society based on natural law, the law of nations and the nature of the Christian religion'). This volume included Locke's *Letters on Toleration*; Gerard Noodt's famous address *De religione ab imperio iure gentium libera* of 1706 ('Religion free from domination'); Jean Barbeyrac's annotations on toleration; Benjamin Hoadly's renowned *Sermon on the nature of the Kingdom or Church of Christ*; and, lastly, a sermon on Paul's attitude towards Christians before his conversion by Joannes Drieberge, a disciple of Philipp van Limborch and a predecessor of Van der Meersch at the Remonstrant Seminary. It was the second edition of this volume – the first having appeared in 1734 – and obviously intended by Van der Meersch to show that the pro-toleration arguments were still very relevant to his own times.[37]

By way of preface Van der Meersch added a tract of his own on the principles of freedom and of the magistrate's rights concerning religion.[38] By establishing a civil society, man has tried to guarantee his own safety. Reli-gion, which is defined as respect for divine providence, has been free from the beginnings of mankind and has remained free in a civil society. Religion is a matter of the individual's conscience; religion can never be forced upon someone, it can only be taught. Toleration has to be based upon the right of each individual to judge for himself. Furthermore, each citizen ought to pos-sess the same civil rights, regardless of his religious affiliation. In other words, not surprisingly Van der Meersch rejects the concept of a privileged religion. Since respect for providence is the criterion for toleration, atheists cannot be included among the tolerated.

Other publications by Van der Meersch, such as his Dutch translation of the well-known attack on ecclesiastical intolerance by the enlightened printer and writer from Berlin, Friedrich Nicolai, entitled *Het leven en de gevoelens van den eerwaarden heer Sebaldus Nothanker* ('The Life and Work of Sebas-tian Nothanker') (1775–6), show that the Resolution of the States of Holland of 1773 did not hinder him from continuing his battle against intolerance. As Warburton wrote to him,

The Ministers of the Calvinistical Church of Holland do not, nor are ever likely to abate their *intolerant* principles, yet in this enlightened Age (for which it is principally indebted to your Heroes) it is hoped, your Magistrates will no longer add terror to their *brutum fulmen.* Go on, Reverend Sir, in supporting the Truth.[39]

How did the orthodox Calvinists react to this Remonstrant opposition? Hofstede published an extensive defence of his critical judgement of the *Bélisaire*, as well as a Dutch translation of a treatise by the Swiss theologian Johann Jacob Zimmerman, in which it was concluded that the Christian religion was superior to the philosophy of Socrates.[40] That he was opposed by a 'sect' which was only 'tolerated' proved too much for Hofstede: how did the Remonstrants dare to attack a preacher of the ruling Church which had the backing of the national authorities? They had to sing another tune. This arrogant reaction occasioned a bitter row about the position of the Remonstrants and other dissenting confessions in the Republic. Strange as it may seem at first sight, this theme was closely connected with the issue of the salvation of virtuous pagans. Since the Remonstrants allowed morally respectable non-Christians to enter heaven so easily, they, the Remonstrants, should not be promoted from a 'connived sect' to a denomination with the right to worship freely and publicly.

Hofstede was supported by other orthodox divines, including an author who called himself an 'advocate of the national church'. The ideas which this author (was it Hofstede himself or his close friend Joan Barueth?) propagated in the two volumes of essays published under this name were typical of eighteenth-century 'Reformed Orangism'. Moreover, they are a perfect example of the way Dutch history could be used as a polemical weapon. The Reformed church had been established by William of Orange; it was this church which had been protected by him and his successors up until their own times. The sole aim of the Dutch Revolt had been to establish this Reformed Church. This exclusivist view upon the nation's past occasioned a series of often vehement reactions. Authors used such original pseudonyms as 'the advocate of the Protestant Church' or 'the advocate of the Roman-Catholic Church'. Apparently the discussants felt at home in the courtroom, since an 'attorney-general of the national church' came forward with a history of the Synod of Dort, while another gave his pamphlet the title 'A Statement of Grounds of Appeal presented to the Honorable Gentlemen RELIGION, PIETY, JUSTICE, WISDOM, TRUTH, IMPARTIALITY, FREEDOM AND CHRISTIAN LOVE on behalf of the Remonstrants, Lutherans, Mennonites, Collegiants, Moravians, Quakers and any other non-Reformed Church'.

The exclusivist view on Dutch history met with fierce criticism from liberal Reformed intellectuals. The Dutch Revolt had been a struggle for freedom and liberty, not only for the Reformed part of the population but also for other inhabitants, including Roman Catholics. Of course, the Union of Utrecht was often referred to; in view of the bicentenary of this 'constitution' in 1779 the interpretation of the Union of Utrecht became even more popular.

Among those liberal Reformed who joined the dissenters in their plea for unlimited tolerance were Professor Petrus Burman of Amsterdam and the novelist Elisabeth Wolff-Bekker. Burman was the centre of a circle of free-spirits, strongly anti-*Stadholder*-minded, which met at his country estate 'Santhorst' (near Wassenaar). At Santhorst they honoured Remonstrant heroes such as Oldenbarneveldt and Grotius. For example, Burman translated Vondel's poem on Oldenbarneveldt's walking-stick into Latin, reciting it on 13 May, 1771, the day on which Oldenbarneveldt's death was commemorated at Santhorst. This walking-stick with which the statesman had climbed up to the scaffold on 13 May, 1619 was kept as a relic at Santhorst, this 'cloister of tolerance' as they called it.[41]

No nuns were allowed to enter the cloister of tolerance – the monks would not be that tolerant – yet there was a sister of the Santhorst congregation who published *De onveranderlijke Santhorstsche geloofsbelijdenis* ('The Immutable Santhorst Confession of Faith', 1772), 'printed at the printing business of her Royal Majesty REASON'. Elisabeth Wolff-Bekker – for she was this 'sister' – had never been to Santhorst, but she was befriended by Burman and his circle. In her 'Santhorst Confession', one of her contributions to the Socratic War, she declared: 'we respect the soft laws of a friendly tolera-tion'.[42] Wolff, who was born into a strict Calvinist family and got married to a Calvinist minister, became a great advocate of toleration, using her literary talents to fight orthodox Calvinist divines. One of Wolff's main publications during the Socratic War was her *Brieven van Constantia Paulina Dortsma* ('Letters by Constantia Paulina Dortsma', 1776), a satirical attack on Hof-stede and his circle. Her opponents never forgot her part in this debate; many years later, it was said of one of her heroines that in her heaven surely 'the Sodomite Socrates was president'.[43]

The Socratic War is illustrative of the important changes in political and religious thought in the Republic in the second half of the eighteenth century. This debate shows us to what extent, and in what manner, toleration and Enlightenment came to be seen as mutually dependent concepts. The fact that Deism was seen as the expression of Enlightenment religion was of crucial importance to the eighteenth-century Dutch toleration debate. It was this per-spective which determined the nature of the debate.

As we saw, the arguments for or against a universal tolerance were often derived from the national past. However, the arguments presented by Noodt and others, based on natural law, slowly but steadily gained force. Yet the growing popularity of natural law was still not acceptable to the Reformed divines in the 1770s, as the case of Frederik Adolf van der Marck made clear: in 1773 this Groningen professor of law was forced to resign his chair because of his insistence on natural law as the basis for toleration and human rights. In this *cause célèbre* Hofstede played his anti-tolerant role convincingly; a part he would play till his death in 1803.[44]

In the 1780s the battle between Orangists and Patriots broke loose, only to end in 1795 with the Batavian Revolution. With this 'revolution' the matter of human rights became a central issue in the young Batavian Republic. Toleration appeared no longer to be sufficient: equality became the goal to be striven for. This would be achieved after the Batavian Revolution, when, in January 1795, the *Declaration of Human Rights* was issued, leading to the separation of Church and State in August 1796. This decree implied an important caesura in Dutch ecclesiastical and political history.

The separation of Church and State occasioned an optimistic atmosphere among non-Reformed such as the Remonstrants. In the autumn of 1796 they attempted to unite all Protestant Churches in the Batavian Republic, but failed miserably. Other such 'ecumenical' attempts also led to nothing.[45] In the late 1790s the spiritual climate in the Netherlands was permeated with a radical anti-religious feeling: the *Staatsregeling* of 1798, the first constitution of the young nation, hardly paid any attention to religious matters. Yet it was denied that the Dutch people, given their national character, would ever turn into atheists as the French had done.[46] Soon this radical wave was over. In the first decade of the nineteenth century the Restoration set in and it seemed as if there was a return to the good old days of the ancien régime.

In 1823 the young Romantic poet and scholar, Isaac Da Costa, launched a ferocious attack on the Enlightenment in a booklet entitled *Bezwaren tegen den geest der eeuw* ('Objections to the Spirit of the Age'). According to Da Costa, one of the most horrible results of the Enlightenment was its proclamation of toleration, 'that magic word'. In his romantic view it was only a return to the Calvinist dogmas and values of the seventeenth century which could save the so-called enlightened Dutch. Da Costa praised the national Synod of Dordrecht of 1618–19 (which had been commemorated in 1819) in particular. His admiration for orthodox Calvinism is all the more striking if we bring to mind that he was a recent convert to Christianity. Be this as it may, his attack on toleration and his plea for a return to the Golden Age of the Dutch Republic brought Da Costa overnight fame.[47] We might interpret Da Costa's offensive as an apt expression of Romanticism – which it certainly was – but in his arguments we encounter a striking similarity with arguments put forward by orthodox Calvinists, who waged war upon the Enlightenment in the eighteenth century. It shows the continuity between the anti-tolerant parties of the eighteenth and nineteenth centuries. They would become active time and again over the course of the nineteenth century, fighting against the offspring of the Enlightenment, showing that ecclesiastical intolerance could rear its head whenever the inner confessional coherence of the Reformed church seemed in danger. However, the pro-toleration party which had fought so bitterly for its ideal had won by 1795: equality had been obtained. Their victory would prove to be of lasting value in the Netherlands.

Notes

1 For Spinoza, see J. Israel, 'Spinoza, Locke and the Enlightenment Battle for Toleration', this volume: 102–13.

2 For the debate on toleration in the French periodical press see J.N.J. Schillings, *Het tolerantiedebat in de franstalige geleerdentijdschriften uitgegeven in de Republiek der Verenigde provinciën in de periode 1684–1753*, Amsterdam and Maarssen, 1997. See also A. Rotondò, *Europe et Pays-Bas, Evolution, réélaboration et diffusion de la tolérance aux XVIIe et XVIIIe siècles. Lignes d'un programme de recherches*, Firenze, 1992; J.I. Israel, 'The Intellectual Debate about Toleration in the Dutch Republic', in C. Berkvens-Stevelinck, J.I. Israel and G.H.M. Posthumus Meyjes (eds), *The Emergence of Tolerance in the Dutch Republic*, Leiden, 1997: 3–36; H. Bots and R. van de Schoor, 'La tolérance à travers les dictionnaires dans les décennies autour de 1700', in Berkvens-Stevelinck, Israel and Posthumus Meyjes, *The Emergence of Tolerance*: 141–53.

3 P.J. Barnouw, *Philippus van Limborch*, The Hague, 1963: 33, 34 and 39–48; J.I. Israel, *The Dutch Republic. Its Rise, Greatness and Fall, 1477–1806*, Oxford, 1995: 674–6; Israel, 'Spinoza, Locke and the Enlightenment Battle', this volume: 102–13. On the early seventeenth-century toleration debate see J.I. Israel, 'Toleration in Seventeenth-Century Dutch and English Thought' in S. Groenveld and M. Wintle (eds), *The Exchange of Ideas. Religion, Scholarship and Art in Anglo-Dutch Relations in the 17th Century. Britain and the Netherlands*, XI, Zutphen, 1994: 13–30.

4 E. Labrousse, *Pierre Bayle*, II, The Hague, 1963: 540–1. E. Labrousse, 'Note sur la théorie de la tolérance chez Pierre Bayle', *Studies in Eighteenth-Century Culture*, IV, 1975: 205–8; C. Berkvens-Stevelinck, 'La tolérance et l'héritage de P. Bayle en Hollande dans la première moitié du XVIIIe siècle', *Voltaire–Rousseau et la tolérance. Actes du Colloque Franco-Néerlandais des 16 et 17 Novembre 1978 à la Maison Descartes d'Amsterdam*, Amsterdam, 1987: 11–28.

5 T. Paine, *Thomas Paine Reader*, ed. M. Foot and I. Kramnick, Harmondsworth, 1987: 231–2.

6 See J. Michman, *The History of Dutch Jewry during the Emancipation Period 1787–1815. Gothic Turrets on a Corinthian Building*, Amsterdam, 1995; H. Berg (ed.), *De Gelykstaat der Joden. Inburgering van een minderheid*, Amsterdam, 1996.

7 See, for example, W.W. Mijnhardt, 'De Nederlandse Verlichting', in F. Grijzen-

hout, W.W. Mijnhardt and N.C.F. van Sas (eds), *Voor vaderland en vrijheid. De revolutie van de patriotten*, Amsterdam, 1987: 53–80; W.W. Mijnhardt, 'The Dutch Enlightenment: Humanism, Nationalism, and Decline', in M.C. Jacob and W.W. Mijnhardt (eds), *The Dutch Republic in the Eighteenth Century. Decline, Enlightenment and Revolution*, Ithaca and London, 1992: 197–223; E.G.E. van der Wall, *Verlicht christendom of verfijnd heidendom? Jacob van Nuys Klinkenberg (1744–1817) en de Verlichting*, Leiden, 1994; Israel, *The Dutch Republic*: 1038–66.

8 See, for example, M.C. Jacob, *The Radical Enlightenment: Pantheists, Freemasons and Republicans*, London, 1981; M.C. Jacob, 'Radicalism in the Dutch Enlightenment', in Mijnhardt and Jacob, *The Dutch Republic*: 224–40; M.C. Jacob, *Living the Enlightenment. Freemasonry and Politics in Eighteenth-Century Europe*, New York and Oxford, 1991; S. Berti, 'Scepticism and the *Traité des trois imposteurs*', in R.H. Popkin and A. Vanderjagt (eds), *Scepticism and Irreligion in the Seventeenth and Eighteenth Centuries*, Leiden, 1993: 216–29; A.J. Hanou, *Sluiers van Isis. Johannes Kinker als voorvechter van de Verlichting in de vrijmetselarij en andere Nederlandse genootschappen, 1790–1845*, 2 vols, Deventer, 1988. A dissertation is being prepared on the reception of Price, Priestley and Paine in the Dutch Republic by Paul van Gestel MA, Leiden University, Department of Ecclesiastical History.

9 A general account of eighteenth-century Dutch ecclesiastical history is still lacking; cf. W.W. Mijnhardt, 'De geschiedschrijving over de ideeëngeschiedenis van de 17e- en 18e-eeuwse Republiek', in W.W. Mijnhardt (ed.), *Kantelend geschiedbeeld. Nederlandse historiografie sinds 1945*, Utrecht and Antwerp, 1983: 162–205.

10 For their attitude towards the Enlightenment see J.W. Buisman, *Tussen vroomheid en Verlichting. Een cultuurhistorisch en -sociologisch onderzoek naar enkele aspecten van de Verlichting in Nederland (1755–1810)*, 2 vols, Zwolle, 1992.

11 See Israel, *The Dutch Republic*: 361–98, 499–505, 637–76 and 1019–66; W. Frijhoff, 'Dimensions de la coexistence confessionelle', in Berkvens-Stevelinck, Israel and Posthumus Meyjes, The Emergence of Tolerance: 213–37.

12 In the course of the eighteenth century the Dutch Reformed Church grew steadily: around 1800 more than half of the population claimed to be Reformed. The numbers of Lutherans and Mennonites also grew, as did those of Roman Catholics and Jews. Only the Remonstrant Brotherhood declined rapidly. But paradoxically enough, while their numbers decreased, 'Remonstrantism' as a mode of thought would become increasingly popular, cf. Israel, *The Dutch Republic*: 1019–29.

13 C. Sepp, *Johannes Stinstra en zijn tijd*, 2 vols, Amsterdam, 1865; J. van Eijnatten, *Mutua Christianorum Tolerantia. Irenicism and Toleration in the Netherlands: The Stinstra Affair, 1740–1745, Studi e Testi per la storia della tolleranza in Europa nei secoli XVI–XVIII*, II, Florence, 1998.

14 C.H. Trotz, *Oratio de libertate sentiendi dicendique consultis propria*: 1741. In 1743 a Dutch translation was published which was received well in Remonstrant circles, see Sepp, *Johannes Stinstra*, II: 105–8.

15 A second edition of the Dutch translation appeared only a month later, in October 1764.

16 On this affair and the role of De Cock's patron, Baron Schwartzenberg, see J. van Sluis, 'Verlicht en verdraagzaam? De kerkelijke sluipwegen van grietman G.F.

130 *Ernestine van der Wall*

Thoe Schwartzenberg en Hohenlansberg', in S. Zijlstra, G.N.M. Vis and D.J.M. Zeinstra (eds), *Vroomheid tussen Vlie en Lauwers. Aspecten van de Friese kerkgeschiedenis*, Delft, 1996: 149–70. Van Sluis suggests that Schwartzenberg is the translator of the *Traité sur la tolérance*.

17 Quoted in H.H. Zwager, *Nederland en de Verlichting*, Haarlem, 1972, 2nd edn 1980: 87.

18 J.C. de Bruïne, *Herman Venema, Een Nederlandse theoloog in de tijd der Verlichting*, Franeker, 1973; J. van den Honert, *Oratio de mutua Christianorum tolerantia*, Leiden, 1745. It was translated into Dutch: *Academische redenvoering over de onderlinge verdraagzaamheid der christenen*. See also Van Eijnatten, *Mutua Christianorum Tolerantia*.

19 R.A. Bosch, *Het conflict rond Antonius van der Os predikant te Zwolle 1748–1755*, Kampen, 1988.

20 *Examen van het ontwerp van tolerantie om de leere in de Dordrechtse synode anno 1619 vastgesteld met de veroordeelde leere der remonstranten te verenigen, voorgesteld in eenige samenspraken door een genootschap van voorstanders der Nederlandse Formulieren van Eenheid, geschreven tot versterking van de liefhebbers der waarheid om door de vleijende naamen van 'liefde' en 'verdraagzaamheid' van de suiverheid des Evangeliums niet afgeleid te worden*, Amsterdam 1753–9.

21 See Israel, *The Dutch Republic*: 392; F. Grijzenhout, 'De patriotse beeldenstorm', in Grijzenhout, Mijnhardt and Van Sas, *Voor vaderland en vrijheid*: 131–56.

22 Gisbertus Bonnet, *Oratio de tolerantia circa religionem, in vitium et noxam vertente*, Utrecht, 1766; it was translated into Dutch as well as into French (by R.M. van Goens); D. van der Kemp, *Oratio de bona spe, quae etiamnunc Ecclesiae Batavae supersit*, Leiden, 1766. See A. van den End, *Gisbertus Bonnet. Bijdrage tot de kennis van de geschiedenis der gereformeerde theologie in de achttiende eeuw*, Wageningen, 1957: 20–2 and 44–65.

23 See E.G.E. van der Wall, 'De vaderlandse kerk en het vaderlandse verleden. De Socratische oorlog over voorrechten en verdraagzaamheid, ca. 1769–ca. 1780', in P.H.A.M. Abels *et al.* (eds), *De kerk in de kop. Bouwstenen tot de kerkgeschiedenis van Noord-West Overijssel*, Delft, 1995: 11–32; E.G.E. van der Wall, 'Marmontel et la ''querelle socratique'' aux Pays-Bas'. *Mémorable Marmontel 1799–1999*. Etudes Réunis par K. Meerhoff et A. Jourdan, Amsterdam 1999 (CRIN 35); 83–96. I am at present preparing a book on the Socratic War.

24 J. Renwick, *Marmontel, Voltaire and the Bélisaire affair (Studies in Voltaire and the Eighteenth Century*, CXXI), Oxford, 1974. A recent edition of the *Bélisaire* is provided by Robert Granderoute, Paris, 1994.

25 In a typical Voltairean fashion Marmontel observes: 'Error has an immensity of space, and truth is like a mathematical point in the prodigious void. And who has hit that point? Each man assumes that happiness to himself; but upon what proof?' *Belisarius*: 217. An English translation of the *Bélisaire* appeared in March 1767, which was reprinted several times. Quotations are from the 1783 London edition.

26 *Belisarius*: 220–2.

27 'A good and upright king has a more powerful empire over the hearts of men than all the pious friends of persecution collected together.' *Belisarius*: 224.

28 *Belisarius*: 209.

29 W. Gobbers, *Jean-Jacques Rousseau in Holland. Een onderzoek naar de invloed van de mensen en het werk (ca. 1760–ca. 1810)*, Gent, 1963: 353 and 449.

30 J.P. de Bie, *Het leven en de werken van Petrus Hofstede*, Rotterdam, 1899. Hofstede edited a literary journal, entitled *De Nederlandsche Bibliotheek* ('The Dutch Library'), which he used as an instrument to spread his Calvinist orthodox opinions on national and international publications. Thus it served as an orthodox counterpart to an older, important enlightened literary journal, entitled *Vaderlandsche letteroefeningen* ('Dutch literary exercises'), which was edited by dissenters.

31 Hofstede, *Den Belisarius . . . beoordeeld*: 229 and 230.

32 Hofstede, *Den Belisarius . . . beoordeeld*: 238–40; cf. De Bie, *Petrus Hofstede*: 195–6; C. Berkvens-Stevelinck, 'La réception de *l'Historie der Reformatie* de Gerard Brandt et son influence sur la conception de la tolérance hollandaise', in Berkvens-Stevelinck, Israel and Posthumus Meyjes, *The Emergence of Tolerance*: 131–40.

33 C. Nozeman, *Socrates eere gehandhaafd*, 1769. For Nozeman, see E.G.E. van der Wall, 'Cornelis Nozeman en de Socratische oorlog', in H.D. Tjalsma and E.H. Cossee (eds), *Remonstranten en de Verlichting*, Amsterdam 1998: 13–24. Among Nozeman's fields of interest were biology, botany, ornithology, medicine, printing and, last but not least, theology. Nozeman translated Swiss and English theological writings (Warburton) into Dutch.

34 Nozeman, *Socrates eere gehandhaafd*: 130.

35 See B. Böhm, *Sokrates im achtzehnten Jahrhundert. Studien zum Werdegang des modernen Persönlichkeitsbewusstseins*, 1928; 2nd edn Neumünster, 1966; R. Trousson, *Socrate devant Voltaire, Diderot et Rousseau. La conscience en face du mythe*, Paris, 1967; M. Montuori, *The Socratic Problem. The History – The Solutions from the 18th Century to the Present Time*, Amsterdam, 1992.

36 Warburton: 'I would call them saints, tho' not of the Roman fabric, yet made of better stuff, of Erasmus's own texture; but stronger . . .'. See J. Tideman, 'Briefwisseling tusschen den hoogleeraar A.A. van der Meersch en den bisschop van Gloucester, William Warburton (1761–1771)', *Kerkhistorisch Archief*, III, 1862: 417–25; C. van Boheemen-Saaf, 'The Fiction of (National) Identity: Literature and Ideology in the Dutch Republic', in Jacob and Mijnhardt, *The Dutch Republic*: 241–52, esp. 245–6.

37 The 1734 edition of this volume, entitled *Verzameling van eenige verhandelingen over de verdraagzaamheid en vrijheid van godsdienst* ('Collection of several tracts on Toleration and Freedom of Worship'), had been published by the Mennonite publisher Isaac Tirion. Van der Meersch added to this volume Locke's *Second Letter on Toleration*, about seventy of Barbeyrac's references and Drieberge's sermon. Drieberge translated Hoadly's sermon into Dutch. On both editions of this toleration volume, see Van Eijnatten, 'Gerard Noodt's Standing in the Eighteenth-Century Dutch Debates on Religious Freedom', *Nederlands Archief voor Kerkgeschiedenis/Dutch Review of Church History*, 79, 1999/2: 74–98.

38 R.D.B.G.D.L.H.M.V. (ps.), *Een vertoog ter inleidinge waarin zo de grondbeginselen van die vrijheid en van het regt der overheid omtrent haar zorge voor den godsdienst als de oorsprong der dwalingen nopens de heerschappij ver denzelven wordt aangeweezen.*

39 Leiden University Library, RS 162, 4 April, 1771; quoted in Van Boheemen-Saaf,

'The Fiction of (National) Identity', in Jacob and Mijnhardt, *The Dutch Republic*: 246.

40 *De beoordeling van den Belisarius . . . verdedigd*, Rotterdam, 1769; J.J. Zimmerman, *De voortreffelijkheid des christelyken godsdienst vergeleken met de philosophie van Socrates*, Rotterdam, 1770. One of Hofstede's opponents suggested that the statue of Erasmus in Rotterdam should be pulled down and replaced by one of Hofstede, since Erasmus had dared to cry out 'O Saint Socrates pray for us'.

41 Burman launched an attack on the *Advocate of the national Church* in a poem entitled *Rhytmus Monachicus ad Ecclesiae advocatos*.

42 P.J. Buijnsters, *Wolff & Deken. Een biografie*, Leiden, 1984: 93–117. Elisabeth Wolff was closely befriended by Herman Noordkerk and Cornelis Nozeman.

43 Buijnsters, *Wolff & Deken*: 227. See also van Boheemen-Saaf, 'The Fiction of (National) Identity': 248–51.

44 See J. Lindeboom, *Frederik Adolf van der Marck. Een achttiende-eeuwsch leeraar van het natuurrecht*, The Hague, 1947: 49–101. Cf. C.J.H. Jansen, *Natuurrecht of Romeins recht. Een studie over het leven en werk van F.A. van der Marck (1719–1800)*, Utrecht, 1987; W.J. Zwalve, 'Het Recht en de Verlichting. De juridische hooglerar Fredrik Adolf van der Marck (1719–1800)', in G.A. van Gemert, J. Schuller tot Peursum-Meijer and A.J. Vanderjagt (eds), *'Om niet aan onwetendheid en barbarij te bezwijken. Groningse geleerden 1614–1989'*, Hilversum, 1989: 83–100; H.W. Blom, ' "Zet de ramen open!". De natuurrechtsleer van Van der Marck (1719–1800)', in H.A. Krop, J.A. van Ruler and A.J. Vanderjagt (eds), *Zeer kundige professoren. Beoefening van de filosofie in Groningen van 1614 tot 1996*, Hilversum, 1997: 163–74.

45 S. Vuyk, *De verdraagzame gemeente van vrije christenen. Remonstranten op de bres voor de Bataafse Republiek 1780–1800*, Amsterdam, 1995.

46 E.G.E. van der Wall, 'Geen natie van atheïsten. Pieter Paulus (1753–1796) over godsdienst en mensenrechten', in *Jaarboek van de Maatschappij der Nederlandse Letterkunde te Leiden 1995–1996*, Leiden, 1997: 45–62.

47 See the recent edition of the *Bezwaren* by G.J. Johannes, *Isaac da Costa. Dwaasheid, ijdelheid, verdoemenis! Een keuze uit het werk*, Amsterdam, 1996. It called forth many reactions, positive as well as negative (for example, 'The Advantages of the Spirit of the Age').

7. Toleration and Citizenship in Enlightenment England: John Toland and the Naturalization of the Jews, 1714–1753

Justin Champion

In the early summer of 1689, after much parliamentary wrangling and debate, the statute of 1 William and Mary Caput 18 'An Act for exempting their Majesties protestant Subjects, dissenting from the Church of England, from the penalties of certain laws' took away many of the legal restraints against religious conscience. Commonly called the 'Toleration Act', the statutory reform amounted to little more than the repeal of penalties against Protestant dissidents like Quakers, Baptists and other varieties of sectarian who refused to conform to ritual, ceremonial or doctrinal elements within the Anglican constitution. The passage of the Act has very often been linked with the intellectual defence of the liberty of conscience articulated famously by John Locke in his first, and subsequent, letters *Concerning Toleration* (1689).[1] That there was a gap between Locke's radical defence of the rights of Christian conscience, and the mere taking away of certain penalties against religious worship, was clear to the man himself. As he wrote, in June 1689, to Phillip van Limborch in the Low Countries,

> Toleration has now at last been established by law in our country. Not perhaps so wide in scope as might be wished for by you and those like you, who are true Christians and free from ambition and envy. Still it is something to have progressed so far. I hope that, with these beginnings, the foundations have been laid of that liberty and peace in which the Church of Christ is one day to be established.[2]

The 1689 Act took away the penalties against those who did not attend the Church of England, it removed the imposition of subscription to the articles of faith, but it did not break the link between civic liberties and religious identity. So, for example, while Quakers were no longer in danger of eradication by persecution (as long as they registered as non-conformists), they were still exempt from holding local, civic or national offices which were still protected by statutory tests of conscience.[3] The 'Toleration' Act gave no liberties to non-Protestant confessions: as article XVII insisted:

> Neither this act, nor any clause, article, or thing contained, shall . . . extend to give any ease, benefit, or advantage to any papist or popish recusant whatsoever, or any person that shall deny in his preaching or writing the doctrine of the blessed Trinity, as it is declared in the aforesaid articles of religion.[4]

As many recent studies of the politics of religion have emphasized, although the act of 1689 established some measure of relief to private conscience, battles over the legitimacy of the imposition of religious tests and oaths persisted throughout the eighteenth century. Whether focused on the question of subscription to doctrinal articles, conformity to the Test and Corporation Acts, or the debate about the validity of the Trinity, from the 1710s through to the 1790s there were periodic and furious controversies both within and without parliament.[5]

Even though the Act of 1689 was not informed by Lockean principles it has been treated historiographically as a watershed.[6] Although the politics of both national and local society in the eighteenth century was still driven by the rival aspirations of Tory conformists and Whig tolerationists, in legal terms a Christian pluralism of religious practice was established. The point to stress here is that the statutory provision established a liberty of worship rather than an equality of civic identity to a limited religious confession. To some extent, England remained a confessional state: the Toleration Act (1689) and succeeding acts in Scotland (1712) and Ireland (1719), while establishing rights to public worship to Protestant dissenters, did not break the connection between religious identity and civil rights. Penal laws removed did not enfranchise even Protestant dissenters to participate in local and national office: the Test and Corporation Acts (1673, 1661) meant that to be a fully competent subject all individuals had to swear oaths of allegiance and supremacy to the Crown and certificate that they had taken Anglican sacraments. These statutory requirements excluded not only the obvious minorities – Catholics, Quakers, Jews, Muslims, atheists – but also many of the more mainstream Protestant dissenters. This compromise between full toleration of a diversity of religious beliefs and the restriction of full civil liberties to the Anglican confession was the result of the theological origins of the Toleration Act itself.[7] The statutory legislation of 1689 was the result of complex and careful negotiation between Anglican and dissenting interests rather than the conclusion of conceptual considerations about the rights of conscience.[8] Such statutory provisions were calculated to avoid much more dangerous alternatives being advanced: the overwhelming imperative was to preserve the authority and legitimacy of the 'true' Anglican religion.

The conceptual origin of many of the arguments advanced in favour of toleration in the period was premised upon theological imperative. Even in its most radical and acute philosophical form, as articulated by John Locke, arguments in defence of free conscience were ultimately drawn from the powerful injunction to sincere religious belief.[9] The starting point for much of this discourse was the reality of true religion and the duty of the individual to engage with it. Arguments against persecution of religious belief insisted that because there was a true religion, toleration of belief was the best epistemological strategy for approaching that truth. Although such a strategy would more than likely have positive effects in terms of civic society, such pluralism was not the objective.[10] At the core of these theories was the notion that the human soul existed in the *saeculum*: the will to believe religious truth was a necessary and unavoidable imperative. One corollary of this position was that theories of toleration were (and perhaps still are) bound intimately with intellectual positions that place a profound sense of value upon religious sensibility, expression and conviction. One product of these conceptual origins may be that the translation of such tolerationist theory into practical social policy resulted in provisions that were limited by the imperatives of theology. The intellectual and cultural conditions of the eighteenth century meant that it was difficult to establish a consistently tolerant policy based upon Christological foundations.

In contrast to Lockean tolerationist theory, which was underpinned by both a stress upon the ethical sincerity of belief and by the exclusion of ignorant and politically deviant belief (Catholics and atheists), there was an alternative account of the rights of freethinking, or *libertas philosophandi*, articulated in its most radical form by Spinoza in his *Tractatus Theologico-Politicus*. As discussed by Jonathan Israel in Chapter 5 of this volume, Spinoza developed an anti-theological account of the rights of thinking: toleration was to be constructed as a civic rather than a religious process. The defence of *libertas philosophandi* attributed to each individual promoted the cause of civic equality rather than a theological tolerance of diversity. In Spinoza's thought an anti-dogmatic, anticlerical attack upon intolerance was conceived as part of a republican civic agenda. This defence of a freedom to think rather than a right to worship, was premised upon metaphysical foundations that were profoundly unorthodox. Unlike Locke, who ultimately sanctioned his understanding of toleration upon a belief in the veracity of Revelation, Spinoza, undercutting the epistemological competence of Scripture, established his principles upon 'philosophy'. The notion that equality of thought and expression thus became a fundamental expression of social policy was a distinct legacy of such Republican discourses. One consequence of such a position was that rights were devolved to all citizens regardless of theological quality: Catholics, Jews, atheists. As Ernestine van der Wall has indicated, this movement to the advocation of civil equality for minorities (such as the Jewish community) was enshrined in the legislation of 1796 prompted by the Batavian Revolution. Treating all individuals as equal in civic identity, regardless of a religious test, was a significant achievement in the history of Enlightened toleration. Arguments ascribing rights of religious expression to non-Christian, or even anti-Christian individuals and communities will be used in this chapter as a litmus test to determine the coherence of tolerationist arguments. By exploring the history of arguments for Jewish emancipation in

England in the eighteenth century, it will be possible to highlight the radical non-Christian intellectual premises of such discourses.

I

In June 1753, an Act enabling Jewish Naturalization passed into statute with relatively little parliamentary or public attention. By November of the same year the Act was repealed in the face of both massive popular agitation and concerted parliamentary opposition. 'The great clamour of 1753' was the opportunity for the rehearsal of much polemic in defence of the 'Church in Danger': Tory gentlemen allied perhaps uneasily with City Merchants to oppose the threat of religious and economic ruin posed by the Act. Many London Merchants, who had been amongst the earliest to organize petitions against the Bill even before it received Royal assent in May 1753, feared that their trading privileges might be eroded by newly naturalized competitors. The threat identified by the Tory gentlemen was not only a corrosion of Anglican imperatives but also an attempt to reinforce Whiggish principles of religious toleration. Indeed in the debate over the repeal, the Act was tainted as dangerous because it clearly set precedence for the toleration of 'socinians, Arians, Deists, and other prohibited sects'.[11] Debate and popular agitation convulsed England in the summer of 1753. Broadsheets, pamphlets, petitions, newspapers and sermons were all employed to engage with the key issues.[12] 'No Jews; Christianity and the Constitution', a slogan adopted by Jackson's *Oxford Journal*, was typical of the anti-Semitic idiom of public discourse.[13] Although much of this popular literature rehearsed the standard hostile anti-Jewish stereotypes embedded in early modern Christian discourse that represented the dangers of cultural and religious pollution posed by Judaism, the point of such language was not to attack 'real' Jews but to disable the public authority of the Whig government of the time. As Perry has put it, 'the ''anti-Jewish'' clamour of 1753 was meant, even at its ugliest, to prepare the ground not for a pogrom, but for a general election'.[14] Even the most 'economic' of polemical writings advanced by the City Merchants took the religious threat of Judaism as a keystone of its case. One consequence of the centrality of religious issues to the debate was a public discursive slippage in pejorative vocabulary: the labels 'Jew' and 'Whig' became interchangeable in the period 1753–4. Figures like Josiah Tucker, who had contributed a moderate defence of the Act in his *Letter to a friend concerning naturalisation*, were burned in effigy and derided as Josias ben Tucker ben Judas Iscariot. Whigs, Jews and Deists were represented as conspiring confreres.[15] A short examination of one of the broadsheet prints – *Vox Populi Vox Dei or the Jew Act Repealed* – rejoicing in the repeal of the Act in November 1753 will usefully illustrate some of the patterns of polemic.

The very title itself indicates the Tory attempt to capture Whig language: 'Vox populi, vox dei' had been appropriated by the radical Whigs in defence of the Glorious Revolution of 1689, here it was turned to defend the Christian constitution of Church and State. The print represented the Cross 'protected by the Eye of Providence' under threat from a 'mob of Jews & Deists' bearing arms. In the background, presumably indicating the role of the City Merchants in agitating against the statute, lay 'London preserved'. The hand of providence held a set of scales tipped in favour of 'The Gospel and Magna Charta' and against bags of money. In the right foreground a prostrate Jew bemoans 'It was ill timed all our ambitions hopes are fleed'. In the left foreground those politicians and bishops who promoted the Act of Naturalization are lambasted by two Godly ministers declaiming 'Wo unto you whose mouths speak great swelling wonder havings mens persons in admiration because of advantage' and 'Thou Mitred Infidel has dignity made thee forget God'. The text under the image reinforces these themes of devious collaboration between Jews and Deists being defeated by providence: 'God's word declares the Jews a Vagrant race, till they their King Messias' Laws embrace, Therefore Deistical attempts are Vain, still must they Wander like that murderous Cain.' The Jew had been 'foold & Baffled with disgrace'.

The episode of popular disorder and political crisis provoked by the Naturalization Act has been the subject of much historical investigation. The most intensive study by Perry, arguing against Namierite accounts of the non-ideological nature of English politics in the mid eighteenth century, has suggested that the anti-Semitism of the affair should be considered secondary to the infrastructure of party politics that framed the conflict. For Perry, as indeed for many contemporaries, the crisis was indicative of the persisting importance of what can be called the 'politics of religion' in the period. The violence of agitation and political discourse was prompted by confessional anxieties very similar to the crisis that convulsed England in the Sacheverell Trial in the earlier part of the century. Clearly English xenophobic traditions colluded with deep-seated convictions about the nature of the religious and political constitution. Such interpretations are undeniably acute, but to emphasize the ideological structures of the crisis at the expense of exploring the meaning of the religious languages articulated at the time is ultimately to marginalize the confessional dimensions of the moment. As many commentators have pointed out, the language provoked by the statute was grotesque and prejudiced: although these anti-Jewish discourses may have been the instruments of a more political or secular purpose it is still necessary to enquire about why and how such hostile language could be adapted to more particular objectives. The moment of 'madness' surrounding the reception of the Naturalization Act may indeed tell us much about the nature of conflict between Whig and Tory accounts of the relationship between Church and

State, or between individual and community, or about the structure of parliamentary politics and the importance of public opinion in national politics. In another way the episode also provides an opportunity for considering a different set of issues related to the commonplace attitudes towards religious dissidents or minorities (Jews, Deists) and to the cultural and political limits put on the nature of toleration established by the revolution of 1689.

II

It is possible, as the evidence of the controversy surrounding the Jewish Naturalization Act may indicate, to approach the question of toleration from a different and perhaps incommensurable conceptual position. Studies of the origins of the Act show how those politicians involved in drafting and enacting its provisions assumed that it was an uncontroversial matter: a question of simply regularizing a series of complex and expensive procedures already available to allow Jewish aliens to become denizens or subjects. Native-born English Jews were subject to a similar panoply of disabilities that discriminated against other non-Anglican communities, rendered perhaps more difficult because even civil oaths of allegiance and supremacy would have been tendered upon the authority of the New Testament. Jews born abroad, treated as aliens, suffered further disabilities, in particular they could not legally own or inherit property, nor undertake colonial trade. For those who did engage in foreign trade, heavy duties were levied. Naturalization, 'the granting to an individual of the status of a liege subject of the Crown', was a legal process, achieved either by Royal Letters patent or by private parliamentary bill, by which Jewish individuals could circumnavigate some of the more invidious disabilities against property and commercial interests.[16] This process of naturalization, after Calvin's Case (1609), was expensive and complicated by the fact that legally it was an option open only 'to such as are of the religion now established in this realm'.[17] Regardless of these legal and religious obstacles some Jews did gain naturalized status in the seventeenth century. By 1740 there was a further legal means by which aliens could gain naturalized status: under the provisions of the Plantation Act, any who emigrated to the colonies and were resident for seven years so qualified.[18] The objective of the 1753 Naturalization Act was to create a process whereby Jews, after a residence qualification and the evidence of two supporting witnesses, could 'upon application for that purpose, be naturalised by Parliament, without receiving the Sacrament of the Lord's Supper'.[19]

As historians of the 'Jew Bill' have established, the proposals were regarded as unexceptionable. Leading Whig figures such as Lord Halifax, Henry Pelham, the Duke of Newcastle and the Earl of Hardwicke gave their support and influence. Politicians of such acuity foresaw no great reaction and indeed the bill passed through parliament with little obstruction between April and May of 1753. By December, in the face of massive opposition, the Act was repealed. In order to try and understand why such agitation and hostility could be generated by the passage of a statute that would have affected a tiny minority of the nation, it is worth pausing to think about the proposals not simply as a matter of regularizing a complicated and iniquitous legal procedure but perhaps to conceive of the Act as a method of toleration under another name. The intellectual consequences of the Naturalization Act to many contemporaries were regarded as a threat to the Christian constitution of the nation: this is perhaps one of the reasons why (as in the broadsheet discussed above, but also in much of the printed literature) the Act was regarded as a conspiracy of Whig Deists and Jews. The latter by faith rejected Christianity, the former by the authority of their ungodly reason. Although conceived as a measure designed to facilitate social and economic matters, the statute was (mis)understood as a challenge to the very nature of the Christian state. An essentially civil proposal was reconceived as a form of religious subversion. The fury of the Tory reaction against the Act is significant in two respects. First, it indicates the limits of social tolerance in mid-eighteenth century 'Enlightenment' England. Second, it could alert the historian to the import of arguments about naturalization as perhaps a more radical (in eighteenth-century terms at least) alternative to more mainstream discussions about toleration. The radicalism of the 'Jew Bill' was that, in some sense, it intended to treat Jews as subjects of the civil state rather than the signifiers of religious meaning. By turning to a much earlier episode where arguments in favour of the naturalization of the Jews were proposed, it will be possible to explore the contours of this intellectual position in much more detail.

III

In October 1714, the printer Bernard Lintot drew up an agreement with the Irishman John Toland: he had already given Toland ten guineas 'for a copy entitul'd Reasons for Naturalising the Jews in Great Britain & Ireland etc'. He also promised to pay a further sum when the first print run of 2,000 copies 'are sold off'.[20] Unusually for Toland's work, only one reply was published the following year even though, as one historian writes, it was a deliberately provocative work.[21] To many contemporaries Toland was a dangerous and subversive figure: a violent 'Republican Atheist' whose politics and religion were profoundly heterodox.[22] Toland's editions of key figures from the republican canon (Harrington, Sidney, Milton and Ludlow) as well as his own theological and philosophical writings identified him as a 'true' Whig, a man committed to political liberty and freethinking. The little attention that has been paid to Toland's contribution to the debate about Jewish disabilities has been found in works devoted to the history of the Jewish community in England rather than in studies of Toland himself. Indeed the place of Toland's *Reasons for Naturalising the Jews* in this historiography is interesting: although there is little effort made to contextualize the work, either with the rest of Toland's writings or with contemporary debates, it is regarded as a key conceptual contribution in the evolution of theories of Jewish emancipation. Ettinger regarded Toland's work as isolated but proleptic of more liberal dispositions towards the Jewish religion.[23] Mayer, in his survey of Enlightenment attitudes towards Jews, complimented Toland's work: his 'pamphlet was the first to go beyond mere toleration of the Jews by urging a decisive improvement in their civil status'. Unlike many of the later polemicists like Voltaire and d'Holbach, who reviled Judaism as a model of intolerance and dogmatism, Toland laid the groundwork for the liberal writings of men like Christian Döhm and Abbé Henri Gregoire.[24] Jacob Katz placed Toland at the intellectual origins of Jewish emancipation: in the *Reasons* Toland 'applied a central principle of European rationalism – the essential oneness of all human nature – to the case of the Jews. This principle later became the cornerstone in the ideology of Jewish integration.'[25] In broader studies of Toland's intellectual relationship with Judaism, historians like Max Wiener have indicated the Irishman's intimacy with Jewish intellectual and theological sources.[26] More recently it has been argued that, immersed as he was in Jewish culture, Toland's philosemitism was key to his critique of organized (and deviant) Christianity: again in Enlightenment coteries Toland's attitudes to Judaism was 'a real exception to the rule'.[27]

It seems then that although Toland's status as a freethinking heterodox thinker is commonplace, consequently he was out of kilter with the broad mainstream of 'Enlightenment' attitudes towards Judaism in advancing a tolerant disposition, if not to historical Judaism, but to contemporary Jews. Manuel's recent survey of early-modern responses to Judaism has underscored this point with particular relevance to the relationship of Enlightenment thinkers like Voltaire, Naigon and d'Holbach, whose polemics can be described as Judaeophobic.[28] Reflecting on the connections made between Jews and Deists in the clamour of 1753 makes Toland's contribution seem even more unique, given that according to the historiography it might be legitimate to expect antagonism rather than collusion between these two groups. The suggestion that Toland may have had philosemitic motivations for advancing the arguments in the *Reasons* may be one way of resolving this conundrum. However, it would mean placing Toland's contribution in the tradition of religious arguments in defence of toleration: that is, that because Toland valued the injunctions of Jewish religion it became the premise of his advocacy of a social policy of tolerance. Toland was, however, a clever and ambiguous thinker who paid very careful attention to the public presentation of his writings. As has been illustrated in studies of his other works, he was skilled at adopting different intellectual positions in both different published works and in public and private contributions, a strategy contrived to provoke reaction in his audiences. Although committed to 'speaking one's mind in public', Toland very often advanced propositions with seeming innocence, that he knew would have provocative repercussions in their reception. One way of exploring the meaning and intentions of his writings is to locate them in both their political and intellectual contexts. Why then did Toland write the *Reasons*?

One clear personal motivation may have been his intimacy with Jewish friends. Certainly one of his close contacts was the Egyptian Jew, physician to Spinoza, Henri Morelli, with whom Toland had contact in the 1700s. Toland, widely travelled, also had contact with Jewish communities in Northern Europe.[29] Toland had little time for people who shunned Jews: for example he berated the landlords of Hampstead who were 'so silly as to let their rooms stand empty, rather than fill them with Jews'.[30] In an intellectual sense Toland was indebted to the thought of Jewish authors such as Baruch Spinoza and Simon Luzzatto. Scattered throughout his works are a series of comments indicating his admiration for the incomparable Moses. His stimulus for writing the text was not simply a benign and protective inclination to associate or engage with Jewish culture. The issue of naturalization was also an important political and ideological concern in the early eighteenth century, in essence an extension of the Whig/Tory divide over the nature of the relationship between the established Church and civil liberties. From the early 1660s the policies of toleration and immigration were intimately related. Economic theorists such as William Petty and Josiah Child argued that expanding the resident population was a route to trading and manufacturing success: a general naturalization of Protestant immigrant refugees was a consistently recommended proposal. Opposition to such proposals originated from religious, ethnic and economic sources: immigrants might bring all forms of cultural and political pollution to the state.[31] In March 1709, the Whig administration enacted, in the face of vociferous Tory opposition, a statute that allowed the naturalization of all Protestant refugees from the Palatinate. By the summer of 1709 over 10,000 refugees had taken advantage of the Act, prompting stentorian prophecies of doom from an enraged Tory press. While Whig sympathists contrived various resettlement schemes to establish communities in England, Ireland and ultimately in the colonies, Tory politicians and churchmen whipped up popular resentment against the economic and religious threat posed by the immigrants. Capitalizing upon this hostility combined with the 'Church in danger' agitation surrounding the Sacheverell Affair, the Tory interest gained power in the General Election of 1710 and moved to repeal the Naturalization Act in early 1711.[32] Toland had vigorously supported the original Act and later, in the reign of George I, defended the principle against the 'bigots'. As he wrote in 1717, 'I despair not of seeing [the Act] revived.'[33] Toland's *Reasons* was published then into an ideological environment, hypersensitive and hostile to discussions of naturalization. The ideological contest between Whig and Tory had already rendered naturalization of Protestant individuals a dangerous prospect: to advance the cause of Jewish naturalization was to be considered beyond the pale.

IV

Indicating the broad intentions of his work, Toland's *Reasons* contained also 'A defence of the Jews against all vulgar prejudices in all countries'. Reiterating this irenic theme, immediately beneath this on the title page was displayed a citation from Malachi 1. 10: 'Have we not all one Father? Has not one God created us? Why do we deal treacherously every one with his neighbour?' Dedicated to the reverend leaders of the Church, Toland, appealing to the learning and piety of the archbishops and bishops, hoped that he 'espous'd a righteous interest'. Drawing a distinction between such Godly men and the 'pernicious maxims of those Priests your predecessors; who, in the following piece, appear to have been the implacable enemies of the Jews, as their superstition made them adversaries to true Religion', Toland encouraged them to use 'your power in the Church, your authority in the Senate, and your influence upon all the people' to be 'friends and protectors [of the Jews] in the Brittish Parliament'.[34] Reinforcing the Jewish origins of Christianity, Toland intended to encourage 'affection' for the 'Jewish Nation'. After all as he pointed out, 'By them you are undeniably come to the knowledge of one God, from them you have receiv'd the holy Scriptures, of them is descended Moses and the Prophets, with Jesus and all the Apostles.'[35] Carefully, Toland attempted to premise the frame of his arguments on religious grounds: the history of the Jewish nation was also the history of Christianity. The bulk of his text, however, eschewed theological arguments in favour of more civil or political reasonings.

What Toland wished to establish were the 'common principles' in favour of a 'General Naturalization'. These 'common reasons for a General Naturalization, are as strong on behalf of the Jews, as of any other people whatsoever'. Toland briefly rehearsed his commitment to such policy, in particular his 'share with others, in persuading and convincing some persons to embrace the right side of the question' and enabling the 'publick law' (of 1709). Lamenting the injurious repeal of the statute, Toland optimistically insisted that this at least provided the opportunity to reform some of the defects of the original provisions by including within its remit 'those who wou'd not only be good subjects, but who wou'd also be as useful and advantageous to the public weal, as any of those Protestant Churches'. Well aware that his proposal would not be popular, he counter-argued that 'I may propose to serve my country . . . [and] the most effectual way to do so, is the promoting of humanity, and the doing good to all mankind.'[36] The first thrust of Toland's defence of these principles was to argue that encouraging secure Jewish settlement in England would not compromise either religion or the economic welfare of the state. Countering Tory insistence that naturalization would pollute Christianity and the established Church, he asserted that, 'no body needs be afraid that any religious party in the nation will thereby be weaken'd or enforc'd'. Jews would make no claims on ecclesiastical benefices or other Church resources. Neither would they ally against either dissenting or established churchmen: 'they'll never join with any party in Civil Affairs, but that which patronises liberty of Conscience and the Naturalization, which will ever be the side of Liberty and the Constitution'. Jews would make good citizens: far from being 'ill subjects, and a dangerous people on any account . . . they are as obedient, peaceable, useful, and advantageous as any; and even more so than many others'. Since the Jews had no country of their own they would bring no foreign 'intanglements', but devote themselves to the defence of their adopted country.[37]

The Jewish community also promised economic benefits: a 'confluence of strangers' far from bringing unfair competition for bread as the 'Vulgar' feared would be the 'true cause of the land's felicity'. The influx of more traders, artisans and brokers would expand production: 'this one rule of *More*, and *Better*, and *Cheaper*, will ever carry the market against all expedients and devices'.[38] For Toland, opportunity was all. The fact that the Jewish nation 'do now almost entirely betake themselves to business of exchange, insurances, and improving of money upon security' was the result of 'necessity' rather than 'any National Institution or Inclination'. Excluded and disabled from handicrafts, public employment and ownership of property forced them to 'trade and usury, since otherwise they could not possibly live'. Toland argued that given the equal footing with others 'not only for buying and selling, for security and protection to their goods and persons; but likewise for arts and handycrafts, for purchasing and inheriting of estates in lands and houses . . . then I doubt not, but they'll insensibly betake themselves to Building, Farming, and all sorts of Improvement like other people'.[39] Jews too could be shepherds, seamen and soldiers. Vulgar prejudice about the 'prevailing notion of a certain genius, or bent of mind, reigning in a certain Family or Nation' should be abandoned. Such 'byass' proceeded 'from Accident, and not from Nature'. Government and environment determined such characteristics: 'The ordinary sentiments and manners of the Portuguese or Italian Jews, differ not from those of the other Portuguese or Italians.'[40] Prejudices about Jewish personal characteristics were 'silly . . . exciting at once laughter, scorn and pity'. For Toland, naturalization was just because Jews were simply like other people: some were 'sordid wretches, sharpers, extortioners, villains of all sorts and degrees' but others were 'men of probity and worth, persons of courage and conduct, of liberal and generous spirits'. Jews as humans deserved to be regarded 'under the common circumstances of human nature' and as 'creatures of the same species'. The diversity of manners 'and especially contrary rites or doctrines in religion' led to hatred, cruel persecution and murder.[41] The Jews' misfortune, simply because of their religious ceremonies which by their nature were matters indifferent, was to have 'had all nations therefore as their enemies'.[42]

The sad experience of the Jews and the concomitant necessity for naturalization was not the result of accident but the design of priests who acted like 'ravenous wolves'. In the middle section of his work Toland turned to history to explain how the Jewish nation had suffered. Importantly, although he exploited the learning of the historian Jaques Basnage and his massive *Histoire des Juifs* (1706) to provide the 'matters of fact' he did not use the providentialist arguments embedded in his source to explain Jewish sufferings. 'Their most inveterate enemies were the Priests' who conspired with rapacious Princes to plunder Jewish property, 'but also to acquire the reputation of zeal and sanctity among the credulous vulgar'. The priests contrived false accounts of Jews and their religion to cultivate popular anxieties about Jewish sorcery and child crucifixion. Such was the fostering of hatred 'that their condition under Christian princes was farr worse than that of their forefathers under Pharao'. Although concerned to document the tragedies of Jewish suffering, Toland was also keen to establish the causes: 'so dangerous and destructive a monster is superstition, when rid by the Mob, and driven by the Priests'.[43] Recommending Basnage's general work for those who wanted to investigate the histories of other nations, Toland turned to concentrate on the annals of English history from the time of William the Conqueror to the eighteenth century. William saw the political benefits of protecting the Jewish community, especially for the revenues he could derive from them in return for protection. 'Political reasons' that William Rufus and Henry I and Henry II adopted too. The first brutality 'chiefly at the instigation of the clergy' was established in the reign of Richard I and continued by John and Henry III. The nadir was achieved by the policy of Edward I, who 'after inhumanities not to be mention'd without horror . . . banish'd 'em quite out of the Kingdom in the year 1290'. The theme of Toland's history was that the Jewish community had continually suffered the most atrocious treatment under the specious motivation of false piety and the 'incessant bawling of the Priests'. It was only with the rule of Oliver Cromwell that Jews were readmitted to England. Since then they had been 'conniv'd at and tolerated, but not authoriz'd by Charter or Act of Parliament'.[44]

Toland rejoiced that England had been 'long since devested of such barbarous and bloody practises'. Abandoning 'narrow and bigotted principles' the promotion of 'common humanity and genuine religion' was now a possibility which would benefit both 'private and public interest'.[45] Toland was aware that many critics would claim that he was blind to the dangers of Jewish religion, but he noted that he had taken 'no inconsiderable pains' to investigate their rites and ceremonies. Indeed, in the latter part of his text, Toland picking up on the theme of 'genuine religion' advanced the suggestion that Judaism was a tolerable and natural religion. Contrary to commonplace Christian accounts, Toland (exploiting certain Jewish authors) insisted that the rites and ceremonies of that religion were 'solely calculated for their own Nation and Republic'. Jews did not wish to convert Christians but simply 'are every where enjoin'd to magnify to all the world the divine goodness, wisdom, and power, with those duties of men, and other attributes of God, which constitute Natural Religion'.[46] Jews, unlike Christians, had no 'Damning Theology' that restrained 'salvation in effect, tho not in words, to the few elect of their own cant and livery'. Naomi would not have encouraged her daughter-in-law Ruth to return to her 'own people and Gods, had she been persuaded there was no salvation out of the Jewish Church'.[47] Jewish religion, as presented by Toland, was the benign inverse of corrupt priestly Christianity, in its tolerance and morality. As he continued, the Jews expected 'no more from the rest of mankind living out of Judea, than, avoiding and detesting the worship of dead men, with all other sorts of Idolatry, to acknowledge and honor one supreme Being, or First Cause, and to obey the Law of Nature, as the adequate rule of their life and manners'. Commanded by Moses 'not to revile the Gods of other nations (Exod.22.28)', Judaism became the normative model of tolerance.[48] Toland simply rebutted the charge of 'Judaizing'.

For Toland, then, Jewish ceremony was irrelevant to the question of tolerance or naturalization. As humans, like others, Jews were 'safe and sociable'.[49] Religious ceremony, as long as it did not prompt execrable persecution like priestly Christianity, was immaterial to the status of individuals in a civic sense. Although Toland had included a very positive account of Jewish religion his defence of toleration was premised not upon this theological credibility, but upon his understanding of the relationship between the individual (*qua* human) and civil society. Toland had opened his work with the assertion that it was his duty to defend naturalization because it was every person's obligation 'to promote the good of . . . [their] country'. Human society was structured by 'ties of kindred, aquaintance, friendship, or confederacy'. Because human beings took longer to rear than other species they were 'absolutely incapable to subsist afterwards without the company of other men'. The web of dependent relations was intimate and social, initially with family relations and then 'in process of time forms notions of acquaintance, neighbourhood, friendship, affinity, association, confederacy, subjection and superiority'. All individuals then attracted three forms of related obligation: to domestic community, to the welfare of the whole species, and thirdly 'in a special manner to the safe and flourishing condition of that country or society to which he immediately belongs'. These obligations were to be achieved by diligent industry and would thus benefit both public and private interests.[50] It was for these reasons, since Jews ought to be treated in the 'common circumstances of human nature', that naturalization was a rational injunction. Consequently, Toland argued that not only should Jews be given security of citizenship in matters of property ownership and livelihood, but also be allowed to hold political, civil, military or local office 'which may indifferently be held by men of all religions'.[51] The Jews should be naturalized 'as, like the Quakers, to be incapacitated in nothing, but where they incapacitate themselves'. Toland's defence of naturalization was very much in terms, then, of the advantages of social policy rather than any particular theological position.

Just as the original motivations of the politicians who drafted the 'Jew Bill' of 1753 were interpreted by hostile contemporaries as a pernicious threat to orthodox Christianity so the one response to Toland's work reviled it in similar terms as 'impious, dangerous and subtle'. The work, *A Confutation of the Reasons of Naturalising the Jews* (London, 1715), rebutted Toland's defence by rehearsing the statutes against Jews and asserting all of the prejudicial commonplaces against Jewish worship and rites. The principle of naturalization would infringe not only religion but the constitution. The 'rights, liberties, customs and privileges' would be violated if 'outlandish men [were put] upon the same footing with the native subjects'.[52] Reprinting the statute of Edward I, the author rehearsed the reasons for the Jews' original banishment: 'stealing and crucifying of Christian children', coin clipping, forgery, impiety, immorality and lastly 'for attempting to pervert Christians to Judaism'. The bulk of the pamphlet consisted of material extracted from the anti-Jewish legislation of the medieval period: the intention was to reiterate the justice of punishment and restraint upon the community. The author denied any conversionist advantages to naturalization: the Jews were stubborn in their denial of Christ and Scripture offered no evidence of providential conversion. Similarly there would be no economic convenience to naturalization: Jews would engross all trade and stocks.[53] Given this antipathetic reaction to Toland's *Reasons*, coupled with his own expressed doubts about the sort of reception his work would encounter, it is perhaps important to ask what was his purpose in publishing the work? Most recently David Katz has suggested that 'Toland's interest in Jews was genuine and not deigned solely to fuel some other Deistic argument, nor to attack indirectly the validity of Christian revelation.'[54] There is no doubt that Toland had a sincere concern for the plight of contemporary Jews: whether this consideration was premised upon a devout theological affinity or upon a more heterodox and deistical understanding of the nature of religion is debatable. One of the pieces of evidence that historians have used to indicate Toland's intimacy with Jewish culture is his use of Jewish sources in both the *Reasons* and his other work. In particular the point has been made that Toland made explicit use of one identifiable Jewish work by Simone Luzzatto, *Discorso circa il stato de gl'Hebrei* (Venice, 1638). Indeed Toland made no secret of his interest in this work which he commented had 'an intention near a kin to mine'. Such was his consideration of the book that he announced he intended to 'in convenient time publish the translation'. Luzzatto was a 'man of extraordinary learning and judgement, very acute and not meanly eloquent'. As Barzilay has shown, much of the argument in defence of Jewish religion was taken from Luzzatto's work.[55] The final paragraph of *Reasons* concludes with a positive recommendation of Luzzatto's work as 'much the handsomest and most reasonable discourse, that ever I read on the subject'.[56] The significance of Toland's regard for Luzzatto's work was more complicated than has been previously appreciated. Most accounts of this intellectual relationship have assumed that Toland was simply borrowing from a relatively uncontroversial (if Jewish) source: in the case of Luzzatto the imputation of orthodoxy was far from the truth.

Luzzatto (d. 1663) was a rabbi in Venice. His written corpus is small, consisting of the *Discorso* (1638) and a philosophical work *Socrate* (1651), both written in Italian, clearly for a non-Jewish audience.[57] As Ruderman has established, the later philosophical work *Socrate* is a profoundly sceptical and erudite text that avoided any account of revelation in its discussion of intellectual discourse: it can hardly be described as orthodox in either Jewish or Christian terms. This ambiguity of theological correctness is also evident in the text Toland had access to. The *Discorso* is more than a work of Jewish apologetic: in the course of defending the Jewish community of Venice, Luzzatto contrived arguments from a number of different intellectual positions. His work was divided into two parts: the first section offered a defence of the role the Jewish community played in the economy of Venice. It was from these sections that Toland drew much of his material. The second section was a more explicit defence of the Jewish religion and the loyalty of the community conceived specifically to rebut the charges Tacitus had laid against them in Book V of his *Histories*. It was in these chapters that Luzzatto contrived a very unorthodox description of the nature of religion and its relationship with the state.[58] Here is not the place to give a detailed exposition of Luzzatto's work but simply to underscore two related themes.[59] As Melamed points out, Luzzatto was one of the first Jewish thinkers to answer the charges laid against the Jewish community by Tacitus in his *Histories*: the latter had reviled the Jews as both superstitious and politically subversive. In his response, Luzzatto made a distinction between Tacitus as a political thinker and him as an anti-Jewish polemicist: as Melamed comments, 'Luzzatto came to bury Tacitus the antisemite by means of praising Tacitus the master of reason of state.'[60] Jewish religion was not politically disruptive but originally adapted to accommodate reasons of state. Luzzatto exploited Machiavellian notions of *prudenza, fortezza* and *virtù* to establish a 'political' reading of the function of religion in the state. The theology constructed by the legislator Moses was 'a political governance patterned after the divine governance of nature'.[61] This Mosaic foundation was calculated to promote a religion that was importantly both rational, and therefore anti-superstitious, and also politically convenient. For Luzzatto the description of Moses as a legislator did not imply an ungodly motive: Moses promulgated 'the law of God . . . [which] provided and cared for the good of our entire species'.[62] Legislators embraced political and moral ambitions: the Jewish example, contrary to Tacitus, established a virtuous, in both the political and religious sense, republic. Judaism as conceived by Moses was a powerful civic theology effective at protecting the interests of nation and state: such religion cultivated a vigorous patriotism and 'rendered the faithful people more lively in its own belief and more militant in defence of its native rites'.[63] Many of the rites and ceremonies which Tacitus objected to had been calculated for such civil objectives. Mosaic injunctions about the sabbath and the prohibition on the consumption of pork had *politicamente* origins either to induce a process of obligation or to encourage military participation. As a consistent part of Luzzatto's argument, in defence of Jewish practices, was his method of establishing a comparison between such manners and Roman equivalents.[64] These related themes, of Moses as a legislator and of Judaism as a rational political religion, were an important influence on Toland's intellectual understanding of Judaism.[65] Importantly, as both Septimus and Melamed have established, Luzzatto's arguments about the nature of Mosaic religion in the *Discorso* also exercised a critical influence on the writings of Spinoza's *Tractatus Theologico-Politicus* (1670) and James Harrington's *Oceana* (1656), texts with which Toland was very intimate.[66]

The suggestion that Moses was a political legislator rather than a religious patriarch was unacceptable to Christian orthodoxy. Machiavelli, both in the *Prince* and the *Discourses*, had treated Moses as a legislator with the same skills and *virtù* as Numa, Solon and Lycurgus.[67] Such an account was considered atheistical: the Mosaic legation was the prophetic foundation of Christianity for orthodox believers. Although Christian theologians insisted Christ had perfected the Mosaic dispensation as a type of prefiguration of the true faith, Judaism was treated as a Godly model.[68] As Ligota has written, '*l'institution mosaïque relève d'une volonté divine qui prend effet dans la profanité de l'histoire humaine'.*[69] Writing histories of Moses was ultimately an apologetic exercise:[70] Toland's excursion in the *Reasons*, with its assertion of the politically rational nature of Judaism was rooted in an essentially counter-orthodox tradition. Indeed the commitment Toland devoted to the sort of account Luzzatto had given in the *Discorso* can be further explored by an examination of his other writings, in particular those composed while Toland lived in the Low Countries between 1708 and 1710. As has already been noted, many historians have suggested that the primary motivation for his defence of the Jewish community was some form of theological appreciation: by contextualizing the arguments of the *Reasons* with the essays he composed towards an account of the *Respublica Mosaica* it will be apparent that Toland's motivation was political rather than spiritual. In this sense then, and contrary to David Katz's suggestions, it may be possible to see some 'Deistical' purpose in his attitude to Judaism. Similarly it will be possible to understand how a non-theological defence of tolerance might be constructed.

V

One of the most obvious hints that Toland held unusual views about Moses can be seen in the frontispiece to his edition of James Harrington's *Works* (1700) where Moses is depicted as the first in the line of great legislators that include successively Solon, Confucius, Lycurgus and Numa. That Toland was intrigued by the significance of potential meanings of Moses's legacy is indicated in his repeatedly announced intention of publishing a major analytical study called *Respublica Mosaica*.[71] Toland promised a full-blown 'political' reading of Moses. Disseminated in manuscript fragments and printed essays, Toland proposed a full-blown assault upon orthodox Christian understandings of Moses as the *vir archetypus*.[72] He rebutted the Christian orthodoxy of works like Huet's *Demonstratio Evangelica* (1679) which took as its motif the Mosaic origins of all philosophical and ethical learning.[73] Toland replaced this Christian *Philosophia Mosaica* with a civic *Respublica Mosaica*.[74] As one critic noted, Toland treated Moses as 'without dispute . . . one of the greatest and wisest Legislators that ever appeared in the world, not excepting Solon, or Lycurgus or Numa'.[75] As understood by Toland, Moses was 'unequivocally . . . a pantheist, or as we in these modern times, would style him, a Spinozist'. Moses maintained that 'no divinity exists separate from the universal frame of nature, and that the universe is the supreme and only God, whose parts you may call creatures, and himself the great creator of all'.[76] Citing Diodorus Siculus, Toland pointed out that Moses himself was 'an Egyptian Priest, and a Nomarch, or Governor of a Province'.[77] Moses was 'learned in all the wisdom of the Egyptians' which indicated his 'priesthood and temporal dignity' and 'not his skill in magic and miracles'.[78] Indeed, Moses instituted a simple non-ceremonial religion that upheld the injunctions of natural religion. Most of the rites and ceremonies of Judaism were introduced by post-Mosaic figures 'from superstitious motives'.[79]

Toland's re-reading of Moses as a political legislator and of Judaism as a religion adapted to civic circumstances was reviewed in brief in his 'Two Problems', originally included in the collection of clandestine manuscripts circulated on the continent post-1708, but published as an appendix to his controversial *Nazarenus* (1718). Toland claimed that he was half a year away from completing his *Respublica Mosaica*: it would surpass the volumes of Sigonius and Cunaeus. Moses's 'plan' of government, if it had been success-fully established in Judea, 'cou'd never have been afterwards destroy'd, either by the internal sedition of subjects, or the external violence of enemies, but should have lasted as long as mankind; which is to make a Government Immortal, tho it be reckon'd one of the things in nature the most subject to revolutions'. Toland proposed to discuss whether this immutability was based on 'any promise and miraculous concurrence of God; or on the intrinsic nature and constitution of the form itself' by posing two questions about the nature of Judaism. The first question enquired why, given that the ancient institutions of the Egyptians, Babylonians, Greeks and Romans had disinteg-rated long ago, had the Jews 'preserved themselves a distinct people with all their ancient rites'? Secondly, why, after the collapse of their republic had they persisted in their hostility towards idolatrous practices? Toland encour-aged answers that did not have 'recourse to miracles, or to promises drawn from the Old Testament'. In his own view Moses's system was to be explained by using Cicero's *de Republica* rather than providential arguments: such an achievement meant that it was necessary to 'allow MOSES a rank in the politics farr superior to SALEUCAS, CHARONDAS, SOLON, LYCURGUS, ROMULUS, NUMA, or any other Legislator'.[80] As Toland concluded, indicating that he always contrived some practical implication from his intellectual speculations, such was the 'original purity' of the Mosaic republic, that if the Jews ever happened to be 'resettl'd in Palestine upon their original foundation, which is not at all impossible; they will then, by reason of their excellent constitution, be much more populous, rich and powerful than any other nation now in the world'.[81] It was apparent from the reception of this corpus of works on Moses that Toland's attitudes were regarded by contemporaries as dangerously perfidious towards Christian observance.[82] In the English language reviews Toland got a similarly jaun-diced reception. Works like *Origines Judicae* were described as 'such an outrageous libel upon God's word, prophets and people'. One writer, Samuel Parker, was astonished at Toland's relation of Moses: 'one would think, it might have satisfy'd Mr Toland to transform him into an Egyptian priest,

without loading his memory so far as to tell us again and again, that with
some people he pass'd for a Pantheist or Spinozist, in plainer words, a down-
right Atheist'.[83] As Carabelli's bibliographical study shows, Toland's writings
about Moses received extensive reviews in the major journals of the republic
of letters and were the subject of intensive and lengthy rejoinders in larger
theological works and academic disputations published in the Low Countries,
Germany and France. The point by now should be clear. Toland, although
without doubt fascinated by the example of Moses and the origins of the
Hebrew state, could not (and cannot) be regarded as having an orthodox (in
any sense of the word) appreciation of Judaism.

VI

As a context for exploring the advocacy of the naturalization of Jews
advanced in the *Reasons* (1714) Toland's earlier and later researches on the
Respublica Mosaica seem to support a suggestion that his philosemitism was
of an unusual type. Contrary to David Katz's counsel that there were no
Deistical implications in his defence of naturalization, it seems that Toland's
appreciation was founded upon a profoundly political understanding, not just
of Judaism, but of all religion. This is not to propose that the *Reasons* ought
to be considered as an instrument contrived for a different agenda of corrod-
ing Christian confessionalism, but that it was an attempt to provoke a change
in social policy premised upon a genuinely non-theological understanding of
the nature of community and religion. As has been seen above, one of the
key works exploited in Toland's development of his attitude towards Judaism
was the apologetic of the Venetian rabbi, Simone Luzzatto. The latter work,
premised as it was upon a Tacitean understanding of the political value of
religion to the civic community, was a genuine defence of the Jewish community. Although Toland extended the 'political' dimensions of Luzzatto's
understanding of the Mosaic foundation, his defence of the humanity (and
consequent equality) of Jews was sincere. Toland's justification of naturalization was based upon what would come to be regarded as an 'Enlightenment'
understanding of the nature of religion, which implied that it was an important form of cultural meaning but was not to be privileged as a form of tran-
scendence. The determinants for ascribing value to religious expression or
identity were not to be found in theological languages of providence, salvation or truth but in a civic vocabulary of tolerance, virtue and communal
affection. Thus there were profoundly philosophical foundations to Toland's
promotion of naturalization that went beyond the obvious objective of
defending the Jewish community. Importantly, his advocacy of such a proposal also indicates the practical dimensions of his thought. The fact of the
clamour that inundated a similar political measure some forty years after

Toland's suggestions likewise emphasizes both the radical innovation of his proposals and the persisting confessionalism of English society.

Notes

1 For an account of the political history of the Toleration Act see H. Horowitz, *Parliament, Policy and Politics in the reign of William III*, Manchester, 1977.
2 See E.S. de Beer (ed.), *The Correspondence of John Locke*, Oxford, 1978: III, 633 and 689.
3 See D.L. Wyckes, 'Friends, Parliament and the Toleration Act', *Journal of Ecclesiastical History*, XLV, 1994: 42–63.
4 See E.N. Williams (ed.), *The Eighteenth-Century Constitution 1688–1815. Documents and Commentary*, Cambridge 1970.
5 See J. Walsh, C. Heydon, S. Taylor (eds), *The Church of England c. 1689–c. 1833. From Toleration to Tractarianism*, Cambridge, 1993; K. Haakonssen (ed.), *Enlightenment and Religion. Rational Dissent in Eighteenth-Century England*, Cambridge, 1996; B.W. Young, *Religion and Enlightenment in Eighteenth-Century England*, Oxford, 1998.
6 See, for example, the important collection: O. Grell, J. Israel, N. Tyacke (eds), *From Persecution to Toleration*, Oxford, 1991.
7 See M. Goldie, 'The Political Thought of the Anglican Revolution' in R. Beddard (ed.), *The Revolutions of 1688*, Oxford, 1991: 102–36.
8 See J.G.A. Pocock, 'Religious Freedom and the Desacralisation of Politics: from the English Civil Wars to the Virginia Statute' in M.D. Petersen and R.C. Vaughan (eds), *The Virginia Statute for Religious Freedom. Its Evolution and Consequences in American History*, Cambridge, 1988: 43–73.
9 See J. Dunn, 'The Claim to the Freedom of Conscience: Freedom of Speech, Freedom of Thought, Freedom of Worship' in Grell *et al.* (eds), *From Persecution to Toleration*; J. Marshall, *John Locke. Resistance, Religion and Responsibility*, Cambridge, 1995; J.A.I. Champion, ' "Private is in secret free": Hobbes and Locke on the Limits of Toleration, Atheism and Heterodoxy' (forthcoming).
10 For some very astute comments see P. King, 'Justifying Tolerance', *History of Political Thought*, X, 1989: 733–43.
11 T.W. Perry, *Public Opinion, Propaganda and Politics in Eighteenth Century England: a study of the Jew Bill of 1753*, Cambridge Mass., 1962: 156.
12 See G. Cranfield, 'The "London Evening Post" and the Jew Bill of 1753', *Historical Journal*, VIII, 1965: 16–30.
13 Perry, *Public Opinion, Propaganda*: 97.
14 Perry, *Public Opinion, Propaganda*: 75.
15 See I. Gilmour, *Riot Risings and Revolution. Governance and Violence in Eighteenth Century England*, London, 1992: 288–9.
16 See J.M. Ross, 'Naturalization of Jews in England', *Transactions of the Jewish Historical Society of England*, XXIV, 1969–73: 59–72. See also N. Perry, 'Anglo-Jewry, the Law, Religious Conviction, and Self-interest (1655–1753)', *Journal of European Studies*, XIV, 1984: 1–23.
17 Perry, *Public Opinion, Propaganda*: 87. The necessity of a religious test for certification of naturalization was withdrawn in 1845, see N. Perry, 'Anglo-Jewry': 12.

18 As D. Katz points out in *The Jews in the History of England 1485–1850*, Oxford, 1994: 244, some 189 Jews took advantage of this lengthy process, but only a handful actually took up residence in England.

19 The best overview of the content of the bill is to be found in Katz, *Jews*: 244–6.

20 See BL Add Mss 4295 f 26. October 28, 1714. The irony is that only two copies of the work now survive. There are, however, two modern editions. See P. Radin (ed.), *Pamphlets relating to the Jews in England in the 17th and 18th Centuries*, California State Library, 1939; and H. Mainusch (ed.), *Grunde für die Einbürgerung der Juden in Grossbritannien und Ireland*, Stuttgart, 1965. All references are to the latter edition.

21 See D. Statt, *Foreigners and Englishmen. The Controversy over Immigration and Population, 1660–1760*, Newark, 1995, who comments (at 195) that the 'tract, though enlightened in its arguments, represents little more than a gesture of provocation'.

22 See S. Parker, *Censura Temporum*, 1709: 564.

23 See S. Ettinger, 'The Beginning of the Change in Attitude of European Society towards the Jews', *Scripta Hierosolymitana*, VII, 1961: 193–219, discussion of Toland at 216–19.

24 See P.H. Mayer, 'The attitude of the Enlightenment towards the Jew', *Studies on Voltaire and the Eighteenth Century*, XXVI, 1963: 1161–205 at 1165. Mayer's contribution is a valuable survey, although he mis-characterized Toland as a devout Dissenter reverent of all Scripture and especially the Old Testament.

25 See J. Katz, 'The term "Jewish Emancipation": its Origin and Historical Impact' in *Emancipation and Assimilation. Studies in Modern Jewish History*, New York, 1972: 21–46, on Toland see 28–9. Many thanks to David Feldman for drawing my attention to this work.

26 See M. Wiener, 'John Toland and Judaism', *Hebrew Union College Annual*, XVI, 1941: 215–42.

27 See S. Berti, 'At the Roots of Unbelief', *Journal of the History of Ideas*, LVI, 1995: 555–73 esp. 567–73.

28 See F. Manuel, *The Broken Staff. Judaism through Christian Eyes*, Cambridge Mass., 1992.

29 J. Toland, *Reasons for Naturalising the Jews*, London, 1714 § 17.

30 J. Toland, *A Collection of Several Pieces of Mr John Toland*, 2 vols, London, 1726: II, 110–11.

31 See Statt, *Foreigners and Englishmen*: 57; and *idem*, 'The City of London and the Controversy over Immigration, 1660–1722', *Historical Journal*, XXXIII, 1990: 45–61.

32 For an account see H. Dickinson, 'The poor Palatines and the Parties', *English Historical Review*, LXXXII, 1967: 464–85, and *idem*, 'The Tory Party's Attitude to Foreigners: a Note on Party Principle in the Age of Anne', *Bulletin of the Institute of Historical Research*, XL, 1967: 153–65; see also G. Holmes, *British Politics in the Age of Anne*, London, 1967; and C. Robbins, 'A note on the General Naturalization under the later Stuarts', *Journal of Modern History*, XXXIV, 1962: 168–77.

33 Toland, *The State Anatomy of Great Britain*, 1717: 56.

34 Toland, *Reasons*: 36 and 38.

35 Toland, *Reasons*: 36.

36 Toland, *Reasons*: 52, 46 and 44.
37 Toland, *Reasons*: 52 and 54.
38 Toland, *Reasons*: 82 and 84.
39 Toland, *Reasons*: 56.
40 Toland, *Reasons*: 60.
41 Toland, *Reasons*: 62.
42 Toland, *Reasons*: 64.
43 Toland, *Reasons*: 68.
44 Toland, *Reasons*: 82 and 80.
45 Toland, *Reasons*: 82.
46 Toland, *Reasons*: 96.
47 Toland, *Reasons*: 98, citing Ruth 1.15.
48 Toland, *Reasons*: 100.
49 Toland, *Reasons*: 100.
50 Toland, *Reasons*: 42.
51 Toland, *Reasons*: 88–90.
52 Anon., *A Confutation of the Reasons for Naturalising the Jews*, London, 1715: 1.
53 *A Confutation*: 28–30 and 33–5.
54 Katz, *Jews in History*: 235.
55 I.E. Barzilay, 'John Toland's borrowings from Simone Luzzatto', *Jewish Social Studies*, XXXI, 1969: 75–81.
56 Toland, *Reasons*: 102.
57 See D. Ruderman, 'Science and Skepticism. Simone Luzzatto on Perceiving the Natural World' in *Jewish Thought and Scientific Discovery in Early Modern Europe*, New Haven, 1995: 153–84.
58 See B. Ravid, *Economics and Toleration in Sixteenth Century Venice. The Background and Context of the Discorso of Simone Luzzatto*, Jerusalem, 1978: esp. 19–22 which outlines the structure of the work.
59 The following paragraphs draw upon B. Septimus, 'Biblical Religion and Political Rationality in Simone Luzzatto, Maimonides and Spinoza' in I. Twersky (ed.), *Studies in Medieval Jewish History and Literature*, Cambridge, Mass., 1979: 399–434; A. Melamed, 'Simone Luzzatto on Tacitus: Apologetica and ragione di stato' in I. Twersky (ed.), *Studies in Medieval Jewish History and Literature*, II, Cambridge, Mass., 1984: 143–70. I am grateful to the latter for correspondence on the subject.
60 Melamed, 'Luzzatto': 158.
61 Cited in Septimus, 'Biblical Religion': 411.
62 Cited in Septimus, 'Biblical Religion': 425–6.
63 Cited in Septimus, 'Biblical Religion': 423.
64 See Septimus, 'Biblical Religion': 422; Melamed, 'Luzzatto': 164.
65 That Toland was aware of these themes is indicated in the *Reasons*: 94 where he commented on Luzzatto's defence 'against the calumnies of the celebrated historian, Cornelius Tacitus'.
66 For Harrington, see A. Melamed, 'English Travellers and Venetian Jewish Scholars. The Case of Simone Luzzatto and James Harrington' in G. Cozzi (ed.), *Gli Ebrei e Venezia secoli XIV–XVIII*, Milan, 1987: 507–26.
67 For discussion of Machiavelli and Moses see A. Brown, 'Savonarola, Machiavelli and Moses. A Changing Model' in A. Brown, *The Medici in Florence. The exer-*

cise of Language and Power, Florence, 1992: 263–79. See also N. Wood, 'Machiavelli's concept of virtù reconsidered', *Political Studies*, XV, 1967: 159–72 at 162 and 168.

68 See Manuel, *The Broken Staff*; A. Katchen, *Christian Hebraists and Dutch Rabbis*, Cambridge, Mass., 1984; P. van Rooden, *Theology Biblical Scholarship and Rabbinical Studies in the Seventeenth Century*, Leiden, 1989; *idem*, 'Conceptions of Judaism as a Religion in the Seventeenth Century', *Studies in Church History*, XXIX, 1992: 299–308; E. Horowil, 'A different mode of civility: Lancelot Addison on the Jews of Barbary', *Studies in Church History*, XXIX, 1992: 309–25.

69 C. Ligota, 'Histoire à fondement théologique: La République du Hébreux' in *L'Ecriture Sainte au temps de Spinoza et dans le système Spinozist*, Paris, 1992: 149–67 at 158.

70 Cited in L.A. Segal, 'Jacques Basnage de Beauval's L'Histoire des Juifs: Christian Historiographical Perceptions of Jewry and Judaism on the Eve of the Enlightenment', *Hebrew Union College Annual*, LIV, 1983: 303–24 at 317; see also J.M. Elkin, 'Jacques Basnage and the History of the Jews: Anti-Catholic Polemic and Historiographical Allegory in the Republic of Letters', *Journal of the History of Ideas*, LIII, 1992: 603–30. For a detailed study see G. Cerny, *Theology, Politics and Letters at the crossroads of European Civilisation. Jacques Basnage and the Baylean Huguenot Refugees in the Dutch Republic*, Dordrecht, 1987.

71 See 'Projet d'une Dissertation sur la Colonne de feu et de Nuée des Israélites: dans une Lettre à Megalonymus', Austrian National Library, Vienna, ONB 10325: 4–5. Toland reiterated his intention of publishing such a work in *Nazarenus* (1718) Appendix 2, and in *Tetradymus* (1720).

72 For a detailed account of this work, and its relationship with clandestine works see J.A.I. Champion, 'John Toland and Le Traité des trois imposteurs' (forthcoming); for context see S. Hutton, 'Edward Stillingfleet, Henry More, and the decline of Moses Atticus: a Note on Seventeenth-Century Anglican Apologetics' in R. Kroll *et al.* (eds), *Philosophy, Science, and Religion in England 1640–1700*, Cambridge, 1992: 68–84; for a general discussion of this context see Champion, *Pillars*, 154–8.

73 See P. Rossi, *The Dark Abyss of Time. The History of the Earth and the History of Nations from Hooke to Vico*, Chicago, 1987: esp. 152–7.

74 See D.B. Sailor, 'Moses and Atomism', *Journal of the History of Ideas*, XXV, 1964: 3–16 for the persistence of the orthodox veneration of Moses in the eighteenth century.

75 See *Two Essays sent in a letter from Oxford*, 1695: 15.

76 The eighteenth-century manuscript translation of *Origines Judicae*, The Hague, 1709 [hereafter, *OJ*] located in the John Ryland's Library, Manchester [call mark 3 f 38] has been used here. The manuscript is not paginated or foliated: reference will be made to page openings and paragraph number. See *OJ* 16 § 6.

77 *OJ* 39 § 14.

78 *OJ* 42 § 14.

79 *OJ* 52 § 18.

80 *Nazarenus*, 1718: Appendix I, 2–3, 4–5 and 6–7.

81 *Nazarenus*, 1718: Appendix I, 8.

82 For a full bibliography of the responses to *Origines Judicae* see G. Carabelli, *Tolandiana*, Florence, 1975.

83 S. Parker, *Censura Temporum*, 2 vols., London, 1708–9: 547–64 cited at 548, 559 and 560–3. For further English reviews see *The History of the Works of the Learned*, XI, 1709: 376–8.

8. Citizenship and Religious Toleration in France

Marisa Linton

In common with most of Europe, both Catholic and Protestant, in France there was very little support for religious toleration at the start of the eighteenth century. France was unique amongst the major Catholic powers in having a sizeable Calvinist minority which had developed without the protection of a civil power. This meant that the question of toleration could not be ignored as it was in those countries where religious uniformity prevailed. In some ways France appeared to take a step backward in this respect, in that a measure of official toleration had existed in the shape of the Edict of Nantes of 1598 which was then revoked in 1685. But the Edict was never intended as an endorsement of the principle of toleration. On the contrary, it was a pragmatic measure to end the religious wars of the sixteenth century and a recognition of the military force of the Huguenots, rather than a positive statement of toleration. Nevertheless, the Revocation of the Edict meant that the situation for France's Calvinist minority at the start of the eighteenth century was in many ways worse than it had been for much of the seventeenth. In terms of ideas, France is often seen as being at the forefront of the debate on religious toleration during the eighteenth century, as the French *philosophes* such as Voltaire formulated arguments which were to influence much of Europe towards a new recognition of rights of private conscience. But as we shall see, the French monarchy, like other Catholic leaders, tended to be hostile to such ideas. Indeed, when toleration did eventually begin to become government policy this was dictated as much by pragmatic political motives as by the philosophical principles which emanated from the *philosophes*.

Private religious belief was closely bound up with public existence in eighteenth-century France. Religion was the glue which held society together. It was generally thought to be vital for the French people to share the religion of their monarch, God's representative on earth. God, the monarch and his people were brought together by the common bond of the 'true religion', that of the Catholic Church. Religious uniformity was considered necessary on two main counts. The first was the belief that the Catholic Church maintained the only true religion and that anything else was heresy and could not lead to God. The second was the much more pragmatic idea that religious unity was a social and political necessity, essential for social cohesion and to prevent unrest and even civil war. This was a very real fear. No one wanted a return to the religious wars which had devastated France in the sixteenth century. At the beginning of the eighteenth century there was as yet no real acceptance of the idea that individuals might enjoy liberty of conscience and still be loyal subjects of the State. Legal and civil rights as French subjects were conveyed by means of the sacraments, particularly the rites of birth, marriage and (where possible) death-bed absolution. The sacraments were administered and registered by Catholic priests, and without them there was no official acknowledgement of an individual's civil existence. Through baptism an infant became simultaneously one of the Catholic faithful and a member of the French nation. As we shall see, however, during the course of the eighteenth century the bond between religious and civil existence gradually began to weaken as arguments about religious liberty became increasingly linked to the growing theme of citizenship.

From about the mid eighteenth century the word 'citizen' began to appear fairly frequently as an alternative to the more customary term, 'subject'. Two places where the term was to be met with were the official pronouncements of the *parlements* or law courts, and the writings of the *philosophes*. It was a word which had a polemical rather than a strictly legal application. Indeed, there was no real legal distinction between the terms 'citizen' and 'subject' before the Revolution. All French people before 1789 were, by law, subject to the absolute sovereignty of the monarch. But the idea of citizenship could imply a more active level of participation in civil society than did the more passive word subject. Used strategically, the term 'citizen' invoked the notion of a public-spirited man of good intent, who was prepared and able to exercise a responsible role in his community. Citizenship lent itself to the argument that people (mostly men) could play an active role as members of their community because they wanted the public good, the good of the *patrie*. Citizens had duties, both public and private, but they also had rights, by virtue of their responsibility and loyalty, to be treated impartially as a part of that community. One did not need to be a good Catholic in order to be a virtuous citizen. As we shall see, the idea of citizenship became a means by which religious minorities might claim that their spiritual beliefs were a private matter between themselves and their consciences, one which did not affect their rights to public and civil status.[1] The two religious groups who were most affected by this gradual change in attitudes were the French Protestants or Huguenots, and the Jansenists, and we will now look at the position of each of these in turn.

The Revocation of the Edict of Nantes in 1685 (set out in the Edict of Fontainebleau) marked a decisive step away from toleration by the French government and an attempt to impose a religious settlement by coercive means. This piece of draconian legislation removed the effective toleration of the Huguenot (Calvinist) minority in France, a state of affairs which had existed since the purely pragmatic or 'politique' civil and religious compromise that had been agreed as a settlement of the wars of religion which had proved so divisive and destructive. The decidedly spurious justification for this ending of toleration offered was that there were now few Protestants in France, most having already seen the light and converted to Catholicism, a claim belied by the large numbers who sought refuge in other countries, although others stayed in their native country despite the fact that their lives were made more difficult by the spirit of intolerance. The Revocation stated that Calvinist churches were to be closed. Huguenots were forbidden to leave France, with the exception of their clergy who were to be banished if they would not abjure their faith. Calvinist ministers who remained in France would be sent to the galleys. All forms of Calvinist worship were prohibited. Moreover all children born to Huguenot parents must be baptized and brought up as Catholics.

Why did the French monarchy take such a step? It used to be thought that Louis XIV's action arose from a sudden rush of piety in his declining years, fed by Madame de Maintenon and his Jesuit confessors. However, it is generally agreed now that the principal motive was probably political. Louis XIV was determined to eradicate a sect which he saw as latently republican in its sympathies and which had the potential to undermine the French State. At the time the belief that the Huguenots constituted a civil threat was widely accepted. The Revocation was far from being an unpopular move. Most leading figures in French society of the time welcomed it, including Jansenists and Oratorians, and even liberal-minded individual thinkers such as La Bruyère and Fénelon, although the latter was subsequently to modify his position.[2] The Revocation accorded with their assumptions about the relationship between political security and religious conformity.

The arguments against the Huguenots were of three main kinds. Firstly, to the Catholic way of thinking, they were heretics and as such constituted a religious threat by their very existence and especially for the way in which they encouraged independence of thought – a situation which some warned would eventually lead to the challenging of all religious thought and even to atheism. Secondly, they were seen as culturally subversive, cultivating habits of independent thought, and standing for a different set of identity and values from those which had made France a great power. Thirdly, they appeared as a political threat: the link was clear in the minds of Catholic thinkers between religious independence of thought and subversion in the State. The argument was that freedom of conscience and lack of loyalty to the Catholic Church could lead subjects whose loyalty to the State was also questionable to become armed rebels. They might stir up civil contention within the State of France and give their loyalty to other Protestant states. The idea that people whose religious affiliations were elsewhere might also be suspect in their political affiliations and disloyal to the monarchy was not exclusive to France, indeed it was prevalent amongst most of the European powers at this time. The Duc de Saint-Simon expressed this fear in his claim that the Calvinist community, after the Edict of Nantes, had established 'a separate, well organised republican government ... in a word, a state within a state'.[3] In practice it seems that there were republican elements in Protestant thought, but that these came to the fore in times of persecution, that is, before the Edict of Nantes, and again after its Revocation. On the other hand, very few Calvinists were involved in the Fronde.[4]

Ironically, the measures taken against the Huguenots, such as the practice of rounding up Protestant clergy, were in part responsible for the guerrilla war of the Camisards, which reached a peak of intensity in the years 1703–4. The Camisards were Protestant peasants in the remoter regions of the south of France who, bereft of their regular clergy, took to a form of millenarianism and outright rebellion against the Catholic authorities. Memories of the Camisards and their violence lingered on into the eighteenth century and were frequently used to argue that Protestants constituted an 'enemy within' the French State whose presence was potentially dangerous and subversive.

In 1724 the Duc de Bourbon, the young Louis XV's first minister, passed an Act which tightened up the legislation against Protestants even further. It was stated that Catholicism was the only religion existing in France. It provided, amongst other things, for execution of Protestant clergy who preached the faith, and tightened up the laws against Protestant marriages, and against public worship – for which people could be sent to the galleys, perpetually imprisoned and even executed. They were not allowed to hold public office. All children must be baptized within twenty-four hours of their birth by a Catholic priest. Many Protestants were forcibly taken to houses of conversion run by the Catholic clergy.

Despite the prohibitions against leaving France, many Huguenots risked everything to escape. At the time of the Revocation there were approximately 900,000 Calvinists in France, constituting something like 5 per cent of the population. Of these, 200,000 fled in the immediate aftermath, and it is estimated that something like 300,000 Huguenots left in total between 1685 and 1760 at the time of the last wave of persecutions.[5] They went to places as far-flung as Russia and Ireland. But by far the greatest number naturally congregated in those sympathetic Protestant countries which were fairly accessible from France. About 100,000 went to the Dutch Provinces, and 80,000 each to England and to Brandenburg-Prussia. Here they set up communities in exile. The risks and difficulties involved in leaving their homeland meant that these voluntary exiles tended to be strong-minded, independent and educated. To the Dutch Provinces in particular came a number of intellectuals, clerics, writers, editors and publishers. The refugees in Holland were granted civil rights and a secure status. They formed a lively and distinctive community, with a network of readers, correspondents, writers and consumers of pamphlets and books. Not surprisingly, the question of toleration was one which much concerned them. But it took time, even for these exiled Huguenots who, one might assume, would have a vested interest in the pursuit of toleration, to accept it as a laudable principle in itself. Many, such as the pastor Jurieu, were quite as intolerant towards the Catholic authorities as the latter were towards them. Jurieu fed the Catholic belief in the political disloyalty of the French Calvinists by speaking of a 'holy war' to be waged against France under the leadership of William of Orange.

However, others in the Dutch community, such as Henri Basnage de Beauval and, most famously, Pierre Bayle, began to formulate new responses to these issues. Bayle's ideas, contentious in his time, were to help bring about a major shift in ideas about toleration during the course of the eighteenth century. It was Bayle who, independently of Locke, developed the argument of the 'erroneous conscience', that is, that it was possible to err in one's religious beliefs in good faith, and that liberty of conscience should necessarily be respected. Most famously and controversially, he argued in the *Dictionnaire historique et critique* (1697) that it was possible to conceive of a society of virtuous atheists, by which he meant that good citizenship could function independently of religious belief. This claim predictably provoked outrage in some quarters. It was anathema for Calvinists of Jurieu's persuasion as well as for devout Catholics. His opponents claimed that his ideas would set the unwary off on the slippery slope that led to 'freethinking' in religious matters, or even to atheism. Yet Bayle himself was by no means an atheist or a freethinker. He remained true to the Calvinist faith of his birth. Ironically, eighteenth-century freethinkers and rationalists were to claim Bayle as one of their own, though his ideas about the liberty of the 'erroneous conscience' had been formed from the perspective of a religious man. As for the common claim that to permit religious toleration would only encourage political disloyalty, Bayle argued that it was rather the reverse. It was the State's lack of toleration for their beliefs, not the beliefs in themselves, that forced religious minorities to seek the support of foreign powers. If they were officially tolerated and granted a secure civil status, then their loyalty could be assured. The experience of the Dutch Provinces showed that where religious pluralism existed, religion ceased to be a political issue.[6]

For those Protestants who remained in France, their actual position was rather more complex than the official position of intolerance would suggest. A large proportion succumbed to the immense pressures brought to bear on them, and converted, or appeared to do so. But many, at least in secret, remained loyal to their faith and constituted a sizeable underground community. Apart from the issue of public worship, the biggest difficulty to confront them was the status of their marriages. They could marry secretly in a ceremony conducted by a Protestant cleric usually in the open air, and hence known as 'wilderness' marriages. These, of course, were not recognized as marriages by the State and therefore any resulting children would not be legitimate, and could lose their rights to their parents' property. Or they might go through the form of a Catholic marriage and later of baptism for their children – but this was a problem for their consciences, and also for the conscience of the Catholic priest performing the rite who was often aware that he was marrying a Huguenot couple. On the other hand, there was a certain amount of *de facto* toleration accorded to some Protestant minorities in small communities. Such persecution which took place was generally of a sporadic and local nature, the product of specific circumstances.

Differences depended in part on the attitude of the local Catholic clergy. Some stuck very closely to the law and insisted that suspected Protestants who wanted to marry should go through a lengthy process of public denial of their Protestant faith and acceptance of the state religion. In other areas the Catholic clergy took a less rigid view. For example, in the late seventeenth-century community of Layrac in Aquitaine, it appears that the confessional state, typified by the strong views of monarchy and militant Catholic clergy, was not accepted uncritically. Here, in the years after the Revocation, the very small group of Protestants were largely accepted by the local elite, an acceptance strengthened by intermarriage and family ties.[7] Generally speaking, in northern France, where there was a greater concentration of towns and the country was more under surveillance, it was very difficult for Huguenots to avoid detection. In more remote regions, particularly in the southern provinces of Dauphiné, Poitou, Languedoc and Provence, local Protestant communities tended to be more militant and assertive than in the north. Here they were often fairly open in their open-air worship which the authorities might well choose to ignore. Nevertheless, those Protestants who remained in France faced constant uncertainty and problems in their civil existence and in their right to worship. In 1713 the aged Louis XIV had been brought to declare that there were no more Protestants in France which constituted a curious argument for why toleration was no longer necessary. Protestants were officially referred to as *nouveaux convertis* (i.e. new Catholic converts). This denial of a separate status made them entirely subject to Catholic courts, and this legal fiction was maintained until the eve of the French Revolution.

The position of the Jansenist sect in France was still more ambiguous than that of the Protestants. Jansenism had begun life as a purely theological movement founded by Cornelius Jansen, bishop of Ypres, who died in 1638. It was a particularly austere and quasi-puritan branch of Catholicism, with little interest in worldly matters. Jansenists wanted to reform the Catholic Church rather than to secede from it as the Protestants had done. In their own eyes the Jansenists were Catholic, despite many points of proximity to Calvinist belief, especially about predestination and grace. It is notable that, during the seventeenth century and the first half of the eighteenth, Jansenists gave little indication that they felt affinity with the Protestants. Far from supporting the case for the toleration of Protestants, Jansenist thinkers appear to have been as enthusiastic in their denunciation of the Protestant heresy as many of the most conventional Catholics. Their hostility towards the idea of toleration of Protestants was heightened by their eagerness to keep their distance from a sect seen as 'heretical'. In 1686 the leading Jansenist thinker, Antoine Arnauld, had openly welcomed the Revocation of the Edict of Nantes which he claimed was both legally and theologically justified.[8] But in 1713 Louis XIV obtained from the Pope the Bull *Unigenitus*, an official condemnation of Jansenist beliefs which was seen as an authorisation to exclude Jansenists from the Catholic Church, a decision which they themselves would not accept. Thereafter the civil liberties of Jansenists in eighteenth-century France were in some ways almost as contested as those of the remaining Protestants. Indeed, the suppression of Jansenism was generally more consistently carried out during the first two-thirds of the eighteenth century than was the persecution of Protestants.[9] Attempts were made to deny suspected Jansenists the sacraments and thus the right of private conscience. There were three main ways in which Jansenists might react to this persecution. They might capitulate, abandon their Jansenist beliefs and accept the orthodox tenets of the Catholic Church. If, however, they persisted in their Jansenism, they might withdraw further from the material world into the spiritual one. Many chose this second option, avoiding worldly politics and retreating into mysticism, convulsionism and belief in miracles. In the early 1730s many Jansenists sought out the tomb of an austere Jansenist, Deacon Pâris, at Saint-Médard in Paris. It was widely believed that miracles were taking place at his tomb, and believers who gathered there frequently experienced convulsions of religious fervour.[10] The third option was to become more active on behalf of Jansenist rights to practise their religion as they saw fit. This often took the form of organized legal protests against the denial of the last rites and other sacraments.

By the early 1730s a split had widened between the more spiritual Jansenists and those who chose to fight in the public forum. Much of this public defence of Jansenism focused on the principal law courts, the *parlements*. From about 1731 the *parti janséniste*, composed of priests, lawyers and magistrates in the Paris *parlement*, began to emerge as a considerable force for the contestation of the legacy of the Bull *Unigenitus* (1713). Jansenism, which had begun as a purely spiritual movement, was slowly transformed. Increasingly, their arguments were couched in a new kind of language, one of civic rights. This civic rhetoric was to gain its full force during the 1750s, but there were intimations of it in the writings of some campaigners on behalf of Jansenism as far back as the 1730s. Thus, the Jansenist theologian, the *Abbé* Duguet, put together an influential work, *Institution d'un Prince* (written in 1713 for the young Prince of Piedmont, but published in 1739) which was, ostensibly at least, a traditional study of the duties of kingship and not an explicitly Jansenist text. But Duguet conceived of those duties in terms of a political language which laid the emphasis on the responsibility of the king towards his people, making extensive use of such terms as *'patrie'*, 'republic', 'citizen', 'equality', 'public good', *'bienfaisance'*, 'nation' and 'virtue'. He used the authority of the Scriptures to argue that it was the king who served the 'republic' which existed outside himself and was independent of him. From this Duguet concluded: 'It is therefore the same thing to be for the republic and to be king; to be for the people and to be sovereign. One is born for others, since one is born to command them; because one must not command others except in order to be useful to them.'[11] Duguet's concept of a 'republic' was compatible with monarchy, providing that the monarch served the 'public good' *(bien public)*, dispensed justice, maintained equality, rewarded virtue and punished vice, defended his people, and kept them happy.[12] It was the duty of kings to instil morality in the people but Duguet conceived of these moral virtues in terms of secular values rather than of orthodox Catholic doctrine. A prince 'must inspire in his subjects the love of all the virtues on which the good of the State depends', the first and foremost of these virtues being, 'love of the *patrie*'.[13] He continued:

not that I think that the moral virtues are absolutely different from those which have religion as their principle and goal; on the contrary, I see the former as a rough draft of which the latter are the perfection; and in fact it is because I see the former as being like a joyful preparation for the latter that I think that they need great attention.[14]

These moral virtues were identified with the civic virtues of classic republicanism, 'the pagans', and he quoted Saint Augustine to show that such civic virtues are not opposed to Christianity, but were an earthly echo of 'the true Religion'. By learning to love one's *patrie* and by being virtuous citizens in this life, people could prepare themselves to 'become citizens of another *patrie*'.[15] Civic responsibility was thus linked to moral righteousness. Similarly, the concept of the 'general will' was gradually transformed from a theological belief (particularly a Jansenist one) into a political one.[16] Jansenists maintained that they were not attempting to overthrow the social order but trying to win for themselves the right to individual conscience. By adopting a vocabulary which combined elements of both civic and moral virtue they helped to prepare the ground on which others might later build when challenging the authority of the political system. This was seen as an implicit threat, and Duguet's book was banned in 1740 by Louis XV's chief minister, Cardinal de Fleury.[17]

The classic view of the eighteenth-century debate on toleration was that it was the ideas of the Enlightenment which led directly to toleration becoming the accepted policy of governments. The view of the *philosophes* as champions of toleration was one which they themselves promoted. Certainly they had a profound impact in terms of ideas although, as we shall see, other factors also contributed to the change in government stance. In arguing the case for toleration, Enlightenment thinkers in the eighteenth century said relatively little that was original: many of their arguments had first been articulated by men such as Locke and Bayle. Thus Montesquieu (whose wife was a member of the thriving Calvinist community in Bordeaux) and Voltaire argued for the rights of Protestants to religious toleration not because they had much sympathy with their beliefs (Voltaire in particular was somewhat dismissive) but because they believed in liberty of conscience as a natural right. There was a growing interest also in cultures and religious beliefs outside Europe: in Islam, of course, but also in the beliefs of cultures hitherto almost unknown to Europeans, such as Confucianism. For the *philosophes* of the Encyclopédie generation there was an increased awareness of the value of beliefs outside the Christian world, a growing sense of cultural relativism, and an acceptance that other peoples were able to organize their societies in perfectly valid ways and as good citizens on their own terms.

The championship of the *philosophes* for religious toleration was not, however, without its limitations and ambiguities. The case for liberty of conscience was one thing, and this could clearly be justified by arguments based on the tradition of natural rights. Complete civil toleration and public acceptance of religious minorities was more problematic. Not all the *philosophes* by any means were whole-hearted supporters of the idea of the public rights of Protestants to exist as an acknowledged community. Civil toleration in private life (the right to marry, the acknowledgement of the legitimacy of Protestant children) was one issue. But should Protestants also be allowed toleration in public life, and to hold public office? Anxieties in this respect were provoked by the traditional fear of civil unrest, of the loyalties of a community of Protestants within the wider community of Catholics. To put this another way, could Protestants be good citizens?

The argument that Protestants, despite their beliefs, could be both responsible citizens and virtuous individuals in their private and family life was employed in that most notorious of legal cases, the Calas affair. For many, the Calas case came to represent the very epitome of the horrors of intolerance and a symbol of the Enlightenment stand in defence of toleration. Jean Calas, a Toulouse merchant, was condemned to death in March 1762 by the Toulouse *parlement*, on very flimsy evidence, for the murder of his son who, finding his career as a lawyer blocked due to his religious loyalties, had grown very depressed and been found hanged. The case against his father hinged on the claim that the son had been thinking of converting to Catholicism and that, rather than see this happen, his own father had been prepared to murder him. Voltaire, who had at first assumed the father's guilt, became convinced of his innocence and campaigned tirelessly to rehabilitate his memory and to restore to his family their good name and family fortune. The defence of Calas (both before his death and posthumously) undertaken by his lawyers, including the renowned Elie de Beaumont, hinged on two main areas. The first was the failure of those who built the case against Calas to carry out certain procedures. The second was the much wider point that Calas was a worthy citizen, a man of virtue, as was his family. The claim that he and his family had conspired to murder one of their own members was simply implausible. Despite the undoubted injustices of this case, it has been argued that the Calas affair was something of an aberration. Toulouse, by the mid eighteenth century, was relatively tolerant of its small Huguenot community. The persecution of Calas and heightened fear of Protestantism at that time was a temporary revival of old terrors brought about by a combination of circumstances, the effects of the Seven Years War against Protestant England and Prussia, and local events stirred up by the arrest and execution of a Protestant pastor, François Rochette, which led to tension in the city of Toulouse and fears of civil disorder.[18]

In 1763 Voltaire published his *Traité sur la tolérance* which built on his polemical defence of Jean Calas to make a more general statement about the necessity for toleration. He took up the theme of citizenship, claiming that Calas as a citizen had the right of a proper hearing before an impartial court, but he had 'no defence but his virtue'.[19] Natural law, he said, should be the basis of human law: 'All over the earth the great principle of both is: Do not unto others what you would that they do not unto you. Now, in virtue of this principle, one man cannot say to another: "Believe what I believe, and what thou canst not believe, or thou shalt perish." ' The supposed right of intolerance, he said, was 'the right of the tiger; nay, it is far worse, for tigers do but tear in order to have food, while we rend each other for paragraphs'.[20]

Other legal cases in the 1760s also contributed to a change in attitudes, such as the Sirven case in which Voltaire and other writers took up the cause of victimized Protestants. Voltaire was not the only *philosophe* to campaign actively for toleration. A series of polemical articles on this subject appeared in the *Encyclopédie*, penned by authors of very varying backgrounds and beliefs, from the atheist, Diderot, who wrote the article on 'Intolerance', to the Protestant, the Chevalier de Jaucourt, who was responsible for such articles as that on 'Liberty of conscience', and on the '*Patrie*', although his article on 'toleration' was suppressed by the censor. Again, the arguments they used were not particularly original: they were the familiar ones based on natural law and the right to freedom of conscience. But through the *Encyclopédie* such ideas reached a wider audience and gained greater acceptability. Despite its official suppression by the authorities in 1759, and the long years that followed during which its publication was prohibited, the *Encyclopédie* was read by men, from clerics to magistrates, who formed pillars of the French establishment and who were best situated to promote a change in ideas.[21]

The attitude of the *philosophes* towards religious toleration has generated a significant level of historical controversy. The classic view of the *philosophes* is of fearless campaigners for religious and civil freedoms. But their primary motive was hostility to the Catholic Church and its institutionalized power over people's lives. This did not incline them to sympathize with other religious beliefs. The Calvinist community were by no means always grateful for the interventions of the *philosophes*. It was not easy for devout believers of whatever religion to make common cause with *philosophes* who were sceptical about the value of any organised religion – or even of religion at all. Some of the arguments used by the *philosophes* were also felt by Calvinists to be counterproductive. Montesquieu, for example, in *De l'esprit des lois* (1748) had defended the idea of civil toleration for religious minorities, indeed, he was a committed advocate of toleration, although he preferred utilitarian arguments to justify this position. But his remarks linking Protestantism to republics (he argued that the Protestant temperament was more suited both to cold northern climates and to republicanism) revived the old fear that the first loyalty of the Protestant community was not to the French monarchy and was seen by some Calvinists as being detrimental to their cause.[22] Even Voltaire, who for many people appeared as the very embodiment of toleration, had limits to his tolerance and was known, for example, to have anti-Semitic opinions.

Rousseau, despite his own Calvinist upbringing in Geneva, proved something of a disappointment to French Calvinists seeking support in specific cases for those of their brethren who were victimized by the French State in the early 1760s. Paradoxically Rousseau repeatedly showed himself to be unwilling to take up his pen as a polemicist on their behalf, his excuses ranging from ill-health to the negligible extent of his influence with French ministers and officials. The knowledge that Voltaire had often been before him in taking up some cases probably profoundly irritated Rousseau, for the two were at daggers-drawn by this point. In his works Rousseau had generally taken up a general position in favour of religious toleration. This was most outspoken in his *Lettre à Christophe Beaumont* (1763) where he argued the case for civil rights for French Protestants. But he also maintained that it was desirable to conform outwardly to the religion supported by the State, so as to avoid civil disunity. This was the position taken in his most sustained discussion of the subject given to his Savoyard vicar, in *Emile*, and also in the *Social Contract*. Here he stated that all those people who did not conform to a 'purely civil profession of faith' which ensures that they behave as good citizens, should be banished, although he qualified this by adding that such a state religion must not allow religious intolerance: 'tolerance should be given to all religions that tolerate others, so long as their dogmas contain nothing contrary to the duties of citizenship'.[23] It is necessary, he said, to distinguish between the personal religion of man, his private beliefs, and the religion of the citizen, which involves the outward dogmas which preserve the unity of society.[24] It was a position which succeeded in antagonizing both the *philosophes* (who were offended at Rousseau's campaign against scepticism and irreligion) and the religiously devout, both Catholic and Calvinist, who were shocked by his suggestion that the outward forms of religion were not strictly relevant. *Emile* was condemned to be burned for this reason, both by the Paris *parlement*, and by the Calvinists of his native Geneva – a betrayal which Rousseau never forgave. Gradually, however, the idea of toleration began to gain ground amongst a significant proportion of the reading public, an influence which extended far beyond the confines of philosophic circles. Indeed, many members of the Catholic clergy also endorsed the idea of religious toleration, a fact which in itself indicates a fundamental sea change in attitudes during the second half of the eighteenth century.[25]

But arguably it was not the *philosophes* alone who were responsible for the change in attitudes towards the toleration of Protestants which took place in the late 1750s and early 1760s. Another reason for change seems to be attributable to the Protestant minorities themselves, who began to show signs of a new militancy and openness. In more remote areas they began to build churches once more, and to worship more publicly. They also began to campaign more actively for toleration. A significant event in bringing about a change in attitudes on the part of the monarchy itself was the Conti affair. In 1755–6, the Prince de Conti offered to help the Protestant community to obtain freedom of worship, and some suspected him of having *frondeur* intentions. It has been claimed that Conti was attempting to stir up rebellion and trying unsuccessfully to enlist the support of the Huguenots. Whether Conti was a would-be rebel or not (and many historians remain sceptical about this), it does appear that the refusal of Protestants to challenge Louis XV at a time of great vulnerability for the French monarchy (on the eve of the outbreak of the Seven Years War against Protestant enemies, England and Prussia in 1756) did much to diffuse Louis's suspicion of his Calvinist subjects' loyalty. All but a tiny minority showed themselves to be loyal French citizens despite their religious beliefs.[26]

The ambiguity of the Jansenists' position involved them in legal disputes which had acquired a political dimension from the mid eighteenth century and, it can be argued, even as far back as the 1720s. Such legal disputes were for the most part played out in the forum of the Paris *parlement* (the most important of the thirteen *parlements*). Disputes over religion had proved a major cause of dissension between the Paris *parlement* and the monarchy. The campaign to suppress the 'errors' of Jansenism was given renewed vigour by the declaration in 1749 by the archbishop of Paris, Christophe de Beaumont, that suspected Jansenists must produce *billets de confession* (that is documents signed by an approved priest, testifying to their having made a satisfactory confession and established their conformity to the official doctrine of the church and acceptance of the Bull *Unigenitus*) before they could be allowed to receive either the Eucharist, or extreme unction on their death beds. The magistrates of the Paris *parlement* saw this measure not only as an affront to civil liberties but also, and in their eyes more importantly, as a direct challenge to their own area of jurisdiction. They challenged the legality of demanding *billets de confession*. They were encouraged in this stance by the presence amongst the magistrates of a small but well-organized band of Jansenists, the *parti janséniste*, as well as by a network of Jansenist lawyers attached to the Paris *parlement*. It is hard to establish with certainty exactly who was a Jansenist at this time since many people were understandably reluctant to admit their tendencies. Recent historians tend to the belief that Jansenists were far more numerous and politicized, particularly in the *parlement*, than has been given credit in the past. Dale Van Kley has argued very strongly the case for Jansenists as a catalyst for political disputes from the 1750s up until the Revolution; whilst Peter Campbell has shown that Jansenists were a significant presence within the Paris *parlement* as far back as the beginning of the 1730s.[27] It seems clear that the influence of Jansenists and their defence of civil liberties extended far beyond their own ranks to include many members of the *parlement* who were not themselves Jansenist but who resented what they saw as excessive control by the State and the Church over the matter of religious beliefs. The dispute over toleration of Jansenism thus became in some senses a political struggle over the authority of the *parlements*, and their right to defend the independence of the Gallican church. The struggle over the *billets de confession* became a protracted three-sided dispute between the orthodox Catholic Church, the Paris *parlement* and the monarchy.

The *parlements* themselves were far from being a radical force. They wanted to defend their own autonomy and sphere of authority and not infrequently repudiated more radical statements made on their behalf and in their name.[28] It seems probable that most of the magistrates within the Paris *parlement* did not share the more radical ideas of the *parti janséniste* and were very circumspect in their views. Nevertheless, the magistrates of the *parlements* were almost the sole power in the realm capable of even challenging the authority of absolute monarchy. This fact, coupled with their willingness on those occasions when it suited their strategy, to employ the rhetoric of citizenship and to appear as the 'defenders of the nation', meant that the *parlements* had the potential to rally support amongst the wider reading public who read the *Remonstrances* of the *parlements*, and works by Jansenists such as Le Paige and Claude Mey who put the case for *parlementaire* constitutional rights.[29] By 1771 Jansenists were coming together with non-Jansenists in the course of which they adopted elements of the Enlightenment natural law tradition and Rousseauist ideas of citizenship into an argument which had begun in defence of Jansenist rights to worship, but had now developed into what amounted to political agitation in support of the *parlements* and for a French constitution. Jansenist militancy therefore played its part in leading to what has been characterized as a 'desacralization' of the French monarchy; a process which, though few would argue that it caused the French Revolution, nevertheless helped to make a revolution thinkable, by providing a vocabulary through which it could be conceptualized and justified.[30]

From about the late 1750s leading Jansenist intellectuals (including clerics and magistrates) had abandoned their traditional hostility towards Protestantism and were beginning to campaign for official toleration for Calvinists both in their quasi-official journal, the *Nouvelles Ecclésiastiques*, and through their members within the *parlements*, of whom the most prominent was Robert de Saint-Vincent.[31] Such Jansenists were steering a complex course, for they were understandably unwilling to employ the same kind of arguments as the *philosophes* which they feared would lead to more indifference to religion and the increased secularization of society. Instead, they set up arguments based on the notion of citizenship and what they termed a Christian toleration which did not imply indifference to religion, but implicitly acknowledged that it was both unrealistic and counterproductive to try to coerce people into specific religious beliefs. They made the Augustinian division between the earthly and the heavenly city and spoke of the need for a strong but paternal and loving king, devoted to the best interests of his people, in ways that echoed the *Abbé* Duguet many years before.[32]

By the time that Louis XVI came to the throne the idea that citizenship conferred the right to religious toleration had gained ground amongst the reading public, whether they obtained such ideas from the writings of the *philosophes* or from the remonstrances of the *parlements*. In about 1784 an informal alliance was formed which had the goal of obtaining legal toleration of Calvinists. This alliance involved the highest officials and ministers including Loménie de Brienne and the Baron de Breteuil. Another powerful advocate came in the shape of the former minister, Malesherbes, whose support of Protestant toleration was of long-standing. He wrote two treatises, one in 1776 entitled 'Mémoire sur les affaires de religion', the other in 1779, 'Mémoire sur le mariage des Protestants' which circulated privately. He argued that the Revocation of the Edict of Nantes, far from having removed Protestants from the French nation, had done the reverse and created a separate nation within a nation. The only way to resolve this problem was not by coercion but by establishing a secular civil settlement based on common rights to citizenship and leaving religious beliefs to individuals' private consciences.[33] In the 1780s he returned to the fray, more outspokenly this time with two *Mémoires* published in 1784 and 1785 which argued still more strongly the Protestant case. He was careful, however, to exculpate Louis XIV from any blame, claiming that it had not been the king's intention to drive the Protestants from France.[34] Another campaigner was the Marquis de Lafayette. Like many others, he was inspired by the experience of the American Revolution and the fairly liberal attitude of the American revolutionaries towards minority religious beliefs which had culminated in the legal separation of Church and State. These sympathetic figures formed links with some Protestant pastors, including Jean-Paul Rabaut Saint-Etienne. These men met and, to some extent, made common cause and discussed tactics. Malesherbes wanted to go further: given the chance, he would have wished to include Jews and other non-Christians in the provisions for toleration. But he was also a pragmatic man, with a keen sense of what was achievable, and he concentrated his energies on the Calvinists and particularly what he felt to be the most pressing issue, that of the recognition of Protestant marriages. There were three main places where pressure might be brought to bear: in the king's council, in the Paris *parlement*, and in the Assembly of Notables which was convened in February 1787. All three were tried. In the *parlement* Robert de Saint-Vincent, the Jansenist magistrate, spoke stirringly on behalf of Protestant toleration in February 1787, and helped to secure *parlementaire* support for this measure.[35] Even so, the situation dragged on, and it was a combination of two final factors which won over much wavering opinion. The first of these was the *cause célèbre* of the Marquise d'Anglure who, in July 1787, was the subject of a legal brief published by the famous lawyer Target in the fight to have the mixed marriage of her parents recognized as lawful, and hence her legitimacy and right to inherit from her father. The second factor in the precipitation of change was the diplomatic crisis in the Low Countries in the autumn of 1787.[36]

Eventually, the monarchy itself accepted this change in public opinion and felt a consequent moral pressure to take action. Louis XVI was convinced enough of the justice of the Protestants' cause to grant an Edict of Toleration on 19 November, 1787. This long-awaited edict proved to be a half-measure for France's Protestant community, and it failed to end the debate which was to continue until the Revolution. The Edict provided for the civil toleration of Protestants, particularly in acknowledging their right to marry, the legitimacy of their children and their right to hold and inherit property. But it was less satisfactory on the subject of their religious toleration. They were still denied the official right to worship as they wished, nor were their clergy given official acknowledgement. Their civil rights also stopped short of letting them hold public office: they were excluded from judicial and municipal office, and were not permitted to become teachers.

Full toleration for Protestants came finally with the French Revolution. The Declaration of the Rights of Man spelt out the principles of equality and civic right. Article 10 of the Declaration stated that 'No one should be disturbed for his opinions, even in religion, provided that their manifestation does not trouble public order as established by law.'[37] This was not to be the end of the matter, of course. There were many ways in which the issue of toleration was still to prove problematic during the revolutionary period.[38] But in the context of the late eighteenth century, when even the principle of religious toleration was still not acknowledged by most powers in Europe, it was certainly an impressive beginning.

Notes

1 On the relationship between religious status and civil status see J. Merrick, 'Conscience and Citizenship in Eighteenth-Century France', *Eighteenth-Century Studies*, 21, 1, Autumn 1987: 48–70.
2 G. Adams, *The Huguenots and French Opinion, 1685–1787: the Enlightenment Debate on Toleration*, Waterloo, Ontario, 1991: chap. 2.
3 Cited by Adams, *The Huguenots and French Opinion*: 39.
4 For a useful summary of much of the debate on toleration and Protestantism, see Adams, *The Huguenots and French Opinion*. For the wider context one can consult the classic study by H. Kamen, *The Rise of Toleration*, London, 1967. On the republican tendencies of the Huguenots, see Adams, *The Huguenots and French Opinion*: 9–10.
5 *Ibid.*: 35.
6 On the differences between Bayle and Jurieu, see E. Labrousse, *Bayle*, Oxford, 1983: 33–9.

7 G. Hanlon, *Confession and Community in Seventeenth-Century France. Catholic and Protestant coexistence in Aquitaine*, Philadelphia, 1993.

8 See R. Birn, 'Religious Toleration and Freedom of Expression', in D. Van Kley (ed.), *The French Idea of Freedom: the Old Regime and the Declaration of Rights of 1789*, Stanford, 1994: 287.

9 R.R. Palmer, *Catholics and Unbelievers in Eighteenth-Century France*, Princeton, 1939: 15.

10 J. Dedieu, 'L'Agonie du Jansénisme (1715–1790)', *Revue d'histoire de l'Eglise de France*, 14, 1928: 162–214. Van Kley also discusses the interactions between religious and political Jansenism, though starting from a later period, in D. Van Kley, 'The Jansenist Constitutional Legacy in the French Prerevolution, 1750–1789', *Historical Reflections/Réflexions Historiques*, 13, 1986: 393–454; also R. Tavenaux, 'Jansénisme et vie sociale en France au XVIIe siècle', *Revue d'histoire de l'Eglise de France*, 54, 1968. On the convulsionaries see B.R. Kreiser, *Miracles, Convulsions and Ecclesiastical Politics in Early Eighteenth-Century Paris*, Princeton, 1978.

11 J.J. Duguet, *Institution d'un Prince: ou Traité des qualitéz, des vertus et des devoirs d'un souverain*, London [Rouen?], 1739: 10.

12 *Ibid.*: 9–11.

13 *Ibid.*: 232–42 and 249–59.

14 *Ibid.*: 233.

15 *Ibid.*: 233–4.

16 P. Riley, *The General Will Before Rousseau: the Transformation of the Divine into the Civic*, Princeton, 1986.

17 E. Carcassonne, *Montesquieu et le problème de la constitution française*, new edition, Geneva, 1970: 38.

18 This is the argument put forward by D. Bien, *The Calas Affair: Persecution, Toleration and Heresy in Eighteenth-Century Toulouse*, Princeton, 1960.

19 Cited in L. Hunt (ed. and trans.), *The French Revolution and Human Rights: a Brief Documentary History*, Boston, 1996: 38–9.

20 *Ibid.*: 39–40.

21 On the readership of the *Encyclopédie*, see R. Darnton, *The Business of Enlightenment: A Publishing History of the Encyclopédie, 1775–1800*, Cambridge, Mass., 1979.

22 Adams, *The Huguenots and French Opinion*: 69.

23 J.-J. Rousseau, *Social Contract*, G.D.H. Cole (ed. and trans.), London, 1973: Book IV, chap. 8, 277.

24 *Ibid.*: 272 and 276–7.

25 A classic study of a gradual shift in attitudes amongst the Catholic clergy is that by Palmer, *Catholics and Unbelievers*.

26 J.D. Woodbridge, *Revolt in Prerevolutionary France: the Prince de Conti's Conspiracy against Louis XV, 1755–1757*, Baltimore, 1995.

27 See the many works by D. Van Kley, especially *The Damiens Affair and the Unravelling of the Ancien Régime, 1750–1770*, Princeton, 1984; also P.R. Campbell, *Power and Politics in Old Régime France, 1720–1745*, London, 1996; P.R. Campbell, 'Aux Origines d'une forme de lutte politique: avocats, magistrats et évêques. Les crises parlementaires et les jansénistes', in C. Maire (ed.), *Jansénisme et Révolution*, special issue of *Chroniques de Port-Royal*, Paris, 1990.

28 See, for example, K.M. Baker, *Inventing the French Revolution*, Cambridge, 1990: chap. 6, 'A classical republican in eighteenth-century Bordeaux: Guillaume-Joseph Saige'.

29 Van Kley, 'The Jansenist Constitutional Legacy': 393–454.

30 D. Van Kley, *The Religious Origins of the French Revolution*, New Haven, 1996: 11–13.

31 See C.H. O'Brien, 'The Jansenist Campaign for Toleration of Protestants in Late Eighteenth-Century France: Sacred or Secular?', *Journal of the History of Ideas*, 46, 1985: 523–38; and Adams, *The Huguenots and French Opinion*: 231.

32 O'Brien, 'The Jansenist Campaign', esp. 527–8 and 538.

33 See Birn, 'Religious Toleration and Freedom of Expression': 293–5.

34 *Ibid.*

35 Adams, *The Huguenots and French Opinion*: chap. 18.

36 *Ibid.*: chap. 19.

37 Cited in Hunt, *The French Revolution and Human Rights*: 79.

38 On this subject see, for example, the articles in Van Kley (ed.), *The French Idea of Freedom*, esp. S.M. Singham, 'Betwixt Cattle and Men: Jews, Blacks, and Women, and the Declaration of the Rights of Man', and R. Birn, 'Religious Toleration and Freedom of Expression'.

9.   A Tolerant Society?

Religious Toleration in the Holy Roman Empire, 1648–1806

Joachim Whaley

In his essay of 1802 on the German constitution, Hegel commented that one of the many regrettable features of the Holy Roman Empire after 1648 was that it sanctioned the legality of intolerance.[1] Paradoxically, the religious troubles of the sixteenth century and the Thirty Years War had strengthened the links between religion and the State. 'Even civil rights are linked with religion', he noted. Both Catholics and Protestants attempted to 'exclude one another from civil rights and to gird and establish this exclusion with every kind of legal pedantry'. Only Frederick the Great and Joseph II 'put a higher value on freedom of conscience in religion than on the barbarity of legal rights'. Their toleration decrees contravened Imperial law but accorded with 'the higher natural rights of freedom of conscience and the non-dependence of civil rights on faith'. These isolated acts, Hegel believed, pointed the way forward to the state of the future in which Church and State would be separated and man's conscience therefore truly free.

Hegel's comments place him on a watershed in the history of religious toleration in the German lands. He looked back on an era in which, since 1648, the rights of Catholic, Lutheran and Calvinist communities established before 1624 were guaranteed by Imperial law. For the rest, however, toleration was a precept of prudent government, an instrument used by rulers and magistrates to maintain political and social stability or to promote prosperity. Religious freedom was granted from above by decree; its beneficiaries remained in no doubt about the fragility of their rights. What Hegel looked forward to was an age in which religious freedom would ultimately be recognized as a natural fundamental right which precedes the State, a right no longer granted by the State but recognized and guaranteed by it. The change from one system to the other was gradual. Criticism of the old regime had been growing since the 1760s when writers like Lessing began to formulate radical demands for emancipation and to envisage a future in which human beings might not even need government at all, a world in which even atheists might be tolerated.[2] The events of the French Revolution, the reorganization of the German territories after 1803 and the transformation of their administrations then created a new framework in which fundamental rights became a pressing political issue for the first time, though their translation into law was not fully complete until the later decades of the nineteenth century.

The protagonists of change at the end of the eighteenth century were often scathing in their criticism of the past. The new ideas that they espoused have become so fundamental to the very idea of modern society that the eighteenth century toleration system, like the Imperial system of which it was an integral part, was underrated and misunderstood. Indeed it is only in the last few decades that historians have begun to revise the nineteenth-century view of the Holy Roman Empire which unthinkingly accepted Pufendorf's description of it as '*monstro simile*'. In a scholarly tradition dominated by Prussian-German nationalist preconceptions, the Reich used to be regarded as a decayed and chaotic institution, corrupt to the core. Now, however, it is recognized as a system which worked relatively effectively. Under the Holy Roman Emperor as *Schutz- und Schirmherr*, it fulfilled a vital role as a *Rechts-, Verteidigungs- und Friedensordnung* in central Europe after 1648.[3] As a *Verteidigungsordnung* its very existence both guaranteed the peace and stability of Europe as a whole and ensured the survival of the myriad small German states, most of which would have been incapable of survival as independent units in the competitive world of the European powers. As a *Friedensordnung*, the *Reich* both ensured protection from external threat and served to prevent conflict between the states. As a *Rechtsordnung*, it provided mechanisms to secure the rights both of rulers and, more extraordinarily, of subjects against their rulers. Its institutions, such as the Imperial courts, provided legal safeguards for many of the inhabitants of the German states.

Quite crucial to an understanding of how the *Reich* functioned is the recognition that its constitution or fundamental law after 1648, the Peace of Westphalia, was essentially a religious peace. The treaty marked the end of over a century of bitter religious conflict and religious wars.[4] It provided an effective framework for peaceful coexistence between the various warring parties. This has led some historians to conclude that after 1648 the foundations for a tolerant society were laid, even that the federal and cooperative institutional structures of the *Reich* might be regarded as a model for the contemporary efforts to create a federal European union or for a satisfactory resolution to intractable ethnic and religious conflicts such as that in Bosnia.[5] Such judgements are, however, rather dubious. They ignore the severe limits on the degree of religious freedom which actually prevailed in early-modern Germany, from a late twentieth-century point of view at least. They fail also to take into account the fact that the Peace of Westphalia only applied to the three major Christian denominations. Above all, they make it difficult to understand the late eighteenth-century debate over toleration and freedom of conscience.

On the other hand, the Peace of Westphalia did in fact prevent a renewed outbreak of religious war, and its provisions account largely for the marked decline of religious persecution after 1648 and its virtual absence in the eighteenth century. In that sense the toleration system it created matches perfectly the definition of the kind of toleration regime that Michael Walzer has recently suggested may well be the best that can be aspired to at most times: a legal system which secures the religious rights of a variety of groups, is capable of being extended, and which, by virtue of being a juridical structure, does not depend on the unlikely prospect of the majority of the population developing the personal virtue of tolerance.[6] Indeed, the system established by the Peace of Westphalia bears many of the characteristics of the consociation as described by Walzer: a system where 'each group lives in relative security' and where 'mutual toleration depends on trust, not so much in each other's good will as in the institutional arrangements that guard against the effects of ill will'.[7] Participation in the system was specifically limited to Catholics, Lutherans and Calvinists. In some territories, however, circumstances developed which resulted in the formal extension of toleration to others. This in turn resulted in laws which transcended the limited system of 1648 (which recognized only groups and communities) and ultimately established the rights of individuals.

I

One of the distinctive features of the German debate about religious toleration was its legal rather than theological character.[8] At root it was a debate about the implications of extending the principles and provisions enshrined in the Peace of Westphalia. The aim of the treaty was to remedy the defects of the terms of the Peace of Augsburg. That settlement had established the principle of *cuius regio, eius religio* and placed authority in confessional matters (the *jus reformandi*) firmly in the hands of the princes and magistrates. In doing so it gave both Catholics and Lutherans hopes of extending their powers by converting or reconverting individual rulers. The only right given to those who did not share the faith of the ruler was that of emigration on payment of compensation or allowing three years for the orderly disposal of property. Equally problematically it did not recognize Calvinism as a legitimate Christian Church and thus almost immediately generated extreme tension at the level of Imperial institutions.

The ambiguities inherent in the Peace of Augsburg undoubtedly contributed to the constitutional crisis of the *Reich* in the late sixteenth century which, in the context of growing international tension, exploded in the Thirty Years War. On the other hand it is significant that some influential Imperial politicians responded to these tensions with an irenic concern for the unity of the *Reich*, and with arguments similar to those of the *politiques* in France.[9]

The Imperial military commander, Lazarus von Schwendi, for example, who had conducted the brutal siege of the Lutheran 'rebels' at Magdeburg in 1550–2, argued in the 1570s that religion should play no part in the politics of the Empire. Similarly, the influential master of the Imperial mint, Zacharias Geizkofler, argued in 1613 that toleration was imperative both because it was impossible to force man's conscience and because history showed that attempts to extirpate religious beliefs merely led to their wider dissemination and to the ruin of the ruling house. The true politician should be guided by the lessons of history, by an assessment of damage sustained through past conflicts, and by the dictates of reason. Such views clearly did not avert the catastrophe of the Thirty Years War. They do, however, seem to be representative of an increasingly pragmatic approach to religion. Above all, they reflect a widespread concern for the future of the *Reich*, a clinging to the reality of a common cause and to the hope that it might also ultimately be possible to restore unity in religion (*concordia*) by means of moderation (*tolerantia*).

Such considerations shaped the settlement of 1648. The Peace of Westphalia recognized all three major Christian confessions and guaranteed certain rights for all their members in the *Reich*. At the level of Imperial institutions it ensured parity between Catholics and Protestants: regardless of numerical circumstances, votes in the *Reichstag* which involved religious matters could only be decided by the agreement of both parties. The procedure of *itio in partes* (dividing into parties at the request of either Catholics or Protestants), together with the injunction to reach decisions '*amicabilis compositio*' was expressly designed to protect the interests of the Protestant minority. At the level of imperial institutions religious conflict was thus avoided by 'secularizing' Imperial law.

Considered from this point of view, it is clear that the Peace of Westphalia was not intended to promote toleration in any straightforward sense but rather ensure that peace would prevail until the divided Christian Churches were re-united. Furthermore this goal was primarily political and legal, rather than theological, in nature.[10] The unity of the *Reich* took precedence over purity of dogma, and for this reason the papacy strenuously objected to the treaty and never recognized it. In the following decades, several re-unification projects were launched, primarily by Catholics and strongly supported by the Emperor Leopold I after 1658.[11] Count Ernst of Hessen-Rheinfels, for example, a convert to Catholicism and author of the irenic *Der discrete Catholische*, preached toleration as the precondition for the reconciliation of all German Christians, the reform of the *Reich* and the establishment of perpetual peace. He exercised a major influence on the Elector Archbishop Johann Philipp von Schönborn who commissioned Leibniz to formulate plans which ultimately extended far beyond the *Reich* to the uniate and orthodox churches.

The idea of a reformed *Reichskirche* as a vehicle for a revived *Reich* retained its fascination until its demise in 1803: it runs through the thinking of Hontheim (Febronius) and later Dalberg, and subsequently resurfaced in the German opposition to Napoleon.[12] While such plans were largely Catholic in inspiration, they also received enthusiastic support from many Protestants such as Leibniz, Johann Michael von Loen, Johann Friedrich Wilhelm Jerusalem and Justus Möser, to name but a few.[13] They were, however, no more successful than efforts made in the eighteenth century to unite the two major Protestant churches or more effective than the irenic attitudes of pietism in restoring a community of all believers. Common to most of these reunification schemes was an emphasis on the ideal of political unity, a willingness to make concessions on dogmatic and liturgical matters, and an underlying hostility to the curia in Rome. All of them foundered, not least precisely because their inspiration and intent was primarily political and because their protagonists underestimated the entrenched theological differences that had to be overcome. On the other hand they did arguably contribute to the creation of an intellectual and religious framework which gradually fostered the elaboration of more systematic arguments for toleration. While those who opposed the extension of religious toleration could always appeal to the restrictions implicit in Imperial law, the proponents of change justified their arguments by the fact that it also expressly fostered cooperation and reconciliation, and forbade religious polemics.

II

This debate took place in the territories where the Peace of Westphalia also laid down the framework for the next 150 years. Within each territory authority in religious matters was ceded unambiguously to the princes and magistrates.[14] Their freedom to determine the extent of religious freedom in the territories under their jurisdiction was, however, to be limited henceforth by the principle that the yardstick by which legitimate claims to rights and ownership were to be measured was the *status quo* of 1 January, 1624, the so-called *Normaljahr*. This applied both to territories as a whole and to individuals or groups within them. It was now no longer possible for a prince who converted to oblige his subjects to follow him into another church. Any minority which enjoyed privileges or owned property in a given territory before 1624 was granted protection in perpetuity by Imperial law. Minorities which had no status before 1624 were guaranteed the right to emigrate without being deprived of their property. Each group enjoyed a different degree of freedom of worship. The official or dominant faith enjoyed the *exercitium religionis publicum* (churches with spires and bells); those with rights dating from before 1624 could enjoy the *exercitium religionis privatum* (chapels without bells); those without such rights had only the *exercitium religionis domesticum* (prayers in the family home and the right to visit churches in a neighbouring principality).

The limitations of the treaty considered as a toleration law arose from its aim of securing the unity of the *Reich* by mediating between the combatants of the previous century. Its provisions concerning religion applied only to Catholics, Lutherans and Calvinists. Sectarians were excluded; the myriad small Protestant churches such as the Mennonites enjoyed no rights and, according to some commentators such as Johann Jakob Moser, the treaty implicitly prohibited the toleration of such groups anywhere in the *Reich*.[15] Also excluded were the Jews, who were not treated as a religious group at all. They were subject to special laws deriving from the medieval Imperial protectorate over the Jews, which ultimately gave rise to arguments over whether the question of their treatment was in any sense at all a theological issue, or whether it was not simply a legal and administrative matter.[16]

For the majority of the population, however, the treaty did at least provide a safeguard against religious wars and freedom from persecution. Indeed in doing this it generated an extraordinary variety of provisions, all enshrined in the public law of the *Reich*. While most territories had a single dominant, if not exclusive, church, others emerged with more complex arrangements. In some Imperial cities such as Augsburg, Biberach, Dinkelsbühl and Ravensburg, both Catholics and Lutherans enjoyed equal rights in a system where absolute parity was guaranteed from the city council down to the bodies which appointed church caretakers.[17] A unique form of parity prevailed in the bishopric of Osnabrück where a Catholic bishop alternated with a ruler from the Protestant house of Braunschweig-Lüneburg, during whose rule the episcopal jurisdiction was exercised by the archbishop of Cologne as Metropolitan.[18] In other cities and territories the treaty favoured one faith yet secured the rights of the other. One of the most bizarre and distorted examples of this principle was the Lutheran episcopal seat of Halberstadt which contained six Catholic monasteries with about 100 monks and 35 nuns to serve a Catholic minority of only 750 inhabitants.[19] In other towns the same church might be used by two confessions, sometimes with complex wrought iron gates and internal fences to mark out the space to which each was entitled. There were even examples of Protestant pastors being appointed by Catholics. In Wetzlar, for example, there was a particularly complicated arrangement which specified the induction of a Protestant pastor by a Catholic dean who solemnly supervised the oath of loyalty to the true Protestant faith taken at the hand of the Catholic deacon in full liturgical dress.[20] Similar highly specific arrangements prevailed in many rural areas. In the village of Goldenstedt, for example, between Bremen and Münster, Catholics and Lutherans who had fought over the village church for decades, and destroyed it on several occasions, developed a *de facto* 'Simultanaeum' after 1650: Lutherans attended the Catholic high mass; hymns taken from the Lutheran hymnal were accompanied by the Catholic organist; the Catholics sang some of the hymns, while the Lutherans simply remained silent during the Latin responses; the Catholic priest had instructions from his superiors not to stress those dogmas that might upset the Lutherans.[21] Even single religious foundations might be shared between various denominations, such as the noble convent of Schildesche near Bielefeld which housed six Catholic, six Lutheran and six Calvinist noblewomen. The community survived in perfect harmony into the nineteenth century and followed the kind of heterodox Christian liturgy, reflecting practices of all three denominations, which regularly prompted astonished and outraged commentaries in the letters of the papal nuncios to Rome.[22]

The complexity and variety of inter-confessional structures which developed in the German territories was unique in Europe (the only parallels are in Jerusalem and Ethiopia). It is, however, not easy to assess the significance of this state of affairs in the extension of greater religious toleration in the eighteenth century. For one thing, controversies over the interpretation and application of particular agreements threatened to plunge the *Reich* into war on several occasions until about the 1720s.[23] The expulsion of 20,000 Protestants from Salzburg in 1732 showed just how brutally the right of emigration could be transformed into an instrument of persecution.[24] The conversion of individual princes, or the succession of a ruler of a different confession also continued to generate tensions which at times threatened to explode in internal strife and civil war. The succession of the Catholic line of Neuburg to the Calvinist Palatinate in 1685 led to a particularly bitter and often violent struggle during which many Calvinist clergy and congregations were driven into exile and the peace of the *Reich* as a whole was threatened on several occasions. After decades of wrangling matters came to a head when the Elector Karl Philipp, who succeeded in 1716, transferred his court from Düsseldorf to Heidelberg in 1718: he promptly banned the Heidelberg Catechism and expelled the Calvinists from the Heilig-Geist-Kirche, removing the wall that had partitioned the Calvinist-occupied nave from the chancel which had been occupied by the Catholics since 1705. An outcry on the part of the *corpus evangelicorum* forced him to restore the *status quo* in 1720, whereupon he simply moved his Catholic court to Mannheim. For several more years, however, the wider issues continued to destabilize the politics of the *Reich*, as the Protestant princes continued to dispute the legality of the so-called 'Ryswick clause', whereby in lands occupied by France during the war years 1688–97 Catholic worship should be permitted to continue openly even if this had not been laid down in 1648. In the Palatinate itself, relations between Calvinists and Catholics remained charged with resentment until the end of the eighteenth century.[25] Other princely conversions and successions of rulers from a line which did not share the dominant faith had no less wide-ranging implications. When Augustus the Strong of Saxony converted to Catholicism in 1697, followed by his son and heir in 1712, a major political crisis in the *Reich* was averted by the transfer of the leadership of the caucus of Protestant princes to other hands. Within Saxony itself, however, the conversion marked the beginning of protracted and bitter wrangling over the Elector's right to introduce Catholic worship for himself and his court.[26] Similarly, the succession of a Catholic line in Protestant Württemberg in 1733 marked the start of a conflict which, under the irresponsible and despotic rule of Karl Eugen, culminated in 1770 in the duke's deposition and temporary imprisonment by the Imperial courts.[27]

Even in cities such as Augsburg where absolute parity, both religious and civil, was guaranteed by the Treaty of Westphalia, ideas of religious toleration as such did not necessarily gain ground. Some have been tempted to see these communities as 'bridgeheads of religious tolerance' on the 'long road to toleration'.[28] In reality they were dead-end byways. Augsburg may have remained peaceful, but it became gripped by what one historian has called 'parity mania' and, by the end of the eighteenth century, enlightened observers had nothing but scorn for the 'city of Catholic and Protestant pig sties'.[29] Legally established parity guaranteed by Imperial law almost invariably led to communities where two or three denominations were often far too obsessed with fanatical adherence to the *status quo* even to contemplate the extension of tolerance to those of other faiths than their own.

III

The most significant arguments for change, both Protestant and Catholic in origin, focused on the position in the German territories rather than on the *Reich* or on the cities or institutions where parity or inter-confessional arrangements had been specified in 1648. Significantly, these arguments were also primarily concerned with the position and powers of rulers and the needs of the State rather than with the rights of individual subjects.[30] Pragmatic political and economic considerations rather than the radical theological ideals of religious dissenters were crucial in extending the principles laid down by the Peace of Westphalia.[31]

In Protestant Germany, the development of natural law theories was crucial to the emergence of new and more powerful arguments for extending the limited toleration of the Peace of Westphalia. Pufendorf, for example, combined a conservative view of the rights and duties of a ruler with a recognition that confessional uniformity was not an absolute prerequisite for successful government and a stable society.[32] Thomasius went further and explicitly rejected the episcopal rights of Protestant princes, which he viewed as a relic from the Catholic past.[33] The tendency of Protestant natural law was to deny that rulers had an obligation to make their subjects virtuous or to worry about their salvation. Thomasius stressed the needs of the State, which required toleration on pragmatic grounds in order to promote peace and prosperity. No prince had the right to lay down the law on theological matters. Similarly no theologian had the right to dictate to dissenters. The most that a prince might do in the interest of maintaining domestic peace would be to offer a dissenting theologian the possibility of emigration, though without loss of property or infringement of civil rights.[34]

Similar views also developed in Catholic Germany. The papacy itself never even recognized the Peace of Westphalia. Yet, even before 1648, theologians such as the Netherlands-born Viennese court preacher Becanus, comparable to Bellarmine in his implacable opposition to Lutheranism, conceded that there were circumstances in which a Catholic monarch might tolerate Protestants.[35] If a ruler could not stamp out heresy without stirring up civil war then an irenic approach would both maintain stability in the short term and ultimately promote the cause of reconciliation, i.e. the return of the heretics to the Catholic Church. Such views gained ground steadily after 1648. In the 1670s, for example, the Austrian, Benedictine Ludwig Engel, urged that Catholics in the *Reich* should recognize the validity of the Peace of Westphalia, though regard it as subordinate to canon law.[36] By the middle of the eighteenth century the influential Würzburg canon lawyer, Johann Caspar Barthel, made a widespread impact with his acceptance of Imperial law. For the first time in Catholic circles, and in conscious opposition to Rome, Barthel recognized Imperial law as the equal of canon law and proceeded to elaborate arguments which justified toleration on the basis of natural law.[37] In these areas too, the legal framework of the Peace of Westphalia created a situation quite unlike that anywhere else in Western Europe. Imperial law and, later, aspirations to create State churches, reinforced pragmatic arguments for toleration (invoking peace and prosperity) which owed little to enlightened thinking and clearly contradicted the wishes of the curia.[38]

All these specific arguments developed, of course, within an intellectual context that was increasingly favourable to the idea of greater religious toleration. In the Protestant world, pietists and other more radical sectarians both promoted irenic views and opened up the first cracks in the edifice of orthodoxy.[39] Also influential was the reception in Germany of the ideas of Locke, Bayle, and later Voltaire and the development of systems of natural religion.[40] In Catholic Germany, movements such as Jansenism, Muratorian reform Catholicism and later Febronianism had a similar impact, reinforcing opposition to the papacy and strengthening the desire to accommodate, ultimately to re-unite, at least the three major Christian denominations within the

Reich.[41] The existence of indifference and natural religion amongst some educated elites was also significant. In Electoral Trier, for example, the circle of friends of Chancellor La Roche and his wife Sophie at the court of Ehren-breitstein in the 1770s created an atmosphere influenced by ideas of the young Goethe and Jacobi, which clearly influenced the reforms of the Elector Clemens Wenceslaus in the 1780s.[42] In both Catholic and, above all, Protestant areas more general *Aufklärung* attitudes generated amongst clergy and educated laity alike a sensitivity to the common ground between religions and a desire to put behind them the rigid and intolerant attitudes which had generated so much bloodshed in the past.[43]

By the middle of the eighteenth century, the issue of toleration had thus become one of the central themes of Enlightenment thinking. Two points should, however, be emphasized. Firstly, there is a clear distinction between most notions of toleration and religious indifference. In the context of the ideas outlined above, for example, Lessing's vision of a society in which all might be permitted, even encouraged, to strive in their different ways for the same truth appears as radically utopian, impossibly remote from contemporary reality. More in tune with that reality were those ideas which concentrated on the legal and political problems posed by tolerating three Christian denominations in the *Reich*. Secondly, it is important not to overestimate the impact of any of these ideas on real conditions. Early-modern toleration edicts in the German lands were almost invariably granted from above for largely pragmatic reasons. They cannot be seen as a response to popular demand from below or even from highly educated and enlightened intellectual elites.[44]

In some Protestant areas at least the incidence of such decrees pre-dates the development of the theory that justified them. The most prominent example is Brandenburg, where the Electors pursued a policy of toleration from the early seventeenth century.[45] The first general decree, the *Lästeredikt* of 1614, aimed purely and simply at ensuring the cohesion of a scatter of predominantly Lutheran territories after the conversion of the Elector Johann Sigismund to Calvinism in 1613. Later decrees were all aimed at specific groups – Catholics in territories acquired since 1648 (though not in Brandenburg until the reign of Frederick William I, 1713–40); Jews expelled from Vienna in 1670; the Huguenots expelled from France in 1685; or the Protestants driven out of Salzburg in 1732. The explicit intention of this *Peuplierungspolitik* was to encourage the settlement of communities which might contribute to prosperity and growth. In the eighteenth century, as Brandenburg-Prussia grew in power, a more pronounced political motive also emerged: the desire to pose as the antithesis of Habsburg, the guardian of all who might be threatened by either the political ambitions or the religion of the Imperial house.[46]

For all his oft proclaimed indifference to religion, even Frederick the Great did not deviate from the policies of his predecessors in these matters. He might flaunt his scorn for Christianity by referring to Christ as the 'hero' of a 'sect'; yet his *Generalreglement* for the Jews of 1750 was harshly repressive, and aptly described by Mirabeau as 'worthy of a cannibal'.[47] At the level of philosophical reflection, Frederick was clearly a rationalist agnostic. He was contemptuous of all religion, especially Catholicism, and once declared that adherents of all faiths, even Turks and heathens, should be free to seek salvation in their own way in his kingdom. All he demanded of his subjects, as he told Maria Theresa, was 'civil obedience and loyalty'.[48] There was, however, a difference between the freedom of expression that the king encouraged in non-political matters (including theology, as Kant emphasized) and the policies actually pursued in confessional matters. If the former was boldly innovative and rightly praised by many contemporaries, the latter followed a more traditional pattern.[49]

Until the end of Frederick's reign, religious toleration was for the most part still a political regime of licences or decrees granted by royal fiat to communities or groups. Like his immediate predecessors, the king behaved entirely in the tradition of Thomasian territorialism, asserting the authority of the State over religion. This was true even of the most significant area of confessional policy during his reign: the treatment of the Catholic population of the Silesian territories annexed 1740–2. In his philosophical writings, the king expressed nothing but contempt and scorn for the Catholic Church and the papacy. On the other hand that did not prevent him from authorizing and promoting the construction of a Catholic cathedral, the Hedwigskirche, in Berlin. Indeed, Hohenzollern tradition and political necessity dictated a distinctly prudent and calculating policy towards his new Catholic subjects. The Peace of Breslau (1742) confirmed the rights of the Catholic Church in Silesia, as set out in the Peace of Westphalia. The king subsequently failed in his attempts to substitute a Prussian general vicariate or bishopric for the existing bishopric of Breslau which spanned both Prussian and Habsburg Silesia after the partition. That did not, however, prevent him from promoting the reform of the Church on Prussian territory, often by exercising his royal right of veto on episcopal and papal decrees. The most spectacular example of that was his decision to forbid the publication in Prussia of Clement XIV's bull banning the Jesuits in 1773, a move motivated by the need to preserve the educational system. Political motives also led Frederick to issue a declaration guaranteeing the security of monastic institutions in October 1782 – a clear response to the outrage generated amongst Catholics by Joseph II's decree ordering the dissolution of many monasteries in November 1781.

These policies, similar to those pursued in territory gained from the first partition of Poland in 1772, were all designed to assert the territorial supremacy of the Prussian monarchy, to ensure peace in all parts of the kingdom and a workable administration of the whole, and to secure the loyalty of new, and initially reluctant, subjects. They went no further than they needed to; neither the privileges he granted nor the rights that many believed were implicit in them were codified during his reign. The first general Prussian toleration edict, which formally established the equal legal status of the three major Christian Churches, was published in 1788, two years after his death, while the principle of freedom of conscience was enshrined in the *Allgemeines Landrecht* of 1794. This removed the restrictive intent of the law of 1788 which had aimed to counteract the influence of the *Aufklärung* on Protestant theology.[50]

The kinds of pragmatic and political considerations which characterized the policies of the Brandenburg Electors also moved many other German territorial rulers. The counts of Wied, for example, tolerated sectarians of all kinds in order to promote their new town Neuwied after 1662.[51] The kings of Denmark did the same in Altona on the Elbe in an attempt to compete against the economically superior, yet intolerant, Lutheran free Imperial city of Hamburg.[52] Such obvious economic considerations were also often linked with more complex political motivations. The power to grant religious freedom, like the power to extend protection to individuals or groups generally, was, after all, one of the most significant attributes of *Landeshoheit*. Nothing demonstrated the authority of a prince more effectively than the exercise of that power in the face of opposition from subordinate town magistrates and the like. This seems, for example, to have been a significant factor in determining the policy of Count Friedrich Ernst of Solms-Laubach in imposing toleration on the magistrates of Laubach, and on the counts of Solms-Rödelsheim with whom he shared jurisdiction over the town, when they tried to expel radical sectarians in 1699 and 1700.[53] It is difficult to assess the degree of religious conviction which undoubtedly played a part in most, if not all, of these cases. Yet religious idealism alone was rarely a motor of change, and changes motivated exclusively by it were rarely lasting. That is illustrated by the case of the mixed Lutheran and Catholic duchy of Sulzbach (in the northern Oberpfalz, east of Nuremberg) under Christian August who, after his own conversion from Lutheranism to Catholicism in 1655–6, introduced religious freedom for all manner of sects, including the Jews, in preparation for an eventual union of all faiths. Here, the theological studies and personal piety of the duke created a unique island of religious freedom in a minuscule territory until his death in 1708. Thereafter, however, the irenic projects initiated by Christian August were neglected and many of the freedoms he had granted were restricted or withdrawn as his successors gave precedence to the Catholic religion of the court.[54]

Most of these localized toleration regimes shared three common characteristics. Firstly, their toleration edicts often went far beyond what was technically permitted by the Peace of Westphalia. Secondly, they were the work of territorial rulers exercising full use of their *jus reformandi*. The 'modernizing' impetus did not come from relatively free urban societies such as Hamburg. There, pragmatic economic arguments, often also informed by the latest philosophical wisdom, foundered repeatedly on the implacable opposition of the Orthodox Lutheran clergy in alliance with the guilds.[55] For most of the eighteenth century, Hamburg, like Augsburg and other Imperial cities, remained paralyzed by what had been decreed at Westphalia in 1648. Thirdly, the typical early-modern toleration edict showed little concern with the rights of the individual as such. The individual was only granted limited rights or privileges piecemeal, and generally by virtue of being a member of a community, if that was perceived to be in the economic or political interests of the State, which were paramount at all times.

IV

It was not until the 1780s that initiatives were launched to formulate more systematic toleration regimes. Joseph II led the way with his edict for Lutherans, Calvinists and Greek Orthodox Christians of 1781 and a groundbreaking edict for the Jews in 1782.[56] These measures reflected all the conventional pragmatic and economic arguments for religious toleration. The emphasis was not on religious freedom as such, but on strengthening the position of the state church by imposing control on other churches. That had implications for the Emperor's ability to assert his position (against Prussia) in the *Reich* and in Europe: even limited freedom was considered sufficient to dispel the reputation of intolerance and to secure the loyalty of otherwise possibly disaffected minorities. In the case of the Jews specifically, the aim was to control the activities of the various communities and to restrict the east–west migration which it was feared might bring unwelcome numbers to Vienna.[57] Furthermore, Joseph II's attitude to the Jews, typical of the *Aufklärung*, was at root informed not by the spirit of toleration but by the ambition of assimilation. Of course, Enlightenment ideas provided a following wind and helped shape the language of reform, but Joseph's desire to forge out of the heterogeneous Habsburg territories a unified state capable of standing up to Brandenburg-Prussia was fundamental. A unitary state required 'unitary' subjects.

Joseph II's example inspired many other rulers. Electoral Trier and Mainz, for example, both took steps to clarify the legal position of Protestants, particularly those with economic potential.[58] Remarkably, these new policies in Trier and Mainz also extended to the Jews: physiocratic ideas were employed to encourage them to engage in agriculture and other 'useful' and productive occupations as the first step towards removing the stigma attached to them and towards their integration into Christian society.[59] Similar toleration initiatives were undertaken in other states at this time.[60] By 1785 even the Senate of Hamburg was able persuade its citizens to emulate the example of the Holy Roman Emperor and grant the right of private worship to Calvinists and Catholics, though not to the Jews.[61]

These initiatives were more systematic largely because they applied to several groups simultaneously. They were subsequently extended and subsumed within the legal codes which began to appear from the last decade of the eighteenth century. In Prussia, for example, which did not follow the example of Joseph II's toleration edicts, the legal code commissioned in 1780 brought into being a systematic toleration system for all but the Jews when it was published as the *Allgemeines Landrecht* in 1794.[62] That legal code safeguarded the needs of the State on the one hand and guaranteed the rights of the individual on the other. The State was obliged to grant freedom of religion and conscience to all. At the same time, however, it retained the right to privilege the 'state' religion and to control other religious societies and to ensure that their teachings did not subvert the State. The abandonment of the principle of the closed confessional state was only partial: other Christian denominations were licensed as 'societies', free associations of like-minded subjects, exercising their individual freedom of conscience privately within the constraints defined by the State.

These reforms represented a radical extension of religious toleration in many areas. Yet the limitations remained severe. In most smaller territories the principle of licensing particular groups prevailed. Many groups, including the Jews in most areas, were excluded. Furthermore, even those included were restricted to specified forms of private worship and often still limited in their civil and legal rights. In Austria, for example, those who were granted limited toleration in 1781 and 1782 were only given full legal and civil rights in 1811. In Prussia the position of the Jews was only regulated in 1812.[63]

V

The Enlightened absolutist legislation of the 1780s and 1790s remained incomplete and its implications were never fully tested for it was overtaken by events. The whole situation in the German territories was transformed during the period of upheaval which followed the French revolutionary wars: the secularization of the *Reich* in 1803–4, followed by its dissolution in 1806, the territorial reorganization of the Confederation of the Rhine, all of which was reflected in the Vienna Settlement of 1815. The French constitution of 1791 had laid down unqualified freedom of conscience and belief for all (including the Jews) as a fundamental right of all free citizens and proclaimed the indifference of the State to all religion.[64] After 1800 this became the foundation of French government in all occupied German territories (for example, the left bank of the Rhine and the Hanseatic cities). It was also accepted as the guiding rule in all German states which came within the French sphere of influence, and it also influenced the reforms in states such as Prussia and Austria outside that sphere.[65]

On the other hand, the consequences for the period after 1815 were distinctly uneven. The constitution of the German Confederation proclaimed the equality of all Christians as a fundamental principle and envisaged the formulation of an equivalent principle for the Jews at some future date. The rights of Christians were to be secured in constitutions, but not all states implemented constitutions in the following years, and the question of the rights of the Jews was shelved almost everywhere. Within the rather open framework created by the Act of Confederation, the various states pursued widely different policies. Some rescinded legislation introduced in the French period and reverted to the principles laid down in the Peace of Westphalia. Others adapted French or French-inspired legislation. Only those states which inherited territory from former ecclesiastical principalities were obliged to guarantee full confessional parity in those areas, though not necessarily elsewhere in their states.

In general, it is striking that the most 'progressive' states were those which gained territory as a result of the secularization process after 1803, or which inherited substantial territories from the French empire.[66] Bavaria, for example, became a multi-confessional state as a result of the acquisition of Protestant lands in Franconia and the Palatinate, while Württemberg acquired a significant Catholic population: each state passed toleration decrees in 1803 which granted both freedom of worship and equal political rights to all Christians. Likewise, Prussia emerged from the 1815 settlement with substantial territories inherited from the French empire in the Catholic Rhineland. Even more extreme was the case of the duchy of Nassau which, between 1806 and 1815, absorbed no less than twenty-three previously independent entities, resulting by 1816 in a population composed of 160,000 Protestants and 125,000 Catholics.[67] Here, extending religious toleration was fundamental to the construction of a new unitary administration for the duchy and to the task of gaining the loyalty of new subjects. The creation of the Nassau union (of the Lutheran and Calvinist Churches) in 1817 and the negotiations to establish a single Nassau bishopric in Limburg (finally achieved in 1827) were both part of a process of state building founded on the parity principle, which began in the school system with mixed Protestant and Catholic school boards, joint use of schools and the introduction of a common curriculum of religious instruction. In Nassau, as elsewhere, 'modernization' and greater toleration was the by-product of reconstruction and integration, driven by the needs of the State rather than by theological considerations or by recognition of the rights of man.[68] By contrast, some predominantly north German territories, where boundaries did not change and there was consequently no need for new legislation, behaved like closed confessional states until the twentieth century: Mecklenburg-Schwerin only granted the right of public worship to Catholics in 1903; the free city of Lübeck followed suit a year later.[69] The principles laid down by the Peace of Westphalia proved to be nothing if not durable.

VI

The nineteenth-century history of religious toleration in the context of the relationship between Church and State and the struggle for Jewish emancipation are beyond the scope of this chapter. However, they help provide a perspective on the degree of toleration which prevailed in the period of the Holy Roman Empire. To the end of the *Reich* the situation remained dominated by the limited toleration defined by the Peace of Westphalia, limited both in the degree of freedom allowed and in the number of groups to which it was extended. In this sense, religious toleration in the Holy Roman Empire was the product of the need to resolve a political problem: to facilitate co-existence between the estates of the *Reich* and to ensure the survival of the system as a whole. It was not brought about by the application of any abstract or idealistic principle, but arose simply out of the need to maintain some form of community between Catholics, Lutherans and Calvinists.

The limits set out in the Peace of Westphalia were extended in some states for pragmatic reasons, notably by Austria and Prussia, but also in many smaller territories where sectarians or Jews were tolerated. Yet even the most systematic reforms of enlightened absolutism in the 1780s and 1790s rested on somewhat contradictory theoretical foundations: on the one hand a recognition of the individual right to freedom of conscience and belief; on the other hand an insistence on the authority of the state over religious organizations. This contradiction was not fully resolved in favour of the rights of the individual until the twentieth century. Indeed, even today the general social acceptance of the legal principles of toleration is far from complete.

At the end of the eighteenth century the ideal of a tolerant society still remained remote. Hegel was not alone in identifying the continuing link between Church and State, between religious belief and civil rights, as the core of the problem. He was, however, misleading when he claimed that the Holy Roman Empire was an intolerant society. After all, the evidence for a marked decline in persecution is clear. The views of two other leading thinkers of the time indicate deeper reasons for dissatisfaction and indeed suggest a sense of unease about any system of toleration that needs to be enshrined in, and enforced by, law. In one of his *Maximen und Reflexionen*, Goethe wrote that 'Toleration should really only be a transitory attitude; it must lead to recognition. To tolerate is to insult.'[70] Some years earlier,

Schiller had implied a similar indictment of his own times when he wrote of his vision of a new age when 'toleration has become superfluous'.[71] Such aspirations have lost none of their appeal in the last 200 years. If Schiller were to revisit the world in the last years of the twentieth century, one suspects that he might find the distance from that new age not much diminished.

Notes

1 *Hegel's Political Writings*, trans. T.M. Knox, Oxford, 1964: 189–95.

2 On Lessing's views on toleration, see H. Schultze, *Lessings Toleranzbegriff. Eine theologische Studie*, Forschungen zur systematischen und ökumenischen Theologie, vol. 20, Göttingen, 1969: esp. 42–7. For the debate generally, see J. Whaley, 'Pouvoir sauver les apparences: The Theory and Practice of Tolerance in Eighteenth-Century Germany', *British Journal for Eighteenth-Century Studies*, XIII, 1990: 1–16; H. Schultze, 'Toleranz für Europa. Theologische und philosophische Einsichten nach der Aufhebung des Edikts von Nantes', in M. Stolpe and F. Winter (eds), *Wege und Grenzen der Toleranz. Edikt von Potsdam 1685–1985*, Berlin, 1987: 112–30.

3 See G. Schmidt, *Der Dreissigjährige Krieg*, Munich, 1995: 7–8 and 94–8; C. Dipper, *Deutsche Geschichte 1648–1789*, Frankfurt a. M., 1991: 252–62.

4 J. Whaley, *Religious Toleration and Social Change in Hamburg, 1529–1819*, Cambridge, 1985: 4–6.

5 C.P. Hartmann, 'Bereits erprobt: Ein Mitteleuropa der Regionen', *Das Parlament*, No. 49–50, 3/10 December, 1993: 21; Wolf Gruner, *Die deutsche Frage in Europa 1800 bis 1990*, Munich and Zurich, 1993: 82–7.

6 M. Walzer, *On Toleration*, New Haven and London, 1997: 8–36, 52–82 and 92.

7 *Ibid.*: 23–4.

8 See Whaley, *Religious Toleration*: 4–6; W. Grossmann, 'Religious Toleration in Germany, 1648–1750', *Studies on Voltaire and the Eighteenth Century*, CCI, 1982: 115–41; I.W. Frank, 'Einleitung', in *idem* (ed.), *Toleranz am Mittelrhein*, Quellen und Abhandlungen zur Mittelrheinischen Kirchengeschichte, vol. 50, Mainz, 1984: 1–10; K.O. v. Aretin, *Das Alte Reich 1648–1806*, 3 vols, Stuttgart, 1993–7: i, 44–56.

9 W. Schulze, *Deutsche Geschichte im 16. Jahrhundert, 1550–1618*, Frankfurt a. M., 1987: 161–93 and 258–64. For the origins of French politique ideology, see Q. Skinner, *The Foundations of Modern Political Thought, vol. 2: The Age of Reformation*, Cambridge, 1978: 249–54.

10 v. Aretin, *Das Alte Reich*: i, 316–38.

11 *Ibid.*; see also H. Raab, 'Toleranz im Kur- und Erzstift Trier', in Frank, *Toleranz am Mittelrhein*: 21–43, esp. 29–32.

12 *Ibid.*: 345; K.O. v. Aretin, *Das Reich. Friedensordnung und europäisches Gleichgewicht 1648–1806*, Stuttgart, 1986: 409–19; v. Aretin, *Das Alte Reich*: ii, 391–400; H. Raab, 'Kirchliche Reunionsversuche', in H. Jedin (ed.), *Handbuch der Kirchengeschichte*, vol. 5, Freiburg, Basel and Vienna, 1970: 554–70.

13 K.H. Welker, *Rechtsgeschichte als Rechtspolitik. Justus Möser als Jurist und Staatsmann*, 2 vols, Osnabrück, 1996: ii, 341–50.

14 For the following, see v. Aretin, *Das Alte Reich*: i, 44–8; W. Grossmann, 'Toleration – *exercitium religionis privatum*', *Journal of the History of Ideas*, XL, 1979: 129–34; U. Scheuner, 'Die Auswanderungsfreiheit in der Verfassungsgeschichte und im Verfassungsrecht Deutschlands', in *Festschrift Richard Thoma zum 75. Geburtstag am 19. xii. 1949. Dargebracht von Freunden, Schülern und Fachgenossen*, Tübingen, 1950: 199–224.

15 H. Conrad, *Deutsche Rechtsgeschichte* vol. II, *Neuzeit bis 1806*, Karlsruhe, 1966: 177. For a similar view held by J. Möser, see Welker, *Rechtsgeschichte als Rechtspolitik*: i, and 350–5; J.B. Knudsen, *Justus Möser and the German Enlightenment*, Cambridge, 1986: 89–93. Möser envisaged the possibility of extending toleration on a juridical as opposed to a philosophical basis, provided that new groups were willing to conform to the principle which informed the legal framework of the Peace of Westphalia.

16 Conrad, *Rechtsgeschichte*: 223–6; F. Battenberg, *Das europäische Zeitalter der Juden*, 2 vols, Darmstadt, 1990: i and 101–11.

17 P. Warmbrunn, *Zwei Konfessionen in einer Stadt. Das Zusammenleben von Katholiken und Protestanten in den paritätischen Reichsstädten Augsburg, Biberach, Ravensburg und Dinkelsbühl von 1548 bis 1648*, Veröffentlichungen des Instituts für Europäische Geschichte Mainz vol. 111, Wiesbaden, 1983; B. Roeck, *Eine Stadt in Krieg und Frieden. Studien zur Geschichte der Reichsstadt Augsburg zwischen Kalenderstreit und Parität*, Schriftenreihe der Historischen Kommission bei der Bayerischen Akademie der Wissenschaften vol. 37, Göttingen, 1989: 844–68 and 949–74; E. François, *Die unsichtbare Grenze. Protestanten und Katholiken in Augsburg*, Abhandlungen zur Geschichte der Stadt Augsburg, Sigmaringen, 1991.

18 H. Nottarp, 'Zur *communicatio in sacris cum haereticis*. Deutsche Rechtszustände im 17. und 18. Jahrhundert', in *idem, Aus Rechtsgeschichte und Kirchenrecht. Gesammelte Abhandlungen*, ed. F. Merzbacher, Cologne and Graz, 1967: 424–46, esp. 433. The complex and uneven arrangements at the parish level are indicated by Knudsen, *Justus Möser*: 89–93 and Welker, *Rechtsgeschichte als Rechtspolitik*: ii and 922–8.

19 *Ibid.*: 429–30.

20 *Ibid.*: 430–2. For an account of the friction which this situation generated in Wetzlar, see H.-W. Hahn, *Altständisches Bürgertum zwischen Beharrung und Wandel. Wetzlar, 1689–1870*, Stadt und Bürgertum vol. 2, Munich, 1991: 91–8.

21 Welker, *Rechtsgeschichte als Rechtspolitik*: i and 250. The term 'Simultaneum' was originally used in the sixteenth century to denote the authorization of two or more religious communities in the same territory; after 1648 it was restricted to the right of two or more congregations of differing faiths to use the same ecclesiastical building: see *The Oxford Dictionary of the Christian Church*, ed. F.L. Cross and E.A. Livingstone, 2nd edn, Oxford, 1974: 1278.

22 François, *Die unsichtbare Grenze*: 230; Nottarp, '*communicatio in sacris cum haereticis*': 439–46.

23 v. Aretin, *Das Alte Reich*: i and 54–6.

24 M. Walker, *The Salzburg Transaction. Expulsion and Redemption in Eighteenth-Century Germany*, Ithaca and London, 1992; W.R. Ward, *The Protestant Evangelical Awakening*, Cambridge, 1992: 93–115.

25 v. Aretin, *Das Alte Reich*: ii and 263–95.

26 *Ibid.*: i and 54.

27 *Ibid.* See also G. Haug-Moritz, *Württembergischer Ständekonflikt und deutscher Dualismus. Ein Beitrag zur Geschichte des Reichsverbands in der Mitte des 18. Jahrhunderts*, Veröffentlichungen der Kommission für geschichtliche Landeskunde in Baden-Württemberg, Series B, vol. CXXII, Stuttgart, 1992: 43–121 and passim.

28 P.F. Barton, 'Der lange Weg zur Toleranz', in *idem* (ed.), *Im Lichte der Toleranz. Aufsätze zur Toleranzgesetzgebung des 18. Jahrhunderts in den Reichen Joseph II., ihren Voraussetzungen und ihren Folgen. Eine Festschrift*, Studien und Texte zur Kirchengeschichte und Geschichte, Second series vol. IX, Vienna, 1981: 11–32, esp. 22.

29 François, *Unsichtbare Grenze*: 21; Warmbrunn, *Zwei Konfessionen*: 404; v. Aretin, *Das Alte Reich*: i and 49–50.

30 Frank, 'Einleitung': 9–10.

31 Grossmann, 'Religious Toleration': 116–17.

32 H. Klenner, 'Toleranzideen im siebzehnten Jahrhundert', in Stolpe and Winter (eds), *Wege und Grenzen der Toleranz*: 80–93, esp. 86–9; Grossmann, 'Religious Toleration': 132–4.

33 Schultze, 'Toleranz für Europa': 122–4; Grossmann, 'Religious Toleration': 133–5.

34 For similar views, expressed in a Leipzig legal dissertation by G.E. Lessing's grandfather in 1669, see T. Lessing, *De Religionum Tolerantia. Über die Duldung der Religionen*, ed. G. Gawlick and W. Milde, *Kleine Schriften zur Aufklärung*, II, Wolfenbüttel and Göttingen, 1991.

35 H. Mathy, 'Toleranz im Kur- und Erzstift Mainz', in Frank (ed.), *Toleranz am Mittelrhein*: 45–77, esp. 48–9.

36 K. Schwarz, 'Die Toleranz im Religionsrecht des Heiligen Römischen Reiches Deutscher Nation, in Brandenburg-Preußen und in Österreich', in Stolpe and Winter (eds), *Wege und Grenzen der Toleranz*: 94–111, esp. 105.

37 *Ibid.*: 105–6; Raab, 'Toleranz im Kur- und Erzstift Trier': 38–9; K. Schreiner, 'Toleranz', in *Geschichtliche Grundbegriffe. Historisches Lexikon zur politisch-sozialen Sprache in Deutschland*, ed. O. Brunner, W. Conze and R. Koselleck, 7 vols, Stuttgart, 1972–92: vii and 445–605, esp. 553–64.

38 Jedin, *Handbuch der Kirchengeschichte*: v, 123 and 511–14.

39 Grossmann, 'Religious Toleration': 126–30; see also Ward, *Protestant Evangelical Awakening*: 116–240.

40 C. Link, 'Toleranz im deutschen Staatsrecht der Neuzeit', in P.F. Barton (ed.), *Im Zeichen der Toleranz. Aufsätze zur Toleranzgesetzgebung des 18. Jahrhunderts in den Reichen Joseph II., ihren Voraussetzungen und ihren Folgen. Eine Festschrift*, Studien und Texte zur Kirchengeschichte und Geschichte, Second series vol. VIII, Vienna, 1981: 17–38.

41 v. Aretin, *Das Reich*: 403–33.

42 Raab, 'Toleranz im Kur- und Erzstift Trier': 35–8.

43 See, for example, the evidence cited by M. Maurer, *Die Biographie des Bürgers. Lebensformen und Denkweisen in der formativen Phase des deutschen Bürgertums (1680–1815)*, Veröffentlichungen des Max-Planck-Instituts für Geschichte vol. CXXVII, Göttingen, 1996: 212–25.

44 Barton, 'Der lange Weg zur Toleranz': 13–15.

45 H. Rudolph, 'Öffentliche Religion und Toleranz. Zur Parallelität preußischer Religionspolitik und josephinischer Reform im Lichte der Aufklärung', in Barton (ed.), *Im Zeichen der Toleranz*: 221–49; Schwarz, 'Toleranz im Religionsrecht des Heiligen Römischen Reichs': 99–105.

46 Rudolph, 'Öffentliche Religion und Toleranz': 227–31.

47 J.H. Schoeps, 'Aufklärung, Judentum und Emanzipation', *Wolfenbütteler Studien zur Aufklärung*, IV, 1977: 75–102, esp. 79; Battenberg, *Das europäische Zeitalter der Juden*: ii and 65–7.

48 Quoted by T.C.W. Blanning, 'Frederick the Great and German Culture', in R. Oresko, G.C. Gibbs, H.M. Scott (eds), *Royal and Republican Sovereignty in Early Modern Europe. Essays in memory of Ragnild Hatton*, Cambridge, 1997: 527–55, at 543.

49 *Ibid*.: 544–7. Blanning, however, places religious toleration on a par with the encouragement of intellectual freedom in non-political matters, which underestimates the element of continuity between Frederick and his predecessors in confessional policy.

50 A. Schindling, 'Friedrichs des Großen Toleranz und seine katholischen Untertanen', in P. Baumgart (ed.), *Kontinuität und Wandel. Schlesien zwischen Österreich und Preußen*, Sigmaringen, 1990: 257–72; H. Conrad, 'Religionsbann, Toleranz und Parität am Ende des alten Reiches', *Römische Quartalschrift*, LVI, 1961: 167–99, esp. 189–96.

51 W. Grossmann, 'Neuwied-am-Rhein: Town Growth and Religious Toleration. A Case Study', *Diogenes*, CX, 1980: 20–43; *idem*, 'Religious Toleration': 123–4.

52 Whaley, *Religious Toleration*: 35–6.

53 B. Hoffmann, *Radikalpietismus um 1700. Der Streit um das Recht auf eine neue Gesellschaft*, Frankfurt a. M., 1996: 56–82 and 186. The counts of Solms-Rödelsheim, cousins of Count Friedrich Ernst, had inherited one-fifth of the rights over Laubach, which they lost no opportunity to assert, both in person and by means of their officials. Their support for the hard line of the magistrates and guilds against the sectarians was a typical example of their strategy.

54 V. Wappmann, *Durchbruch zur Toleranz. Die Religionspolitik des Pfalzgrafen August von Sulzbach 1622–1708*, Einzelarbeiten aus der Kirchengeschichte Bayerns, vol. LXIX, Neustadt a.d. Aisch, 1995.

55 Whaley, *Religious Toleration*: 164–8.

56 See the numerous contributions in Barton (ed.), *Im Lichte der Toleranz* and Barton (ed.), *Im Zeichen der Toleranz*.

57 J. Karniel, 'Die Toleranzpolitik Kaiser Josephs II.', in W. Grab (ed.), *Deutsche Aufklärung und Judenemanzipation*, Jahrbuch des Instituts für Deutsche Geschichte Supplement 3, Tel-Aviv, 1980: 155–77.

58 Raab, 'Toleranz im Kur- und Erzstift Trier': 35–43; Mathy, 'Toleranz im Kur- und Erzstift Mainz': 59–77.

59 Battenberg, *Das europäische Zeitalter der Juden*: ii and 63–5.

60 See the survey in Schreiner, 'Toleranz': 506–9 and 537–47.

61 Whaley, *Religious Toleration*: 164–8.

62 Rudolph, 'Öffentliche Religion und Toleranz': 231–49; Conrad, 'Religionsbann, Toleranz und Parität': 167–99.

63 *Ibid*.: 189–99.

64 *Ibid*.: 196–7.

65 Frank, 'Einleitung': 3–10. See also W. Demel, *Vom aufgeklärten Reformstaat zum bürokratischen Staatsabsolutismus*, Enzyklopädie deutscher Geschichte, vol. XXIII, Munich, 1993.

66 W.D. Gruner, 'Deutschland zwischen Revolution, Reform und Restauration 1770–1830', *Tijdschrift voor Geschiednis*, CII, 1989: 368–400, esp. 394; G. Pfeiffer, 'Die Umwandlung Bayerns in einen paritätischen Staat', in *Bayern: Stadt und Kirche, Land und Reich*, Munich, 1962: 35–109.

67 K. Schatz, 'Toleranz im Fürstentum Nassau', in Frank (ed.), *Toleranz am Mittelrhein*: 79–94.

68 *Ibid.*; see also W. Jäger, 'Der Strukturwandel des Staates und die Kirchen in Nassau zwischen Revolution und Restauration', in K.O. v. Aretin and K. Härter (eds), *Revolution und konservatives Beharren. Das Alte Reich und die Französische Revolution*, Mainz, 1990: 175–95.

69 Frank, 'Einleitung': 7.

70 Quoted by Schultze, *Lessings Toleranzbegriff*: 11.

71 Quoted by Schreiner, 'Toleranz': 601–2.

10. Enlightenment in the Habsburg Monarchy: History of a Belated and Short-Lived Phenomenon

Karl Vocelka

Traditionally, Austrian historiography defines the reign of Maria Theresa, Joseph II and Leopold II (1740–92) as the period of Enlightened Absolutism, whereas the period before 1740, under the rule of Charles VI, could be defined as late Baroque and was characterized by a Counter-Reformist atmosphere. Although one can identify a short-lived influence of enlightened ideas before 1740, the spread of enlightened ideas remained an elitist phenomenon. To understand the intellectual situation in the Habsburg Monarchy we have to glance back briefly at the preceding two centuries. In the sixteenth century, the ideas of Luther's Reformation reached the Habsburg Monarchy very quickly and established themselves firmly. The Reformation – sometimes referred to as the first wave of rationalism in Europe – was adopted, above all, by aristocrats who used it as a weapon against centralism and the incipient absolutism of the Catholic Habsburg dynasty, but it was also taken up by the citizens in the major cities. As the peasant population generally followed the religion of their manorial lords – an Austrian version of the *cuius regio, eius religio* principle from the religious peace of Augsburg in 1555 – a great part of the population converted to Protestantism in two waves (one in the 1520s and a second one in the 1560s). From the very beginning, the Habsburg rulers did their best to arrest the growing trend toward Protestantism, and somewhat later – in the middle of the sixteenth century – even to reverse the situation. Nonetheless we can estimate that in 1600 approximately 70 per cent of the population in Eastern Austria and up to 90 per cent of the Bohemian inhabitants were no longer Catholics. The majority of them were Lutherans, but there were also some Calvinists and in Bohemia some remnants of the Hussite movement. The situation in Hungary was more complicated as Hungary was divided into three parts at that time and only the small western portion was ruled by the Habsburgs. Lutherans and Calvinists dominated in Hungary as a whole and could never be converted and disciplined as they were in Bohemia and Austria. The reasons for this difference are manifold, extraordinarily complicated and include the presence of the Turkish menace in Hungary.

In the late sixteenth century, and more successfully in the early seventeenth century, the Habsburgs implemented and reinforced Counter-Reformist measures in their territories. The political and religious tensions culminated in the outbreak of the Thirty Years War, but the victory of the Catholic Emperor Ferdinand II in the Battle of the White Mountain in 1620 marked a turning point. The defeat of the Protestant Bohemian estates opened the way for the strict and often brutal recatholicization of Bohemia, as it was later practised in the Austrian Hereditary Countries, and to an absolutist rule of the Habsburg dynasty. In this period there was no such thing as religious toleration in the Habsburg monarchy.[1]

The complete triumph of the Counter-Reformation in the slowly developing Baroque culture meant – in highly simplified terms – the suppression of all religions except Catholicism, less emphasis on books and reading and more on the fine arts and music. Virtually all of the various orders of the Catholic Church settled in the Habsburg Monarchy, the most important being the Jesuits who controlled most of the educational system. Nearly all the universities in the Habsburg-ruled countries were in the hands of the Jesuits who shared their power with the Piarist order in the preparatory school system.[2]

Both the educational system (which did not share the Protestant emphasis on reading) and the general perception of the world at the time contributed significantly to the belated and cautious reception of the ideas of the Enlightenment. However, political animosities also played an enormous role in diminishing the influence of the Enlightenment in Austria. Most of the philosophers advocating the modern ideas were French, but France had been in permanent conflict and frequent war with the Habsburgs since the late Middle Ages. This is especially noticeable in the late seventeenth century during the reign of Leopold I when French – at that time the *lingua franca* of the European elite – was outlawed at the court of Vienna in favour of Italian or Spanish as a second language in addition to Latin.

The education of the Habsburg princes – as of many aristocrats – lay in the hands of clergymen and therefore most often in the hands of Jesuits. One can easily imagine that this did not enhance the probability that the texts of the enlightened philosophers would become a focal point within the educational programme. But Joseph I's education was different. He was not raised by Jesuits, but rather influenced by secular thought and imperial and enlightenment ideas.[3]

When Leopold died in 1705, Joseph began his rule in a new, more efficient, progressive and modern style, but unfortunately he died unexpectedly six years later. Exhausted by hunting animals in the forests and pursuing women at the court, he was an easy victim of smallpox. His brother Charles – struggling for the Spanish succession and titling himself King of Spain, though not really in control of that country – was forced to renounce Spain in order to succeed his brother in the hereditary countries. The Spanish realm was lost and in the Habsburg Monarchy the cultural winds shifted – Charles's rule was very Catholic, very Baroque and far removed from any modern ideas.

However, Joseph I was not the only person in the Habsburg Monarchy influenced by enlightened philosophy. Another figure who was probably as important as the emperor himself was Prince Eugene of Savoy, the famous commander-in-chief of the Imperial army. Apart from Prince Eugene, there were also other aristocrats interested in the ideas of Enlightenment, but they constituted an infinitely small minority and carried practically no influence.

When the Habsburg male branch of the family died out with Charles VI in 1740, his elder daughter Maria Theresa succeeded him. The Enlightenment in Austria has been discussed until now almost solely in the context of the reforms of Maria Theresa and her sons, without asking whether there was enough enlightened public to successfully carry out those reforms.[4] In accordance with the normal discourse of Austrian historiography I shall first discuss the enlightened reforms put into effect by the Habsburg rulers and then attempt to analyse how these reforms and the Enlightenment in general affected the various groups in society. An analysis of the socio-intellectual situation will help us understand why the reforms were relatively unsuccessful.

In assessing Maria Theresa's rule, one can take two different points of view. On the one hand she was a very Baroque ruler: her lifestyle was pious and followed the family traditions. In a famous letter to Joseph II she warned him against reading the books of the French philosophers whose ideas opposed the Catholic dogmas.[5] On the other hand, in her political activities – especially the reforms that she instigated immediately after the end of the War of Succession – modernization is apparent and the influence of enlightened ideas is clearly visible. In spite of the fact that the reforms were only very partially her own doing – numerous advisors were instrumental in creating and implementing the reforms – her position as 'mother of the country' (reflecting the sixteen children she bore) helped to characterize and uphold her legend as a *good* female ruler.

Before analysing the reforms, we need to take a look at Maria Theresa's main advisors, first and foremost her husband, Francis Stephen of Lorraine. Although he is sometimes treated by historians as an unimportant Prince Consort in the shadow of his wife, his role was far more significant than this stereotype suggests. He was raised in Lorraine and only later moved to Vienna, remaining French in many aspects for his entire life. Francis Stephen travelled extensively. On a trip to the Netherlands in 1731–2 he was accepted into a masonic lodge, which introduced him not only to the ideas of Enlightenment but also to the progressive elite. Francis Stephen's economic abilities are well known, most of the private fortune of the Habsburg family was

accumulated by him. But apart from this his most important talent was his
ability to recognize able advisors and to introduce and recommend them to
his wife, above all Friedrich Wilhelm von Haugwitz who coined the first
phase of the reforms, Wenzel Anton Kaunitz-Rietberg who later replaced him
and Gerard van Swieten, whose educational reforms transformed the Habsburg Monarchy intellectually. In addition to these prominent reformers many
other aristocrats in key political positions were influenced by enlightened
ideas and were often members of masonic lodges.[6]

Although the reforms defined by historians as 'Reforms of Enlightened
Absolutism' encompassed many different trends during Maria Theresa's forty
years of rule, they took place in four basic areas:

1. Centralization of administration to make it more effective, particularly
   with regard to taxation.
2. Economic and social measures.
3. Judicial reforms.
4. Educational reforms.

The general interpretation of Maria Theresa's rule considers all these
reforms to be 'enlightened', a view with which I would disagree. The creation
of an intermediate level of administration, the so-called *Kreisämter*, had, for
instance, a completely different goal: to reduce the power of the local aristocrats. These district offices (*Kreisämter*) were to report on the economic,
demographic and political situation in the district, which provided the central
administration with more information regarding measures of mercantilism
and in turn helped to control the local aristocracy. The district offices also
served as a court of appeal for serfs found guilty by the courts of law of their
manorial lords. Many other reforms – above all the new direct taxation
system which excluded the estates from any influence on the collection of
taxes – can also be interpreted as absolutist rather than enlightened measures.[7]
The same applies to the second group of measures concerning the economic
and social situation of the population, especially the discussion regarding the
abolishment of serfdom in Bohemia which was finally put into practice under
Joseph II. Particularly important was the attempt to unify the legal and judicial situation in the monarchy which was composed of various kingdoms,
duchies and other territories, each of which had retained their own historical
laws.

One fact, which is still included in all Austrian schoolbooks, supposedly
proves the enlightened rule of Maria Theresa: the abolition of torture in 1776.
What is usually not mentioned, however, is that the original law regulating
torture, the *Constitutio Criminalis Maria Theresiana* published by Maria
Theresa in 1769, not only carefully described and defined the use of torture;
it was a very old-fashioned book of laws which still contained crimes such

as witchcraft and 'leze-majesty'. The abolition of torture in 1776 was finally attained only under the influence of Joseph II and Joseph von Sonnenfels, one of the most important enlightened figures at the court in this period.

Finally, we need to discuss the reforms in the field of education, of central importance to the majority of the enlightened philosophers. As opposed to other areas, these reforms were really founded on Enlightenment ideas, although one might again argue that the reforms of the Habsburg Monarchy's educational system also met the needs of an absolutist state, as an increasingly sophisticated and complicated society and economy required new administrators, officers, diplomats and specialists in virtually every area.

Until this time some primary schools had existed, but they were organized by villages, towns and cities or run by the Catholic Church with its different orders and monasteries. The novelty consisted in the fact that Maria Theresa introduced a general, compulsory and secular network of primary schools, at least theoretically every child now had to be educated. Although the basic idea was certainly good, it did not succeed in all respects. If we take a look at the statistics of the nineteenth century we can see how inefficient and unsatisfactory this general education remained. In some parts of the country over 100 years after Maria Theresa's reforms more than half of the population was still illiterate.[8]

In matters of religious tolerance – which should be the real proof of the enlightened attitude of a state administration – there was very little progress during Maria Theresa's rule. Although she was obviously influenced by Jansenist ideas (Jansenism is a theology based on Augustine and in many aspects close to Protestantism, which stressed the intrinsic piety more than Baroque representation),[9] and therefore had a different approach to religious piety than her predecessors, Maria Theresa still was of the opinion that all of her subjects should believe in the only saving church – the Roman Catholic Church. All others were – in her opinion – '*in dem unglücklichen Religionsirrthum verfallene Untertanen*' (subjects addicted to the unfortunate heterodoxy).[10] Converts to Catholicism continued even during her period of reign to receive 'pensions' – one could say that 'religious belief' could be bought by the government.

Although the Counter-Reformation had been highly successful in the Austrian hereditary countries, nevertheless some Protestants had been able to survive secretly in remote valleys of the Alps. Maria Theresa did not exile them to Germany, as the Archbishop of Salzburg had done several years before, but resettled them in Hungary, which was already religiously diverse and where a few more Protestants would make no difference. The ambiguity of enlightened reforms is obvious in these measures. She could not tolerate non-Catholics in the hereditary countries, but on the other hand practical demographic considerations prevented her from exiling them from the Habsburg Monarchy. Economic interests here[11] were as important as religious ideas. Only the threat of her son Joseph abdicating in 1777 as Emperor and co-ruler of the monarchy prevented the expulsion of Moravian Protestants. Maria Theresa finally had to grant them, at least, a sort of toleration by allowing private worship.[12]

Some measures – including the reduction of the influence of the Jesuits and other religious orders or raising the age of admittance into a monastery to twenty-four – influenced indirectly the religious situation in the monarchy.[13] However, the real attacks against the dominant position of the Catholic Church in the Habsburg Monarchy only began under Joseph II. With the exception of Hungary, where the Counter-Reformation was not successful, the Habsburg Monarchy under Maria Theresa consisted of an empire in which only the Catholic religion was allowed.

Maria Theresa paid particular interest to the question of the Jews who, in spite of a certain degree of tolerance, had suffered frequent pogroms and two very brutal waves of expulsion in Vienna, one in the Middle Ages and another in 1670. Maria Theresa herself was highly prejudiced against the Jews. She wrote: '*Ich kenne keine ärgere Pest für den Staat als diese Nation, welche Betrug, Wucher und Geldvertragen, Leut in Bettelstand zu bringen, alle üble Handlungen ausüben, die ein anderer ehrlicher Mann verabscheuete*' (I do not know of a worse plague for the country than this nation, which practises fraud, usury and money business, turns people into beggars and commits all kinds of evil deeds which any honest man would abhor).[14] Her Patent for the Jews in 1764 still contained old discriminations: only the house-father was allowed to marry whereas all others had to remain single, four times a year all persons living in a Jewish household had to be registered, they were not allowed to live in the suburbs of Vienna, men had to be bearded (a relict of the old badges and special clothing for Jews), they were required to vacate the street when a priest with the Holy wafer passed by and they were not allowed to leave their houses on Sunday before noon. There were, however, parts of the monarchy – such as Triest, Gorizia or Hohenems in Vorarlberg – where the Jews fared better. The restrictions under which Jews were 'tolerated' were economic: they had to prove that they had sufficient wealth, they were to be 'useful' to society by founding factories and they were required to pay the so-called '*Toleranzgeld*' (money of toleration) every year. In 1744, Maria Theresa even ordered the expulsion of the Bohemian Jews, although the order was revoked at the last minute.[15] One example of Maria Theresa's anti-Jewish sentiment was the commission sent to Galicia-Lodomeria after the country was created from the spoils of the first Polish partition in 1772. The commission, composed of anti-Semites selected personally by Maria Theresa, was instructed to give mandatory second names to all Jews. Many of the typical Galician Jewish names such as 'Gesäßgezwitscher' still convey a story of religious intolerance and humiliation.

Taken as a whole the reforms of Maria Theresa appear more absolutist and centralist than enlightened, even if one must admit that the influence of enlightened ideas is visible to a certain degree. The entire situation appears very different if we analyse Joseph's reforms, often called Josephinism. The term Josephinism can include all the reforms of Joseph II, but it can also be limited to those reforms concerning religion and in the narrowest sense it refers only to Joseph's influence on the Catholic Church.[16]

In many ways, Joseph's reforms continued and radicalized the reforms of his mother. Joseph never denied that his efforts at administrative reform continued the tradition of Absolutism. He himself coined the slogan 'All for the people but nothing through the people', a principle which, of course, did not conform with the progressive ideas of the Enlightenment. On the contrary, during Joseph's reign the control over the population increased. He even wanted to establish a file for every citizen comparable to the files of the army containing all the 'necessary' information concerning each subject. On the other hand – and here again the enormous ambiguity of the period is apparent – Joseph abolished censorship at least for a short period of time, and he tolerated – although not necessarily supported – the Freemasons.

Joseph's politics of tolerance were characterized on the one hand by an enlightened, but on the other hand by a clearly utilitarian, approach towards confessional politics. Whereas his mother still maintained the tradition of confessionalization which had characterized politics in central Europe since the sixteenth century, trying to force all territories to conform religiously, Joseph issued two patents of tolerance in 1781 and 1782 for the three major dissenting faiths. Under certain narrowly defined circumstances the Protestants (both Lutheran and Calvinist), the Orthodox and the Jews were tolerated. The impetus for this decision certainly lies in the economic situation, which was still dominated by the ideas of mercantilism and proto-industrialization. In this way all three religious groups became important factors in economic achievement. The Jews controlled a good part of the money-lending business in the Habsburg monarchy, the Protestants, who came to Austria from England and western Germany brought not only money but also technical know-how and the Orthodox controlled most of the trade with eastern Europe.

In spite of the magnitude of the gesture, Joseph's patent of tolerance for Protestants was still very limited. Only private worship was permitted and Protestant churches were not allowed to have spires and entrances directly from the street. People wishing to be registered officially as Protestants had to undergo six weeks of religious instruction by a Catholic priest, whose job was of course to try to convert them to Catholicism.[17]

Joseph's 1782 patent for the Viennese Jews was intended to serve as a model for the socially and economically more advanced sections of the Jewish population. He abolished specific taxes (*Leibmaut*) and discriminating restrictions concerning the freedom to live, travel or study where one chose and access to schools. All his measures were intended to integrate Jews into a nascent bourgeois society. Nonetheless some discriminating taxes for Jews remained, e.g. on Kosher meat (*Koscherfleischaufschlag*) or Shabbat candles (*Lichtzündungssteuer*). The measures for the Jews in Bohemia and especially in Galicia were less progressive – the Jewish communities there were very different from those in the urban centres – but even here separate jurisdiction and administration for the Jews was eventually eliminated. The Hungarian Jews were also included in the patents of tolerance, but none of these measures assured any form of equality and Jews continued to remain without full civic rights.[18] The limits of Enlightenment and toleration can be seen by using the Moravian 'Deists' – the successors of the Moravian Brothers or Baptists – as an example: Joseph II refused to grant them religious freedom.

The debate on the phenomenon of Josephinism has centred in the past around the works of the Jesuit historian, Ferdinand Maaß, and the 'Marxist' historian Eduard Winter. At the core of Josephinism are the reforms concerning the Catholic Church. Maaß interpreted Josephinism as a violation of the rights of the Catholic Church, whereas Winter emphasized the progressive aspects of Josephinism as a movement which reformed the Baroque Church. What did the Josephine reforms of the Catholic Church consist of?
1. Administrative reforms.
2. Dissolution of 'useless' monasteries.
3. Centralization of the education of priests.
4. Abolition of Baroque forms of piety.
In regard to the first point Joseph attempted to found new parishes because, in his opinion, no one should live farther than one hour away from a church. Having reshaped the parish structure – an undertaking financed by the dissolution of monasteries, about which more below – he reorganized the number and territories of the dioceses in the Habsburg Monarchy. Generally speaking the borders of the dioceses should correspond with those of the provinces. In one specific case a political question was also involved: two provinces of Austria – Lower- and Upper-Austria – were religiously administered by Passau which lay outside the borders of the Habsburg Monarchy. Joseph grasped a golden opportunity. He founded three new dioceses: Linz for Upper Austria, St. Pölten and Vienna, which already existed as a diocese, but was now significantly enlarged.[19]

At the beginning of Joseph's rule, the Habsburg Monarchy contained innumerable monasteries, many of which had no social function such as running a hospital or a school or supporting parishes. These monasteries, e.g. those of the Carthusian or the Camalduan order, were exclusively contemplative. Joseph ordered the dissolution of all 'unnecessary, useless' monasteries. Altogether about 700 different monasteries ceased to exist. The landed property of these monasteries formed the *'Religionsfonds'*, a fund which was used to cover the wages of the priests and other needs of the parishes which Joseph had founded.[20]

The education of the priests was now concentrated in state-run seminars, the so-called *'Generalseminarien'*, in which the priests received not only their religious education, but also became so-called 'state officers in a black dress'. In the Habsburg Monarchy the Catholic Church was responsible for numerous areas of state administration. It not only registered births, baptisms, marriages and burials, it also offered an important network for influencing public opinion. The priests of the Josephine era were given orders by the State on what to include in their sermons, which in turn meant that these sermons were not exclusively on religious topics. They included such varied subjects as how to plant potatoes, how to harvest saffron and how to inoculate people against smallpox.

Last but not least, while the measures concerning the abolition of different forms of Baroque piety may not have constituted the core of the reforms, they were in many cases the most visible symptoms and therefore met with a great deal of resistance. One of the most famous measures, quoted in nearly every book on Joseph II, was Joseph's decision to save 'useful' material by no longer burying people in coffins, but rather in sacks. This measure also had the advantage that decomposition took place more quickly. Joseph proposed using a coffin with a hinged bottom (*Klappsarg*), dropping the body into the grave, meaning that the coffin could be reused and hence money and material would not be wasted. Public outcry, however, forced him to withdraw this Patent after only a very short period of time. Joseph was bitterly disappointed by the insistence of the people on a beautiful ceremonial funeral, even if it meant their financial ruin. Even today the Viennese are known for their fascination with elaborate funeral ceremonies ('a *schoene Leich*' as they call it).

None the less Joseph was successful in at least reducing the Baroque pomp and activities which his predecessors had established with the sole intention of making the newly enforced Catholic Church attractive to the population. He abolished brotherhoods and processions, forbade pilgrimages which lasted more than one day – he also knew they consisted not only of prayer and ascetic behaviour but also often led to *'Ausschweifungen'* (mostly sexual excesses) – and even regulated the number of candles to be burned in church services. A measure which severely affected the working population was the reduction of the number of holidays: Catholics enjoyed almost twice as many holidays as Protestants. Joseph and his advisors argued that Catholics did not work for about one-third of the year, which was probably true in the country-side. In view of Max Weber's thesis concerning the relationship between Calvinism and capitalism we can assess the economic importance of the issue of holidays. Even the representatives of the Church supported a reduction of holidays. An initial reduction had taken place in 1753–4 and was intensified in 1771.[21] All these measures breathed the spirit of Enlightenment and met with a positive response among a good portion of the clergymen in the Habsburg countries.

At the end of his life Joseph himself was convinced that his attempts at reform had failed – and there was indeed good reason to think so. Resistance against his reforms had grown throughout the entire population because they had been implemented too quickly and too radically. The masses simply could not understand them. Revolutions had broken out in two separate parts of the Empire – Hungary and the Austrian Netherlands – and the latter appeared lost for the Habsburgs. Joseph composed an epitaph for himself: 'Here lies Joseph who failed in everything he undertook.'

However, even after Josephinism died as a reform movement along with its inventor, a stratum of old Josephinists survived in the priesthood, in the intelligentsia and especially in the staff of state administration. Many of the events in the nineteenth century and many of the achievements of liberalism in the 1860s would not have been possible without this important group of 'old Josephinists', whose best-known symbol was the famous Austrian author Franz Grillparzer. Grillparzer even had himself carried into the parliament in a wheelchair in 1868 to vote for the so-called confessional laws which re-established at least some principles of Joseph's reforms after a long conservative interruption.[22]

The only genuinely constitutionally inclined monarch of the Habsburg family was Joseph's younger brother Leopold. In 1765 Leopold, or 'Pietro Leopoldo', began his rule in Tuscany in close cooperation with a group of reformers in Florence. The motto of his rule was *'riforma, riforma e più riforma'* (reform, reform and more reform). Instead of centralization, which created a large and expensive apparatus of state officials, Leopold preferred self-government by the estates, the participation of the ruled in the ruling system, religious toleration and the complete abolition of censorship. This was a very different programme in comparison to the centralistic and absolutist approach of his older brother.

The most important difference seems to lie in the fact that Leopold was a pragmatic politician with a feeling for feasibility. The tempo of his reforms corresponded to the ability of the population to accept them. Even today in Italy Pietro Leopoldo is still revered as a highly positive figure and respected ruler.[23]

When Joseph died in 1790, Pietro Leopoldo left Tuscany – where his reforms continued – and became Leopold II, the ruler of the Habsburg Monarchy and Emperor of the Holy Roman Empire. Leopold ruled for only two years, but they were very decisive. The political situation he faced upon his return to Austria was difficult. Joseph's hasty and radical reforms had shocked a great part of the population and a spirit of resistance had been awakened. In two parts of the Habsburg Monarchy – Hungary and the Netherlands – open rebellions were in progress. In Hungary – where the ceremony of the coronation and the symbolic value of the crown of Saint Stephan were so important – Joseph had deeply injured the feelings of the aristocratic elites by refusing to be crowned. A loather of all ceremonies, he had simply had the crown of Saint Stephan sent to the Viennese treasury. As in Hungary, the attempts at centralization and absolutist control also provoked resistance in the Netherlands. Here – as elsewhere – Leopold was able to effect a compromise because of his strong constitutional background and his pragmatic approach. By sacrificing some of the more radical positions he was able to preserve many of the important reforms – including religious tolerance – of Josephinism, which remained in effect more or less until the middle of the nineteenth century.

In contrast to the majority of the historians who have viewed Leopold as the ideal enlightened ruler, modern researchers such as Gerda Lettner[24] have shown that he also cooperated very closely with counter-enlightenment groups. The most important personality within these groups was Leopold Alois Hoffmann who published the *Wiener Zeitschrift*, the mouthpiece of counter-enlightenment. Leopold appears to have prepared a turnabout in 1792 shortly before his death, but by this time powerful groups, influenced by enlightened ideas, had already formed. Hoffmann faced a great amount of resistance within the country and provoked even a kind of students' protest demonstration at the University of Vienna.

After the death of Leopold II in 1792, his son took over as the young Emperor Francis II/I, but he had neither the intellectual ability of his father or uncle nor were the circumstances favourable for a continuation of the politics of enlightened reform. The French Revolution of 1789 had left a deep impression on the rulers of Europe in general and on the Austrian Habsburgs in particular. In 1793, Marie Antoinette – Francis's aunt – was executed in Paris, and the political turmoil deepened the rift with the Habsburg Monarchy – already in conflict with revolutionary France. As a result, the ideas of the French Revolution were banned in the Habsburg Monarchy, the Jacobites were persecuted and the influence of the Enlightenment was halted, at least at the level of state politics.

The discussion of the Enlightenment in Austria is normally centred – as my chapter paper mirrors – on the reforms of the rulers. This is, of course, based on the fact that the reception of the Enlightenment was more or less restricted to the elite. Nevertheless I would like to discuss briefly some aspects of the question: 'Was there an enlightened public in the Habsburg monarchy?'

We can differentiate three groups: the freemasons, the bourgeoisie and the clerics.

The most important group were the freemasons. The first Great Lodge was founded in London in 1717 and the idea and the institution spread soon to the continent. Count Hoditz founded the first lodge in the Habsburg Monarchy in Vienna called 'The three cannons' (*'Zu den drei Kanonen'*) on September 17, 1742. Whereas Maria Theresa persecuted the masons and dissolved the lodge, her husband and other members of the family not only protected it, some of them even became members. As the lodges represented Enlightenment ideas such as tolerance, humanity and charity, their members – mainly aristocrats and some representatives of an incipient bourgeoisie – also constituted a public for enlightened politics. The most important lodge was founded by a man who became a legend of freemasonry – Ignaz von Born – the model for Sarastro in Mozart's *The Magic Flute*. Most of the masons were aristocrats, including the lower stratum of the aristocracy, but some bourgeoisie, intellectuals and artists such as Mozart were also members.[25]

The second group poses a definition problem: Was there a bourgeois public (*bürgerliche Öffentlichkeit*) as Jürgen Habermas defined it, which would have constituted the right group for the reception and discussion of enlightened ideas?[26] While in England and France a new bourgeoisie was in the process of forming, the Habsburg Monarchy was still very backward in comparison. Here society remained feudal – the aristocracy playing the most important role – preventing the development of proto-industrialization and therefore also of a new, self-aware bourgeois group. The reason can only be explained within the context of the differences in industrialization in Europe. In central Europe – since the beginning of the early-modern era, far from the main continental trade routes which were centred on the Atlantic – no accumulation of capital took place for various reasons.[27] The owners of most of the proto-industrial factories which were founded in the late seventeenth and eighteenth centuries were not Austrians, but rather immigrants from western Germany, France and to some extent England, who brought money and technical know-how with them. The negative economic situation helps to explain the lack of a capitalist and intellectual elite and therefore also the lack of an infrastructure for the distribution of ideas: a free press did not exist before Joseph's reforms. At first he tried to abolish censorship completely, but reintroduced it partially when he himself was publicly criticized. None the less, times had changed. To borrow Leslie Bodi's title of his book on the literature in this period, which modifies an oft-quoted phrase by Ilja Eisenburg, 'A Thaw in Vienna' (*Tauwetter in Wien*) had arrived.[28] But other institutions necessary for the formation of a bourgeois public, such as clubs and coffeehouses, were still only partially in existence. The coffeehouses for which Vienna is now famous were not places for political discussion in the eighteenth century, but simply venues to drink coffee. The lack of a bourgeoisie, the small intelligentsia and the absence of a free press did not create a climate conducive to public political discourse as in western Europe.

The third group were the clerics, who were surprisingly open to enlightened ideas. Of course a great part of the clergy – especially the monks and nuns of the monasteries – were still very Baroque in their attitudes. Within the clerical group, however, one of the few intellectual elites open to all classes, at least a small segment of priests was influenced by enlightened ideas. This is also the group which carried on Josephine reforms. This group was represented on all levels of the Catholic hierarchy in the Habsburg Monarchy; some bishops were Josephinists who helped to carry out the reforms and many clergymen in lower positions recognized the advantages of such reforms. Those priests who were in contact with the masses were the instruments of the spreading of enlightened ideas.[29]

But most importantly, the reforms of enlightened absolutism have to be discussed in the context of the social situation. The rulers – who were only partly influenced by enlightened ideas – are only one aspect of the belated and short-lived phenomenon of Enlightenment in the Habsburg Monarchy. The backward economic and social development in the Habsburg Monarchy contributed far more to this defect.

In the long run, the lack of success of the Enlightenment in Austria led to the fact that the Habsburg Monarchy remained an absolutist state until 1848 – when the revolution briefly interrupted absolutism – and until the 1860s when an equally belated constitutionalism finally appeared. It was particularly during this process of constitutionalization and liberalization in the nineteenth century that the leaven of enlightened elites – as small as they may have been – was working. Joseph II served as a model and hero for the revolutionaries of 1848 and the old Josephinists played an important role in the new orientation of the Habsburg Monarchy towards a more democratic and humanistic political system.

Notes

1 For the general situation see G. Mecenseffy, *Geschichte des Protestantismus in Österreich*, Graz and Köln, 1956; and J. Lenzenweger *et al.*, *Geschichte der Kirche*, Graz, Wien and Köln, 1990.

2 H. Engelbrecht, *Geschichte des österreichischen Bildungswesens. Erziehung und Unterricht auf österreichischem Boden*, 5 vols, Wien, 1982–8; and B. Duhr, *Geschichte der Jesuiten in den Ländern deutscher Zunge*, Freiburg, 1907.

3 C. Ingrao, *In Quest and Crisis: Emperor Joseph I and the Habsburg Monarchy*, West Lafayette, 1979: 20ff.; and chapter 2 in K. Vocelka and L. Heller, *Die Private Welt der Habsburger. Leben und Alltag einer Familie*, Graz, Wien and Köln, 1998.

4 For bibliographical information see: K. Vocelka, I. Mayer and M. Wakounig, 'Auswahlbibliographie zur Zeit Maria Theresias und Josephs II', in *Österreich im Europa der Aufklärung. Kontinuität und Zäsur in Europa zur Zeit Maria Theresias und Josephs II*, II, Wien, 1985: 969–1063. Useful texts for a general introduction are E. Garms-Cornides, 'Rivalutatione del Settecento. Versuch einer Literaturübersicht', *Römische Historische Mitteilungen*, XII, 1970: 197–278; H. Reinalter, *Die Aufklärung in Österreich. Ignaz Born und seine Zeit*, Frankfurt a. M., 1991; and E. Winter, *Frühaufklärung. Der Kampf gegen den Konfessionalismus in Mittel- und Osteuropa und die deutsch-slawische Bewegung*, Berlin, 1966.

5 J. Schmidt, 'Voltaire und Maria Theresia', *Mitteilungen des Vereines für Geschichte der Stadt Wien*, XI, 1931: 73–115.

6 G. Klingenstein (ed.), *Staatskanzler Wenzel Anton von Kaunitz-Rietberg 1711–1794. Neue Perspektiven zur Politik und Kultur der europäischen Aufklärung*, Graz, 1996; F.A.J. Szabo, *Kaunitz and Enlightened Absolutism 1753–1780*, Cambridge, 1994; F.T. Brechka, *Gerard van Swieten and his World 1700–1772*, The Hague, 1970; P. Hersche, 'Gerhard van Swietens Stellung zum Jansenismus', *Internationale kirchliche Zeitschrift*, LXI, 1971: 33–56.

7 R. Reinhardt, 'Zur Kirchenreform in Österreich unter Maria Theresia', *Zeitschrift für Kirchengeschichte*, LXXVII, 1966: 105–19; R. Reinhard, 'Maria Theresia und der Josephinismus', *Zeitschrift für katholische Theologie*, LXXXIX, 1957: 201–13; H. Benedikt, 'Der Josephinismus vor Joseph II', *Österreich und Europa. Festgabe für Hugo Hantsch*, Graz-Wien-Köln, 1965: 183–201; and F. Maaβ, *Der Frühjosephinismus*, Wien and München, 1969.

8 A. Egger, *Die Reform der österreichischen Volksschule unter Maria Theresia*, Brixen-Innsbruck, 1912, and U. Krömmer, *Johann Ignaz von Felbinger. Leben und Werk*, Freiburg-Basel-Wien, 1966.

9 H. Wagner, 'Der Einfluβ von Gallikanismus und Jansenismus auf die Kirche und den Staat der Aufklärung in Österreich', *Österreich in Geschichte und Literatur*, XI, 1967: 521–34; P. Hersche, *Der Spätjansenismus in Österreich*, Wien, 1977; and P. Hersche, 'War Maria Theresia eine Jansenistin?', *Österreich in Geschichte und Literatur*, XV, 1971: 14–25.

10 R.J. Wolny, *Die josephinische Toleranz unter besonderer Berücksichtigung ihres geistlichen Wegbereiteres Johann Leopold Hay*, München, 1973: 115.

11 G. Otruba, *Die Wirtschaftspolitik Maria Theresias*, Wien, 1963.

12 P.F. Barton (ed.), *Im Zeichen der Toleranz. Aufsätze zur Toleranzgesetzgebung des 18. Jahrhunderts in den Reichen Josephs II., ihren Voraussetzungen und ihren Folgen. Eine Festschrift*, Wien, 1981; P.F. Barton (ed.), *Im Lichte der Toleranz. Aufsätze zur Toleranzgesetzgebung des 18. Jahrhunderts in den Reichen Josephs II., ihren Voraussetzungen und Folgen. Eine Festschrift*, Wien, 1981.

13 B. Duhr, 'Die Etappen bei der Aufhebung des Jesuitenordens nach den Papieren von Simancas', *Zeitschrift für katholische Theologie*, XXII, 1898: 432–54; B. Duhr, 'Die Kaiserin Maria Theresia und die Aufhebung der Gesellschaft Jesu', *Stimmen der Zeit*, CX, 1926: 207–21; F. Maaβ, 'Die österreichischen Jesuiten

zwischen Josephinismus und Liberalismus', *Zeitschrift für katholische Theologie*, LXXX, 1958: 6–100.

14 G. Wolf, *Aus der Zeit der Kaiserin Maria Theresia*, Wien, 1888: 62.

15 N. Vielmetti, 'Vom Beginn der Neuzeit bis zur Toleranz' in A. Drabek *et al.* (eds), *Das österreichische Judentum. Voraussetzungen und Geschichte*, Wien and München, 1974: 59–82; P.P. Bernard, 'Joseph II and the Jews. The origin of the Tolerance Patent of 1782', *Austrian History Yearbook*, IV/V, 1968–9: 101–19; W. Bihl, 'Zur Entstehungsgeschichte des josephinischen Patents für die Juden Ungarns vom 31. 3. 1783', in H. Fichtenau and E. Zöllner (eds), *Beiträge zur neueren Geschichte Österreichs*, Wien, 1974: 282–98; and W. Häusler, *Das galizische Judentum in der Habsburgermonarchie. Im Lichte der zeitgenössischen Publizistik und Reiseliteratur von 1772–1848*, Wien, 1979.

16 F. Maaβ, *Der Josephinismus, Quellen zu seiner Geschichte in Österreich 1760–1790*, Wien, 1951–61; E. Winter, *Der Josephinismus und seine Geschichte. Beiträge zur Geistesgeschichte Österreichs 1740–1848*, Brünn, München and Wien, 1943; E. Winter, *Der Josephinismus. Die Geschichte des österreichischen Reformkatholizismus 1740–1848*, Berlin, 1962; and F. Valjavec, *Der Josephinismus. Zur geistigen Entwicklung Österreichs im 18. und 19. Jahrhundert*, München and Wien, 1945) R.A. Kann, *Kanzel und Katheder. Studien zur österreichischen Geistesgeschichte vom Spätbarock zur Frühromantik*, Wien-Freiburg-Basel, 1962; G. Holzknecht, *Ursprung und Herkunft der Reformideen Kaiser Josephs II. auf kirchlichem Gebiete*, Innsbruck, 1914.

17 C. O'Brien, 'Ideas of Religious Toleration at the Time of Joseph II. A Study of the Enlightenment among Catholics in Austria', *Transactions of the American Philosophical Society*, LIX, 1969: 5–76; Barton, *Im Lichte der Toleranz*; H. Wagner, 'Die Idee der Toleranz in Österreich' in *Religion und Kirche in Österreich*, Wien, 1972: 11–128.

18 W. Häusler, 'Toleranz, Emanzipation und Assimilation. Das österreichische Judentum des bürgerlichen Zeitalters (1782–1918)', in A. Drabek *et al.* (eds), *Das österreichische Judentum. Voraussetzungen und Geschichte*, Wien and München, 1974: 83–140.

19 *200 Jahre Diözese St. Pölten. Ausstellungskatalog zur Jubiläumsausstellung Krems. Minoritenkirche Stein*, St. Pölten, 1985.

20 A. Wolf, *Die Aufhebung der Klöster in Innerösterreich*, Wien, 1871; G. Winner, *Die Klosteraufhebungen in Niederösterreich*, Wien, 1967.

21 P. Hersche, 'Wider "Müßiggang" und "Ausschweifung". Feiertage und ihre Reduktion im katholischen Europa, namentlich im deutschsprachigen Raum zwischen 1750 und 1800', *Innsbrucker Historische Studien*, XII/XIII, 1990: 97–122.

22 K. Vocelka, *Verfassung oder Konkordat? Der publizistische und politische Kampf der österreichischen Liberalen um die Religionsgesetze des Jahres 1868*, Wien, 1978.

23 A. Wandruszka, *Leopold II, Erzherzog von Österreich, Großherzog von Toskana, König von Ungarn und Böhmen, Römischer Kaiser*, vols 1 and 2, Wien, 1965.

24 G. Lettner, *Das Rückzugsgefecht der Aufklärung in Wien 1790–1792*, Frankfurt a. M. and New York, 1988.

25 H. Reinalter, *Freimaurer und Geheimbünde im 18. Jahrhundert in Mitteleuropa*, Frankfurt a. M., 1983; R. Feuchtmüller and E. Krivanec, *Die Freimaurer in Öster-*

reich. Zur Geistesgeschichte des 18. Jahrhunderts. Museum Schloβ Rosenau bei Zwettl, Schloβ Rosenau bei Zwettl, 1975; H. Reinalter, 'Joseph II. und die Freimaurerei im Lichte zeitgenössischer Broschüren', *Unsere Heimat*, LI, 1980: 193–206; and H. Wagner, 'Die Lombardei und das Freimaurerpatent Josephs II. von 1785', *Mitteilungen des Österreichischen Staatsarchivs*, XXXI, 1978: 136–53.

26 J. Habermas, *Strukturwandel der Öffentlichkeit. Untersuchungen zu einer Kategorie der bürgerlichen Gesellschaft*, Neuwied, 1962.

27 For the Austrian economic situation see R. Sandgruber, *Ökonomie und Politik. Österreichische Wirtschaftsgeschichte vom Mittelalter bis zur Gegenwart*, Wien, 1995.

28 L. Bodi, *Tauwetter in Wien. Zur Prosa der österreichischen Aufklärung 1781–1795*, Frankfurt a. M., 1977.

29 There is a series of dissertations on bishops of the period, e.g. V. Einspieler, *Johann Karl Graf von Herberstein, Bischof von Laibach. Sein Leben, Wirken und seine Stellung in der Geschichte des Josephinismus*, Diss. Wien, 1951; M. Windhagen, *Ferdinand Graf von Hallweil, Bischof von Wiener Neustadt, 1706–1773*, Diss. Wien, 1970; P. Lackner, *Joseph Adam Graf von Arco, Bischof von Seckau, 1780–1802. Ein Beitrag zur Geschichte des Josephinismus in der Steiermark*, Diss. Graz, 1961; and K. Raitbauer, *Erzbischof Johann Joseph Trautson*, Diss. Graz, 1955. An important study is: F. Wehrl, 'Der "Neue Geist". Eine Untersuchung der Geistesrichtungen des Klerus in Wien von 1750–1790', *Mitteilungen des Österreichischen Staatsarchives*, XX, 1967: 36–114.

11. Toleration in Eastern Europe: the Dissident Question in Eighteenth-Century Poland–Lithuania

Michael G. Müller

Even admirers of eighteenth-century Poland and its last king Stanislaw August Poniatowski, such as the French historian Jean Fabre, have agreed that, in terms of religious tolerance, the Polish–Lithuanian Commonwealth was among the nations which most radically rejected the concept of modernity. At a time when almost everywhere in Europe, including Russia, the idea of freedom of belief took root as one of the commonly shared values of the Enlightenment, in Poland religious emotions seemed to run higher than ever before. In the course of the eighteenth century, the Republic of Nobles ultimately abandoned its own tradition of constitutionally asserted religious tolerance as established in the famous Warsaw Confederation of 1573 and embarked instead on implementing, and stubbornly defending, a concept of nobilitarian nationhood that firmly linked the idea of citizenship to the Catholic faith. It could therefore not be denied, as Fabre argued, that not least the nobilitarian nation itself was to be held responsible for the catastrophe that ended in the first partition of Poland in 1772. Quite legitimately Catherine II and Frederick II could claim that by intervening on behalf of the persecuted Polish dissidents the partitioning powers had defended the principles of the *philosophes* – even though the intervention led to what otherwise was to be considered an act of arbitrary and barbarian violation of international law and the rights of nations.[1]

The very fact that religious toleration in Poland–Lithuania had been in steady decline ever since the early seventeenth century is beyond question. With the Counter-Reformation essentially completed after the re-conversion of the vast majority of the Protestant aristocracy around 1600, gradually increasing pressure was brought to bear on the remaining non-Catholic communities, namely the Protestant ones. Since the 1630s, restrictions on church building and public worship by Protestants were introduced in growing numbers. The second half of the century witnessed intensified prosecution of Protestants for blasphemy and apostasy. From 1717 national jurisdiction curtailed the dissidents' rights of political representation and of access to public office. A point of crisis was reached with the so-called Torun disturbances or, in the terminology of German historiography, the Torun Massacre (*Thorner*

Blutgericht) of 1724. The death sentences carried out on several members of the Torun town council, for allegedly having encouraged anti-Catholic street riots, led not only to heated public debates but also to immediate and vehement protests from neighbouring non-Catholic states including Russia.[2] Ever since, the neighbours' concern to defend dissident rights and to protect their respective Polish co-religionists has been high on the agenda of great-power politics in Eastern Europe. At the same time, religious tension within the country steadily grew as the vast Catholic majority of the Polish *szlachta* mobilized against foreign interference, and put even more pressure on those among their compatriots who, willingly or not, were the cause for the Republic's ill fame among the European states, and the external pressure resulting from it. From there it was, at least at first sight, only a short step to the outbreak of open conflict in the 1760s. In reaction to new anti-dissent legislation the courts of Petersburg and Potsdam issued, in 1767, a joint ultimatum to fully restore the constitutional rights of dissidents. The result was the outbreak of a full-scale war of religion in 1768 that ended with the defeat of the defenders of the Catholic faith united in the Confederation of Bar and with the partition of 1772.

Do these facts, however, justify the outstandingly harsh verdict of religious intolerance and the rejection of modernity in eighteenth-century Poland issued by the vast majority of contemporary commentators and later historians alike? Was the Polish–Lithuanian Commonwealth indeed the only state in Eastern Europe that had failed to learn the lesson of the Enlightenment and that, in terms of the development of modern, 'civilized' attitudes towards religion, had been objectively overtaken – and therefore maybe rightfully dismembered – by the more rationally governed absolutist states in its neighbourhood? And had the Commonwealth's alleged 'failure' to adopt the projects of statehood and civil society as represented by enlightened despotism at all to do with its attitudes towards religion and confessional conflict; or, in other words, was Poland's constitutional and cultural *Sonderweg* as a non-absolutist Commonwealth actually at the roots of what appears to be *Sonderweg* with respect also to the development of religious tolerance? A number of observations have led us to doubt the hitherto dominant narratives, in particular, if the Polish case is put more systematically in a comparative perspective.

Looking more closely at the realities of interconfessional relations in early-modern Poland–Lithuania one realizes that the decline of religious tolerance in the Commonwealth was by no means a linear or all-encompassing process. Oppression and persecution on religious grounds occurred not only much later than usually assumed, but also in a much less general way. While, in numerical terms, the Protestant communities saw themselves reduced to a marginal position, and the scope of free public worship outside the Roman

Catholic Church had been markedly narrowing ever since the early seventeenth century, the constitutionally acknowledged status of the dissidents remained essentially untouched until the political crisis during the Great Northern War. And even after the so-called Silent Diet of 1717 had, for the first time, introduced explicitly anti-dissident legislation, the scope of toleration was reduced only under specific aspects. Anti-dissident mobilization, as well as foreign intervention, primarily focused not on religious practices by non-Catholics as such, but rather on the issue of political representation for the dissenting elites. In any case, the contexts in which religious tolerance became an issue of public controversy and of conflict varied enormously in the seventeenth and eighteenth centuries, and these contexts merit careful differentiation.

Throughout the eighteenth century, Poland–Lithuania remained culturally as much a multiconfessional state as it had been in the seventeenth century. As late as the 1770s, prior to the first partition, an estimated 18 per cent of the Commonwealth's overall population, and about 3 per cent of its noble citizenry, openly adhered to religious communities other than the Roman Catholic Church. However, the Catholic majority was far from representing a confessionally homogeneous group, since the distinct religious identity of the Uniates, or Catholics of the Eastern Rite, accounting for well over one-third of the Catholic population, had by no means disappeared.[3] Moreover, in spite of continuing efforts by the Catholic hierarchy to extend their influence and, in particular, their judicial control over the non-Catholic population, the very existence of the dissident communities was never actually threatened – at least not under circumstances where dissident landowners or urban magistrates continued to provide the financial means to maintain the respective church organizations. Thus, with the exception of the Arians, none of Poland's dissident groups suffered a fate similar to that of the French Protestants after the Revocation of the Edict of Nantes, or that of the Russian Jews who were subject to violent persecution and expulsion under Catherine I and her immediate successors. Nor were Polish dissidents confronted with a territorial segregation of confessional groups as practised in the German territories on the basis of the *cuius regio* settlement in the Holy Roman Empire.

Compared with Poland's absolutist neighbour-states in Eastern Europe, the Commonwealth did not pursue a fundamentally different policy of toleration and discrimination that could be qualified as a *Sonderweg*. As in most parts of Europe, enlightened rulers engaged in cautiously, and selectively, accommodating certain minority confessions for mainly utilitarian reasons without, however, abandoning the idea that, in principle, the *cura religionis* was with the sovereign and that the control over, and limitation of, religious freedom remained a necessary pre-requisite of good government. Policies of tolerating and privileging individual religious denominations – similar to those adopted by Poland in relation to the Orthodox peasantry and the Jews – were therefore as frequent, and as consistent with the concept of enlightened despotism, as were acts of intervention and selective persecution. As late as 1744–5 the Austrian Empress, Maria Theresa ordered the expulsion of the whole of Bohemian Jewry – a decision that the Empress long firmly defended against all criticism and that, at least for Prague, was thoroughly executed until its revision five years later.[4] In Russia, after the first partition of Poland in 1772, the government of Catherine the Great fought a fierce *Kulturkampf* in order to subordinate the Catholic and Uniate bishoprics to the control of the Empire's 'Holy Synod', and to eliminate any kind of ecclesiastical autonomy in the region or of direct influence from Rome.[5] Even Frederick the Great's declared indifference with respect to the religious belief of his Prussian subjects proved to be limited when, as in the case of the newly conquered province of Silesia, central control of the Church hierarchy seemed in question. Furthermore, while the East European absolutist rulers eventually did acknowledge the principle of freedom of belief in one way or the other – albeit hesitantly and, as in the Russian case, very cautiously and inconspicuously – their commitment to religious toleration never included the political sphere. The claims raised by the future partitioning powers in 1767 that the Polish dissidents should be granted full civil and political rights as citizens of the Republic were never seriously considered, let alone openly discussed with respect to Prussia, Russia or the respective lands of the Habsburg Empire.

At least with respect to the last decades of the eighteenth century, the Poles may also rightly claim to have developed, and to some extent implemented, their own project of enlightened tolerance. Remarkably enough, the partitioning powers of 1772 lost virtually all interest in the dissident question in Poland–Lithuania once the territorial dismemberment of the Republic had been executed; in fact, none of the parties involved now insisted on the respective stipulations of the Polish–Russian treaty of 1768, although they were solemnly confirmed in 1773. Instead, the question became an issue of internal debates over state reforms in Poland–Lithuania precisely when the external pressure diminished. Among the positive results of the 'spiritual revolution' in Poland under the rule of Stanislaw August Poniatowski one should consider the attempts, after the 1770s, at consolidating the legal and administrative status of the Jews; most important, however, was the May Constitution of 1791, that in fact fully acknowledged the principle of toleration and argued precisely along the lines of pro-dissident propaganda after the middle of the century.[6]

Nevertheless, the fact remains that in the Polish case, the issue of religious toleration became increasingly divisive over the course of the eighteenth century, and that the Republic of Nobles ultimately proved unable to politically control interconfessional tension in a similar way to what had been success-fully achieved in the neighbouring absolutist states. It needs to be examined more closely to what extent, and in what respect, developments in Poland–Lithuania differed from those in other multiconfessional states in Eastern Europe after all – and it needs to be clarified whether or not the constitutional structure and cultural profile of the Polish–Lithuanian Commonwealth was of some significance in this context.

The following two assumptions may serve as a starting point for a discus-sion of these questions. On the one hand, it can probably be argued that the steady increase in religious tension in Poland reflects a very much universal trend towards the formation of ideologically homogeneous majorities within early-modern societies – in the context of proto-national elite integration. As, over the course of the seventeenth century, the project of nationhood became increasingly associated with the idea of cultural homogeneity, religion appears to have gained new importance as a marker of majority identity – and, in consequence, also as a major factor in the emergence of a quite new phenomenon: that of minorities. In the Polish case, the concept of *Sarmatism* as the guiding ideology of the ruling noble class throughout the seventeenth and most of the eighteenth centuries, represents the development in question very clearly. *Sarmatism* linked the constitutive elements of Polishness – republican liberty, nobilitarian culture and the Polish language – not merely to the Catholic faith as such but, much more specifically, to a national concept of religiosity and the respective religious practices.[7] Thus Poland, like other states, underwent in this period a process of re-confessionalization that was very much associated with what appears to be a genuinely modern process of the 'nationalization' of religion.

On the other hand, one may assume that both the constitutional structure of the Commonwealth and its (increasingly precarious) position in East-European power relations accounted, at the same time, for a rather unique dynamic of re-confessionalization. The constitutional aspect seems relevant, since the Polish system of government relied to a much greater extent than any other in Eastern Europe on the participation of, and mediation between, large segments of the society – and consequently, much earlier than in, for example, Russia, the religious beliefs and emotions of a nobilitarian 'public' developed an immediate impact on state politics. Foreign affairs, in turn, were crucial in that Swedish and, at a later stage, Russian and Prussian strategies to systematically exploit the dissident question as an instrument to interfere with Polish politics can largely be held responsible for the steady escalation of confessional conflict during the century. The often arbitrary claims by neigh-bouring powers in favour of their respective Polish co-religionists were increasingly – and, incidentally, quite rightly – perceived as being part and parcel of an overall scheme to undermine Polish sovereignty. Predictably, the Catholic nation reacted by developing ever more rigid mechanisms of religious exclusion. In this sense, it can be argued that the decline of tolerance in eighteenth-century Poland is very much a side effect of what historians have come to call the Republic's 'Crisis of Sovereignty' that originated from the realignment of East European powers in the course of the Great Northern War and was to culminate in the first partition of Poland in 1772.

In the following paragraphs, three aspects of the problem will be discussed based on the following: the constitutional and legal framework in which confessional relations developed since the sixteenth century, the social contexts and connotations of emerging intolerance and the political circumstances under which, in the eighteenth century, religious tension developed into crisis. The argument will largely be based on a re-reading of evidence that has long been accessible. Some substantially new information has, however, been produced by recent research, particularly in relation to the eighteenth century, by Wojciech Kriegseisen's thorough account of the history of the Polish Protestants in the 'Saxon period'.[8] With respect to some narrow aspects, namely the issue of foreign intervention on religious grounds in the period immediately preceding the partition of 1772, the author also draws on his own archival research.

At first sight, the development of the formal position of the Polish–Lithuanian dissident groups might appear rather contradictory. While the restrictions, legal and practical, implemented against non-Catholics rapidly multiplied from the 1630s onwards, their constitutional status remained essentially untouched. At every interregnum until the end of the seventeenth century the *pax inter dissidentes* of the Warsaw Confederation had been solemnly renewed, and even after 1700 there was no question of its formal revocation. Moreover, in Lithuania – otherwise notorious for the religious zeal of its Catholic and Uniate nobility – the Warsaw Confederation was formally incorporated into the land's separate law-code, and remained so until the partitions, thus acquiring even higher constitutional validity than in the lands of the Crown of Poland. The explanation for this paradox does not simply lie in the discrepancies between 'theory and practice' in the Commonwealth's constitutional and legal culture. It should much rather be understood as the natural, and legally consistent, consequence of the constitutional choices that had been made when the principle of toleration was established by the Warsaw Confederation of 1573.

The specificities of the Polish *pax inter dissidentes* of 1573 become immediately evident when we compare it with the Peace of Augsburg of 1555.[9] It represented a more 'modern' solution than the latter in that it straightforwardly acknowledged the individual's freedom of belief rather than seeking to establish a *modus vivendi* for the dissenting *Reichsstände* that provided for mutual toleration between, but not within, the territories of the Holy Roman Empire. Furthermore, the Warsaw Confederation was not concerned with theological justifications of confessional pluralism, nor with regulating the relationship between secular rule and *cura religionis* – issues that in the *Reich*, at least until the Peace of Westphalia, created major problems of legal interpretation; instead it was a purely secular law providing for the individual's protection against persecution and oppression on religious grounds. In the perspective of the non-dominant religious communities and their respective churches, on the other hand, the Polish model provided significantly less security than the German *Religionsfriede*. Not only did the Warsaw Confederation fail to specify whether its guarantees for the individual's freedom of belief applied to anybody outside the limited field of the noble citizenry, but, more importantly, it also lacked any explicit recognition of the very existence of confessional communities or ecclesiastical organisations outside the Roman Catholic Church. Due to the strictly secular nature of the Polish settlement, the legitimacy of confessional churches could not become the object of constitutional consideration.[10]

How fragile the Polish settlement of 1573 actually was as a legal framework for confessional co-existence, became evident as soon as the quantitative relationship between the Catholic and the dissident nobility substantially changed after the establishment of the Uniate church in Poland's Eastern lands and the mass re-conversion of the Protestant nobility in Northern Poland and Lithuania around 1600. If deprived of their aristocratic protectors and patrons, dissident congregations could only survive under exceptional circumstances – be it, in analogy with the situation of the Jews, due to toleration by influential magnates, or be it, as in the case of Royal Prussia, under the protection of major towns and their Protestant patricians. But even where noble families persisted in their dissident faith, their respective congregations often lacked the indispensable support of consolidated church organizations – a disadvantage that could hardly be compensated materially or politically by backing from co-religionists abroad. This is not to say that the rapid decline of the once numerous dissident congregations occurred without external pressure brought about by the agencies of the Counter-Reformation in Poland. Such pressure had been extreme ever since the end of the sixteenth century, and it continued to grow steadily afterwards. It is, however, important to understand that the Polish Counter-Reformation achieved its major aims without necessarily violating the constitutional principles laid down in 1573.[11] By its very nature, the Polish constitutional model of religious toleration was an inadequate tool for the protection of minority confessions, and most of the innumerable restrictions that the dissident churches and their congregations had to face over time could still be considered consistent with the fundamental idea of the individual citizen's freedom of conscience.

The primary objective of anti-dissident legislation, and its ever more restrictive interpretation by the national diets, had, until the beginning of the eighteenth century, been essentially to 'freeze' the confessional landscape after the Counter-Reformation, i.e. to strictly confine dissident presence and dissident religious life, as far as the Christian confessions were concerned, to the positions actually held around 1630. The constitution of 1632, banning the building of new Protestant and Orthodox churches in royal towns, eventually came to be interpreted as a rule applying to the Republic's entire territory (town, royal demesne or noble estate), and, after 1700, as a ban even on the repair of already existing dissident churches. Similarly, a law of 1668 against public dissident worship in the presence of the court or the national diet was, by 1700, regarded as a legal basis for generally denying, even to dissident noblemen, the right to public worship outside their home congregation. Other legal precautions against any possible strengthening of dissident influence were: the rule *rex catholicus eso*, the exclusion of non-Catholics from nobilitation, the introduction of Catholic censorship of any publications with religious content, not least the Constitutions of 1668 and 1670 ruling that apostasy as well as sacrilege committed by Jews should be prosecuted under the laws against Arianism.[12]

Almost as threatening to the status of the Christian dissidents as was the anti-dissent legislation of national diets was the normative power of the jurisdiction by the (elective) Crown Tribunal in religious matters. Although formally without any normative competence, the tribunal had a particularly powerful position in this respect as a result of seventeenth-century legislation against Arianism. It had established the so-called Arian Register which comprised a list of religious offences that the Tribunal was obliged to prosecute by office – and with priority over secular cases. In its original function, the Register could hardly be considered very harmful to dissident concerns, since Arianism had always been excluded from the Protestant *Consensus Sendomirensis* of 1570 and the Warsaw Confederation alike. Things changed however, as the list of offences incorporated into the Register by the Tribunal grew longer. By 1726, the Register not only mentioned a number of other groups to be automatically prosecuted alongside the Arians (such as the Mennonites and the Polish Brethren), but it also defined the category of general offences concerned in a much broader way than two generations earlier: virtually all matters of religion such as sacrilege, blasphemy or heresy should now be subject to the court's ruling; at the same time, the term 'heretic' acquired an ever broader meaning being, in the eighteenth century, also applicable to, for example, Calvinists.[13]

The effects on the dissidents, in particular on the Protestants in the lands of the Polish Crown, were significant. As early as 1688, the Crown Tribunal tried the minister of a Calvinist congregation near Cracow for having celebrated mass in a place other than an 'old' (i.e. existing prior to 1632) Protestant church; in fact, the local church had been demolished by Catholic students from Cracow in 1626, and the congregation had benefited thereafter from the hospitality of a nearby manor. In 1713, a Lutheran captain of the Masowian Cavalry was sentenced to death and executed after allegedly having started a theological dispute in a Lublin tavern. In the same year two alleged members of the community of Polish Brethren were arrested in Lublin; only one of them escaped imprisonment by agreeing to be baptized by the local Jesuits.[14] Such cases were to play an important role as precedents for a large number of trials to follow in the 1720s and 1730s.

Even now, however, the practice of semi-constitutional religious persecution remained selective. If the forces behind the Polish Counter-Reformation had pursued a long-term strategy of re-conquering ground from the dissident elites by gradually limiting the legal scope of toleration, they had certainly been successful with respect to the major domains of conflict. Wherever the dissidents were, on the local level, in a clear minority position, and saw themselves confronted with determined Catholic action, they eventually proved unable to defend their rights on a legal basis. Where, on the other hand, local traditions of religious dissent remained dominant, and the regional elites – wealthy burgher communities and magnates – continued to support dissident ecclesiastical life, the impact of anti-dissident legislation and jurisdiction was much less marked. Neither the Protestant strongholds in Prussia and parts of Lithuania, nor the Orthodox core regions in the east witnessed a similar level of confrontation as in Poland proper; here, attempts by Catholic authorities to implement anti-dissident laws and court rulings as rigidly as in the lands of the Crown of Poland largely failed.

It also seems noteworthy that the restrictions of religious freedom in the Commonwealth imposed by legislation and judicial practice were apparently not sufficiently spectacular to raise, prior to the Great Northern War, major objections from the non-Catholic powers and to provoke foreign political intervention.[15] This was only the case when, after 1717, *Sejm* legislation specifically targeted the political prerogatives of the non-Catholic nobility thus adding a new, explicitly political dimension to the issue of religious dissent. In fact, the anti-dissident stipulations in the constitutions of 1717, 1733, 1736, 1764 and 1766 marked a turning point in that, contrary to previous legislation, they challenged in substance the constitutional principle of tolerance as established in 1573. The so-called 'Mute Diet' of 1717 that ratified the conditions for the return to the Polish throne of Augustus II, ruled that the king should not designate persons of questionable noble status, foreigners, or dissidents as royal dignitaries in the Commonwealth – thus making not only the senatorial offices in the Republic fall under a monopoly of the Catholic nobility, but also the award of so-called Royal Estates (*królewszczyzny*) representing a major source of income for the majority of the magnate families. If, however, the restrictions introduced in 1717 primarily concerned the higher strata of the dissident nobility – those eligible, due to their magnate status, for senatorial dignity and the function of *starosta* – political discrimination of the non-Catholic citizens took a much more general form in the context of the political struggle after the death of Augustus II. The Constitutions of the Convocation Diet of 1733 and the *Sejm pacyfikacyjny* of 1736 made participation in the system of noble representation as a whole dependent on the individual's confessional status; in the future, the dissidents would also be denied the right to vote as deputies to the lower chamber of the Diet or as members of elective tribunals and commissions – the right to vote, *nota bene*, or the *activitas*, but not necessarily the right to be elected.[16] In spite of this subtle difference, however, dissident presence in the elective bodies of the Republic *de facto* ceased shortly thereafter. It was in the 1740s that the last Protestant deputies to the Diet and the Crown Tribunal faced formal exclusion by their Catholic colleagues from the deliberations of the respective bodies. The overall confirmation of the perfect commitment of the Republic's institutions to the Catholic faith by the constitutions of 1764 and 1766, in this respect, only acknowledged an existing practice.

At least two conclusions may be drawn from this brief overview of the development of the legal and constitutional status of the dissidents. It is obvious, on the one hand, that Poland's constitutional tradition of tolerance did not survive the eighteenth century intact, not even in its narrow interpretation of the later seventeenth century. By denying to its dissident citizenry the full rights of participation in the Commonwealth's institutional system, the Republic had ultimately abandoned the principles of 1573. In the religious and ecclesiastical sphere, on the other hand, the decline of toleration followed a somewhat different logic, and developed a different dynamic. What had been true for the late sixteenth century, essentially applied for the eighteenth century as well. The scope of legally secured tolerance that different dissident confessions could benefit from depended largely on their numerical strength and their social backing, and also on the degree to which religious divides became associated with other lines of conflict. Thus, even now the multiconfessional character of the Republic was not seriously questioned with respect to the Orthodox peasantry or even to the sizeable Jewish population – quite in contrast to the allegedly much more rationally governed states of the Habsburgs and the Romanovs. The opposite was true for the Polish Protestants who although representing, in quantitative terms, only a marginal confessional minority were at the centre of the social and political conflict – and became indeed the main target of anti-dissident legislation and jurisdiction.

One of the major changes that occurred in Poland–Lithuania between the late sixteenth and the eighteenth century was that religious affiliations acquired increasingly clear social connotations. While after the Reformation, and well into the seventeenth century, religious dissent in Poland–Lithuania cut across virtually all social layers of the Republic's population, subsequently both the social distribution of dissent and, perhaps even more importantly, its public perception changed substantially. The Orthodox faith became as much associated with Poland's Eastern peasantry as the Jewish confession had been associated, even in the past, with petty tradesmen, pedlars or inn-keepers, particularly in the regions east and south-east of the Vistula. The Protestant faith, instead, was increasingly perceived as being primarily an affair of the urban population in the Commonwealth's western and northern areas; namely the economically powerful towns of Royal Prussia and their patrician elites who came to be considered as most prominently representing the Protestant (Lutheran) element – a view that was also influenced by the fact that both the social and cultural lifestyle of the mainly German-speaking urban elites in Prussia seemed to underline their 'otherness'. In general, the perception of religious dissent by the Catholic majority developed towards identifying it essentially with groups that, in the understanding of the eighteenth-century Polish nobility, were not part of 'the nation'.

To a large extent, obviously, this picture simply reflects the factual social shifts in confessional allegiances that had taken place as a result of the church-union of Brest and the Counter-Reformation, namely the rapid melting-away of a nobilitarian dissident party after the defeat of the Protestant-supported Zebrzydowski rebellion of 1607.[17] As can be observed in the case of the Prussian patricians, however, the change in perspective also had to do with the cultural redefinition of the nation. In their self-perception, these urban elites had always represented, and in some respects continued to do so even in the eighteenth century, very much an aristocratic group clearly separated from the *milieu* of craftsmanship and urban trade. Moreover, in various contexts they had long shared, and actively participated in, Poland–Lithuania's aristocratic, if not magnate elite culture; this was not only true of the patricians' economic and social performance and general lifestyle but also of their educational concepts and career patterns, and not least of their acting within the same personal and political networks. Polish attitudes towards the urban aristocracy changed, however, as, in the course of the seventeenth century, the major Prussian towns became increasingly perceived as economic and, eventually, also political competitors and, more importantly, as potential agents of the foreign powers that threatened national sovereignty.[18]

The mechanisms of social exclusion thus coming to bear against the patricians, in particular those of Royal Prussia, are clearly reflected in a wave of anti-urban and, at the same time, anti-dissident polemics during and after the Great Northern War. As an anonymous pamphlet of 1718 stated, the Poles must have either failed to grow up, to reason or to have entirely lost their common sense to tolerate the fact that dissidents of dubious origin claimed a right to rule over them – and in fact already manipulated the country's political life. 'Indeed, not only Oxonian, Genevan or even Frankfurt Doctors, but also poor little grammar school students from Torun insist on spreading their baccalaurean wisdom in the chamber of deputies, and in the senate tradesmen, brewers and tailors wish to rule in the manner of lord mayors.'[19]

In the first decades of the eighteenth century, in particular, the social argument in anti-dissident polemics became supplemented by a new rhetoric of 'alienness' that not only referred to the Protestant burghers but also to the second, even more important group in question: the remaining dissident nobility. The term 'alien' in this context covered much more than the fact of religious diversity as such. The rhetoric of 'alienness' in fact established a link between religious dissent on the one side, and practically the entire complex of other attributes that were considered incompatible with, and dangerous to, Polishness on the other. It largely identified Protestantism with competing social and political loyalties and suggested that genuine Poles were Catholics 'by nature' – implying that the term 'dissident nobility' was a *contradictio in adiecto*: a dissident nobleman was bound to be of dubious, at best semi-aristocratic, and most probably foreign descent.

Precisely the last argument was emphasized most strongly by anti-dissent pamphlets. The text of 1718 cited above stresses the categorical inequality of Catholic and dissident nobility in its very title, identifying the pamphlet as the 'Catholic response' by 'Roman Staropolski, a szlachcic with ancient forefathers' to the unjustified allegations of the 'Dissident Protestant nobleman recently here appeared, Pan Skartabella'. The title of a leaflet circulated the following year, in 1719 reads very similarly: 'Reply by the honourable Christian Katolicki to the supplication submitted by the honourable dissident newcomers to the nobility at the Diet of Grodno . . .'.[20] But it was also in other contexts that the topos appeared. When, in a senate meeting in 1726, Minister Jan Jerzy Przebendowski tried, as on earlier occasions, to moderate anti-Protestant emotions and cautiously argued in defence of the Torun Lutherans, he was immediately accused of being a false Catholic, and of having been bribed by the dissidents.[21] Potentially, the argument worked both ways: while affiliation to a dissident confession could be treated as an adequate reason to question one's nobilitarian Polish origin and loyalty to the Commonwealth, allegedly 'un-Polish' behaviour could, in turn, justify doubts with regard to the individual's commitment to the Roman Catholic Church.

During the reign of Augustus III, when external political influence and pressure on the Republic became paramount in Polish politics, this process of 'nationalization of religion', i.e. of a religiously underpinned elitist nation-formation in Poland–Lithuania, seems to have reached its culmination.[22] With the dissidents, both indigenous and non-indigenous, theoretically eliminated from the political life of the republic as well as from its higher military and administrative structures, the political nation could perceive and represent itself as a socially and culturally homogeneous body for which Catholicism (as a national tradition of religiosity) functioned as one of the central markers – alongside *szlachta* identity and lifestyle, republican tradition and the Polish language. On the other hand, however, such elite integration had its specific limitations. Especially concerning the public and the ideological sphere it seemed to lack, even by the mid eighteenth century, the all-encompassing disciplining process that characterized the project of confessionalization, whether Catholic or Protestant, in many other early-modern societies. Only in very limited social and regional contexts did a centrally defined programme of Catholic religiosity actually become instrumental in enforcing homogeneity of, and control by state authorities over, significant segments of the population; given the regional diversity and the lack of agencies of central power in the Commonwealth, neither the Polish king nor the Church had the means to implement a policy of Catholic confessionalization comparable to that of the Habsburgs or the Bourbons. Furthermore, even in the sphere of *szlachta* ideology and the political public the degree of commitment to the Catholic cause seems to have largely depended on specific political contexts. While religious emotions ran high in the years of foreign intervention and civil war under Augustus II as well as during the War of Polish Succession, Catholic propaganda against the dissidents was gradually toned down after the 1740s, and only re-emerged almost a generation later when, in the interregnum after the death of Augustus III, foreign diplomatic intervention put the issue of the dissidents' representation back onto the agenda. It therefore seems to be a valid assumption that *Sarmate* religious zeal was often an expression of specific anti-Protestant or anti-Orthodox emotions, and of xenophobia in general, much more than of a positive programme of Catholicism as such.

The process of confessional elite integration in Poland–Lithuania seems to represent a rather unique phenomenon after all. While the 'nationalization of religion' implied in the shaping of *Sarmate* religiosity appears to have gone further, and developed more prominent features than in most other parts of Europe, the unifying effects of the process, including its impact with respect to toleration, remained remarkably selective and 'contextual'. Unlike Austria and Bohemia or France and Spain, the Polish–Lithuanian Commonwealth was not a country of Catholic confessionalization *sensu strictu*.

It has already been pointed out that the origins both of explicitly anti-dissident legislation in the republic and of the 'dissident question' as an issue of international politics can be dated precisely to the year 1717. This very fact seems to support the assumption that the eighteenth-century conflict over the status of the Polish dissidents had little to do with the long-term evolution of inter-confessional relations from the seventeenth century, but that it developed out of a different, genuinely political logic.

The danger of a new front of religious conflict opening up for the Commonwealth had been imminent since the election of Augustus II to the Polish throne, and it materialized in the aftermath of the civil war that ended with the Saxon elector's restitution to the Polish throne in 1716. While in the seventeenth century the 'dissident threat' had, in the eyes of the *szlachta*, mainly consisted in the native Protestants being potential 'agents' of foreign, especially Swedish influence and interference, such worries diminished as Polish–Swedish tension eased and, at the same time, the number of noble dissidents decreased; even if granted full constitutional rights, and morally supported by Prussia and Russia, the dissidents as a 'party' would, in the future, hardly have been able to influence political decision-making to any significant degree. The dynastic union between Poland–Lithuania and Protestant Saxony, however, gave new weight to the question of potential dissident influence. The election diet of 1697 had, in fact, taken all possible precautions in order to prevent the King from subordinating the republic to a 'Saxon' government. In practice, however, the King's Saxon entourage soon acquired influence on Polish matters as Augustus II involved his trusted German followers both in a formal and an informal way in the government of the kingdom. A critical point was reached when Augustus II, in 1714, attempted an absolutist coup d'état, with the intention of extending the Electorate's system of government to the Polish and Lithuanian lands; civil war and Russian military intervention in support of the unpopular Saxon king were the consequence.

At the centre of subsequent negotiations over a new constitutional compromise between king and country was the concern to reduce the opportunities for Saxon interference in Poland to a minimum. The restrictions imposed on the dissidents in 1717 immediately belonged in this context: they were part and parcel of a political compromise by which the Polish opponents of the Saxon dynasty accepted Augustus's return to the Polish throne – in return for a constitutional settlement that ultimately deprived the elective king of most of his political prerogatives in the Commonwealth, including the right to nominate foreigners and/or dissidents to republican offices.[23] In spite of this settlement, tension over 'unconstitutional' nominations persisted until the end of Augustus's rule and beyond. His son Augustus III, who followed him on the Polish throne after the Polish War of Succession, had to accept, in

1736, that the principles excluding 'foreigners' from Polish political life were confirmed, and spelled out even more restrictively. He also engaged, however, in plans for an absolutist turnover backed by his Saxon followers, and continued to use the services of German-Protestant confidants for his activities in Poland–Lithuania. A good example is the case of his Saxon first minister, Count Brühl, who *de facto* acted as Polish Chancellor and was eventually awarded, against strong opposition, the title of an indigenous Polish nobleman.[24]

The political dilemma that Poland's last king, Stanislaw August Poniatowski, had to face in the 1760s was thus, in many ways, predictable. After the experiences of the Saxon period, it seemed unrealistic to try and convince the *szlachta* nation that it would be wise to compromise with pro-dissident claims from abroad, while the events of the recent interregnum of 1764 had reinforced rather than dispelled public anxieties about foreign interference. No wonder therefore that the decisions of the Coronation Diet frustrated the hopes of the king-elect to avoid formal confirmation of the anti-dissident laws passed since 1736. On the other hand, the foreign protectors of the dissidents seemed, even more than in the past, determined to pursue the issue of toleration against the reluctant majority of the Polish nobilitarian nation – and to instrumentalize the question in the context of their respective political schemes. As an instruction for the Russian envoy to Poland, issued in the name of Catherine the Great by her minister, Count Nikita Panin, in August 1767, pointed out: religious and ecclesiastical matters were of no concern to the Empress's policies.

For us, the dissident question in Poland is not about wanting to support the dissidents and spread our faith or that of the Protestants; it serves us exclusively as an opportunity to interfere in all matters of Polish politics . . . The Protestant confession, in particular, in no way merits our support, since it might become instrumental in helping Poland to overcome superstition, to improve education, in short: to contribute to a more rational and more efficient organization of the Polish state – so undesirable to us.

Improving, on the other hand, the position of Poland's Orthodox population would make the republic only more attractive to Russian serfs, and encourage them to flee across the border in even larger numbers than at present. While pressing the issue with the Polish government, the Russian envoy should therefore refrain from immediate contacts with, or commitment to, the dissident groups concerned.[25]

Indeed, both Russian and Prussian diplomacy had followed this rationale since 1764 with respect to the dissident question. When the two powers publicly demanded the full restitution of the dissident nobility's constitutional rights, and religious emotions among the Catholic *szlachta* ran high in response, it soon became obvious that a majority in the republic would rather go to war than straightforwardly accept a Prusso–Russian ultimatum. A compromise instead – although perfectly conceivable even after the outbreak of civil war in 1768 – appeared hardly promising in a situation where the poorly concealed intention of Russia and Prussia was precisely not to let the opportunity for armed intervention pass.

Nevertheless, a diplomatic initiative for compromise on the dissident issue ensued, when Westminster offered mediation and the British diplomats started consultations with the parties concerned in Warsaw and Petersburg in 1769.[26] They rapidly discovered that a pragmatic solution to the religious problem as such would have been in close reach. Representatives of both the Orthodox and the Protestant nobility offered to voluntarily renounce the political privileges in question, and to issue a public declaration to this effect – in exchange for a more formal confirmation of their religious freedom which the government of king Stanislas Augustus, in turn, was perfectly prepared to grant. It took the British mediators somewhat longer, however, to understand that the numerous Russian and Prussian objections, primarily in procedural matters, could not be overcome. Negotiations in Petersburg dragged on for months – and were finally broken off in the late summer of 1770 when, after major Russian victories in the Turkish war, Catherine II's policy in the Polish question shifted towards a definite understanding with Prussia with regard to a partition. The British diplomats could therefore easily understand Count Panin's declaration of early September that the stubbornness of the Polish ministers had ultimately moved the Empress to no longer consider a compromise over dissident rights, and to abandon the suggested peace plan 'at least for the present'.[27]

Thus at almost no stage of the dissident conflict in the eighteenth century had the republic had much of a rational chance to escape the impact of a purely instrumental confessional policy as practised by Russia and Prussia. Polish reactions, ideological and political, to foreign interference in religious matters appeared by no means excessive, let alone exceptional, if compared to standards in most other European states at the time. However, it was not the degree of practised religious intolerance in Poland–Lithuania which proved crucial for the fate of the Commonwealth, but the circumstances that allowed for an exceptional degree of politicization of the dissident issue through foreign interference.

Notes

1 J. Fabre, *Stanislas Auguste Poniatowski et l'Europe des lumières*, Paris, 1952: esp. 311ff.

2 S. Salmonowicz, 'O toruńskim tumulcie z roku 1724', *Odrodzenie i Reformacja w Polsce*, XXVIII, 1983: 161–84.

3 J.K. Hoensch, *Sozialverfassung und politische Reform. Polen im vorrevolutionären Zeitalter*, Köln and Vienna, 1973: 90 and 186–94.

4 S. Plaggenborg, 'Maria Theresia und die böhmischen Juden', *Bohemia*, XXXIX, 1998: 1–16.

5 I. der Madariaga, *Russia in the Age of Catherine the Great*, London, 1981: 503–18.

6 Article 1 of the May Constitution confirmed the status of the Catholic faith as the 'ruling religion' and granted, at the same time, 'to everybody irrespective of his confession freedom of belief and the government's protection'. *Volumina Legum*, IX, Cracow, 1889: 220–5.

7 For an introduction see M. Bogucka, *The Lost World of 'Sarmatism'. Custom as a Regulator of Polish Social Life in Early Modern Times*, Warsaw, 1996.

8 W. Kriegseisen, *Ewangelicy polscy i litewscy w epoce saskiej: 1696–1763*, Warsaw, 1996.

9 Cf. the contribution by J. Whaley, Chapter 9 in this volume.

10 For an overview M.G. Müller, 'Protestant confessionalisation in the towns of Royal Prussia and the practice of religious toleration in Poland–Lithuania', O.P. Grell and B. Scribner (eds), *Tolerance and intolerance in the European Reformation*, Cambridge, 1996: 262–81.

11 As a regional case-study see M.G. Müller, *Zweite Reformation und städtische Autonomie im Königlichen Preußen: Danzig, Elbing und Thorn in der Epoche der Konfessionalisierung (1557–1660)*, Berlin, 1997.

12 Kriegseisen, *Ewangelicy polscy*: 19–49.

13 M. Wajsblum, 'Ex regestro arianismi. Szkice z dziejów upadku protestantyzmu w Malopolsce', I, *Reformacja w Polsce*, VII/VIII, 1935–6: 245–308; II, *Reformacja w Polsce*, IX/X, 1937–9: 89–408.

14 For detailed accounts of judicial practice Wajsblum, 'Ex regestro arianismi', and Kriegseisen, *Ewangelicy polscy*: esp. 22ff. and 206–26.

15 Namely German historiography has, in the past, clearly overrated the relevance of foreign concern for the Polish dissidents – in the attempt to justify Prussia's interventionist policy towards the Republic. For an example see G. Rhode, *Brandenburg-Preußen und die Protestanten in Polen, 1640–1740: Ein Jahrhundert preußischer Schutzpolitik für eine unterdrückte Minderheit*, Leipzig, 1941.

16 *Volumina legum*, VI: 622 and 677.

17 The most comprehensive study of the motives and circumstances of the reconversion of the Polish nobility still is G. Schramm, *Der polnische Adel und die Reformation*, Wiesbaden, 1965.

18 Cf. M.G. Müller, 'Städtische Gesellschaft und territoriale Identität im Königlichen Preußen um 1600. Zur Frage der Entstehung deutscher Minderheiten in Ostmitteleuropa', *Nordost-Archiv*, VI, 1997: 565–84.

19 Cited after Kriegseisen, *Ewangelicy polscy*: 174f.

20 *Ibid.*

21 In fact, as a very young man Przebendowski had been a Protestant; since his conversion to Catholicism, however, roughly sixty years had passed by then. Polski Slownik Biograficzny, XXVIII: 649–58.

22 For a new interpretation of the political and cultural profile of the Polish elites in the period after 1736 see J. Staszewski, *August III. Kurfürst von Sachsen und König von Polen*, Berlin, 1996: 221–60.

23 The broader political context is analysed by J. Staszewski, *August II Mocny*, Warsaw, 1998.
24 M.G. Müller, *Polen zwischen Preußen und Rußland. Souveränitätskrise und Reformpolitik, 1736–1752*, Berlin, 1983.
25 *Sbornik Imperatorskago Russkago Istoričeskago Obščestva*, LXVII: 409f.
26 For an evaluation of British archival sources concerning the British mediation M.G. Müller, 'A Very Rational and Wise Plan. Noch einmal zur Frage der britischen Friedensvermittlung in Polen und Rußland im Jahre 1770', W. Borodziej (ed.), *Między Niemcami a Rosją*, Warsaw, 1997: 98–110.
27 Charles Cathcart's report from the Russian court, 11 September, 1770, Public Record Office, State papers Russia, vol. 84.

12. Toleration in Enlightenment Italy

Nicholas Davidson

In 1789, on the eve of the French Revolution, Tommaso Vincenzo Pani published a defence of the Inquisition entitled *On the Punishment of Heretics*. Pani was a Dominican; in 1789, he was employed as Inquisitor in the city and diocese of Faenza in the Papal States. His book was designed to show that without an active Inquisition, the survival of the Catholic faith would be put at risk, and the established political and social order would collapse. At one point, he takes a swipe at the writers who had criticized the work of the Inquisition at the time, referring to the 'ridiculous innovators and the philosophers who lack all judgement, the fashionable scholars and the ignorant politicians who, with their idle talk and their lies, without authority and reason do all they can to discredit the tribunal of the faith'.[1]

Pani no doubt considered that the events of the following few years in France amply corroborated his argument, and in 1795, he published an expanded second edition of his book. Just over 200 years later, we in our turn might be inclined to view the publication and republication of such a text as evidence that intellectual life in Italy at the end of the eighteenth century was still significantly affected by the threat of censorship and persecution. Certainly, there were Italians throughout the century who complained of the threat posed by the Inquisition. In 1715, for example, Paolo Alessandro Maffei observed that in Rome, 'anyone who becomes known as a scholar immediately earns the title and reputation of (a heretic)'.[2] And Italians who travelled abroad often remarked on the contrast between the intellectual and religious freedom they believed existed in some other countries and its absence at home. The contrast was drawn most frequently with England, where – according to Antonio Cocchi, writing in London in 1724 – it was 'permitted for everyone to say whatever they think'.[3] The workings of this apparently tolerant society were reported in more detail by Alessandro Verri, during an extended visit to London in 1766–7. 'Nobody even talks about religion here', he wrote in a letter to his brother Pietro on 21 December, 1766, when describing how members of different denominations did business together daily without making any reference to their contrasting religious convictions. Individuals are free to believe as much or as little as they like;

and such freedom extends even to questions of politics: 'Do you want to say that the King is an arse? Go ahead – my servant says it one hundred times a day.' '*In somma*', he concludes, '*qui la libertà*', here is freedom: freedom to believe, freedom to discuss, freedom to publish.[4] Similar conditions were occasionally reported by Italians in more distant lands. Travelling in the Lebanon in 1767, Giovanni Mariti observed the situation in Beirut, where the grand emir, a Druse, allowed 'the most perfect tolerance in religion, so that everyone can practise their own religions without giving rise to any disputes or disturbance'. Even changes in religion were permitted, he claimed: apostasy and heresy were no crimes.[5]

Up to a point, the impression of Italian backwardness conveyed by evidence of this kind is borne out by the survival of book censorship and Inquisition tribunals throughout the eighteenth century. The Roman Congregation of the Index (founded in the sixteenth century) continued to issue its periodic Indices of Prohibited Books, listing titles that Catholics were not permitted to read;[6] additional condemnations of newly published books were issued regularly by both the Congregation and local inquisitors, who also ordered prohibited titles to be burned in ritualistic public ceremonies.[7] Many of the most celebrated works of the Enlightenment were condemned by Rome: Montesquieu's *L'Esprit des lois* (in the French original and in Italian translation) in March 1752; Voltaire's entire output to date in February 1753 (condemnations of his subsequent books were issued as they were published: the *Traité sur la tolérance* in February 1766, for example); the *Encyclopédie* in September 1759; Rousseau's *Du contrat social* in June 1766; d'Holbach's *Système de la nature* in November 1770. Italian authors suffered the same fate: Pietro Giannone's *Istorie civile* was condemned in July 1723; Cesare Beccaria's *Dei delitti e delle pene* in February 1766; Carlo Antonio Pilati's *L'esistenza della legge naturale* in June 1766.[8] And outside the Papal States, secular governments employed their own systems of censorship to review and ban new and imported publications. Authors therefore had in theory to secure the approval of both Church and State before their works could be put on sale in any Italian city.[9]

Local inquisitors continued their investigative work, too. Some trials gave rise to widespread debate and publicity at the time – one thinks for example of the celebrated trials of the Neapolitan 'atheists' which began in 1688, and of the Florentine poet Tommaso Crudeli in 1739.[10] Occasionally, victims of the Inquisition left autobiographical accounts of their experiences in their own writings.[11] And at the same time, the papacy continued to condemn perceived dissident groups, and to justify the Church's continued use of force to constrain and punish those in error.[12] In such circumstances, it is hardly surprising that authors and editors might sometimes exercise a degree of self-censorship in public, and reveal their real views only with caution, even in private.[13] As Giovanni Lami observed, the trial of Tommaso Crudeli was 'a great example to teach us to be more modest and circumspect in what we say'.[14]

Given this institutional evidence of censorship and repression, it comes as something of a surprise to read Charles de Brosses' conclusion on the situation in Rome after he had visited the city in 1739:

> the freedom to think in matters of religion, and sometimes even to discuss them, is at least as great in Rome . . . as in any other city I know. You should not believe that the Holy Office (of the Inquisition) is as black as the devil; I never heard stories of anyone brought before the Inquisition and treated with severity.[15]

But when we examine the evidence more closely, it is apparent that neither official censorship nor inquisitorial prosecution were usually considered to be very effective methods of control, and certainly not after the early years of the eighteenth century. The Church had always undermined its own attempts to control what was read by its willingness to issue special licences to allow named individuals to possess books condemned by the Inquisition or listed on the Index. Giuseppe Valletta, for example, was granted such a licence; and he allowed other scholars free access to his library.[16] The work of government censors was similarly compromised by the frequent determination of their employers to protect the economic health of the local printing industries. Then, as now, the scandalous sold well, and helped to boost not just the profits of the industry but also the tax revenues of the governments. In Venice, for example, the magistracy responsible for supervising the book trade sometimes gave permission to publish a text, notwithstanding the condemnation issued by its own censors, as long as its title-page bore a false (and foreign) place of publication.[17] In any case, the preoccupations of government and Church censors often failed to coincide. Governments were most concerned about challenges to their own authority, while the Church was more anxious to prohibit works that rejected elements of Catholic doctrine and morality. The result was that the authorities of Church and State could frequently be found accusing each other of excessive leniency, or ignoring each other's condemnations. Thus, the *Encyclopédie* was never banned in Venice, even though it was put on the Index in 1759; indeed, the Venetian authorities gave permission on a number of occasions for an Italian translation of the entire work to be published in the Republic![18]

There were also many ways to evade the established controls on the publication and ownership of prohibited and unlicensed titles. Clandestine and anonymous publications were common; the official censors could identify them as dangerous only after they had been printed and put on sale – by which time it was too late to prevent their circulation. Books bought or published abroad could be imported with ease from one state to another, since it was impossible to check the luggage of every traveller crossing the (often ill-defined) boundaries between them, let alone all the parcels delivered every day to private citizens and retailers.[19]

The Italian records are therefore full of references to the wide availability of prohibited books, both Italian and foreign, in the eighteenth century: bookshop inventories, library catalogues, scholarly correspondence and censors' reports all give the same impression.[20] Banned books often appeared in new editions, even after they had been added to the Roman Index. An edition of Rousseau's *Contrat social* was published in Livorno by Marco Coltellini in 1764, for example, using a false place and date of publication.[21] By the middle of the century, ecclesiastical attempts to ban books were gradually being scaled down. During the pontificate of Benedict XIV (1740–58), influential figures within the Curia, such as Cardinals Angelo Maria Querini, who was Prefect of the Index, and Domenico Passionei, as well as the Pope himself, used their power to reduce the number of titles prohibited by the Church; and in 1753, Benedict altered the procedures of the Congregation so that authors were allowed an opportunity to defend their texts before a decision to ban them was made.[22] Benedict's successors did not all agree with his new approach; but even before his election, a number of secular governments had begun to remove responsibility for the licensing of non-religious books from clerical censors, and to reduce the number of books explicitly banned from their own territories.[23] By 1768, Pietro Verri could write: 'I believe that in no Italian city – nor even in any French city – is there such freedom for books as we now have in Milan.'[24]

The activity of ecclesiastical inquisitors was also reduced. Few modern scholars have explored the trial records that survive from the Inquisition in Settecento Italy, but the work that has been done seems to confirm the judgement of William Monter and John Tedeschi that in the eighteenth century, 'the various branches of the Roman Inquisition were somnolent'.[25] The total number of cases investigated was only a fraction of the figures in previous centuries, and in most states, the tribunals were gradually run down. The first closure was in Naples in 1746. The inquisitors in Parma and Piacenza were expelled by their government in 1768, and their tribunal closed in 1769.[26] Restrictions on the Lombard inquisitors were introduced at about the same time, and in 1771, the local government ordered that no new inquisitors should be appointed in the Duchy when the existing office-holders died or resigned. The activities of those inquisitors still in office were then formally suspended in 1775, and the tribunals finally abolished in 1782, in the wake of Joseph II's celebrated Patent of Toleration issued the year before.[27] The abolition of the Tuscan tribunals was even more gradual. The Grand Duke had initially suspended Inquisition activities in the state as early as 1743; but after negotiations with the papacy, the tribunals were reopened by Francis

Stephen in 1754 under new and more restrictive regulations. They were formally abolished in 1782, in the same year as the Sicilian tribunals.[28] Even in
those parts of the peninsula where the Inquisition survived until the 1790s,
such as the Venetian Republic and the Papal States, it is clear that the scale
and severity of tribunal activities had been significantly diminished. In the
1770s, for example, Carlo Antonio Pilati (no friend of the Inquisition) could
report that 'Heretics (in Rome) are not obstructed in any way, but allowed to
do as they please. They kneel neither to God nor to the Pope, yet no one
reviles them for that reason.'[29]

What I have tried to present so far is a swift overview of the institutional
framework within which to set the history of toleration in Enlightenment
Italy. I have not yet said very much about the Italian Enlightenment itself,
but one of the most striking features of the period in Italy is just how marginal
a role the question of toleration seems to play in the published works of
Italian Enlightenment writers. Italians do not appear frequently in historical
discussions of toleration in the eighteenth century. Many Italian authors
ignored the subject altogether in their published work, and there is certainly
no obvious text to set beside Voltaire's celebrated *Traité sur la tolérance* in
France. The question of toleration was clearly not a significant preoccupation
within Italian intellectual circles. The number of religious non-conformists
was not high in the Italian states: Piedmont contained a number of Walden-
sian communities, brought within an early toleration statute in the 1690s;[30]
and there were important Jewish communities in the bigger towns and cities,
as well as smaller numbers of Greek Orthodox Christians and Protestant
migrants. By the eighteenth century, though, as we have seen, the inherited
methods of control and repression were generally ineffective; Inquisition tribunals seem to have spent most of their time investigating cases of magic and
religious indiscipline, rather than individuals with unacceptable intellectual
beliefs. Although some writers in the early years of the century did suffer
from an active inquisitorial prosecution (most notably Pietro Giannone and
Alberto Radicati), most were able to rely on their high social status or the
protection of powerful patrons to escape serious investigations. Giovanni
Alberto De Soria, for instance, a professor at the University of Pisa who did
much to spread awareness of Locke's work in Tuscany, and who was a suspected Deist, was protected by Cardinal Gian Francesco Negroni.[31] Where
there was only a limited persecution, there was no need for a developed
literature of toleration.

But this does not mean that the issue of toleration never appears in the
work of Italian Enlightenment writers; and in fact the arguments advanced
by Italians between the 1690s and the 1780s for the establishment of a greater
toleration in the peninsula tend to share a number of similar characteristics.
The first is that they all deal with the question above all in terms of practicalit-

ies. The tone was set by the Neapolitan jurist Giuseppe Valletta, in his *Letter in Defence of the Modern Philosophy*, written between 1691 and 1697, in the wake of the Neapolitan 'atheist' trials. Valletta argues that the persecution of individuals with dissident beliefs simply does not work: the body can be enslaved, but not the mind. In addition, he claims, the sort of intellectual dissent that had been persecuted in the past had not always been demonstrably in error anyway.[32] Valletta was directing his criticism here at the recent inquisitorial prosecution of Cartesian philosophers; but his suggestion that the inquisitors often persecuted the wrong people reappears in a number of later writers,[33] and it is stated most strikingly in the wonderfully ironic Chapter 39 of Beccaria's *On Crimes and Punishments*, first published in 1764, and reissued in its definitive form in 1766. The chapter is entitled, rather vaguely, 'Of a Particular Type of Crime', and opens with an admission that he has said nothing elsewhere in the book about crimes which lead to punishment by death at the stake. However, he explains,

It would take too long, and would take me too far from my topic to show, the example of many countries notwithstanding . . . how opinions, which differ only on a few very subtle and obscure points no human intelligence can grasp, can nevertheless overthrow the public good if one view is not preferred by authority to another.

In the same chapter, Beccaria also suggests that the attempt to control opinions is bound to fail, 'its only achievement being hypocrisy and hence moral degeneration'.[34] And since persecution of this kind is bound to fail, the use by the Church of torture and the death penalty for religious offences is also condemned by implication, for Beccaria's central principle is that 'The purpose (of punishment) is nothing other than to prevent the offender doing fresh harm to his fellows and to deter others from doing likewise.'[35] By the later 1760s, therefore, the ineffectiveness of religious persecution had become a familiar theme of Italian writers. Pilati's *Reflections of an Italian on the Church*, published in 1768, argued that '(physical) punishments do not enlighten or persuade or convince the intellect'; and in the later 1770s, Alessandro Verri mused admiringly on the religious tenacity of the Jews, despite centuries of obviously ineffective persecution throughout the Christian world.[36]

The second characteristic of these discussions is the regular use of the term *libertà* – liberty, freedom. Valletta's *Letter*, for example, refers frequently to *la libertà nel filosofare, la libertà di teologare, la libertà dell'opinare*.[37] His use of the infinitive form of the verbs in such phrases, rather than their matching noun forms (*filosofare* rather than *filosofia*, for instance), provides us with a clue to his main concern: the principle he was seeking to defend was not so much the freedom of belief itself as the freedom of intellectual debate. And this preoccupation is obviously consistent with the argument already mentioned, that what had been persecuted in the past had not always been demonstrably wrong, for as Valletta himself insisted, 'philosophies are no more than opinions'.[38] The importance of the freedom of debate appears frequently in later writers. In 1770, for example, Giuseppe Gorani's *The True Despotism* presented untrammelled debate – especially in print – as the best method for exposing error and bad argument.[39] The same point had been made a few years earlier by Beccaria: 'opinions are clarified by being bandied and debated so that the true rise to the top and the false sink into oblivion'.[40]

The significance of this insistence on the freedom of debate should not be underestimated, for it involved a decisive step away from the long-established idea that a public consensus of religious belief was essential for the maintenance of social and political stability.[41] The writers I have discussed did not believe that the debate between conflicting opinions would pose any danger to the established order, as long as it was pursued in good faith. There was therefore no need for persecution in matters of opinion. Pilati made the point most forcibly in his celebrated text *On the Reform of Italy*, first published in 1767: 'Those who disagree with us now believe themselves to be in the right and to be on the road to truth, just as we believe ourselves to be. Therefore, instead of persecuting them, let us seek to persuade them from their errors.'[42] Indeed, according to Pilati, far from realizing uniformity, persecution actually encouraged division in society, and so served to damage its cohesion and welfare.[43]

However, we should not overestimate the significance of the argument about the freedom of debate either. Since religious persecution involved the exercise of ecclesiastical power, its elimination was likely to lead to a consequent strengthening of the authority of secular government. Italian writers in the Enlightenment were aware of this. The conflict between Church and State jurisdiction was a well-established theme in Italian political thought in the early-modern period, and discussion in the eighteenth century was bolstered by the calculated recovery of the work of earlier writers such as Paolo Sarpi.[44] In the 1720s, for example, Alberto Radicati set his attack on the work of the Inquisition in just such a jurisdictional context: the Church had used religious persecution in the past, he claimed, to increase its power at the expense of the State.[45] Giannone similarly criticized the Church's exploitation of its doctrinal and disciplinary authority to protect and enhance its temporal power;[46] and Gorani's *True Despotism* made the explicit statement that the establishment of religious toleration would secure the sovereign's authority once and for all.[47] As Pietro Verri argued towards the end of the century,

it was really an absurdity to see established a jurisdiction independent of the Sovereign, with access to the use of force, prisons, tortures and confiscations; (and) to read edicts issued in the name of the inquisitor which were reinforced with the threat of confiscations and physical punishments against all and sundry . . . yet in which the Sovereign had played no part at all.[48]

So we should be wary of equating a call for religious toleration in Enlightenment Italy too easily with a call for unlimited freedom of belief. What was involved was more a demand for a redrawing of the boundary between Church and State, a demand that took the writers of the eighteenth century well beyond the parameters of the debate established by Giuseppe Valletta.[49] Cosimo Amidei made an absolute distinction in his study of *The Church and the Republic*, first published in 1768, between the spiritual responsibilities of the one and the earthly responsibilities of the other: 'there is an infinity between the one and the other power'.[50] Pilati took the idea still further in his *Reflections*. Not only was there a great gulf fixed between the concerns of the Church and the State; there should also be a total distinction of methods. The Church was a community, whereas the State was a hierarchy; within the Church, there could therefore be no superior and no inferior, and hence no obedience or disobedience.[51]

It is also important to recognize that Italian Enlightenment writers continued to advocate a degree of religious uniformity in society, despite their criticisms of persecution by the Church. In the privacy of their own studies, some might at times have developed Deist or anti-Christian convictions;[52] but in their published work, they all continued to insist on the maintenance of clear limits to religious toleration. From Valletta in the 1690s to Filangieri in the 1780s, Enlightenment writers extended their toleration only to those who accepted both the existence of God and the existence of an afterlife in which the good were rewarded and the evil punished. At the end of the seventeenth century, Valletta took belief in God and in the afterlife to be the two basic principles of religion, and identified them not only in Christianity but also in Platonism.[53] A century later, Gaetano Filangieri similarly insisted in his *Science of Legislation*, first published in 1780, that the idea of the godhead and belief in an afterlife were the core elements of all religions.[54] Pilati put the common argument most clearly: 'Any religion that professes a single God, teaches the virtues, and insists on the prospect of punishments and rewards in the future life will serve the good of the State and the security of the citizens within it.'[55]

In other words, these writers still saw a minimum of religious teaching as essential to secure order in society. What we find in the Italian Enlightenment therefore, is not so much a demand for complete toleration, as a redefinition of what can be tolerated. Since any belief system that teaches the existence of God and the afterlife should be left unmolested, Protestants, Greeks and Jews can be brought within its range. But other groups will continue to be excluded – most notably Deists and atheists – and their continued persecution is to be encouraged. Furthermore, as a consequence of the institutional redefinition that had altered the position of the boundaries between Church and State, that persecution could now be enforced only by the State, since the very nature of the Church precluded its use of force. As Pilati explained, members of every 'religion' should be tolerated – but individuals who 'reason badly', and who spread teaching that is contrary to virtue and the good of the State are never to be tolerated.[56]

Despite their significant limitations, these arguments might still be seen as marking a decisive move away from the positions traditionally adopted in the early-modern period. Paradoxically, though, and at exactly the same time, very similar arguments were also being developed by a number of self-consciously Catholic writers. A loss of faith in the likely benefits to be gained from the use of force was perhaps only to be expected within Catholicism given the failure of centuries of religious persecution and war to eliminate the enemies of the Church. Indeed, the reduction in the scale of censorship and inquisitorial investigations that we have already noted in eighteenth-century Italy might even be attributable to just such a loss of faith. Many Catholic intellectuals were therefore prepared to acknowledge that the Inquisition had often targeted the wrong people in the past. This was perhaps most tellingly exemplified in the very public debate about magic and witch-craft that raged (for the most part in the north-east of the peninsula) around the middle of the century. Although the participants in the debate disagreed on many points of detail, there was a widespread recognition that the witch-trials that had scarred Europe for so many centuries had been a dreadful mistake: a 'terrible slaughter', as Girolamo Tartarotti called them in his book *On the Nocturnal Congress of the Witches*, published in 1749.[57] A matching recognition can be traced even in the policies of some eighteenth-century popes. Benedict XIII and Clement XIV tried to counter the myth of Jewish ritual murders; Benedict XIV began to remove from the Index the titles of all books that supported the heliocentric theories of Copernicus and Galileo.[58] In his unpublished *Letter of Ippofilo fiorentino*, written around the middle of the century, Giovanni Lami widened the scope of this debate to insist that it was almost always wrong to accuse a person of heresy just because he or she disagreed with some aspect of current Roman policy.[59] Like Beccaria later, Lami believed that most disputes within the Church concerned problems that were ultimately insoluble, and that attempts to prosecute those who partici-pated in them were therefore pointless. He argued instead that Catholic scholars should be permitted to pursue research and debate without fear of the Inquisition.[60]

This willingness to engage in debate within the Church was extended still further by some leading Catholics to include those outside it as well. Pope Benedict XIV ventured on a celebrated correspondence with Voltaire, for example, and Cardinals Angelo Maria Querini and Domenico Passionei corresponded regularly with Protestants and other non-Catholics throughout their careers.[61] As the former Jesuit, Giovanni Battista Roberti observed towards the end of the century, 'are they not for the most part Christians too, cleansed by the same baptism (as us)? They are divided from the unity of the Church by heresy and schism – but do they not also read, hear and spread the Gospel?'[62] Roberti's emphasis on what was shared by all Christians, and his recognition of the good faith of non-Catholics, reflects a broader desire expressed in many reform circles in the Italian Church to cut away what were seen as the non-essential accretions acquired by Christianity since the days of the Apostles, and to return the faith to its core beliefs.[63] One of the most thorough-going expressions of this thinking was provided in the course of lectures prepared by Angelo Fabbro for the academic year 1771–2 at the University of Padua, where he held a chair in ecclesiastical law. The notes for these lectures reduce the Church to nothing more than 'the congregation of those who recognize Christ as head and author of their religion, who profess him as their Lord, who accept the mysteries revealed by him and venerate the sacraments he instituted'. Anyone who held to that core of beliefs in good faith, he argued, should be tolerated.[64]

This call for toleration, like that of the Enlightenment authors I discussed earlier, was, of course, of only limited application. Anyone who did not hold the newly delimited core of Christian teaching was by definition still excluded and liable to prosecution. And again, as in the work of many Enlightenment writers, responsibility for that prosecution was entrusted by these Catholic reformers to the State rather than the Church. As early as the 1740s, Giovanni Lami had come to the conclusion that the activities of the Inquisition reduced the proper completeness of the State's control of justice. He therefore argued that the Inquisition should be abolished; responsibility for dealing with heresy within the Church should be given instead to the local bishops, and any subsequent prosecutions should be entrusted to the authorities of the State.[65]

That such ideas, so close to those of Enlightenment writers, should appear in the work of Church reformers, is certainly worth noting in a discussion of toleration in Enlightenment Italy. But the most sustained Italian discussion of the case for toleration appears in the work of a Jansenist theologian called Pietro Tamburini. He was born in Brescia in 1737, and began his career at the seminary in his home town. He subsequently took a post at the Irish College in Rome, and then moved to a chair at the University of Pavia in Lombardy, where he remained until his death in 1827.[66] His ideas on toleration appear in three books published in the 1780s, most notably in a publication of 1783 entitled *On Ecclesiastical and Civil Tolerance*. Tamburini starts from the recognition that religious persecution simply does not work. Centuries of violence by the Inquisition have in fact had the opposite effect of that intended, and have served only to increase doubt and unbelief within the Church. Intellectual errors are inappropriate targets for such methods, for terror has never assisted the acceptance of truth; in any case, it had to be admitted that the Church has often mistakenly directed its fire against the truth rather than against those who were genuinely in error. Toleration is therefore the only practical policy for a Christian. This does not mean that Christians should abandon their own convictions; but they must be prepared to allow for the honest expression of opinions they do not accept themselves. The truth has to be loved, not feared; it can be propagated only by persuasion – by preaching, example and debate.[67]

The Church should thus continue to condemn error; but men and women who are in error must be tolerated. This conclusion is reinforced by Tamburini's understanding of the nature of the Church. Both in his book *On Ecclesiastical and Civil Tolerance*, and in his *Reflections* published in 1786, Tamburini insisted on the radical difference between religious and civil society. 'Our Divine Redeemer founded a religion based on humility, on gentleness, on love', he wrote. 'Admonitions, humble prayer and learning are the means by which the Church should maintain the faithful in the way of the Lord; chains, shackles, prisons and the stake are the methods of secular government.' When the Church seeks to punish heretics by force, therefore, it corrupts the true spirit of Christianity and confuses the economies of two separate societies. And since the Church should not desire the physical elimination of heretics, neither should the secular ruler.[68]

But that does not mean that secular government has no role to play. Tamburini's ideas about toleration are addressed to the problem of intellectual error: as long as heretics observe the law, they should be left in peace. It is only if they seek to disrupt the social order that the ruler should act against them. And here Tamburini arrives at an argument familiar from my earlier discussion. Secular government must always act against atheists, he says, since atheism 'destroys all religion, and kills (all) virtue . . . and subverts the majesty of the law'.[69] Tamburini's conclusion is therefore that the Church should never be involved in religious persecution, and – in line with many Enlightenment writers – he applauds the abolition of the Inquisition. But he still wants to exclude some identifiable beliefs from his call for toleration, and allows for their continued persecution by the State.[70]

Tamburini's ideas are clearly not unique. Some of them appear also in the work of other Italian Jansenists; and they are certainly reflected in the decrees of the Synod of Pistoia, held in September 1786 under the presidency of his close friend Scipione de' Ricci, who was then bishop of the Tuscan city.[71] Ricci shared Tamburini's belief in the radical separation of Church and State,[72] and the Synod's decrees state clearly that Christ 'did not wish to found a kingdom or a temporal monarchy'. For the Church to use 'force and violence to demand . . . submission to its decrees' is therefore an abuse of its authority, and the Synod consequently condemned 'the exaction by force of what depends on persuasion and the heart'. 'The mind cannot be persuaded by force, nor the heart reformed by prison and the fire.'[73]

It would obviously be possible to develop this investigation of the literature on toleration produced in the eighteenth century. But I hope I have said enough to demonstrate that the arguments adopted by Enlightenment and ecclesiastical writers in support of toleration were remarkably similar. Persecution does not work; debate is not to be feared; persuasion is more effective than force. Their conclusions were similar too, for all the writers I have discussed suggested that there was a reduced core of beliefs that were considered essential before an individual could qualify for toleration. They did not all agree on what that core consisted of; but none of them put forward an argument for a complete freedom of belief, and nobody advocated toleration for unbelievers. When dealing with atheists, it seems, persecution does work; debate is dangerous; and persuasion must give way to force. Indeed, the writers I have discussed here probably all viewed atheism as the greatest danger. From all sides, warnings were sounded against the growth of unbelief in Italian cities. In a letter of 1752, for example, Pope Benedict XIV expressed his urgent desire that Catholic theologians should abandon their internecine squabbles, and turn their energies instead 'against the materialists, the atheists, the Deists, who seek to uproot our holy religion from its foundations'.[74] Fifteen years later, the author of an anonymous *Ecclesiastical Plan* published in Venice opined that 'Luther and Calvin would have had very little impact if they had had to deal with the indifferentism that rules today. Most people think only about their daily life, and nothing else.'[75]

Enlightenment and Catholic reformers were therefore at one in their attempts to draw together around a shared set of basic beliefs, and to entrust the prosecution of all who rejected those beliefs to the State. In 1791, for example, Giuseppe Compagnoni published an article in the *Notizie del mondo* in Venice in which he praised Joseph II's Patent of Toleration, and at the same time attacked intolerance as 'a sacrilege against the Christian religion, which can alone inculcate peace and fraternal love among men'.[76] And here it is interesting to note the tendency of Enlightenment and Catholic writers to refer approvingly to each other in their publications. Pietro Tamburini, for example, quoted Montesquieu as an authority in his *Reflections* of 1786 when discussing the need for an absolute separation of Church and State;[77] Carlantonio Pilati made extensive use of the German theologian Febronius, as well as the French philosopher d'Holbach, when preparing his text *On the Reform of Italy*.[78]

Now I am not trying to suggest that contributors to the Italian Enlightenment were all closet Catholics.[79] They had of course all been brought up as Catholics, and educated in a school system dominated by the Church; and they were all undoubtedly aware of developments in contemporary Catholic thinking, not least because the periodical publications which they read, and to which they contributed, contained reports and reviews on all recent controversies. On the other hand, several of them had moved well beyond Catholicism in their own beliefs. Their support for the continued protection by the State of a core of approved religious teaching had less to do with its doctrinal validity than its perceived social utility. In his notes on Rousseau's *Social Contract*, compiled in the later 1760s, Francesco Dalmazzo Vasco made it abundantly clear that he was not concerned with the truth-claims of religion: 'membership of one religious community or another has nothing to do with the purpose for which religion is bound to the political system'. Who can decide on the truth of a religion anyway, he asks: 'certainly not a human being'. What matters instead is that religion should serve the good of society; and it is for the government to determine what that religion should be. 'Anyone who believes as he ought to' can be tolerated; but 'the government should not allow any changes to that religion', and 'anyone who seeks to attack that religion openly should be regarded as a disturber of the public order'.[80]

In other words, the call for greater toleration that appears in the work of both Enlightenment and Catholic writers in eighteenth-century Italy carries with it a call for a new system of persecution. And if we look more closely at the government legislation that abolished the old instruments of repression, we find that that is exactly what was established. In Parma in 1769, and in Lombardy in 1775, responsibility for prosecuting dissent was taken from the inquisitors and passed to a new alliance of bishops and government.[81] It is true that Joseph II's Patent of Toleration in 1781 allowed some non-Catholic groups to practise their religion in private; but he continued to insist on the prosecution of Deists, and in 1787, he summarily abolished all Catholic lay confraternities in Lombardy – hardly the action of a ruler dedicated to complete religious toleration.[82] Peter Leopold's edict of 1782 abolishing the Inquisition in Tuscany refers explicitly to the prince's duty to maintain religion; and while urging the bishops of his state to monitor the beliefs of the faithful, the grand duke insisted that 'whenever the circumstances of a case require it, we must proceed with severity; and when the use of the secular arm is needed, we shall consider it our duty to intervene'.[83] Almost everywhere in the same period, the role of the Church in the censorship of books was replaced by that of the State.[84]

So was there a causal link between published discussions on the question of toleration and the legislative changes introduced by governments? There are some parts of the peninsula where it might be argued that intellectual developments had significantly altered the climate of opinion among the elites of Church and State, thus preparing the way for decisive institutional change later; but in many other areas, the intellectuals' calls for the abolition of the Inquisition tribunals were published only after the legislative campaign against them had already begun. A convincing argument for the importance of intellectual debates can certainly be made in the case of Peter Leopold in Tuscany. He was aware of the work of both Enlightenment and clerical reformers, and he made good use of their ideas in his edict of 1782. But here, as in Sicily, where the Inquisition was abolished in the same year, legislative action was crucially influenced by the decisions of Joseph II in Austria the year before; and it must also be remembered that Peter Leopold's predecessors – who were not necessarily impressed by the arguments of reformers – had already closed the Florentine tribunal between 1743 and 1754. When Peter Leopold's father re-opened the tribunal in Florence, he was acting against the preferences of his reforming adviser Giovanni Lami, who had for years urged its complete abolition. In Venice, on the other hand, where many of the most outspoken writers lived and published, the Inquisition was abolished only after the defeat of the Republic by Napoleon in 1797.

The situation in Italy on the eve of the French Revolution was thus neatly summarized by Pietro Verri in a letter to his brother written on 11 May, 1782:

Today we are oppressed only by an evil sovereign. Yesterday we faced that threat, and also a threat from the Inquisition. But which condition is better, do you think: that of a man placed between a lion and a tiger; or that of a man facing a lion on its own?[85]

Notes

1 T.V. Pani, *Della punizione degli eretici e dei tribunale della Santa Inquisizione: lettere apologetiche*, Faenza, 1789: II, vii.

2 Quoted by F. Waquet, *Le Modèle français et l'Italie savante: Conscience de soi et perception de l'autre dans la République des Lettres*, Rome, 1989: 192–3; for a similar view from a foreign visitor a few years earlier, see p. 52. Compare also the worries expressed by Pope Benedict XIV in his letter to Cardinal de Tencin on 20 August, 1749: E. Morelli (ed.), *Le lettere di Benedetto XIV al Card. de Tencin*, Rome, 1955–84: II, 193.

3 A. Cocchi, *Opere*, Milan, 1824: I, 451.

4 G. Gaspari (ed.), *Viaggio a Parigi e Londra (1766–1767): Carteggio di Pietro e Alessandro Verri*, Milan, 1980: 168–9. Verri's description of the Royal Exchange in this letter echoes Voltaire's report published more than thirty years earlier: see F. Deloffre (ed.), *Voltaire: Lettres philosophiques*, Paris, 1986: 60–1. (I am grateful to Dr Robert Wokler for alerting me to this resemblance.)

5 G. Mariti, *Viaggio da Gerusalemme per le coste della Soría*, Livorno, 1787: II, 27–31, 35. Compare also the comments of the Papal Nuncio Antonio Eugenio Visconti in 1766 on proposals for religious toleration in Poland: A. Theiner (ed.), *Vetera monumenta Poloniae et Lithuaniae*, Rome, 1864: IV, 94–5.

6 The British Library holds copies of nearly twenty Roman Indices published between 1681 and 1796.

7 See for example Alessandro Verri's report on the burning of two books in the

Piazza Minerva, Rome, in August 1782: E. Greppi, A. Giulini and G. Seregni (eds), *Carteggio di Pietro e di Alessandro Verri*, Milan, 1923–42: XII, 364.

8 The dates of condemnation are taken from the *Index librorum prohibitorum. . . Pii Sexti pontificis maximi jussu editus*, Rome, 1786: 95, 101, 122, 177, 226, 227, 255, 284, 306; cf. H. Gross, *Rome in the Age of Enlightenment: The Post-Tridentine Syndrome and the Ancien Regime*, Cambridge, 1990: 261.

9 Compare comments of Waquet, *Le Modèle français*, 227–8; L. Braida, *Il commercio delle idee: editoria e circolazione del libro nella Torino del Settecento*, Florence, 1995: 84–6.

10 For the Neapolitan trials, compare N. Davidson, 'Unbelief and Atheism in Italy, 1500–1700' in M. Hunter and D. Wootton (eds), *Atheism from the Reformation to the Enlightenment*, Oxford, 1992: 83–4. An account of the Crudeli trial appears in M. Rastrelli, *Fatti attinenti all'Inquisizione e sua istoria generale e particolare di Toscana*, Florence, 1782: 173–239.

11 See especially the reports of Alberto Radicati in his *Factum*, published in R. Ajello *et al.* (eds), *Politici ed economisti del primo Settecento: Dal Muratori al Cesarotti*, Milan, 1979: 69–76; of Pietro Giannone, in S. Bertelli (ed.), *Pietro Giannone: Vita scritta da lui medesimo*, Milan, 1960: 277–92; and of Filippo Mazzei, in B. Romani (ed.), *Memorie della vita e delle peregrinazioni del fiorentino Filippo Mazzei*, Rome, 1944: 89–111.

12 The Freemasons were condemned by Clement XII in 1738, for instance: *Bullarum diplomatum et privilegiorum sanctorum Romanorum Pontificum*, Turin, 1872: XXIV, 366–7. For the use of force, see Pius VI's *Auctorem fidei* of 1794: A. Barberi and R. Segreti (eds), *Bullarii Romani continuatio*, Rome, 1845: 395–8.

13 Compare Ludovico Muratori's reluctance in 1726 to include a text on the Inquisition submitted for publication in the *Rerum italicarum scriptores*, 'for fear that the volume might be condemned by Rome: something that would not please me, and even less the gentlemen in Milan responsible for printing it' (quoted in Waquet, *Le Modèle français*: 227).

14 Quoted in F. Venturi, *Settecento riformatore: Da Muratori a Beccaria*, Turin, 1969: 128.

15 Y. Bezard (ed.), *C. de Brosses: Lettres familières sur l'Italie*, Paris, 1931: II, 134; these comments were probably written between 1745 and 1755 (compare volume I, page x).

16 Waquet, *Le Modèle français*: 231; D. Carpanetto and G. Ricuperati, *Italy in the Age of Reason, 1685–1789*, London, 1987: 80–1.

17 See F. Piva, *Cultura francese e censura a Venezia nel secondo Settecento: Ricerche storico-bibliografiche*, Venice, 1973: 28, 46, 50, 171–2; cf. also A. Machet, 'Censure et librairie en Italie au XVIIIe siècle', *Revue des études sud-est européennes*, 10, 1972: 466, 472–9. The fifth edition of Beccaria's *Dei delitti* was published in Livorno in 1766, but copies credited either Lausanne or Harlem as the place of publication: R. Bellamy (ed.), *Beccaria: On Crimes and Punishments and Other Writings*, Cambridge, 1995: xlii–xliv.

18 Piva, *Cultura francese*: 24–5, 88–9, 144–5. The translation of the *Encyclopédie* was eventually published in Padua in 1781. Compare Machet, 'Censure et librairie', 479; and 468 on the translation of Voltaire's *Lettres anglaises* in 1760. The Neapolitan authorities refused to recognize Rome's condemnation of Giannone's *Istorie civile*: Bertelli (ed.), *Pietro Giannone: Vita*: 88. Compare also the extraord-

inary reprimand delivered on the orders of the Senate to the Venetian Inquisitor in April 1766 recorded in Venice, Archivio di Stato, *Santo Uffizio*, b. 156, reports of Zan Antonio da Riva and Francesco Morosini dated 30 April, 1766. For Piedmont, see Braida, *Il commercio delle idee*: 91–4.

19 Machet, 'Censure et librairie': 468, 471, 483; Piva, *Cultura francese*: 89, 106, 115–16, 182–94; Braida, *Il commercio delle idee*: 124–8, 155; compare Waquet, *Le Modèle français*: 231–2.

20 For some examples, see E. Cochrane, *Tradition and Enlightenment in the Tuscan Academies, 1690–1800*, Rome, 1961: 96; Machet, 'Censure et librairie': 465–6; Piva, *Cultura francese*: 14, 20–2, 45–6, 87–9, 97–9, 144–51, 168, 171, 175–80, 198–203; G. Tabacco, *Andrea Tron e la crisi dell'aristocrazia senatoria a Venezia*, Udine, 1980: 211–19; Waquet, *Le Modèle français*: 95–7, 230; Braida, *Il commercio delle idee*: 157–62, 176–8, 181–219.

21 F. Venturi, 'Un'edizione italiana del Contrat social e della Lettre à Christophe de Beaumont de Jean Jacques Rousseau', *Rivista storica italiana*, 87, 1975: 51–4. Compare also for example G. Compagnino, *Gli illuministi italiani*, Rome and Bari, 1974: 113; Waquet, *Le Modèle français*: 162–3.

22 M. Rosa, *Riformatori e ribelli nel '700 religioso italiano*, Bari, 1969: 71, 75–6.

23 For reforms in Tuscany in the 1740s and 1760s, and in Lombardy under Maria Theresa, see F. Valsecchi, *L'Assolutismo illuminato in Austria e in Lombardia*, Bologna, 1934: II, 178–9, 248–51; Venturi, *Settecento riformatore: Da Muratori a Beccaria*: 307–8; Carpanetto and Ricuperati, *Italy*: 165, 171, 218–19. The Venetian government regularly ignored the recommendations of its clerical *revisori*, and included only fourteen titles in its definitive list of prohibited books issued in 1772; by the 1780s, the practice of ordering the destruction of banned books by burning had been abandoned: Piva, *Cultura francese*: 22–4, 49–55, 65, 73–4, 77, 91.

24 Greppi, Giulini and Seregni (eds), *Carteggio*: I, par. 2, 236; compare also X, 92 and XII, 129.

25 E.W. Monter and J. Tedeschi, 'Toward a Statistical Profile of the Italian Inquisitions, Sixteenth to Eighteenth Centuries' in G. Henningsen, J. Tedeschi and C. Amiel (eds), *The Inquisition in Early Modern Europe: Studies on Sources and Methods*, Illinois, 1986: 133.

26 See Carpanetto and Ricuperati, *Italy*: 184, 190–1. Du Tillot's decision in the Duchy of Parma was reversed in 1780: Greppi, Giulini and Seregni (eds), *Carteggio*: XI, 134–5.

27 See Greppi, Giulini and Seregni (eds), *Carteggio* I, par. 2: 170; Valsecchi, *L'Assolutismo illuminato*: II, 177–8, 225.

28 For the last years of the Tuscan tribunals under Grand Dukes Francis Stephen and Peter Leopold, see Rastrelli, *Fatti*: 163–72; for the Sicilian Inquisition, see F. Renda, *L'espulsione dei Gesuiti dalle Due Sicilie*, Palermo, 1993: 36.

29 C.A. Pilati, *Voyages en differens pays de l'Europe en 1774, 1775, et 1776*, The Hague, 1777: II, 42; compare the similar assessment of Alessandro Verri in Greppi, Giulini and Seregni (eds), *Carteggio*: VIII, 194, 234. For the tribunal in Venice, see de Brosses' comment in the 1730s: 'L'inquisition a lieu à Venise; mais elle a les ongles tellement rognés, que c'est à peu près comme s'il n'y en avait point': Bezard (ed.), *C. de Brosses: Lettres*: I, 203.

30 The text of the edict of 23 May, 1694 is printed in M. Viora, *Storia delle leggi sui Valdesi di Vittorio Amedeo II*, Bologna, 1930: 217–19.

31 Venturi, *Settecento riformatore: Da Muratori a Beccaria*: 347; Cochrane, *Tradition and Enlightenment*: 124.

32 G. Valletta, 'Lettera in difesa della moderna filosofia e de' coltivatori di essa', in M. Rak (ed.), *Giuseppe Valletta: Opere filosofiche*, Florence, 1975: 148, 162, 164, 168, 214–15.

33 Giannone's autobiography repeatedly criticizes the inquisitors for their ignorance: see for example Bertelli (ed.), *Pietro Giannone: Vita*: 89–90.

34 Here and elsewhere in this chapter, I quote from the excellent translation of Beccaria's *Dei delitti e delle pene* by R. Davies and V. Cox in Bellamy (ed.), *Beccaria*; Chapter 39 appears on 99–100. For the Italian text, see F. Venturi (ed.), *Illuministi italiani*: III, *Riformatori lombardi, piemontesi e toscani*, Milan, 1958: 27–105.

35 Bellamy (ed.), *Beccaria*: 31. Beccaria's chapters on secret denunciations, torture and the death penalty are all of relevance for this discussion: see Bellamy (ed.), *Beccaria*: 37–44 and 66–72. Pilati also opposed the use of torture: see his *Ragionamenti intorno alla legge naturale e civile*, Venice, 1766: 134–9.

36 C.A. Pilati, *Riflessioni di un italiano sopra la Chiesa*, 'Borgo Francone', probably Basle, 1768: 211, quoted by F. Venturi, *Settecento riformatore*: II, *La chiesa e la repubblica dentro i loro limiti, 1758–1774*, Turin, 1976: 297; Greppi, Giulini and Seregni (eds), *Carteggio*: IX, 119–20. Compare also the comments of Francesco Dalmazzo Vasco's *Suite du contrat social* transcribed in F. Venturi, *Dalmazzo Francesco Vasco (1732–1794)*, Paris, 1940: 95–129, and in Venturi (ed.), *Illuministi italiani*: 844.

37 Rak (ed.), *Giuseppe Valletta*: 168, 214.

38 *Ibid.*: 214.

39 G. Gorani, *Il vero dispotismo* ('London', actually Geneva, 1770), I, ch. 25.

40 Bellamy (ed.), *Beccaria*: 99.

41 For an example of this thinking, see the anonymous review of the Italian translation of the *Questions sur la tolérance*, attributed to J. Tailhé and G.N. Maultrot, published in the *Novelle della repubblica letteraria* in 1760; M. Berengo (ed.), *Giornali veneziani del Settecento*, Milan, 1962: 58.

42 I quote from the second edition: C.A. Pilati, *Di una riforma d'Italia*, 'Villafranca', probably Coira, 1770: 48–9. Compare also the interesting attempt of Pietro Verri in 1775 to imagine himself into the position of a victim of persecution in an Islamic state: Greppi, Giulini and Seregni (eds), *Carteggio*: VIII, 165.

43 Pilati, *Di una riforma*: 44–7. Compare also the arguments of Elia Morpurgo in favour of toleration for the Jews: *Discorso pronunziato da Elia Morpurgo, capo della nazione ebrea di Gradisca*, Gorizia, 1782: at 92; and the notes of Alfonso Longo on the Italian edition of Mirabeau's *Les devoirs*, Milan, 1780: 190, printed in Venturi (ed.), *Illuministi italiani*: 286.

44 For Sarpi, see Davidson, 'Unbelief': 77–8, with references, and more recently V. Frajese, *Sarpi scettico: Stato e Chiesa a Venezia tra Cinque e Seicento*, Bologna, 1994. Eighteenth-century discussions include G. Nave (a pseudonym for Giuseppe Giacinto Maria Bergantini), *Fra Paolo Sarpi giustificato: dissertazione epistolare*, 'Colonia', probably Venice, 1752, which was put on the Index in 1754; F. Griselini, *Memorie anedote spettanti alla vita ed agli studj del sommo filosofo e giurisconsulto*

F. Paolo Sarpi, 'Losana', probably Venice, 1760, which was also quickly put on the Index, but subsequently reprinted under the title *Del genio di F. Paolo Sarpi*, Venice, 1785.

45 A. Radicati di Passerano, 'Discours VIII', in his 'Recueil de pièces curieuses' published in Ajello, *Politici ed economisti*: 51–68.

46 Bertelli (ed.), *Pietro Giannone: Vita*: 91, 289–90, 292; the argument is repeated in his *Triregno*, for which see Carpanetto and Ricuperati, *Italy*: 111. Pilati also cast doubt on the motives for persecution in *Di una riforma*: 43–4.

47 Gorani, *Vero dispotismo*: ch. 21.

48 P. Verri, 'Memoria cronologica dei cambiamenti pubblici dello stato di Milano, 1750–1791' in C. Casati (ed.), *Lettere e scritti inediti di Pietro e di Alessandro Verri*, Milan, 1879–81: IV, 360–1; compare also his comments in the letter to his brother of 20 March 1782: Greppi, Giulini and Seregni (eds), *Carteggio*: XII, 228. Many of the contemporary debates about book censorship turned on the question of jurisdiction: see for example the anonymous work now usually attributed to Cosimo Amidei entitled *La chiesa e la repubblica dentro i loro limiti*, s.l., 1768: 142–8.

49 Compare the observations of M. Rak, *La parte istorica: Storia della filosofia e libertinismo erudito*, Naples, 1971: 18–19.

50 Amidei, *La chiesa*: 16.

51 A summary of the text is provided by Venturi, *Settecento riformatore*: II, 296–7. Not surprisingly, the Roman Inquisition ordered the book to be burnt: 301.

52 A case of this kind could certainly be made for Radicati for much of his career, and for Giannone at the end of his life. For Radicati, see the classic studies by F. Venturi, *Saggi sull'Europa illuminista I: Alberto Radicati di Passerano*, Turin, 1954; and 'La conversione e la morte del conte Radicati', *Rivista Storica Italiana*, 75, 1963: 365–73.

53 See for example Rak (ed.), *Giuseppe Valletta*: 133.

54 G. Filangieri, *La scienza della legislazione*, Naples, 1807: book V, ch. 8.

55 Pilati, *Di una riforma*: 47–8; compare Gorani, *Vero dispotismo*, ch. 24.

56 Pilati, *Di una riforma*: 47.

57 G. Tartarotti, *Del congresso notturno delle Lammie*, Rovereto, 1749: xxvi. Compare Scipione Maffei's explanation of the witch-trials as a direct consequence of the imposition on the laity of the mistaken beliefs of the inquisitors: *Arte magica dileguata*, Verona, 1750: 48; and Muratori's criticism of the use of torture to extract confessions in witchcraft cases: Carpanetto and Ricuperati, *Italy*: 131.

58 M.S. Anderson, *Europe in the Eighteenth Century, 1713–1783*, London, 1976: 412; U. Im Hof, *The Enlightenment: An Historical Introduction*, Oxford, 1994: 176–7.

59 Quoted in M. Rosa, 'Atteggiamenti culturali e religiosi di Giovanni Lami nelle *Novelle letterarie*', *Annali della Scuola Normale Superiore di Pisa: Lettere, storia e filosofia*, 25, 1956: 273.

60 *Novelle letterarie* (1741), col. 827; see also Rosa, 'Atteggiamenti': 278, 281–3, 296. Compare the attempts of Muratori to protect Giannone from the Inquisition: L. Marini, 'Documenti dell'opposizione curiale a Pietro Giannone', *Rivista Storica Italiana*, 79, 1967: 696–732.

61 See Morelli (ed.), *Le lettere di Benedetto XIV*: I, 314–15 for Benedict's report on his correspondence with Voltaire; quoting St Jerome, he explained that 'com-

mendavimus Philosophum non dogmatistam'. For Querini, see for example his correspondence between 1751 and 1753 with the Wittenberg professor G.G. Kirchmaier in N. Coleti (ed.), *Epistolae Eminentissimi et reverendissimi D.D. Angeli Mariae Quirini*, Venice, 1761: 570–3 and 606–12. For Passionei, see the study by A. Caracciolo, *Domenico Passionei: tra Roma e la repubblica delle lettere*, Rome, 1968: 84–7, 151–3. Cf. also Gross, *Rome*: 261, 278–9.

62 'Annotazioni sopra la Umanità del secolo decimottavo', in G. Roberti, *Opere*, Bassano, 1797: VIII, 299.

63 Compare Maffei's criticism of belief in magic in *Arte magica*: 3–6, 27, 30–1, 34, 47; and Tartarotti's contribution to the *Novelle letterarie*, 1743: cols. 675–6. Further discussion on this tendency can be found in Rosa, 'Atteggiamenti': 266, 272–3, 278, 282; Waquet, *Le Modèle français*: 188–9.

64 The text is printed in B. Brugi, 'Una gloria politica della Serenissima', *Atti del Reale Istituto veneto di scienze, lettere ed arti*, ser. 8, vol. 12, 1909–10: 188–93.

65 *Novelle letterarie*, 1744, cols 184–5, 235–6; compare also Rosa, 'Atteggiamenti': 321–3. Fabbro similarly believed that the government of the Church rested with the prince: Brugi, 'Una gloria': 188–93.

66 Brief biographical details can be found in C.A. Bolton, *Church Reform in Eighteenth-Century Italy*, The Hague, 1969: 60, 146. Cf. also Gross, *Rome*: 263, 282–4.

67 Tamburini's texts on toleration are very difficult to find in Britain; I therefore quote here from the full discussion in A.C. Jemolo, *Il giansenismo in Italia prima della Rivoluzione*, Bari, 1928: 304–9.

68 Jemolo, *Il giansenismo*: 306–7.

69 *Ibid.*: 307–8.

70 *Ibid.*: 304–5. Interestingly, Tamburini's *Lettere teologico-politiche*, published in Pavia in the early 1790s, present a reasoned defence of government absolutism: Jemolo, *Il giansenismo*: 323.

71 Tamburini served as *Promotore* of the Synod, and stayed at the bishop's palace: Bolton, *Church Reform*: 60.

72 N. Rodolico, *Gli amici e i tempi di Scipione dei Ricci: saggio sul giansenismo italiano*, Florence, 1920: 74–5. Compare also the views of Antonio di Montagnacco in Venice: Tabacco, *Andrea Tron*: 61–2.

73 *Atti e decreti del Concilio diocesano di Pistoja*, Florence, 1788: 80–1. Ricci and his supporters longed for the reunion of all Christians: Bolton, *Church Reform*: 123, 159.

74 Morelli (ed.), *Le lettere di Benedetto XIV*: II, 473; cf. the comment of Ignazio De Giovanni in 1794: 'Il problema di Bayle, se una società d'atei possa sussistere, ci fece orrore . . .' (quoted in Braida, *Il commercio delle idee*: 193). See also the preaching campaigns of the Jesuit Cristoforo Muzani, discussed by A. Prandi, *Religiosità e cultura nel '700 italiano*, Bologna, 1966: 83–4.

75 *Piano ecclesiastico per un regolamento da tentare nelle circostanze de' tempi presenti*, Venice, 1767, quoted in Venturi, *Settecento riformatore*: II, 114–15.

76 G. Compagnoni, 'Prospetto politico dell'anno 1790', *Notizie del mondo*, 1791, printed in Berengo (ed.), *Giornali veneziani*: 530; compare the anonymous article from the *Magazino italiano*, 2, 1768: 181–6, in Berengo (ed.), *Giornali veneziani*: 308; and the comments of Gorani, *Vero dispotismo*: chs 24–5.

77 Jemolo, *Il giansenismo*: 309; he also made use of social contract thinking in his

De tolerantia (Jemolo, *Il giansenismo*: 320). Cf. also the quotation from Filippo Alticozzi in Cochrane, *Tradition and Enlightenment*: 229–30.

78 Carpanetto and Ricuperati, *Italy*: 278. Interestingly, the Jesuit Francesco Antonio Zaccaria included a reference to Pilati in his assault on Febronianism, *Anti-Febronio*, first published in 1768: Venturi, *Settecento riformatore*: II, 287.

79 Though compare the comments of Owen Chadwick, 'The Italian Enlightenment', in R. Porter and M. Teich (eds), *The Enlightenment in National Context*, Cambridge, 1981: 90; and of Richard Bellamy, 'Italy', in J.W. Yolton, R. Porter, P. Rogers and B.M. Stafford (eds), *The Blackwell Companion to the Enlightenment*, Oxford, 1991: 247.

80 Venturi, *Dalmazzo*: 110–11. Compare also the implications of Pilati's *L'esistenza della legge naturale*, Venice, 1764, discussed in Venturi, *Settecento riformatore*: II, 254–6; and of the unfinished book V of Filangieri's *Scienza della legislazione*.

81 Carpanetto and Ricuperati, *Italy*: 190–1; Valsecchi, *L'Assolutismo illuminato*: II, 178.

82 Valsecchi, *L'Assolutismo illuminato*: II, 237–8; W. Doyle, *The Old European Order, 1660–1800*, Oxford, 1990: 202.

83 The text of the edict is printed in Rastrelli, *Fatti*: 167–71.

84 In general, see Machet, 'Censure et librairie': 459–90; and Braida, *Il commercio delle idee*: 8–9, 73–140 for Piedmont.

85 Greppi, Giulini and Seregni (eds), *Carteggio*: XII, 290. Compare also Verri's criticisms of Joseph II – written after the Emperor's death – in his *Pensieri sullo stato politico del Milanese nel 1790*, printed in S. Romagnoli (ed.), *Illuministi settentrionali*, Milan, 1962: 378–87.

13. Inquisition, Tolerance and Liberty in Eighteenth-Century Spain

Henry Kamen

The Iberian world is peculiarly difficult to fit into a discussion of toleration, because there was in Iberian society no longer any pluralism of culture after the expulsions of the Jews (1492 from Spain, 1497 from Portugal) and the Muslims (1609–14), and therefore no problem of tolerance that might call for either new legislation or new intellectual concepts. The expulsions of these minorities were preceded in each case by impassioned discussions about the rights and wrongs of permitting (that is, tolerating) them within society; thereafter, quite obviously, toleration was not a major issue. But Spain cannot be written off in considering the matter, even though it is habitual to do so.[1] Moreover, the case of Spain allows us to consider in general the interesting differences between northern and Mediterranean Europe, and the reasons for the total absence of toleration theory in the Mediterranean.[2] Spain, Italy and associated states in the Mediterranean were, until the twentieth century,[3] in the forefront of the perennial war against Islamic Africa, a fact that has often been offered as an explanation of Spain's aggressive stance towards non-Christian faiths. Yet there was also a perennial war against Islam in Transylvania and associated border states, which managed none the less to accept some toleration in the sixteenth century; and Italy for long periods tolerated its Jews in a way that the Spaniards since 1492 considered impossible. The Spanish case, evidently, is not easy to explain.

We may consider at least three main aspects of Spanish attitudes in the eighteenth century: retrospective reflections on the country's historical experience; new philosophical approaches; and appreciations of foreign thought. Finally, some attention should be paid to the role of the now declining Inquisition.

Because Spain was the centrepoint of a worldwide empire, and in particularly close touch with the two great sources of western culture, Italy and the Netherlands, it was always to some extent aware of foreign trends of thought. In practice, the poor quality of its universities and the unfamiliarity of most of the elite with any working language other than Spanish, limited contacts largely to Italy, an area which, by the eighteenth century, was losing the cultural supremacy it enjoyed in Renaissance times. The fact that writings on toleration were usually produced by northern European heretics, and were all too often in inaccessible languages, excluded the theme from the framework of normal discourse. Toleration theory, it is clear, had no place in the peninsula. However, it is important to recall that despite the permanent war against Islam a form of cultural plurality had always been a part of the Spanish tradition. Sixteenth-century writers, aware of the blood shed in religious wars elsewhere, had reason to reject the possibility of plurality within a single Christian faith, which they saw as completely unworkable. Leading Jesuit writers of the epoch of Philip II tended to cite the bloodshed of the French wars of religion as an irrefutable argument against the feasibility of toleration among Christians. However, legally sanctioned respect for the culture of Muslims, Jews and American natives, had firm roots within Spanish tradition, which explains why individuals (such as the famous Bartolomé de las Casas and many others) could always be found supporting cultural plurality in opposition to the generally predominant mentality of repression. When pressed by hard political reality, Spaniards could also be constrained into accepting a degree of toleration for Protestants, as even Philip II almost did in the case of the Netherlands.[4] This pluralistic outlook was a permanent feature not only of Spain but also of other European societies with experience of cultural diversity, and it is not difficult to find it surviving into the age of the Enlightenment.[5]

When the French minister Neckar complained in 1790 to the Spanish ambassador in Paris about the banning by the Inquisition of his book, *L'importance des opinions religieuses*, the ambassador responded that 'in France, where so many people doubt the existence of God, a book that demonstrated his existence might have its uses; but in a country where no one doubts it, and where religious unity prevails, to publish would be futile and even dangerous'.[6] The statement serves to remind us that in the theme of toleration we are dealing with two very different worlds: that of northern Europe and the Atlantic, where plurality of belief had slowly and painfully come to be widely accepted since the middle of the sixteenth century; and that of the Mediterranean, where plurality also existed but had never been officially accepted. It is significant that the 1996 volume on *Tolerance* (Grell and Scribner) steers completely clear of southern Europe, which is a pointer to the complete absence of studies on, or interest in, that geographical area.

But is it true that there was authentic religious unity in Spain, as the ambassador claimed? In the Iberian lands the question of toleration of beliefs must be carefully distinguished from a quite different principle, that of freedom to dissent *within* a specific faith. In late medieval Iberia, freedom to dissent did not exist within any of the three official religions. This did not affect the reality that the practices of *other* religious groups were normally respected, not because of a wish for toleration but because the other groups had been, prior to the forced conversions of an earlier epoch, separate political entities under a separate system of laws and jurisdiction. A similar situation can be found among the multicultural communities on the Islamic fringes of the Holy Roman Empire in the Reformation period. Under Christian rule in late medieval Iberia this principle of toleration for other cultures normally continued to be observed. The independent communities of Jews and Muslims who lived in their settlements (*aljamas*) under Christian lords, were always autonomous in religion because they were autonomous in law. When the Christian rulers Ferdinand and Isabella accepted the surrender of Muslim Granada in 1492, the principle was further guaranteed for the entire Muslim population of that realm. No principle of toleration or of intolerance was involved: coexistence was an exclusively legal obligation.[7] The protection given to the *aljamas* by Christian lords was by nature contractual: in return for protection, the Muslims and Jews paid taxes. Because there was no unitary political authority in Spain, for example, the seigneurs felt free to allow their Muslims to observe their own cultural customs, long after the Spanish crown had officially abolished the legal existence of Islam (in 1500 in Castile, in 1526 in the Crown of Aragon). The development can be seen as inherent in the nature of pre-modern political systems in Europe. Before the advent of the modern ('nation') state, small autonomous cultural groups could exist without being subjected to persecution, thanks to the protection of local authorities. The coming of the centralizing state, in post-Reformation Europe, removed this protection and aggravated intolerance.

This multicultural background needs to be explained to many who retain the impression that toleration is an issue to be considered almost exclusively within the parameters proposed by Castellio or Acontius or John Locke. Spain, like many parts of eastern Europe, was a plural (and therefore in some sense tolerant) society long before toleration became a philosophical issue. The same was true of Poland, for example. 'There is nothing new about diversity of religion in Poland', a Polish Lutheran stated in 1592. 'Apart from the Greek Christians, pagans and Jews have been known for a long time, and faiths other than Roman Catholic have existed for centuries.'[8] It was therefore possible, within that sort of context, to have *toleration without a theory of toleration*. Even while Christians and Muslims massacred each other for political or economic reasons, they accepted coexistence within the same territory. Toleration was socially possible, but not ideologically acceptable: this was the peculiarity of the Spanish situation. The point is clearly fundamental, and immediately establishes a clear division between northern European societies (the Netherlands, Britain, Germany), where the toleration debate took place within the parameters of Christian belief, and European frontier societies (Spain, Poland, Transylvania), where everyday physical coexistence with non-Christians affected the nature of the debate and in practice produced no significant theories of toleration. The distinction is vital to developments in the sixteenth century, but has less relevance for the eighteenth century, the subject of the present chapter.

In the period of the Enlightenment, on this premise, Spain was a society conscious of its pluralist background but unwilling to develop any approach to the theory of toleration, quite simply because there were no effective minorities claiming the privilege. The passionate attacks made by occasional Spanish Protestants (always in exile!) against the tyranny of Rome in Spain,[9] or similar works by exiled Portuguese Jews, were met (with good reason) by official scorn. No European society had accepted toleration until forced to do so, and in Spain there was no pressure in that direction. Confessional conflict created theories of toleration, and after Spain had expelled its religious minorities there was no confessional conflict.

Yet, there *were* problems, social rather than religious in nature, encapsulated for example in the fate of the *Chuetas*, the small minority of Jewish origin living in Mallorca. As late as the mid-eighteenth century,

although good Catholics, their sons were denied entrance to the higher ranks of the clergy, and their daughters to the religious orders. They were forced to live in a restricted area of the city, and the people calumniated them with the names *Hebreos, Judios, Chuetas*. Guilds, army, navy and public offices were closed to them.[10]

Despite various efforts by the government and some clergy, discrimination continued up to the end of the nineteenth century. In 1858 they were still

refused all public offices and admission to guilds and brotherhoods so that they were confined to trading. They were compelled to marry among themselves, for no one would contract alliances with them nor would the ecclesiastical authorities grant licences for mixed marriages.[11]

Nothing could be done in Spain about the *Chuetas*, because they were an internal problem of the island. However, they exemplified the old situation, common to much of mainland society since the fifteenth century, of social prejudice against people of Jewish origin. The classic method of discrimination had been through the demand for certificates of purity of blood (*limpieza de sangre*) as a condition of access to posts and honours. The practice was still in use during much of the eighteenth century. We may compare it to the severe cultural discrimination practised in Spain against gypsies (and other *races maudites*) since the early sixteenth century.

The existence and growth of discrimination should not be misconstrued as a triumph of racialism in Spain.[12] Antisemitism continued to exist, but the zeal for *limpieza* was – despite mistaken affirmations to the contrary made by many writers – very strictly confined to a few institutions in a limited number of regions. It is a point that I have emphasized in various publications.[13] In brief, the statutes were never part of the public law of Spain and never featured in any body of public law. Their validity was restricted only to those institutions which had them. Throughout these years, then, there was a profound ambivalence about the implementation of exclusion. Antisemitic discrimination was haphazard rather than systematic. There was also considerable opposition to antisemitism from various intellectuals, who made regular references to the subject in the seventeenth and eighteenth centuries. The mixture of tolerance and intolerance prompted a French ambassador to Spain to remark of an auto-de-fé in Madrid in 1680 that

> these punishments do not significantly diminish the number of Jews in Spain and above all in Madrid where, while some are punished with great severity, one sees several others employed in finance, esteemed and respected though known to be of Jewish origin.[14]

Echoes of *limpieza* practice continued in Spain through the eighteenth century. In 1751, nevertheless, a government minister, José de Carvajal, thought a seventeenth-century treatise attacking *limpieza* so convincing that he ordered a copy of it to be made for himself;[15] and a later chief minister, the count of Floridablanca, considered the penalties for impurity unjust because 'they punish a man's sacred action, that is, his conversion to our holy faith, with the same penalty as his greatest crime, that is, apostasy from it'.[16] Despite such criticisms, *limpieza* as a concept survived in the few institutions that had it on their statute books; but for all practical purposes it ceased to be a racialist concept. At the end of the sixteenth century in Barcelona, one religious order was using the notion of genealogical proofs simply as a way of checking on the good medical health and social conduct of new members.[17] So far did purity of blood cease to have any connection with the Jewish problem that in 1788 we find Charles III's minister Aranda using the phrase *limpieza de sangre* in the sense of purity from any taint of servile office or trade, so that the synonymous term *limpieza de oficios* also came into existence by the end of the century.[18]

One conclusion at which we may arrive, then, is that strictly demographic and social factors account for the absence of approaches to toleration in the Mediterranean. There were no cultural groups with significantly different beliefs or social practices. Moreover, in contrast to the countries of northern Europe, there was no influx of dissident immigrants, such as the Huguenots. In contrast to the twentieth century, when certain sects seem to be attracted by the sunshine of the Mediterranean (or of California), in early modern Europe sectarians fled rather to areas (including even North America) that had a climate they knew and where there was no existing state structure to oppress them. When attempting to obtain an overall perspective of the subject, this simple material explanation is so obvious that it may easily be overlooked. Spain as a consequence remained prominent by its absence from the impact of the immigrant problem on the European intellectual and scientific scene. While other nations – the Dutch, the English, the French and Germans – remained acutely conscious of the intellectual issues raised by sectarian prejudice, Spain remained immune to these currents of thought. When the Royal Society of London in the 1660s began to organize its scientific links with intellectuals from the continent, Spaniards did not feature.

However, already from the 1680s on, there were signs in Spain of active contact with European ideas. By the 1750s several Spaniards, albeit hesitantly,[19] were abreast of new trends in medical science and philosophy. They were exceptional: for the most part, the Spanish elite was cut off from cultural contact by an unreformed educational system, and by lack of familiarity with any of the languages in which the new thinking was being published. It is significant that we know of no substantial literary correspondence between Spanish and European intellectuals before the late eighteenth century, when the literary contacts of the Valencian scholar Mayans i Ciscar (who looked to Italy rather than northern Europe for his inspiration) began to take shape. There was therefore a serious intellectual divide between the south and the north. 'If a nobleman wishes to educate his sons', a prominent minister in Madrid reported in 1713, 'he has to send them to colleges in Bologna, Rome, France and other places'.[20] Spain consequently never featured as a desirable component of the Grand Tour: its universities were (explained one pained English visitor in 1664) 'just where our universities were 100 years ago'.[21] There was no apparent reason for going there; like the rest of southern Europe, it remained on the outer confines of the European experience. 'No country is less known to the rest of Europe', Dr Johnson concluded in 1761.[22]

The backwardness of Spanish thought has traditionally been attributed to the Inquisition. My short exposition has suggested, however, that the lack of toleration in late modern Spain had little to do with that tribunal, and everything to do with the absence of a multiconfessional culture. Theories of toleration always came into being because of socio-political necessities and never because of the dispassionate ratiocinations of a philosopher. The Inquisition, for its part, was merely a tribunal at the service of a society; it did not invent norms, but implemented those already in existence. It is of course true that the Inquisition (like all Catholic institutions of that period) was opposed to modernizing influences, as shown particularly by its treatment of a government minister, Olavide, who had tried to reform the universities and was a patron of the Enlightenment. He disappeared into its cells in 1776–8, and emerged as a changed man, a favourer now of Catholic tradition.

During the later eighteenth century the Inquisition became openly political in its hostility to the Enlightenment, and lost the little support it had enjoyed among the progressive elite in Spain. In the epoch following the French Revolution, one of the first acts of the French regime that occupied Spain in

1808 was to abolish the Holy Office on 4 December. The patriotic forces in the country were represented at the Cortes of Cadiz (1810), which on 22 February, 1813 also decreed the abolition of the Inquisition by a margin of ninety votes against sixty. It was an act that provoked considerable opposition from traditionalists, and on 21 July, 1814 Ferdinand VII restored the tribunal, but in name rather than in reality. Effectively the Holy Office was now moribund. On 9 March, 1820 the king was forced by liberal opposition to abolish it yet again. The final decree of suppression, issued by the government of queen Isabella II on 15 July, 1834, was little more than a formality. From this date the Inquisition ceased to exist in the Spanish monarchy.

The Inquisition was not by any means the only barrier to a liberal polity. There are other factors to bear in mind. The contrast between official attitudes in Spain and in the rest of the Catholic world was commented on sharply by Azara, ambassador to Rome in 1769: 'The whole world is concerned to reform abuses and reduce the usurpations of the priests. Only Spain sleeps.'[23] There was a substantial gap between the very small educated elite with European contacts, and the great mass of the largely illiterate public. In matters of religion (which raises a number of questions that cannot be touched on here) many in the elite had become freethinking liberals. By the 1770s, on the eve of the French Revolution, it is no surprise to find considerable religious scepticism among some of them. The ambassador to the Holy See, Nicolás Azara, wrote: 'Though a sceptic I believe in God, but only in his law',[24] meaning that he did not accept the laws of the Church, an attitude he made perfectly clear in his correspondence. Similar quotations can be found for other members of the governing elite. The political reformers, most notably Jovellanos, very commonly declared themselves to be sceptics; but this was little more than an extension of their reformist anticlericalism. For many, the Church was the principal obstacle to all progress, both economic and moral. As a consequence, they looked favourably on the practice of toleration. But we should not imagine that such attitudes were influenced significantly by the Enlightenment or by French philosophy. The liberal Juan Pablo Forner, for example, was a determined opponent of French ideas. Writing in the 1780s, he reacted sharply when attacked by a priest for being a heretic. 'What I can tell you', he wrote, 'is that the basis of religion is charity, and that if religious devotions are not founded on it they are vain superstition'.[25] It was a purely traditional response, opposed, of course, to reactionary and intolerant attitudes, but founded on a traditional Spanish system of respect for others rather than on Enlightenment ideas of religious liberty.

If tolerant attitudes developed in Spain, it was decidedly not for the reason that had prevailed in northern Europe – the need to arrive at a political and philosophical consensus (the basis of the writings of Locke and Bayle) – but because of the collapse of traditional intellectual structures. Sympathy for the persecuted *conversos* and *Chuetas* (both 'new Christians' of Jewish origin), for example, was not based on any understanding of the syncretic religious practices of minorities or on acceptance of the right to dissent, but simply on a direct rejection of coercion in religion. On the same principle, Spanish statesmen down to the present century continually expressed regret for the intolerant expulsion of Jews in the fifteenth century, but were at the same time reluctant to extend freedom of worship to Protestants, who had never formed part of the historic landscape of the peninsula. A student of the Spanish scene has to concede the grim fact that practical toleration of any sort, let alone legal, did not come into existence in the country until the 1960s (for Protestants and Jews), and had to wait for full implementation until the drawing up of the Spanish constitution after Franco's death in 1975. It has been a long wait.

Notes

1 Some aspects of the question in the sixteenth century are considered in Henry Kamen, 'Toleration and Dissent in Sixteenth-Century Spain: the Alternative Tradition', *Sixteenth Century Journal*, XIX, no.1, 1988: 3–23.
2 At a recent Italian conference on toleration, held under the auspices of UNESCO, not a single paper was devoted to early modern toleration within its Italian context. The excellent paper on Italy in the present volume, by Nicholas Davidson, analyses eighteenth-century attitudes but, not unexpectedly, unearths no Italian theories of toleration or any social context within which toleration was conceived as necessary.
3 Until the nineteenth century, Spain considered north Africa as its primary field of colonial expansion, and the Italian obsession with Africa lingered on until the epoch of Mussolini.
4 H. Kamen, *Philip of Spain*, London, 1997: 295.
5 There are no studies on either the theory or the practice of toleration in Spain. But the literature on multicultural relations is immense. A pioneering work on the subject was by Américo Castro, *The Structure of Spanish History*, Princeton, 1954.
6 Cited in J. Sarrailh, *L'Espagne éclairée de la seconde moitié du XVIIIe siècle*, Paris, 1954: 614.
7 I develop this point in 'Toleration and the Law in the West, 1500–1700', *Ratio Jurs*, 10, no.1, March, 1997: 36–44.
8 Cited by J. Tazbir, *A State without Stakes. Polish Religious Toleration in the Sixteenth and Seventeenth Centuries*, Warsaw, 1973: 35.
9 For example, Felix de Alvarado, of Seville, who became an Anglican then a Quaker in England, and translated some interesting English works into Spanish in the early eighteenth century: cited in M. Menéndez y Pelayo, *Historia de los Heterodóxos Españoles*, 1880: V, 116–18.
10 B. Braunstein, *The Chuetas of Majorca. Conversos and the Inquisition of Majorca*, New York, 1972: 123.

11 Cited in H.C. Lea, *A History of the Inquisition of Spain*, New York, 1906–8: II, 314.

12 Repeating an opinion to be found in numerous well-known works, Benzion Netanyahu, *The Origins of the Inquisition*, New York, 1995: 1063, states that 'the limpieza movement progressed until it dominated all Spanish ecclesiastical organizations and a major part of Spain's public opinion'. None of the affirmations in the passage is correct.

13 Cf. H. Kamen, *The Spanish Inquisition. An Historical Revision*, London, 1997: ch. 11.

14 Cited H. Kamen, *La España de Carlos II*, Barcelona, 1981: 489.

15 Carvajal to Joseph de Luyando, 28 September, 1751, Biblioteca Nacional, Madrid, MS.13043 fol.130.

16 A. Dominguez Ortiz, *Los Conversos de Origen judio después de la Expulsión*, Madrid, 1955: 129 n.14.

17 H. Kamen, *The Phoenix and the Flame. Catalonia and the Counter-Reformation*, London, 1993: 272.

18 Dominguez Ortiz, *Los Conversos*: 130.

19 Cf. the presentations by François Lopez and Francisco Sánchez-Blanco, in *Dieciocho: Hispanic Enlightenment*, spring 1997, Charlottesville, Va.

20 Macanaz, cited in Kamen, *Phoenix*: 313.

21 Cited in Kamen, *Carlos II*: 499.

22 J. Boswell, *The Life of Samuel Johnson*, London, 1949: I, 226.

23 Sarrailh, *L'Espagne*: 365.

24 *Ibid.*: 627.

25 *Ibid.*: 698.

Index